XVI CONGRESS OF THE INTERNATIONAL ORGANIZATION FOR SEPTUAGINT AND COGNATE STUDIES

SEPTUAGINT AND COGNATE STUDIES

Editor
Wolfgang Kraus

Editorial Board
Robert J. V. Hiebert
Arie van der Kooij
Siegfried Kreuzer
Philippe Le Moigne

Number 71

XVI CONGRESS OF THE INTERNATIONAL ORGANIZATION FOR SEPTUAGINT AND COGNATE STUDIES

Stellenbosch, 2016

Edited by
Gideon R. Kotzé, Wolfgang Kraus, and Michaël N. van der Meer

Atlanta

Copyright © 2019 by SBL Press

All rights reserved. No part of this work may be reproduced or transmitted in any form or by any means, electronic or mechanical, including photocopying and recording, or by means of any information storage or retrieval system, except as may be expressly permitted by the 1976 Copyright Act or in writing from the publisher. Requests for permission should be addressed in writing to the Rights and Permissions Office, SBL Press, 825 Houston Mill Road, Atlanta, GA 30329 USA.

Library of Congress Cataloging-in-Publication Data

Names: International Organization for Septuagint and Cognate Studies. Congress (16th : 2016 : Stellenbosch, South Africa) |Kotzé, Gideon R., editor. | Kraus, Wolfgang, 1955- editor. | Meer, Michaël N. van der editor.
Title: XVI Congress of the International Organization for Septuagint and Cognate Studies, Stellenbosch, 2016 / edited by Gideon R. Kotzé, Wolfgang Kraus, and Michaël N. van der Meer.
Description: Atlanta, GA, USA : SBL Press, [2019] | Includes bibliographical references and index.
Identifiers: LCCN 2019000486 (print) | LCCN 2019003563 (ebook) | ISBN 9780884143611 (ebk.) | ISBN 9781628372403 (pbk. : alk. paper) | ISBN 9780884143604 (hbk. : alk. paper)
Subjects: LCSH: Bible. Old Testament.
Greek--Versions--Septuagint--Congresses.
Classification: LCC BS744 (ebook) | LCC BS744 .I58 2016 (print) | DDC 221.4/8--dc23
LC record available at https://lccn.loc.gov/2019000486

Printed on acid-free paper.

Contents

Abbreviations vii

Introduction 1
    Gideon R. Kotzé, Wolfgang Kraus, and Michaël N. van der Meer

Josephus, Origen, and John the Baptist: Exposing a Christian
    Apologist's Deceit 7
    Nicholas Peter Legh Allen

The Ending of the *Canticum Mosis* (Deuteronomy 32:43)
    and Its Reception in Hebrews 1:6—A Fresh Look 33
    Elena Belenkaja

Three Elders: Onias III, Eleazar, and Razis as the Embodiment
    of Judaism in 2 Maccabees 53
    Eugene Coetzer

Demetrius and the Early Reception of the Septuagint 67
    Gunnar M. Eidsvåg

Was the Earth Invisible (LXX Gen 1:2)? A Response to
    Pieter W. van der Horst 85
    Robert J. V. Hiebert

A Semiotic Approach to Analyzing the Widows and Orphans
    as an *Index* in 2 Maccabees 3:10 95
    Pierre J. Jordaan

Just Like Puericide: The Greek Translation and Interpretation
    of a Debated Hebrew Phrase in Lamentations 1:20 103
    Gideon R. Kotzé

Psalm 40(39):7–9 in the Hebrew Bible and in the Septuagint,
    with Its Reception in the New Testament (Heb 10:5–10) 119
    Wolfgang Kraus

Samaria's Downfall in the Versions: The Masoretic Text,
    Vaticanus, and the So-Called Lucianic Recension 133
    Jonathan M. Robker

אולי—Perhaps in the Septuagint 145
    Seppo Sipilä

Rethinking the Original Language of the Book of Judith 161
    Satoshi Toda

Visio Dei in the Septuagint 171
    Michaël N. van der Meer

Doublets in the Catena of the Paris Psalter: An Analysis
    of Psalms 1, 3, and 5 207
    Leontien Vanderschelden

The Future Indicative as Imperative in the Septuagint 233
    Anssi Voitila

Contributors 245
Index of Ancient Sources 247
Index of Modern Authors 258

Abbreviations

AASF	Annales Academiae Scientiarum Fennicae
AB	Anchor Yale Bible
AKM	Abhandlungen für die Kunde des Morgenlandes
ANET	Pritchard, J. B., ed. *Ancient Near Eastern Texts Relating to the Old Testament*. 3rd ed. Princeton: Princeton University Press, 1969.
ANEM	Ancient Near Eastern Monographs
ANF	Ante-Nicene Fathers
AO	Analecta Orientalis
AOAT	Alter Orient und Altes Testament
ArBib	The Aramaic Bible
BASOR	*Bulletin of the American Schools of Oriental Research*
BBB	Bonner biblische Beiträge
BBR	*Bulletin for Biblical Research*
BdA	La Bible d'Alexandrie
BDAG	Bauer, W., F. W. Danker, W. F. Arndt, and F. W. Gingrich. *Greek-English Lexicon of the New Testament and Other Early Christian Literature*. 3rd ed. Chicago: University of Chicago Press, 1999.
BEATAJ	Beiträge zur Erforschung des Alten Testaments und des antiken Judentum
BETL	Bibliotheca ephemeridum theologicarum lovaniensium
BEvTh	Beiträge zur evangelischen Theologie
BHK	Kittel, R., ed. *Biblia Hebraica*. Stuttgart: Württembergische Bibelanstalt, 1937.
BHQ	Biblia Hebraica Quinta
BHS	Elliger, K., and W. Rudolph, ed. *Biblia Hebraica Stuttgartensia*. Stuttgart: Deutsche Bibelstiftung, 1997.
Bib	*Biblica*
BIS	Biblical Interpretation Series
BKAT	Biblischer Kommentar, Altes Testament

BN	*Biblische Notizen*
BO	*Bibliotheca orientalis*
BTS	Biblical Tools and Studies
BWANT	Beiträge zur Wissenschaft vom Alten und Neuen Testament
BZAW	Beihefte zur Zeitschrift für die alttestamentliche Wissenschaft
BZNW	Beihefte zur Zeitschrift für die neutestamentliche Wissenschaft und die Kunde der älteren Kirche
CAD	*The Assyrian Dictionary of the Oriental Institute of the University of Chicago.* Chicago: Oriental Institute of the University of Chicago, 1956–2010.
CBET	Contributions to Biblical Exegesis and Theology
CB.OT	Coniectanea biblica: Old Testament Series
CBQ	*Catholic Biblical Quarterly*
CBQMS	Catholic Biblical Quarterly Monograph Series
CEJL	Commentaries on Early Jewish Literature
DCLS	Deuterocanonical and Cognate Literature Studies
DDD	Van der Toorn, K., B. Becking, and P. W. van der Horst, eds. *Dictionary of Deities and Demons in the Bible*. 2nd rev. ed. Leiden: Brill, 1999.
DJD	Discoveries in the Judaean Desert
DSS	Dead Sea scrolls
DULAT	del Olmo Lete, G., and J. Sanmartín, ed. *A Dictionary of the Ugaritic Language in the Alphabetic Tradition*. 2 vols. HdO 67. Leiden: Brill, 2003.
EKK	Evangelisch-katholischer Kommentar zum Neuen Testament
ErIsr	Eretz-Israel
ETL	*Ephemerides theologicae lovanienses*
ETS	Erfurter Theologische Studien
FAT	Forschungen zum Alten Testament
FGH	Jacoby, F., ed. *Die Fragmente der griechischen Historiker*. Leiden: Brill, 1954–1964.
FRLANT	Forschungen zur Literatur des Alten und Neuen Testaments
GELS	Muraoka, T. *A Greek-English Lexicon of the Septuagint*. Louvain: Deutsche Bibelgesellschaft, 2009.
GKC	Kautzsch, E. *Gesenius' Hebrew Grammar*. Translated by A. E. Cowley. 2nd. ed. Oxford: Clarendon, 1910.
HALOT	Koehler, L., W. Baumgartner, and J. J. Stamm. *The Hebrew and Aramaic Lexicon of the Old Testament*. Translated and edited under the supervision of M. E. J. Richardson. 2 vols. Leiden: Brill, 2001.
HAT	Handbuch zum Alten Testament

HBM	Hebrew Bible Monographs
HBS	Herders biblische Studien
HCOT	Historical Commentary on the Old Testament
HdO	Handbook of Oriental Studies / Handbuch der Orientalistik
HNT	Handbuch zum Neuen Testament
HRCS	Hatch, E., and H. A. Redpath. *Concordance to the Septuagint and Other Greek Versions of the Old Testament*. 2 vols. Oxford: Clarendon, 1897. Suppl., 1906.
HThKAT	Herders Theologischer Kommentar zum Alten Testament
HSM	Harvard Semitic Monographs
HUCA	*Hebrew Union College Annual*
IBHS	Waltke, B. K., and M. O'Connor. *An Introduction to Biblical Hebrew Syntax*. Winona Lake, IN: Eisenbrauns, 1990.
ICC	International Critical Commentary
JAOS	*Journal of the American Oriental Society*
JBL	*Journal of Biblical Literature*
JECH	*Journal of Early Christian History*
JETS	*Journal of the Evangelical Theological Society*
JM	Joüon, P. *A Grammar of Biblical Hebrew*. Translated and revised by T. Muraoka. 2 vols. Subbib 14.1–2. Rome: Pontifical Biblical Institute, 2005.
JNSL	*Journal of Northwest Semitic Languages*
JPSTC	Jewish Publication Society Torah Commentary
JSCS	*Journal of Septuagint and Cognate Studies*
Jsem	*Journal for Semitics*
JSHRZ	*Jüdische Schriften aus hellenistisch-römischer Zeit*
JSJ	*Journal for the Study of Judaism*
JSJSup	Supplements to the Journal for the Study of Judaism
JSOTSup	Journal for the Study of the Old Testament: Supplement Series
JSS	*Journal of Semitic Studies*
JTS	*Journal of Theological Studies*
KEK	Kritisch-exegetischer Kommentar über das Neue Testament
KHAT	Kurzer Hand-Commentar zum Alten Testament
KNT	Kommentar zum Neuen Testament
KTU	Dietrich, Manfried, Oswald Loretz, and Joaquín Sanmartín. *Die keilalphabetischen Texte aus Ugarit, Ras Ibn Hani und anderen Orten. Dritte, erweiterte Auflage*. AOAT 360.1. Münster: Ugarit-Verlag, 2013.
LCL	Loeb Classical Library
LHBOTS	Library of Hebrew Bible/Old Testament Studies

LSCG	Sokolowski, Franciszek. *Lois sacrées des cités grecques*, Paris: Boccard, 1969.
LSJ	Liddell, H. G., R. Scott, H. S. Jones, *A Greek-English Lexicon*. 9th ed. with revised supplement. Oxford: Oxford University Press, 1996.
LXX	Septuagint
LXX.H	Handbuch zur Septuaginta
MIFAO	Mémoires de l'Institut français d'archéologie orientale du Caire
MVEOL	Mededelingen en Verhandelingen Ex Oriente Lux
MSU	Mitteilungen des Septuaginta-Unternehmens
MT	Masoretic text
NEB	Neue Echter Bibel
Neot	*Neotestamentica*
NETS	New English Translation of the Septuagint
NICNT	New International Commentary on the New Testament
NIGTC	New International Greek Testament Commentary
NRSV	New Revised Standard Version
NSKAT	Neuer Stuttgarter Kommentar Altes Testament
NTS	*New Testament Studies*
OBO	Orbis Biblicus et Orientalis
OLA	Orientalia lovaniensia analecta
OLZ	*Orientalistische Literaturzeitung*
OTE	*Old Testament Essays*
ÖTK	Ökumenischer Taschenbuch-Kommentar
OTL	Old Testament Library
OtSt	Oudtestamentische Studiën
QD	Quaestiones Disputatae
RBS	Resources for Biblical Study
RdM	Die Religionen der Menschheit
RGRW	Religions in the Graeco-Roman World
RNT	Regensburger Neues Testament
SBLDS	Society of Biblical Literature Dissertation Series
SBLTT	Society of Biblical Literature Texts and Translations
SBTS	Sources for Biblical and Theological Study
SBS	Stuttgarter Bibelstudien
SCS	Septuagint and Cognate Studies
SSI	*Social Sciences Information*
SP	Samaritan Pentateuch
StPB	Studia post-biblica
TBN	Themes in Biblical Narrative
TCL	Textes cunéiformes. Musée du Louvre

ThT	*Theologisch tijdschrift*
TLG	Berkowitz, L., and K. A. Squitier. *Thesaurus linguae graecae: Canon of Greek Authors and Works.* 3rd ed. Oxford: Oxford University Press, 1990.
TWNT	Kittel, G., and G. Friedrich. *Theologisches Wörterbuch zum Neuen Testament.* Stuttgart: Kohlhammer, 1932–1979.
TLNT	Spicq, C. *Theological Lexicon of the New Testament.* Translated and edited by J. D. Ernest. 3 vols. Peabody, MA: Hendrickson, 1994.
TSAJ	Texts and Studies in Ancient Judaism
UF	*Ugarit-Forschungen*
UTB	Urban-Taschenbücher
VT	*Vetus Testamentum*
VTSup	Supplements to Vetus Testamentum
WBC	Word Biblical Commentary
WUNT	Wissenschaftliche Untersuchungen zum Neuen Testament
ZAW	*Zeitschrift für die alttestamentliche Wissenschaft*
ZBK	Zürcher Bibelkommentare

Introduction

Gideon R. Kotzé
Wolfgang Kraus
Michaël N. van der Meer

The sixteenth congress of the International Organization for Septuagint and Cognate Studies (IOSCS) was held in Stellenbosch, South Africa, from 4 to 5 September 2016, in conjunction with the congresses of the International Organization for the Study of the Old Testament (IOSOT), the International Organization for Targumic Studies (IOTS), and the International Syriac Language Project (ISLP). These congresses were cohosted by Stellenbosch University, the Old Testament Society of Southern Africa (OTSSA), and the Southern African Society for Near Eastern Studies (SASNES). This was the first time that IOSCS convened in Africa. Another outstanding and memorable feature of this congress was the joint session with IOTS, where points of contact and convergence in the study of the Septuagint and the targums were discussed. Jan Joosten served as president of IOSCS, while Michaël van der Meer and Gideon Kotzé were responsible for the program and other practical arrangements. They collaborated closely with the president and secretary of IOSOT, Johann Cook and Louis Jonker.

The meeting of IOSCS in Stellenbosch was a happy occasion for Septuagint scholarship in South Africa, where the study of early Jewish writings in Greek is advancing by leaps and bounds.[1] The burgeoning interest in Septuagint studies in South Africa is witnessed by the substantial growth of the Association for the Study of the Septuagint in South Africa (LXXSA) since its inception in 2007, as well as an increasing number of publications on a wide variety of topics and texts.[2]

---

1. Cf. Gert J. Steyn, "Septuagint Research in South Africa: Some Brief Notes on the Development of Five Study Fields," *JSCS* 51 (2018): 52–61.

2. Pierre J. Jordaan and Nicholas P. L. Allen, "Introduction," in *Construction, Coherence and Connotations: Studies on the Septuagint, Apocryphal and Cognate Literature*, ed. Pierre J. Jordaan and Nicholas P. L. Allen, DCLS 34 (Berlin: de Gruyter, 2016), 1–10 provide an overview of LXXSA and discuss its strengths and weaknesses, as well as the opportunities and threats that face this organisation.

An important feature of South African Septuagint scholarship is the diversity of methodologies that have been employed in the analyses of texts. These range from comparative, text-critical, and translation technical methods to cognitive linguistic, rhetorical, narrative, and psychological approaches. Other noteworthy accents in research by South African scholars are the strong focus on the deuterocanonical literature in Septuagint corpora and the use of the Greek Jewish writings in the New Testament. Pierre J. Jordaan of North-West University and Gert J. Steyn, formerly of the University of Pretoria but now Professor in New Testament exegesis and theology at the Theologische Hochschule Ewersbach in Germany, have led the way in these areas of study. Recently, Cook has also become one of the most vocal proponents of research into the theology of the Septuagint.

The rich diversity in topics, texts, and approaches that characterize South African Septuagint scholarship is also a feature of the group of papers that were presented at the IOSCS congress in Stellenbosch. This volume contains many, but not all of the papers. Some of the papers that are not included here have been published elsewhere in scholarly journals, while those that were part of the joint session with IOTS are earmarked for publication in a separate volume.

In the opening essay of this volume, Nicholas P. L. Allen discusses the debated authenticity of the passage about John the Baptist in Josephus's *Antiquities* (*A.J.* 18.5.2 [§§116–119]). He argues that the passage is indeed a later interpolation and that Origen may have been responsible for the forgery.

Elena Belenkaja tackles the question regarding the source of the quotation from the Song of Moses (Deut 32:43) in Heb 1:6. In this passage, the reading ἄγγελοι θεοῦ is important to the argument that the Son is superior to the angels. Belenkaja investigates the complex textual tradition of Deut 32:43, as represented by the MT, 4QDeut^q, the LXX, and Ode 2:43, and highlights the possibility that the author of Hebrews quoted from a version of Deut 32:43 that contained ἄγγελοι θεοῦ, just as Ode 2 does.

Three of the important characters in 2 Maccabees, Onias, Eleazar, and Razis appear at key points in the narrative. All three of them react to a particular threat, but they do so in different ways. In his contribution, Eugene Coetzer points out that a consistent communicative strategy underlies the three elders' different responses, namely, the portrayal of Judaism's resistance as matching the degree of the threat. The stronger the threat, the more severe the response by the elders. In this way, the three characters embody the narrative's picture of the indomitability of Judaism.

Gunnar M. Eidsvåg discusses the use of the Septuagint in the preserved excerpts from the works of Demetrius the Chronographer, who wrote for Jews in Alexandria. Eidsvåg shows that Demetrius attempted to promote the Torah as an important text for Jewish identity, and characterizes this as an apologetic trait of Demetrius's work.

Robert J. V. Hiebert responds to a recent article by Pieter W. van der Horst in which he argues that ἀόρατος in LXX Gen 1:2 means "unsightly, hideous." In the light of lexical, morphological, and literary considerations Hiebert concludes that van der Horst's contention that ἀόρατος in the Genesis passage does not mean "invisible" is not completely convincing.

The mention of widows and orphans in 2 Macc 3:10 is the theme of the contribution by Pierre J. Jordaan. He employs a semiotic method of Umberto Eco and indicates that the phrase χηρῶν τε καὶ ὀρφανῶν functions as an index in the passage.[3] As an index, the reference to widows and orphans is significant for the rhetoric of the passage, because it points to the idea (also found in LXX Ps 67:6) that God will act as the judge of the widow and the father of the orphan.

Gideon R. Kotzé presents a fresh analysis of the debated reading בבית כמות in MT Lam 1:20c. He shows that the LXX translation provides an intelligible interpretation of the passage's subject matter and that its portrayal of death as a personified figure who causes childlessness is comparable to literary representations of Death in ancient Near Eastern texts. Kotzé concludes that the Greek text and information from the Hebrew poem's larger cultural environment allow the text-critic to make sense of the debated reading in MT Lam 1:20c and that this removes the need to emend the Hebrew wording of the colon.

LXX Ps 39 exhibits a number of differences when compared to MT Ps 40, particularly in verse 7. Some of the readings in the Greek manuscripts agree with the citation of the psalm in Heb 10, and Rahlfs changed these readings in accordance with the Hebrew wording of the MT. Wolfgang Kraus investigates the Hebrew and Greek texts of the psalm, as well as the quotation in Heb 10:5–7 and concludes that the differences with the MT were not created by the author of Hebrews but were part of the LXX text tradition. Rahlfs's changes are, therefore, not necessary. Furthermore, Kraus shows that the quotation from LXX Ps 39 plays an important role in the argumentation of the Hebrews passage.

In his contribution, Jonathan M. Robker focuses on the Hebrew text of 2 Kgs 17, as well as the two primary Greek versions of the passages, the kaige text of Codex Vaticanus and the Antiochene text (or so-called Lucianic recension). He presents examples of variant readings in the textual traditions and suggests that neither of the Greek text types exclusively represents the Old Greek wording, while the MT evidences changes that were made by scribes after the translation of Kings into Greek. These suggestions make a contribution to the study of the textual history of Kings, especially the characteristics of textual traditions and their relationship to one another.

Seppo Sipilä studies the Hebrew adverb אולי and how the Septuagint translators rendered it into Greek. אולי, Sipilä says, expresses uncertainty, and this uncertainty is either caused by a lack of necessary information or by previous actions in the text. He shows that the Greek translators used different ways to

---

3. In a text, an index is a sign that directs an audience's attention to something, and it requires some interpretive effort to grasp the implied meaning.

render the Hebrew adverb, but, in most passages, the translations also convey uncertainty. In those instances where this is not the case, there might be a theological reason for the rendering.

Satoshi Toda reconsiders the issue of the original language of the book of Judith. It is often assumed that Judith was originally written in a Semitic language and that the Greek text is a translation. Toda, however, argues that the book might very well have been composed in Greek.

Michaël N. van der Meer contributes to the discussion on Septuagint theology by looking again at the theme of "seeing God" in the Greek translations of Hebrew Scriptures. The Septuagint translators used different strategies to deal with the *visio Dei*. In certain passages, the Greek translations do not alter the Hebrew text, and the characters are said to see God. In other passages, however, the Greek translators rendered the Hebrew wordings in ways that temper the idea that humans can see God directly. According to van der Meer, these strategies should be seen against the religiohistorical backdrop of Egyptian cultic practices during the Hellenistic period. In this environment, it was not impossible for people to behold deities. However, cultic contexts and cultic personnel were necessary to mediate such visions. Therefore, not everyone enjoyed the privilege of seeing the deities.

Leontien Vanderschelden devotes her article to doublets in the catena of the Paris Psalter (*Parisinus graecus* 139). These doublets are excerpts from patristic commentaries that appear more than once in the commentary on a psalm verse. She compares the excerpts with the source texts and the surrounding fragments, and offers an explanation of the occurrence of doublets in Pss 1, 3, and 5.

In the final contribution to the volume, Anssi Voitila examines future indicative verbs with imperative meaning in the Septuagint and compares this use of the verbal form with other ancient Greek material. He draws on linguists' definitions of different modalities and indicates that future indicative directives in the Greek texts express agent-oriented modality,[4] especially when the addressee is the third person, while they represent speaker-oriented modality,[5] particularly when the addressee is the second person.

With contributions by seasoned specialists as well as up-and-comers from four continents (Africa, Asia, Europe, and North America), the volume is truly representative of the international community of Septuagint scholarship. The articles were peer reviewed and present the results of original research that have not appeared elsewhere in print. They contribute to the study of the Septuagint and cognate literature by identifying and discussing new topics and lines of inquiry, or developing fresh insights and arguments in existing areas of research. The intended audience of the contributions in this volume include scholars and students

---

4. An external agent imposes an obligation on the addressee to perform a predicated action.

5. The speaker imposes an obligation on the addressee.

who are interested in different methods of studying the literature included in Septuagint corpora, the theology and reception of these texts, as well as the works of Josephus.

Josephus, Origen, and John the Baptist: Exposing a Christian Apologist's Deceit

Nicholas Peter Legh Allen

Abstract: Recently the author completed a critical appraisal of the three suspected interpolations in Josephus's *Antiquitates Judaicae*. In this context, this paper reports solely on those findings apropos the well-known references to John the Baptist (i.e., *A.J.* 18.5.2 [§§116–119]). Here reference is made to, *inter alia*, the insights of Frank R. Zindler, Robert M. Price, and Nikos Kokkinos as well as certain findings gleaned from a critical reading of Origen's *Contra Celsum*. A number of Origen's key philosophical and theological refutations of Celsus's many anti-Christian claims are highlighted. As a result, the author exposes Origen's conceivable role in the fabrication of this long-suspected fraudulent text. Consequently, two things become evident: It is highly improbable that Josephus had ever heard of John the Baptist, and Origen must be considered the primary suspect for what is most likely a third-century CE Christian forgery.

1. PROBLEM

In Josephus's *Antiquitates Judaicae* (*Antiquitates Judaicae*), ostensibly written in ca. 94 CE, there are three disputed passages:

1. *A.J.* 18.3.3 (§§63–64) (better known as the *TF* [*Testimonium Flavianum*]);
2. *A.J.* 18.5.2 (§§116–119) (which this paper will refer to as the *BP* [*John the Baptist Passage*]); and
3. *A.J.* 20.9.1 (§§200–203) (which this paper will refer to as the *JP* [*James the Just Passage*]).

Although a few, mostly non-Christian and very often highly skeptical scholars[1] have questioned the legitimacy of the *TF*, *BP*, and *JP* respectively, by and large, contemporary, predominantly Christocentric scholarship[2] confirms these passages as having at least some degree of authenticity. In this context, they tend to view these three episodes as either being completely genuine or at worst, original Josephan creations with some degree of amendment or embellishment by well-meaning, pious Christian scribes. Furthermore, based on this kind of assumption, these often more conservative scholars are seemingly content to accept that these three items provide, *inter alia*, historicity of Jesus researchers with a dependable nucleus of historical material. In short, the information that they contain corroborates their shared worldview apropos an historical Jesus of Nazareth, James the Just, and John the Baptist.

Recently, I completed a critical appraisal of all three suspected interpolations.[3] In this context, this paper reports solely on its findings apropos references to John the Baptist in the *Antiquitates Judaicae*. This passage (*A.J.* 18.5.2 [§§116–119])[4] is presented below for the purposes of easy reference:

> Now some of the Jews thought that the destruction of Herod's army came from God, and that very justly, as a punishment of what he did against John, that was called the Baptist: for Herod slew him, who was a good man, and commanded the Jews to exercise virtue, both as to righteousness towards one another, and piety towards God, and so to come to baptism; for that the washing [with water] would be acceptable to him, if they made use of it, not in order to the putting away [or the remission] of some sins [only], but for the purification of the body; supposing still that the soul was thoroughly purified beforehand by righteousness. Now when [many] others came in crowds about him, for they were very

---

1. Cf. Harold Leidner, *The Fabrication of the Christ Myth* (Tampa: Survey Books, 2000); Robert M. Price, *The Incredible Shrinking Son of Man* (New York: Prometheus Books, 2003); Frank R. Zindler, *The Jesus the Jews Never Knew* (Cranford: American Atheist Press, 2003); and Earl Doherty, *Jesus: Neither God nor Man: The Case for a Mythical Jesus* (Ottawa: Age of Reason Publications, 2009).

2. Cf. James H. Charlesworth, *Jesus within Judaism* (New York: Doubleday, 1988), 93; John Paul Meier, *A Marginal Jew: Rethinking the Historical Jesus*, vol. 1 (New York: Doubleday, 1991), 63; Paula Fredriksen, *Jesus of Nazareth, King of the Jews* (New York: Vintage Press, 2000), 249; and Christopher E. Price, "Firmly Established by Josephus: What an Ancient Jewish Historian Knew About Jesus," in *Shattering the Christ Myth: Did Jesus Not Exist*, ed. James Patrick Holding (Maitland: Xulon Press, 2008), 22.

3. Nicholas P. L. Allen. *Clarifying the Scope of Pre-fifth Century C.E. Christian Interpolation in Josephus'* Antiquitates Judaicae *(c. 94 C.E.)* (PhD diss., North-West University, 2015).

4. English translation according to William Whiston, trans., *Flavius Josephus: The Works of Flavius Josephus*, 1895. In *Perseus Digital Library*. Available: http://www.perseus.tufts.edu/hopper/text?doc=Perseus%3Atext%3A1999.01.0146%3Abook%3D18%3Awhiston+chapter%3D5%3Awhiston+section%3D2.

greatly moved [or pleased] by hearing his words, Herod, who feared lest the great influence John had over the people might put it into his power and inclination to raise a rebellion, (for they seemed ready to do anything he should advise,) thought it best, by putting him to death, to prevent any mischief he might cause, and not bring himself into difficulties, by sparing a man who might make him repent of it when it would be too late. Accordingly he was sent a prisoner, out of Herod's suspicious temper, to Macherus, the castle I before mentioned, and was there put to death. Now the Jews had an opinion that the destruction of this army was sent as a punishment upon Herod, and a mark of God's displeasure to him.

It is most significant that this is the *only* extant, secular reference to John the Baptist found outside of scriptural writings. More critical scholars largely agree that, *inter alia*, based on its arbitrary placement in *A.J.* 18, the *BP* gives all the warning signs of being an interpolation by a later Christian hand. To obviate this interpretation, more conservative scholars tend to argue that it is not even a partial forgery, since it is not (like the better known *TF*) reminiscent of a canonical gospel account. However, they tend to ignore the fact that in the first four centuries of Christianity—even before the Council of Nicaea (325 CE)—there existed any number of Antilegomena and Apocrypha. Any one of these might arguably have served as the source for this more atypical version of the better known New Testament Baptist narrative.[5]

2. METHODOLOGY

In my opinion, contemporary scholars continue to fail to reach consensus in most fields of enquiry whilst they pander to their dominant worldviews. By way of example, a scientist who is a confirmed atheist is not likely to believe in tales of miraculous events. By the same token, a person, who by virtue of an irrational belief system maintains that the earth is flat, will not counter say photographic evidence of the earth being geoid. It also needs to be remembered that more typically, ancient texts can and have been altered by, *inter alia*, well-meaning (even pious) scribes as well as individuals quite intent on deliberate deceit.

In the context of any research project, the scholar's choice of a particular methodology, regardless of its epistemological foundation, will more often than not ascertain the particular disposition of any outcomes. Consider an approach favored by Steve Mason,[6] possibly one of the most prominent Josephus scholars. He has made the claim that, based on the text alone, he can better determine when a particular passage contains its original ideas. Mason maintains that little that Josephus says is innocent and substantiates his case by the employment of what he terms "compositional criticism." Mason defines "compositional criticism" as

---

5. Cf. Matt 3:1–12 and 14:1–12; Mark 1:4–9 and 6:14–29; Luke 3:2–20 and 9:7–8.
6. Cf. Steve Mason, *Flavius Josephus on the Pharisees* (Leiden: Brill, 1991), 40ff.

an attempt to "interpret an author's writings in and of themselves, as self-contained compositions. The narrative is assumed to contain within itself the keys to its own meaning."[7]

Within this *sole* context, Mason analyses a Josephan text for any clues apropos the possible significance for his preferred words and/or phrases. Here, the entire text becomes the primary context for what is contained within it. Further, consistent meanings for terms then become the favored arbitrator for their usage elsewhere in the *same* text. Here, Mason seems to claim that, if a text employs what he determines is typically Josephan vocabulary, then it ensures that Josephus *must* be the author. In contrast to this, I believe that this kind of conclusion, when it is based on only a single methodology, should not be taken as the last word on the topic of investigation.[8]

Due primarily to the tendency of many scholars, seemingly capitulating automatically to a majority consensus view, the *TF*, *BP*, and the *JP* are often considered to be either totally genuine Josephan creations or at worse, partial interpolations. As evidence for these kinds of conclusions, scholars will typically refer to, *inter alia*, Josephus's writing style, his literary progression, the length of the suspected interpolations and their character as compared to non-Josephan texts that contain similar content. All of these approaches are seriously flawed, if taken in isolation. Furthermore, they are largely based on the assumption that it is very *difficult* to forge the writings of Josephus.

In sharp contradistinction, Earl Doherty maintains that, if an individual is determined to formulate a fraudulent Josephan passage, they need only examine the genuine text. In short, all the fraudster needs to do is study certain phrases and terms employed by Josephus and apply them.[9] Doherty refers to these characteristic literary aspects as "Josephan fingerprints."[10] Doherty also quotes Charles Guignebert, who states "It may be admitted that the style of Josephus has been cleverly imitated, a not very difficult matter."[11] This makes a fiction of the claim by Meier who believes that to forge Josephus is well-nigh impossible. Even Mason innocently states that to have "created the *testimonium* out of whole cloth would be an act of unparalleled scribal audacity."[12] My response is "yes, it probably was!"

Surely, any intelligent forger would first ensure that they understood the layout and style of a particular work. He would also make note of useful expressions that could be reused for his own devious purposes. In this manner, an interpolator

---

7. Mason, *Flavius Josephus on the Pharisees*, 43.
8. Mason, *Flavius Josephus on the Pharisees*, 40–44.
9. Doherty, *Jesus*, 535.
10. Doherty, *Jesus*, 535.
11. Charles Guignebert, *Jesus* (New York: University Books, 1956), 17.
12. Steve Mason, *Josephus and the New Testament* (Peabody: Hendrickson, 2003), 171.

would be able to (1) compose the fraudulent text, as well as to (2) determine where best to place the forgery within the context of the genuine text.

Consequently, I favor the more reasonable aspects of what is often called an interpretist/constructivist method. This approach allows a researcher to make use of, where relevant and applicable, a wider range of methods, which, when triangulated, may better assist in establishing greater validity of interpretation. This approach, whilst focused on the issue of social constructs, has many advantages. For example, it makes it possible to establish a more plausible context and as far as is possible, shared worldview, within which rational deduction may take place.

Louis Cohen and Lawrence Manion[13] explain that an interpretist/constructivist approach to research has the intention of better understanding the world of human experience because it accepts that reality is, as Donna M. Mertens confirms, "socially constructed."[14] Vincent Pouliot explains:

> A constructivist methodology that is inductive, interpretive, and historical is able to develop both subjective knowledge (from the meanings that social agents attribute to their own reality) and objectified knowledge (which derives from "standing back" from a given situation by contextualizing and historicizing it). While inductive interpretation is necessary for recovering subjective meanings, contextual and historical interpretation is required for their objectification.[15]

Here, it is assumed that the constructed worldviews of *all* role-players will impact on a particular research finding. In addition, this approach allows for greater cross-referencing between the outcomes of various applicable methodologies. Here, according to Noella Mackenzie and Sally Knipe:

> The constructivist researcher is most likely to rely on qualitative data collection methods and analysis or a combination of both qualitative and quantitative methods (mixed methods). Quantitative data may be utilised in a way, which supports or expands upon qualitative data and effectively deepens the description.[16]

---

13. Louis Cohen and Lawrence Manion, *Research Methods in Education* (London: Routledge, 1994), 36.

14. Donna M. Mertens, *Research Methods in Education and Psychology* (Thousand Oaks: Sage, 2005), 12.

15. Vincent Pouliot, "'Sobjectivism': Toward a Constructivist Methodology," *International Studies Quarterly* 51 (2007): 367.

16. Noella Mackenzie and Sally Knipe, "Research Dilemmas: Paradigms, Methods and Methodology," *Issues in Educational Research* 16.2 (2006): 193–205.

3. Zindler's Arguments for Interpolation: A Case Study

The pioneering work of Frank R. Zindler needs to be highlighted here as one of the more plausible arguments that may be employed when attempting to discount the authenticity of the *BP*.

Zindler contends that the *BP* was placed in the *Antiquitates Judaicae* by either a Jewish-Christian or "an apologist for one of the myriad 'heretical' sects which are known to have existed from the earliest periods of Christian history."[17] He also correctly confirms that other written accounts of John the Baptist (i.e., other than those contained in the canonical gospels) must have once existed. In this regard, Zindler reminds his readers that "a decidedly non-gospel type of John the Baptist holds a very prominent place in the Mandaean religion to this day."[18] Certainly, the religious scriptures of the Mandaeans (i.e., the *Genzā Rabbā*) contain the words of wisdom from their revered prophet Yahya ibn Zakariyya (i.e., John the Baptist). These are not found in any other extant source today.[19]

In addition, there exists a brief reference to John the Baptist in the Gospel of Thomas (i.e., Gos. Thom. 46), and Jerome cites a passage that contains a reference to John the Baptist as contained in the once extant Gospel of the Hebrews (cf. *Dialogus Contra Pelagianos* 3.2). Regardless, Zindler gives his five reasons why the *BP* is most likely a forgery:

First Reason: The *BP* disrupts the continuity of the main narrative.[20] If the *BP* (i.e., section 2 [lines 116–119] from chapter 5 of book 18) is removed from the account as it presently appears, then section 1 (i.e., the preceding section [lines 109–115]) and section 3 (i.e., the following section [lines 120–129]) can now be read as a continuous, uninterrupted narrative:

End of Section 1 (line 115):

So Herod wrote about these affairs to Tiberius, who being very angry at the attempt made by Aretas, wrote to Vitellius to make war upon him, and either to take him alive, and bring him to him in bonds, or to kill him, and send him his head. This was the charge that Tiberius gave to the president of Syria.

Beginning of Section 3 (line 120):

So Vitellius prepared to make war with Aretas, having with him two legions of armed men; he also took with him all those of light armature, and of the horsemen

---

17. Zindler, *Jesus the Jews Never Knew*, 96.
18. Zindler, *Jesus the Jews Never Knew*, 97.
19. Zindler, *Jesus the Jews Never Knew*, 88, 97.
20. Zindler, *Jesus the Jews Never Knew*, 96–97.

which belonged to them, and were drawn out of those kingdoms which were under the Romans, and made haste for Petra, and came to Ptolemais.

This action clearly highlights the possibility that section 2 (i.e., the *BP*) is a clumsy interpolation, as its presence disrupts the continuity of the narrative concerning the various interactions between Aretas IV, Herod Antipas, Tiberius, and Vitellius.

Second Reason: The *BP* contradicts previous information written about the fortress of Macherus. In this regard, the fortress was first recorded in section 1 (specifically, it is mentioned twice in section 1, once in line 111 and again in line 112):[21]

In section 2 (i.e., the actual *BP*; lines 116–119), the reader is informed that Herod Antipas sent John to the fortress of Macherus for execution. However, the preceding paragraph (i.e., section 1) seems to stress that this fortress belonged to King Aretas IV who, incidentally, was Antipas's father in law *before* becoming his mortal enemy.

Thus, even if it is somehow proven that, under more normal conditions, Herod Antipas may have had access to this fortress, once he made an enemy of its legitimate owner (i.e., Aretas IV), he would hardly have been able to send his prisoner there for incarceration and subsequent execution.

As an aside, it should also be seen as highly suspicious that the *BP* manages to amplify its tenuous relationship to the preceding text by the statement: "he was sent ... to Macherus, the castle I before mentioned."

Third Reason: The *BP* contradicts the reasons for Herod Antipas's defeat at the hands of Aretas IV as stated in the same book.[22] The *BP* specifically informs the reader that God, displeased by Herod Antipas's atrocious treatment of the Baptist, allowed Aretas IV to have the upper hand in battle. However, section 2 from chapter 7 of book 18 (line 255) states the following:

> And thus did God punish Herodias for her envy at her brother, and Herod also for giving ear to the vain discourses of a woman.

In this regard, Caligula banished Herodias together with her husband, Herod Antipas.

Fourth Reason: John the Baptist is not mentioned in Josephus's earlier work, *B.J.* (*Bellum Judaicum*), even when it discusses Herod Antipas.[23]

---

21. Zindler, *Jesus the Jews Never Knew*, 98.
22. Zindler, *Jesus the Jews Never Knew*, 98.
23. Zindler, *Jesus the Jews Never Knew*, 98.

Fifth Reason: John the Baptist does not feature in the table of contents of the earlier Greek version of the *Antiquitates Judaicae*. He only appears in the later, Latin translations.[24]

If the *BP* is really a forgery (possibly based on some now long forgotten source), we are only left with the canonical gospels, the *Genzā Rabbā*, the Gospel of Thomas, and the Gospel of the Hebrews for any knowledge about the Baptist. In addition, Zindler reminds us that the Synoptic Gospel accounts tend to emphasize the Baptist mostly in terms of quoted biblical prophecy and not as attempts to describe an actual historical personage. In this context, they use the literary descriptions of Elijah and his sayings as well as selected passages from the prophets to inform us about John the Baptist. Certainly, John is clearly portrayed by the gospels as being an incarnation of Elijah.

4. Price's Arguments for Interpolation: A Case Study

Another critique of this passage's claim to be authentic Josephan material is provided by Robert M. Price, who gives two very compelling reasons why scholars should be highly suspicious of this passage.

The first reason given by Price[25] concerns the obvious urgency of the author to "correct a sacramental interpretation" of John the Baptist's baptismal ritual:

> [John] commanded the Jews to exercise virtue, both as to righteousness towards one another, and piety towards God, and so to come to baptism; for that the washing [with water] would be acceptable to him, if they made use of it, not in order to the putting away [or the remission] of some sins [only], but for the purification of the body; supposing still that the soul was thoroughly purified beforehand by righteousness.

Price points out that this is written in the context of the "here and now" rather than as some dispassionate account of a past event. In addition, Price asks why Josephus, as a practicing Jew, would even care about such subtle doctrinal issues (what he calls "sectarian theological hair-splitting"), any more than say Gallio did in the New Testament (cf. Acts 18:14–15)?[26] Given this valid observation, it is astounding how the Christian scholar Claire Rothschild can even begin to suggest that the

---

24. Zindler, *Jesus the Jews Never Knew*, 99.
25. Price, *Incredible Shrinking Son of Man*, 103.
26. Acts 18:14–15 states: "But when Paul was about to open his mouth, Gallio said to the Jews, 'If it were a matter of wrongdoing or vicious crime, O Jews, I would have reason to accept your complaint. But since it is a matter of questions about words and names and your own law, see to it yourselves. I refuse to be a judge of these things'" (ESV).

BP contains *no* Christian interpolations and further, based on this spurious observation, justifies its possible authenticity.[27]

John C. Meager,[28] who is also a committed Christian scholar, tries to rectify the situation by suggesting that Josephus could have drawn from the general knowledge of a Baptist cult in his own day. For some strange reason, Price seems to buy into this doubtful suggestion that such a cult actually existed. Regardless, even if we allow for such a possibility, Price also maintains that he cannot visualize Josephus being that concerned with such issues and suggests that he would have "edited out such extraneous details"[29] In the context of Price's argument, this statement makes little or no sense, because either Josephus relied on this avowed Baptist cult for his information or he did not. If the former is true, it means that here is some vital evidence for the possible historical existence of John the Baptist. If the latter is true, it means that it is far more likely that the *BP* (and its implied import) is just a later Christian invention and interpolation. Again, if the latter possibility is correct, then Josephus knew absolutely nothing about a Baptist cult in his own time, regardless of whether or not it actually existed.

Price's second reason[30] for suspecting interpolation is akin to the observation previously made by Zindler and concerns the presence of a redactional seam. This, as has already been discussed, concerns the uncomfortable placement of the entire *BP* within supporting text whose logical flow is clearly interrupted. However, Price's specific nuance on this observation, which is quite enlightening, concerns the sentence that introduces the *BP*: "Now, some of the Jews thought that the destruction of Herod's army came from God, and that very justly as a punishment of what he did against John." Price suggests that this is a paraphrase of the genuine words of Josephus, which now have been moved to the end of the passage: "Now, the Jews had an opinion that the destruction of this army was sent as a punishment upon Herod, as a mark of God's displeasure against him." Even so, Price[31] still believes that John the Baptist was a historical figure and goes so far as to compare his alleged cult to the hypothetical Qumran sect.

---

27. Claire Rothschild, "Echo of a Whisper: The Uncertain Authenticity of Josephus' Witness to John the Baptist," in *Ablution, Initiation, and Baptism: Late Antiquity, Early Judaism, and Early Christianity*, ed. David Hellholm, Tor Vegge, Øyvind Norderval, and Christer Hellholm (Berlin: de Gruyter, 2011), 271.

28. John C. Meager, *Five Gospels: An Account of How the Good News Came to Be* (Minneapolis: Winston Press, 1983), 37–38.

29. Price, *Incredible Shrinking Son of Man*, 103.

30. Price, *Incredible Shrinking Son of Man*, 103.

31. Price, *Incredible Shrinking Son of Man*, 104–5.

5. New Evidence from Kokkinos's Research

Thanks inadvertently to the recent (2010), mostly numismatic work undertaken specifically on the Herodian Dynasty by Nikos Kokkinos,[32] some additional and previously unrecorded facts have recently surfaced that greatly assist in determining the actual status of the *BP*. To be clear, Kokkinos seems to *accept* the historicity of both Jesus of Nazareth and John the Baptist. However, he argues from the perspective of an individual who is primarily concerned with presenting a more accurate picture of the familial relationships within the Herodian dynasty. He is not overtly concerned with the historicity of Jesus and his associates. Thus, certain of his findings (especially his numismatic evidence) have only inadvertently assisted in the interpolation debate.

Nonetheless, based on his monumental and highly impressive reevaluation of the Herodian dynasty, Kokkinos surmises that Herod Antipas was most likely born in ca. 25 BCE and if he did in fact execute John the Baptist, it would have most likely occurred in 35 CE (i.e., on Antipas's sixtieth birthday).[33] Kokkinos has also identified Antipas's wife, who was the daughter of Aretas IV of Nabataea. Based on numismatic evidence, it transpires that her name was most likely Phasaelis.[34] He also calculates that in ca. 7–6 BCE, at the time of her marriage to Antipas, she would have been about twelve years of age. Antipas divorced her in ca. 33–34 CE. Josephus (cf. *A.J.* 18.5.1 [§109]) merely tells us that she was the daughter of Aretas IV and does not name her. It is also possible, but not certain, that there were no children resulting from this long union—certainly none that were recorded.[35]

Moreover, Kokkinos determines that on hearing of the death of his half-brother (i.e., Philip the Tetrarch), Antipas travelled to Rome in 34 CE. He did this to lay claim to his half-brother's territories. This was only possible because Philip and his wife Herodias most likely had no offspring.[36] As an aside, Kokkinos solves an old mystery here. Most theologians argue that, due to the references to a "Philip" in the Gospels of Mark, Matthew, and Luke, they have determined a

---

32. Cf. Nikos Kokkinos, *The Herodian Dynasty: Origins, Role in Society and Eclipse* (London: Spink, 2010).
33. Kokkinos, *Herodian Dynasty*, 225.
34. Kokkinos, *Herodian Dynasty*, 231–32.
35. Kokkinos, *Herodian Dynasty*, 231–32.
36. Kokkinos, *Herodian Dynasty*, 268.

seeming contradiction between the gospel accounts and that of Josephus. Kokkinos states that the "stubborn insistence" of these scholars to conflate Herod II[37] with "'Herod-Philip' ... is without value"[38]

Before approaching Tiberius to make his petition, Antipas first went to negotiate marriage with his late brother's widow (Herodias). Kokkinos speculates that Herodias acquiesced to his advances, subject to Antipas first divorcing his then current wife, Phasaelis, and subsequently marrying Herodias. Kokkinos stresses that this proposed union had more to do with politics than romance. Certainly, Herodias (ca.15 BCE–after 39 CE) would have been some forty-nine years of age by this time (i.e., in 34 CE). Her motive was purely to guarantee that she remained aligned to a man who would ensure her continued exalted position and status.

Kokkinos cites further evidence to support this conjecture when he refers to the fact that the pro-Nabataean party from Philip's former tetrarchy ultimately betrayed Antipas by siding with Phasaelis's father (i.e., Aretas IV). This action helped bring about Antipas's subsequent defeat. This event is recorded accurately by Josephus in his *Antiquitates Judaicae*, immediately preceding the *BP*.[39]

6. CONTRADICTIONS BETWEEN THE *BP* AND THE NEW TESTAMENT

If the *BP* is in any way authentic, it means that Josephus (regardless of the actual status of the *BP*), is writing about events that he believed happened between 37 and 41 CE. Kokkinos's numismatic-based research confirms these dates. This does not fit at all well with certain primary, albeit traditional, Christian beliefs: Jesus is assumed to have been crucified in ca. 33 CE, even as early as 27 CE in some versions.[40] Nevertheless, these dates (i.e., 27–34 CE) are supposed to have marked the demise of Jesus of Nazareth quite some time *after* John the Baptist was supposedly executed. Thus, more conventional assumptions would place John's death no later than say 28–29 CE. In fact, this issue is taken up by Kokkinos in quite a negative way. Because he does not seem to question the historicity of

---

37. Kokkinos reclassifies Herod II as Herod III in his writings. This point need not detract from the current argument. Cf. Kokkinos, *Herodian Dynasty*, 145, 195, 207, 208, 222, 223, 237, 245, 265–67, 268, 310, 340, 359, 364, and 365.

38. Kokkinos, *Herodian Dynasty*, 223. Here Kokkinos also cites Harold Walter Hoehner, *Herod Antipas* (Cambridge: Cambridge University Press, 1972), 133–36 and Kenneth C. Hanson, "The Herodians and Mediterranean Kinship, Parts 1 and 2," *Biblical Theology Bulletin* 19 (1989): 79.

39. Kokkinos, *Herodian Dynasty*, 268.

40. Cf. Robert C. Newman who allows for a date from 27–34 CE. Robert C. Newman, "Daniel's Seventy Weeks and the Old Testament Sabbath-Year Cycle," *JETS* 16.4 (1973): 229–34. This opinion is supported by Monte F. Shelley, "Excerpts from When Was Jesus Born, Baptized, and Buried? A Review of LDS and Non-LDS Educated Guesses," https://s3.amazonaws.com/academia.edu.documents/3457982/NT_03-When_was_Jesus _Born_Baptized_and_Buried Summary.pdf?

Jesus of Nazareth, he also sees it as necessary to push the date of the crucifixion forward to as late as 36 CE. He does this in order to *preserve* some gospel accuracy. Here again, is a wonderful example of an individual's worldview impinging on his reasoning. Had Kokkinos no need to protect the crucifixion date as occurring *after* John the Baptist's death he would not have needed to have made this conjecture.

Mason offers another intriguing insight. According to the *BP*, Herod Antipas arrested John *primarily* because he was responsible for causing civil unrest. However, the gospel accounts state that Antipas arrested John because he criticized his union with his brother's wife. In this context, Mason questions why Josephus (assuming he was the author) did not see John as a dangerous popular leader. Elsewhere in the *Antiquitates Judaicae*, such typical Jewish *arrivistes* are normally singled out for heavy criticism. Apart from the *Testimonium Flavianum*, in each and every account concerning a political/religious arriviste, Josephus speaks contemptuously, employing negative epitaphs. For example, he refers to the unnamed Samaritan man (*A.J.* 18. 4.1 [§85]) as a "liar" (ψεῦδος). He refers to John son of Levi (*B.J.* 2.21.1 [§586]) as a "ready liar" (ἕτοιμος μὲν ψεύσασθαι) and an anonymous zealot (*A.J.* 20.8.10 [§188]) as a "charlatan," "sorcerer," or "imposter" (γόητος). Finally, Josephus refers to the charlatan, Jonathan the weaver (*B.J.* 7.1 [§437]) as πονηρότατος ἄνθρωπος ("a vile person")—literally, a "man oppressed by toils."

But the author of the *BP* speaks of John in *positive* terms even calling him a good and righteous leader. This in itself is patently un-Josephan in character.[41]

Ironically, one would think that the more typically conservative and certainly fundamentalist Christian scholars would be fighting extremely hard to *discredit* the *BP*. Instead, many appear to be focusing on why they believe the *BP* to be wholly genuine! Indeed, if it really was authentic extra-biblical evidence, then it would also simultaneously do the following:

1. Prove that John the Baptist was a *bona fide* historical personage; and
2. Contradict the New Testament as the Baptist would then have had to have lived quite sometime *after* the Jesus of Nazareth episode.

Thus, it would throw serious doubt on the gospel accuracy and chronology in general. Therefore, if one wants to retain the gospel accounts as being, at the very least, based on some historical truth, then *clearly*, the *BP* is an obvious forgery. If the gospel accounts are pure religious mythology, then either John the Baptist most probably did not exist or his actions have been adulterated and redacted to suit a religious agenda. Either way, the *BP* is again shown up as fraudulent, since it specifically highlights Josephus as being uncharacteristically involved with quite advanced, perceptive, Christian-based, doctrinal issues concerning the role

---

41. Cf. Mason, *Josephus and the New Testament*, 157, 213–25.

of Christocentric baptism. This is obviously in error given that his combined oeuvre consistently confirms that Josephus was a practicing Jew, with very strong leanings towards Pharisaic philosophy.[42]

The only way that one can accept the *BP* as a valid historical account by Josephus is to seriously discredit the gospels' accuracy. In addition, historians would now have to begrudgingly accept that Josephus was nothing short of being a practicing (albeit clandestine) Christian with notions that were not only too advanced for the time but literally prophetic in nature.

7. Origen as Prime Suspect

It is unlikely that Eusebius (ca. 260–340 CE) was the mastermind behind the original formulation of the *BP*. This is because Origen (ca 184–254 CE), who wrote several decades earlier, mentions that Josephus had referred to John the Baptist. The task now is to try to determine at what point in history the interpolation was first made. Of course, this does not rule out Eusebius as having had a final hand in "perfecting" the *BP*.

If we look at the extant writings of earlier church fathers (i.e., other than Origen), we find that Justin Martyr (ca 100–165 CE) (*Tryphone Iudeo Dialogus*, 49; 50; and 84) possibly made use of Josephus. However, like Origen, Justin Martyr makes no mention of the *TF*. He makes some reference to John the Baptist at least eighteen times, mostly in the context of preparing the way for Christ.[43] To support his case, he quotes solely from the LXX and the New Testament. At no time does Justin Martyr make mention of anything resembling the *BP*.

7.1. Origen as Suspected Interpolator

To understand Origen's possible role in the creation of the *BP*, it is first necessary to be aware of a number of interrelated issues which only come to light as a result of a critical reading of his *Contra Celsum* (*Cels.*). This background information should be viewed as important in assisting one to understand the more likely *raison d'être* behind Origen's philosophical discourse whilst refuting Celsus's many anti-Christian claims.

---

42. Cf. Nicholas P. L. Allen, "Josephus and the Pharisees," in *Construction, Coherence and Connotations: Studies on the Septuagint, Apocryphal and Cognate Literature*, ed. Pierre J. Jordaan and Nicholas P.L. Allen (Berlin: de Gruyter, 2016), 259–300.

43. Justin Martyr refers to John specifically as "John the Baptist" on four occasions.

7.2. ORIGEN'S HELLENISTIC WORLDVIEW

As should be obvious, most (if not all) ante-Nicene apologists shared a similar belief in the efficacy of sympathetic magic. They each had their various interpretations apropos the tenets of the then evolving Christian dogma and associated Christology. In addition, they (like many modern Christians) also took for granted the existence of things like wizards, demons, the Devil and hosts of evil spirits. This is especially true of Origen, who clearly accepts that things like sorcerers and magic not only exist but pose a dangerous threat to an individual who seeks spiritual salvation. He also sees himself as having the important task of trying to counter Celsus's vehement accusation (cf. *Cels.* 1.71) that Jesus of Nazareth was *not* divine but a "wicked and God-hated sorcerer."[44] Origen, like most of his peers, well understands the workings of his world in a typically Hellenistic way.[45] For example, he would affirm that water not only washes away dirt in the natural world, but in the right context, it will equally cancel out iniquity in the spiritual (supranatural) domain.

In *Cels.* 4.62, with reference to Plato, Origen explains:

> For the language in the Timæus, where it is said, "When the gods purify the earth with water, shows that the earth, when purified with water, contains less evil than it did before its purification." And this assertion, that there at one time were fewer evils in the world, is one which we make, in harmony with the opinion of Plato, because of the language in the Theætetus, where he says that evils cannot disappear from among men. [Punctuation for greater clarity NPLA][46]

In the same vein, in *Cels.* 2.7, Origen gives his particular embellishment on the gospel account of Jesus washing his disciple's feet:

> [Jesus] who after supper laid aside His garments in the presence of His disciples, and, after girding Himself with a towel, and pouring water into a basin, proceeded to wash the feet of each disciple, and rebuked him who was unwilling to allow them to be washed, with the words, **Except I wash you, you have no part with Me**. [Insertion and emphasis for clarity NPLA]

---

44. English translation according to *Contra Celsus*, book 1 in *New Advent*, http://www.newadvent.org/fathers/04161.htm.

45. Associative thinking and sympathetic magic remain common assumptions/practices even today. However, they received larger acceptance as having validity in the time of the Ante-Nicaean writers.

46. English translations of *Contra Celsus* according to Peter Kirby, *Origen: Contra Celsus* in *Early Christian Writings*, 2014. http://www.earlychristianwritings.com/text/origen161.html.

This passage reveals an obvious conflation of interpretation. The act of washing the disciples' feet is seen as both symbolic, as well as a sacrament, which will ensure that the disciples literally adopt Christ-like qualities, including those of humility and compassion, et cetera. In *Cels.* 3.24, Origen gives an unbelievable account of how Christians, infused with the power of Christ, can undertake all manner of supranatural activities:

> And some [Christians] give evidence of their having received through this faith a marvellous power by the cures which they perform, evoking no other name over those who need their help than that of the God of all things, and of Jesus, along with a mention of His history. For by these means we too have seen many persons freed from grievous calamities, and from distractions of mind, and madness, and countless other ills, which could be cured neither by men nor devils.

Origen also conceives of a God who is not averse to employing natural processes to enact supranatural outcomes. For example, in *Cels.* 4.69, he refers to the biblical account where the Jewish God "administers correction to the world, in purifying it by a flood or by a conflagration." It is important to remember, that in opposition to this, the more rational Celsus would most likely argue that natural events such as floods and conflagrations are not necessarily brought about by some divine need for retribution. Certainly Origen quotes Celsus as elucidating on this very issue in his *Cels.* 4.11.

Again, in *Cels.* 5.48, whilst speaking on the efficacy of Jewish circumcision, Origen accepts the biblical account of an angel intent on the annihilation of uncircumcised Jews and who only allowed those Jews who were physically circumcised to remain unharmed. He also comments on the biblical tale of Zipporah who used a pebble to circumcise her son and then attributed the blood of circumcision as an effective agency against the avenging angel.

An attempt will be made here to demonstrate that Origen's worldview, which accepts the ability of mere mortals to influence the fabric of the supernatural spheres by the employment of religious/magical rituals/rites, clearly underscores his own perspectives as regards the Christian baptism rite; its workings and its claimed efficacy. Origen is also quite capable of stretching the truth when it best suits him, as has already been substantiated. This is essential to ultimately establishing that Origen is the most likely candidate if one seeks the identity of the author of the *BP*.

7.3. CELSUS'S ANTI-JEWISH SENTIMENTS

It is clear that Celsus (cf. *Cels.* 2.76) takes on the *persona* of a Jew in his now lost treatise against Christianity.[47] However, based on a reading of Origen's *Contra*

---

47. I.e., *True Word* a.k.a. Λόγος Ἀληθής.

Celsum, he must also have had a low opinion of Jews in general. This is one of the reasons why Origen needs to defuse Celsus's attempts (cf. *Cels.* 1.22) to discredit Christians by finding fault with the beliefs and practices of their perceived predecessors (i.e., the Jews). In *Cels.* 1.15, Origen strives to affirm the importance of Jewish culture when he makes mention of, *inter alia*, Numenius, the Pythagorean, Hermippus, and Hecataeus, who variously praise the Jews for their antiquity and great piety, as well as ascertaining that their God was "incorporeal" in nature. Origen contrasts this more positive approach to Jews and Judaism with Celsus's recorded negative comments in *Cels.* 1.16:

> I must express my surprise that Celsus should class the Odrysians, and Samothracians, and Eleusinians, and Hyperboreans among the most ancient and learned nations, and should not deem the Jews worthy of a place among such, either for their learning or their antiquity, although there are many treatises in circulation among the Egyptians, and Phœnicians, and Greeks, which testify to their existence as an ancient people, but which I have considered it unnecessary to quote.

Origen also berates Celsus for his seemingly anti-Semitic attitude in *Cels.* 1.16:

> It seems, then, to be not from a love of truth, but from a spirit of hatred, that Celsus makes these statements, his object being to asperse the origin of Christianity, which is connected with Judaism. Nay, he styles the Galactophagi of Homer, and the Druids of the Gauls, and the Getæ; most learned and ancient tribes, on account of the resemblance between their traditions and those of the Jews, although I know not whether any of their histories survive; but the Hebrews alone, as far as in him lies, he deprives of the honour both of antiquity and learning.

In *Cels.* 2.4, Origen falsely explains that the Jews of antiquity, whether they currently accepted it or not, actually prophesied the coming of Christ. Due to the fact that Celsus takes issue with Jewish trustworthiness, Origen needs to justify the notion that the Jewish scriptures genuinely foretold the coming of Christ and the ultimate demise of the rule of Mosaic Law. He also needs to justify the canonized gospels' narratives of John the Baptist (albeit being a Jew), as preparing the way for Christ. After all, from Origen's perspective, many Jews were divinely inspired prophets of Christianity: Isaiah, Ezekiel, and Elijah—the latter also clearly serving as the Christian model for John the Baptist:[48]

> Now, certainly the introduction to Christianity is through the Mosaic worship and the prophetic writings; and after the introduction, it is in the interpretation

---

48. Cf. Isa 35:8; 40:3, Mal 3:1; 4:5, Matt 3:1–3; Mark 1:2–5; Luke 3:2–6; and John 1:23.

and explanation of these that progress takes place, while those who are introduced prosecute their investigations into the mystery according to revelation, which was kept secret since the world began, but now is made manifest in the Scriptures of the prophets, and by the appearance of our Lord Jesus Christ. But they who advance in the knowledge of Christianity do not, as you allege, treat the things written in the law with disrespect. On the contrary, they bestow upon them greater honour, showing what a depth of wise and mysterious reasons is contained in these writings, which are not fully comprehended by the Jews, who treat them superficially, and as if they were in some degree even fabulous. And what absurdity should there be in our system—that is, the Gospel—having the law for its foundation, when even the Lord Jesus Himself said to those who would not believe upon Him: If you had believed Moses, you would have believed Me, for he wrote of Me. But if you do not believe his writings, how shall you believe My words? Nay, even one of the evangelists—Mark—says: The beginning of the Gospel of Jesus Christ, as it is written in the prophet Isaiah, Behold, I send My messenger before Your face, who shall prepare Your way before You, which shows that the beginning of the Gospel is connected with the Jewish writings. What force, then, is there in the objection of the Jew of Celsus, that if any one predicted to us that the Son of God was to visit mankind, he was one of our prophets, and the prophet of our God? Or how is it a charge against Christianity, that John, who baptised Jesus, was a Jew?

7.4. Origen's Known Acts of Pious Fraud

It must also be accepted that Origen, either by dint of personal conviction or blatant duplicity, is quite capable of academic dishonesty whenever there is a dearth of valid substantiation for his dubious opinions. One very good example of his deceit is witnessed in his account in *Cels.* 1.51, where he attempts to substantiate the then prevalent assumption that a particular cave in Bethlehem was Jesus's birth place. Origen needs this to be treated as *prima facie* evidence that Jesus was undeniably of divine birth. Furthermore, he only has recourse to the populist notion, still highly prevalent today, that if enough individuals believe something to be true then it probably is. Thus, he needs to stress that Jesus's claimed birthplace is a certainty and still exists. He also needs to exaggerate the numbers of persons who accept this improbable notion. Further, he strives to expound that this self-same locale for the nativity event was divinely prophesied in Jewish antiquity. Accordingly, to assist his recapitulation, Origen (*Cels.* 1.51) resorts to expressing a blatant falsehood:

> Moreover, I am of opinion that, before the advent of Christ, the chief priests and scribes of the people, on account of the distinctness and clearness of this prophecy, taught that in Bethlehem the Christ was to be born. And this opinion had prevailed also extensively among the Jews.

Again, as has already been witnessed, Origen is not averse to alleging numerous Jewish prophecies that supposedly foretold the arrival Jesus of Nazareth as Christ and undeniably, in *Cels.* 3.28, he typically makes the following ingenuous statement:

> The whole Jewish people who were hanging in expectation of the coming of Him who was looked for, did, after the advent of Jesus, fall into a keen dispute with each other; and that a great multitude of them acknowledged Christ, and believed Him to be the object of prophecy.

These kinds of statements are quite false on many levels, yet Origen confidently employs them as if they were compelling evidence.

7.5. Christianity as a Religion for the Unlearned

In *Cels.* 1.9, Origen accuses Celsus of stereotyping Christians as being wholly uncritical and relying on blind faith to justify their religious standpoint. Origen speaks to Celsus's contentions as follows:

> He [Celsus] next proceeds to recommend, that in adopting opinions we [Christians] should follow reason and a rational guide, since he who assents to opinions without following this course is very liable to be deceived. And he compares inconsiderate believers to Metragyrtæ, and soothsayers, and Mithræ, and Sabbadians, and to anything else that one may fall in with, and to the phantoms of Hecate, or any other demon or demons. For as among such persons are frequently to be found wicked men, who, taking advantage of the ignorance of those who are easily deceived, lead them away whither they will, so also, he says, is the case among Christians. And he asserts that certain persons who do not wish either to give or receive a reason for their belief, keep repeating, "Do not examine, but believe!" and, "Your faith will save you!" And he alleges that such also say, "The wisdom of this life is bad, but that foolishness is a good thing!" [Punctuation for greater clarity NPLA]

It is evident that Origen feels the need to employ what he considers to be sound, logical reasoning to successfully counter Celsus's indictments of typical Christian credulity. However, as has been determined already, he also accepts the power/reality of sympathetic magic, evil spirits, and demons.

One of his principle concerns is that Celsus consistently presents Jesus of Nazareth as an evil sorcerer, whom only the very naïve would consider to be a worker of divine miracles. In addition, Celsus compares Jesus of Nazareth negatively to other alleged wonder-working god-men (e.g., the Bacchæ [*Cels.* 3.34]; Dioscuri, Hercules, Æsculapius, and Dionysus [*Cels.* 3.22]). In this context, Origen desperately needs to find convincing evidence to successfully elevate Jesus far above any other comparable individuals. In short, he needs to be able to corroborate that the miraculous accounts recorded on behalf of Jesus of Nazareth were not due to trickery, deceit, or invention. Origen needs to convince a doubter like Celsus that Jesus's teaching, actions and deeds were primary, tangible, evidence of his highest divine authority as the living God (as claimed by Christians).

Origen also needs to prove that many Christians (who unfortunately, might really be as unlearned and unsophisticated as Celsus has affirmed), were still correct/justified in their chosen belief. Origen needs to be able to demonstrate to someone like Celsus that Christian conversion was a *divine* event and not mere wishful thinking or ingenuous self-delusion. His preferred approach to solving this conundrum is revealed in (*Cels.* 1.9):

> But since the course alluded to is impossible, partly on account of the necessities of life, partly on account of the weakness of men, as **only a very few individuals devote themselves earnestly to study**, what better method could be devised with a view of assisting the multitude, than that which was delivered by Jesus to the heathen? And let us inquire, **with respect to the great multitude of believers, who have washed away the mire of wickedness in which they formerly wallowed, whether it were better for them to believe without a reason,** and (so) to **have become reformed and improved in their habits**, through the belief that men are chastised for sins, and honoured for good works or **not to have allowed themselves to be converted on the strength of mere faith,** but (to have waited) until they could give themselves to a thorough examination of the (necessary) reasons. [Emphases NPLA].

What is alluded to here is that God Himself foresaw the need to "simplify" matters if he was going to succeed in his mission of Christianizing the entire world. He needed to make things easy for both the converts as well as the converters. In this regard, Origen stresses the overriding benefits of Christian baptism as a sympathetic magical rite, which successfully outweighs any other consideration determined by philosophical debate. Unquestionably, it seems as though Origen is equating the contemplated evaluation of even a well-educated individual who ultimately comes to accept Christ (i.e., based on wisdom alone), with the spiritual conversion of any individual who is merely the beneficiary of the divine power of the rite of a Christian baptism.

7.6. THE EFFICACY OF CHRISTIAN BAPTISM

Baptism is not seen here as some symbolic way to wash away sins or exemplify the believer's passage into a new spiritual life. For Origen, any individual (irrespective of their rationale or level of intellect), once baptized, will exhibit behavior patterns that differ significantly from those that they displayed before their conversion. This is the tangible evidence that Origen wants to hold up to Celsus. For example, by the power of Christ, the converts will reveal that they are now virtuous, righteous and Godly. Baptized Christians literally "improve their habits" regardless of their education. Origen does not even bother to give substantiated examples of this claimed change in behavior patterns but merely presents this astonishing phenomenon as undisputed fact.

In *Cels.* 1.64, Origen elucidates through means of generalities and sweeping statements, the changes that occur during the conversion process replete with baptism rite:

> For we ourselves also were sometimes foolish, disobedient, deceived, serving various lusts and pleasures, living in malice and envy, hateful, and hating one another. But after that **the kindness and love of God our Saviour towards man appeared, by the washing of regeneration, and renewing of the Holy Ghost**, which He shed upon us richly, we became such as we are. [Emphasis NPLA]

Another way of understanding Origen's point of view is to regard the act of baptism as having the same weight as a *rational* decision to convert. Origen tries to subtly suggest that even an unlearned person receives new life in Christ; even if he/she does not fully understand the finer philosophical points of the Christian conviction. Thus, an individual's chosen faith is given authority by the Christian rite of baptism, because it results in him/her literally giving over his/her life to Christ/God. In this regard, the rebirth is not symbolic, but actual. The baptism rite marks the very moment when the converted person accepts/receives Christ into his/her life. In this way, Origen develops an argument, based on sympathetic magic, which can be employed against Celsus's more logical and rational observations.

In *Cels.* 3.48, Origen confirms that anyone is welcome to become a Christian whilst countering Celsus's claim that only unintelligent people convert to Christianity:

> Let him who wills [i.e., to be converted] come to us instructed, and wise, and prudent; and none the less, if any one be ignorant and unintelligent, and uninstructed and foolish, let him also come: for it is these whom the Gospel promises to cure, when they come, by rendering them all worthy of God. [Insertion for clarity NPLA]

Origen believes that once baptized, the individual concerned literally receives and/or internalizes Christ/God. As a result, the baptized individual has no choice but to subsequently act in accordance with Christian/Godly principles. Origen confirms this benefit of Christian baptism (which is demonstrated by his claimed tangible changed behavior patterns) in his *Cels.* 1.9:

> For it is manifest that, (on such a plan), all men, with very few exceptions, would not obtain this (amelioration of conduct) which they have obtained through a simple faith, but would continue to remain in the practice of a wicked life. Now,

whatever other evidence can be furnished of the fact, that it was not without divine intervention that the philanthropic scheme of Christianity was introduced among men, this also must be added. For a pious man will not believe that even a physician of the body, who restores the sick to better health, could take up his abode in any city or country without divine permission, since no good happens to men without the help of God.

Related to this, in his *Cels.* 1.46, Origen explains that we should be assured of Christ's divinity due to his miracles and the fact that his disciples, filled with his power, also performed miracles. Most important of all, he cites both the disciples of Christ as well as contemporary Christian's willingness to face the threat of death for their beliefs as evidence of the truth of Christ's teaching. Origen also claims (again without real substantiation), a Christian's ability to cast out demons, foretell the future and cure illness.

7.7. ORIGEN'S EXPLOITATION OF JOSEPHUS

With the aforementioned contexts in mind, it is possible to see that one of the more problematic issues for Origen was the effective neutralization, *inter alia*, of Celsus's derogatory opinions of Jews in general, unlearned Christian naivety, the Christian claim of Jesus's divinity and his supposed virgin birth. This latter claim also appears to have been supported by the gospel account of John the Baptist's baptism of Jesus. This is because, at this event, God (the Father) is recorded as confirming Jesus's divine paternity. The various issues under review thus far, seem to be interrelated in the gospel account of a righteous and pious Jew (John the Baptist) performing the Christian baptism ritual on the Son of God, replete with the bodily appearance of the Holy Spirit (in the form of a dove) and the heavenly voice of God the Father.

Based on Origen's various comments in his *Contra Celsum* (cf. 1, 37, 40), it can be safely determined that Celsus considered this whole Baptist narrative to be a fiction and also takes issue (justifiably so) with the claim that it was the Jews who prophesized Christ and also the ones who wrote the gospels and thus invented Christianity.

Therefore, ostensibly, Origen needs to prove, to Celsus, *inter alia*, the following six points:

1. Jesus is *really* the son of Almighty God who brought him (conception) into the physical world (incarnation) through the medium of a virgin woman;
2. The Holy Spirit appeared bodily (incarnate) as a dove;
3. The Divine Voice from Heaven (God the Father) actually occurred at *the* baptism event;
4. Christian baptism had *real* spiritual efficacy and resulted in its recipient adopting Godly qualities;
5. A person who displays Christ like/Godly behavior subsequent to a Christian baptism is *evidence* of Jesus's divine status; and
6. The gospel accounts of, *inter alia*, the Baptism event are *wholly* true.

The first recorded reference made specifically to the *BP* was made by Origen. In this regard, it is most important to take note that in his *Cels.* 1.47, Origen has the real need to defend the then current form of the Christian practice of baptism. Below is a transcript of the specific passages which refers to John the Baptist in *Cels.* 1.47:

> I would like to say to Celsus, who represents the Jew as accepting somehow John as a Baptist, who baptised Jesus, that the existence of John the Baptist, **baptizing for the remission of sins**, is related by one who lived no great length of time after John and Jesus. For in the 18th book of his Antiquities of the Jews, Josephus bears witness to John as having been a **Baptist**, and as **promising purification to those who underwent the rite**. [Emphases NPLA]

What is even more telling (given that my findings also reveal that, in all likelihood, Origen forged the *JP* as well)[49] is that the above quoted passage from *Cels.* 1.47 immediately precedes Origen's reference to Josephus as the source for his reference to James (i.e., the *JP*). Thus, we have evidence here that *both suspected* interpolations are literally referenced in tandem in the *same* passage.

We have seen how throughout his *Contra Celsum* Origen iterates his particular take on the rite of Christian baptism and Christ-directed changes to an individual's prior unacceptable behavior patterns. However, when it comes to his account of the Baptism of Christ, Origen seems (on the surface) to be neglecting a golden opportunity to talk to his hobbyhorse. Indeed, in *Cels.* 1.47, Origen merely states that John the Baptist baptized "for the remission of sins … promising purification to those who underwent the rite." However, *concurrent* to this brief comment, Origen also makes a *direct reference* to Josephus.

In one sense, Josephus merely serves here as an independent and trusted witness to back up Origen's assertions on a very superficial level. However, if the reader actually bothers to turn to Josephus's *BP* (i.e., *A.J.* 18.5.2 [§§116–119]),

---

49. For a substantiation of the *JP* as interpolation by Origen, see Nicholas P. L. Allen, "Josephus on James the Just? A Re-evaluation of Antiquitates Judaicae 20.9.1," *JECH* 7.1 (2017): 1–27.

he/she will most "conveniently" discover a lengthy, reiteration of those very issues that disprove some of Celsus's claims. In this regard (assuming that Origen perpetrated this forgery), he manages to legitimize Josephus as author of the substantiation by the link to the castle of Macherus and Herod Antipas. Then, he has Josephus confirm (on his behalf) the following two very important details:

1. John the Baptist may have been a Jew, *but* he was not only a proven "good man," he also actively worked towards making *other* Jews "exercise virtue" and practice righteous behavior and "piety towards God";
2. John the Baptist did not practice some form of traditional Jewish purification ritual;[50] he practiced a distinctly Christian baptism, which ensured that the convert subsequently engaged in a divinely directed, behavioral change, that embodied piety, righteousness and Godly virtues. Specifically, he enacted a religious rite which did two interdependent, overtly, Christocentric actions:
   - The remission of sins;[51] and
   - The purification of the body (supposing that the soul was purified beforehand by righteousness).

The latter two points are nothing more than embellishments of the very concepts that Origen had been trying to convince his reader of in his *Contra Celsum* generally and in *Cels.* 1.47 in particular.

In order to substantiate his take on the rite of baptism, Origen needs the *BP*. For convenience, the pertinent passage from the *BP* is reproduced again:

> [John the Baptist] commanded the Jews to exercise virtue, both as to righteousness towards one another, and piety towards God, and so to come to baptism; for that the washing [with water] would be acceptable to him, if they made use of it, not in order to the putting away [or the remission] of some sins [only], but for the purification of the body; supposing still that the soul was thoroughly purified beforehand by righteousness. [Insertion for clarity NPLA]

By making a direct reference to a passage only found in a work by Josephus at this juncture, Origen literally kills two birds with one stone. He proves his point by supposedly referring to a reliable, non-partisan and objective historian (i.e., one who did not accept Jesus as the Messiah). In addition, this impartial witness was "one who lived no great length of time after John and Jesus."

---

50. I.e., a Jewish *mikveh*.

51. From a mainstream Jewish perspective, God immediately forgives iniquity as a result of genuine repentance. From a mainstream Christian perspective, only Christ's death, his blood, and resurrection can remove sin.

Josephus, who would not have known, let alone been bothered by such specific Christian doctrinal minutiae, is clearly made to say what Origen requires. Origen desperately needs an independent, historically valid, witness to back him up. Here, Josephus (*Cels.* 1.47) conveniently steps in and clearly confirms Origen's point of view.

The real possibility here, is that Origen was most likely the creator of the *BP*. This claim is supported by the following evidence:

1. The very precise nature of Origen's specific arguments (i.e., as contained in his *Contra Celsum*);
2. Origen's need to obtain substantiated evidence to counter Celsus's very valid points; and
3. Origen's proven willingness to employ mistruths when it suited his agenda.

The fact that both the *JP* and the *BP* are mentioned in the same passage penned by Origen strengthens this possibility. It is simply too much of a coincidence that in one paragraph this apologist manages to point to two supporting pieces of evidence, supposedly written by the same author. These both expediently substantiate so many aspects of his argument with Celsus. The fact that both of these "corroborations" have independently been recognized as suspicious in nature and candidates for total interpolation, based on other evidence, is also enthralling. The obvious conclusion that must be made here is that Origen is the prime candidate for two of the three abovementioned suspected interpolations in Josephus's *Antiquitates Judaicae*.

8. Conclusions

The following points, especially when taken collectively, mitigate against the *BP* being in any way an authentic Josephan text. If Josephus wrote the *BP*, it follows that he also:

1. contradicts the gospels as regards the date of John the Baptist's activities;
2. contradicts the gospels as regards the reason for John the Baptist's arrest;
3. shows remarkable familiarity and theologically advanced insights into Christian-based baptism rites;
4. contradicts his statements about the range and scope of Jewish-based cults in the holy land due to failure to mention any other Jewish sect even remotely connected with a Baptist cult or Christianity;[52]
5. contradicts his avowed position on the dangers of Jewish religious upstarts;
6. describes an impossible/contradictory situation at the fortress at Macherus;
7. contradicts his previously stated reasons for God's divine vengeance against Antipas;

---

52. This assumes that the *TF* is also an interpolation.

8. seriously disrupts the literary flow of his narration;
9. fails to mention John the Baptist in his earlier work and in the same context (i.e., the *BJ*); and
10. fails to mention John the Baptist in his table of contents (*Antiquitates Judaicae*).

Based on the arguments cited thus far, only the following debatable point supports the *BP* being in some way authentic: only a non-Christian like Josephus would have placed the New Testament events in the wrong order.

However, the latter point can be easily countered by the need of the interpolator to find a suitable context within the *Antiquitates Judaicae* for his forgery. Although an interpolator would have preferred to have had the *BP* precede the *TF*, he felt that his fraud would be less obvious if he could at least place the two interpolations in a more convincing context. As the only suitable places were not in the correct chronological order this gives the appearance of Josephus having placed the events of Christian import in the wrong order.

The Ending of the *Canticum Mosis* (Deuteronomy 32:43) and Its Reception in Hebrews 1:6—A Fresh Look

Elena Belenkaja

Abstract: In Heb 1:6, the reading ἄγγελοι θεοῦ within the quotation of Deut 32:43 is essential to the author's argument. However, from a text-critical point of view, we have to ask ourselves what text and which version underlies the quotation in Heb 1:6. This paper focuses on the complex textual tradition of Deut 32:43 including not only the MT, 4Q44, and the Septuagint version of Deut 32:43 itself, but Ode 2:43 as well. By comparing the different Greek and Hebrew versions of Deut 32:43, an approximation to the solution can be achieved. Possible influences of Ps 96(97):7 are also an issue of debate in modern research.

1. Key Problem

The ending of the *Canticum Mosis* (Deut 32:43) exists in three different versions: the Masoretic Text (MT),[1] the main Greek translation (LXX), and a fragment from Qumran (4QDeut^q [4Q44] 32:43). All three versions differ from each other. Before the discovery of the Dead Sea Scrolls the only possible comparison was between the MT and LXX. Thus, Henry Barcley Swete states in his *Introduction to the Old Testament in Greek*:

> Possibly the Song was circulated in a separate form in more than one translation. The present Greek text seems to be the result of conflation, lines 1 and 3, 2 and 4, 6 and 7, being doublets; line 2 = 4 appears to be an adaptation of Ps. xcvi. (xcvii.) 7.[2]

---

1. It is virtually identical to SP.
2. Henry Barcley Swete, *An Introduction to the Old Testament in Greek* (Cambridge: Cambridge University Press, 1900), 243.

Eduard Riggenbach follows this thesis later in his commentary on the Hebrews.[3] The situation is different with Julio Trebolle Barrera:

> Before the discovery of the Dead Sea Scrolls, it was possible to suspect that the Greek text of Dt 32:43 contained older elements than those present in the Hebrew Masoretic text. The manuscript 4QDeut^q has proved that the Greek text is not an alteration or an incorrect translation.... The Greek translation only transmits a Hebrew text similar to the one now discovered in Qumran.[4]

The discussion about the possible *Vorlage* of Deut 32:43 is not new and still without a satisfactory answer. G. Ernest Wright already pointed out that this verse "simply cannot be reconstructed with certainty."[5] However, this issue is still relevant and requires constant updating, including its reception history in the New Testament.

In the following, I will give three examples to illustrate what attempts at reconstruction there have been since the discovery of the Dead Sea Scrolls. These will be followed by a look at Heb 1:6.

2. The Diverse Attempts at Reconstructing Deut 32:43

2.1. The Reconstruction by Patrick W. Skehan

The discovery of 4QDeut^q has shed some light on the question of the possible original *Vorlage* of Deut 32:43. Although the text does not match the LXX, "several unique readings [which] bear[s] witness to the existence of the variant Hebrew *Vorlage* used by the Septuagint translator"[6] become apparent.

The manuscript 4QDeut^q consists of only a few fragments of the text from Deut 32:37–43 and 32:9–10(?) and probably "originally contained only the Song of Moses (Deut 32:1–43)."[7]

---

3. Eduard Riggenbach, *Der Brief an die Hebräer*, KNT 14 (Leipzig: Deichert, 1922), 20.

4. Florentino García Martínez and Julio Trebolle Barrera, *The People of the Dead Sea Scrolls: Their Writings, Beliefs and Practices* (Leiden: Brill, 1995), 108.

5. G. Ernest Wright, "The Lawsuit of God: A Form-Critical Study of Deuteronomy 32," in *Israel's Prophetic Heritage: Essays in Honor of James Muilenburg*, ed. Bernhard W. Anderson et al. (New York: Harper, 1962), 33 n. 23.

6. Patrick W. Skehan and Eugene Ulrich, "4QDeut^q," in *Qumran Cave 4 IX: Deuteronomy, Joshua, Judges, Kings*, ed. Eugene Ulrich et al., DJD XIV (Oxford: Clarendon, 1995), 138.

7. Skehan and Ulrich, "4QDeut^q," 137.

Patrick W. Skehan concludes that "the new Qumran materials serve to confirm the existence of a divergent ancient Hebrew text which the LXX translators had before them."[8] His reconstruction of the Qumran text reads as follows:

hrnynw šmym 'mw
whšḥtww lw kl 'lhym
ky dm bnyw yqwm
wnqm yšyb lṣryw
wlmśn'yw yšlm
wykpr 'dmt 'mw

When comparing the text with the MT / SP and the LXX, he makes the following observations:

(1) The reading *šmym* should be preferred with the LXX as more original than MT גוים (this forms an inclusio with v. 1: השמים).

(2) The second stich (v. 43b) proves that this passage clearly refers to Ps 97(96):7. Apart from the *waw*, the Hebrew text is identical.[9]

(3) In his opinion *bnyw* is more original than MT עבדיו.

(4) Wherever MT includes only a half-verse of Deut 32:41, the Qumran text and the LXX contain both.

(5) The verb form *wykpr*, however, is in all likelihood secondary in comparison with וכפר in MT and arises from a further evolution of the Hebrew syntax. On the other hand, *'dmt 'mt*, which coincides with the LXX, is necessary for the understanding of the half-line.[10] The absence of the phrase in verse 43b in MT, which is included in the LXX, leads Skehan to the conclusion that the "concept

---

8. Patrick W. Skehan, "A Fragment of the 'Song of Moses' (Deut. 32) from Qumran," *BASOR* 136 (1954): 14.

9. See Skehan, "Fragment," 15 n. 4. This stich could also be a secondary addition in the psalm. Taking into consideration that the translators of the LXX first worked on the Pentateuch, which provided the source for further translations, it seems possible that the author of the psalm used Deut 32:43 as the basis for his translation. There are also no safe assumptions regarding the determination of the age of the Song of Moses. See, for example, Jack R. Lundbom, *Deuteronomy: A Commentary* (Grand Rapids: Eerdmans, 2013), 852–57. Seybold dates Pss 90–118 to the period of the second temple (520–515 BCE). It is entirely possible that they existed earlier. See Klaus Seybold, *Die Psalmen: Eine Einführung*, UTB 382 (Stuttgart: Kohlhammer, 1986), 10.

10. See Skehan, "Fragment," 14. SP differs from MT here and corresponds with 4QDeut[q]. Cf. Arie van der Kooij, "The Ending of the Song of Moses: On the Pre-Masoretic Version of Deut 32:43," in *Studies in Deuteronomy in Honour of Casper J. Labuschagne on the Occasion of His Sixty-Fifth Birthday*, ed. Florentino García Martínez et al., VTSup 53 (Leiden: Brill, 1994), 97. He considers the reading in 4QDeut[q] "a linguistic adaption to later, post-biblical Hebrew usage of which examples are known from 1QIsa[a]."

of the existence together with God of such supernal beings as we now call angels was not without difficulties, both theological and apologetic, for the pious Jew living in a predominantly polytheistic world."[11] He explains the possible inclusion of elements from verse 41 in verse 43 with the fact that they "are a reflex of the difficulty created when the hemistich parallel to 43[a] was lost or excised; and that the intrusion, whether of one or of two hemistich, destroys the proper parallelism between *ky ... yqwm* and the final hemistich of the poem."[12] The alternative reading of this line in the LXX (καὶ ἐνισχυσάτωσαν αὐτῷ πάντες ἄγγελοι θεοῦ / υἱοὶ θεοῦ) presents, in his opinion, not only another Hebrew version but is also most likely the original version. At the same time, he points to Deut 32:3; Ps 29:1; and LXX 96:7.[13]

His reconstruction of the (proto)Masoretic text of Deut 32:43 is the following:

harnînû šāmayim 'immô	Exult with him, you heavens,
wᵉhābû 'ōz lô kōl bᵉnê 'ēlîm:	glorify him, all you angels of God;
kî dam bānā (y) w yiqqōm	For he avenges the blood of his servants
wᵉkippēr 'adᵉmat 'ammô.	And purges his people's land.[14]

2.2. The Reconstruction by Arie van der Kooij in a Debate with Casper Labuschagne and Maurice Bogaert

Some twenty years later, Arie van der Kooij analysed the ending of the Song of Moses in his contribution to the commemorative publication for Casper J. Labuschagne. Here, he notes that the Hebrew text of Deut 32:8, 43 "has undergone presumably in the Hellenistic era, remarkable changes."[15] In verse 8, "sons of God" becomes "sons of Israel" and, in verse 43, "Rejoice you heavens, with Him" becomes "Rejoice you nations, about His people" in MT. Casper L. Labuschagne[16] assumed that this was an earlier version of verse 43, because the

---

11. Patrick W. Skehan, "The Structure of the Song of Moses in Deuteronomy," in *A Song of Power and the Power of Song: Essays on the Book of Deuteronomy*, ed. Christensen L. Duane, SBTS 3 (Winona Lake: Eisenbrauns, 1993), 156–68. For the structure of the Song, see also Solomon A. Nigosian, "The Song of Moses (Dt 32): A Structural Analysis," *ETL* 72 (1996): 5–22.

12. Skehan, "Fragment," 15.

13. Bogaert refers in this context to 1 Chr 16:28. See Pierre-Maurice Bogaert, "Les trois redactions conservées et la forme originale de l'envoi du Cantique de Mose (Dt 32,43)," in *Das Deuteronomium: Entstehung, Gestalt und Botschaft*, ed. Norbert Lohfink, BETL 68 (Leuven: Leuven University Press, 1985), 330 n. 10.

14. Cf. Skehan, "Structure," 164.

15. Van der Kooij, "Ending," 93.

16. Van der Kooij refers here to Casper J. Labuschagne, "The Song of Moses: Its Framework and Structure," in *De fructu oris sui: Essays in Honour of Adrianus von Selms*, ed. Ian H. Eybers et al. (Leiden: Brill, 1971), 85–98.

reading "heavens" in verse 43 is in literary correspondence with verse 1. Thus, the MT version cannot be the original one. In his opinion, the original *Vorlage* ought to be reconstructed from the LXX and Qumran text. He comes to the following result, which has been translated in the New English Bible accordingly:

> Rejoice with him, you heavens,
> bow down, all you gods, before him,
> for he will avenge the blood of his sons
> and take vengeance on his adversaries;
> he will punish those who hate him
> and make expiation for his people's land.

Owing to the repetition in the third and fourth part of the verse of the Greek text, Van der Kooij argues for "an expanded and contaminated text, partly based on the (proto)masoretic version of verse 43."[17] While Labuschagne considers the Qumran text with six cola the earlier version,[18] Pierre-Maurice Bogaert acknowledges the Qumran text as the primary version of verse 43 with only four of them.[19] He omits cola two and five, which have no parallel in MT. Furthermore, Bogaert reads in the first cola the divine designation אלהים instead of שמים. His arguments, however, are not convincing. Since "heaven" of 4QDeut^q and LXX is attested and appears also in Deut 32:1, this reading is probably the original one. Apart from that, Bogaert interprets דם בניו in the first cola as "the blood shed by his sons" and not as "the blood of his sons."[20] Van der Kooij correctly states that nowhere in the Song of Moses does it say that the sons of God had shed innocent blood.[21]

Assuming that the editor has intentionally omitted cola two and five in MT, the question arises, why he did so. Bogaert does not believe in this possibility. However, there are several examples in the Torah of such omissions (cf. Gen 46:20, 27; and Exod 1:5). Therefore, it is quite possible that the editor has abbreviated the text.[22]

Looking at the text as a whole, Van der Kooij notes, as Skehan had done before him, that the second colon has a parallel in Ps 97(96):7 and the fifth colon

---

17. Van der Kooij, "Ending," 96.
18. Meyer had already pleaded for this assumption 1961. Cf. Rudolf Meyer, "Die Bedeutung von Deuteronomium 32, 8f.43 (4Q) für die Auslegung des Moseliedes," in *Verbannung und Heimkehr: Beiträge zur Geschichte und Theologie Israels im 6. und 5. Jahrhundert v. Chr., W. Rudolph zum 70. Geburtstag*, ed. Arnulf Kuschke (Tübingen: Mohr Siebeck, 1961), 197–209.
19. Bogaert, "Trois rédactions," 336.
20. Van der Kooij, "Ending," 97.
21. See Van der Kooij, "Ending," 97.
22. Van der Kooij, "Ending," 98.

recalls verse 41. Therefore, there is the possibility that these were added "at some later stage of the transmission of the text."[23] On the other hand, he rightly points out that the last part of Ps 97(96):7 could be taken from Deut 32 or that both texts simply have a common background. Furthermore, the fourth colon also shows a parallelism with verse 41b.

Another argument he raises is the poetic structure. Without the second stich in the first line of verse 43, the characteristic element of the Song of Moses, which establishes a parallelism between the cola and thus forms bicola, would disappear. The additional second colon in verse 1 creates the first line of verse 43 and establishes a parallelism between "heavens" and "gods" and between "with him" and "him." Also the fifth stich "is needed in order to get a nice structural balance in this part of the verse."[24] Furthermore Van der Kooij points out the chiastic structure of the verse, which is only possible with the fifth colon. "The blood of his sons" then relates to "expiation for his people's land" and "vengeance on his adversaries" relates to "punish those who hate him." Such a conglomeration of thoughts is found in Num 35:33.

The second colon in the LXX differs from 4QDeut^q: כל אלהים ... - ... πάντες υἱοὶ θεοῦ. This raises the question, whether the translator had a different *Vorlage*, that is, כל בני אלהים. Nowhere is it documented that כל אלהים is translated as πάντες υἱοὶ θεοῦ. Therefore, Bogaert assumes that the Hebrew text must have contained בני אלהים.[25] According to Van der Kooij, this deviation could have occurred for various reasons:

(1) In verses 17, 31, and 37, θεοί has a negative connotation and therefore the reading πάντες θεοί is inappropriate.

(2) With υἱοὶ θεοῦ a correlation to verse 8 would be established.[26]

Generally speaking, it is clear that a shorter reading of MT changes the parallelism in the first two cola: "his people / his servants," as in verse 36, whereas no parallel structure exists in the last two cola. Also Van der Kooij makes clear that through the reduction the Song of Moses has a total of 140 cola or 70 lines as well as seventy sons of Israel. These changes in verse 43 are connected to verse 8, where the sons of Israel are mentioned. For this reason, the shorter version of the MT could have been harmonized to fit "the number of the sons of Israel." In his opinion the Qumran version is the original.

---

23. Van der Kooij, "Ending," 98.
24. Van der Kooij, "Ending," 98.
25. Cf. Bogaert, "Trois rédactions," 336.
26. See Van der Kooij, "Ending," 99. He assumes that "sons of God" is the original wording.

2.3. THE RECONSTRUCTION BY JUHA PAKKALA

In his book, published in 2013, Juha Pakkala deals with the questions of omissions in the Hebrew Bible and primarily looks at literary translation. In one chapter, he explores the "omissions as a result of ideological or theological censoring,"[27] to which he counts Deut 32:8 and 43. In his opinion "the reading in the MT / SP is the result of a theological correction that included the omission of disturbing polytheistic elements."[28] These elements he spots particularly in the second cola of 4QDeut[q] and LXX, which are missing in MT / SP and the modification of שמים to גוים. "This change was probably done in order to avoid the idea that שמים refers to animate gods residing in heaven. That gods are in fact meant is implied by its poetical parallel כל אלהים in 4QDeut[q] and in the assumed *Vorlage* of the Greek υἱοὶ θεοῦ."[29]

Furthermore, דם עבדיו could be a correction of דם בניו, because the text implies that Yahweh had sons. That means that 4QDeut[q] and LXX include a polytheistic conception, which is not represented (anymore) in MT / SP. Subsequent additions of such a conception are unusual, according to Pakkala, while their omission is understandable.[30] The double reading of the first lines in LXX he explains as follows:

The first double line has a parallel in 4QDeut[q], while the second is contained in parts of the MT. The sentence ἐνισχυσάτωσαν αὐτῷ πάντες ἄγγελοι θεοῦ is only documented in the LXX and has no parallel, "but this may have been an earlier and separate attempt in the MT to avoid the theological problem: כל אלהים would have been changed to כל מלאכי אלהים (= πάντες ἄγγελοι θεοῦ)."[31] This parallel was omitted from the MT later. It is possible, however, that the reference was made to the angels only in the translation process.[32]

It is striking that in line six of the LXX there are parallels to be found to MT and in line 7 to 4QDeut[q]. Pakkala believes that the LXX at this point is harmonized. But it is also possible that a logical poetic parallelism to verse 41 was intended. This means that the Greek text is the original and 4QDeut[q] and MT contain only a part of this original. "On the other hand, כי דם בניו יקום and וכפר אדמת עמו also seem to form a parallelism, now interrupted by כי דם בניו יקום or ולמשנאיו ישלם."[33] Pakkala concludes that ונקם ישיב לצריו in MT or וכפר אדמת עמו

---

27. Juha Pakkala, *God's Word Omitted: Omissions in the Transmission of the Hebrew Bible*, FRLANT 251 (Göttingen: Vandenhoeck & Ruprecht, 2013), 183, 185.
28. Pakkala, *God's Word Omitted*, 188.
29. Pakkala, *God's Word Omitted*, 188.
30. Pakkala, *God's Word Omitted*, 188–89.
31. Pakkala, *God's Word Omitted*, 188–89.
32. See Pakkala, *God's Word Omitted*, 180 n. 16.
33. Pakkala, *God's Word Omitted*, 189.

in 4QDeut^q are later intrusions that may be influenced by poetic concerns.[34] Hence he arrives at the following reconstruction:

> Give a ringing cry, (you) heavens, with him,
> worship him, (you) all gods,
> for he will avenge the blood of his sons,
> he will purge the land of his people.

This shows two half-verses that are parallel to each other. The given order was finally disturbed in MT or 4QDeut^q by expansions that have been influenced by verse 41. The reason for this remains unclear. It is clear, however, that "the MT / SP version represents a substantially revised tradition where the mythological and theologically offensive elements have been intentionally removed."[35] The second line has been completely removed and שמים changed to גוים.

2.4. CONCLUSION

These three examples are not the only ones. There are many further examples of deviations on which this investigation cannot elaborate. But a reconstruction attempt proposed by Aleander Rofé[36] should be mentioned, whose result was included in the commentary of Jeffrey H. Tigay.[37]

Patrick W. Skehan	Arie van der Kooij/ NEB/Labuschagne	Juha Pakkala	Alexander Rofé
Exult with him, you heavens, glorify him, all you angels of God;	Rejoice with him, you heavens, bow down, all you gods, before him,	Give a ringing cry, (you) heavens, with him, worship him, (you) all gods,	Rejoice heavenly beings with Him And let the divine ones exult,
For he avenges the blood of his servants	for he will avenge the blood of his sons		for He will avenge the blood of His servants

---

34. See Pakkala, *God's Word Omitted*, 189.
35. Pakkala, *God's Word Omitted*, 190.
36. Alexander Rofé, "The End of the Song of Moses (Deuteronomy 32:43)," in *Liebe und Gebot: Studien zum Deuteronomium*, ed. Reinhard Georg Kratz and Hermann Spieckermann, FRLANT 190 (Göttingen: Vandenhoeck & Ruprecht, 2000), 164–72. Allen says that his "4-stich conclusion resembles that of Skehan." David M. Allen, *Deuteronomy and Exhortation in Hebrews: A Study in Narrative Re-presentation*, WUNT 2/238 (Tübingen: Mohr Siebeck, 2008), 49 n. 19.
37. Jeffrey H. Tigay, *Deuteronomy: Devarim*, JPSTC (Philadelphia: Jewish Publication Society, 1996).

	and take vengeance on his adversaries; he will punish those who hate him	for he will avenge the blood of <u>his</u> <u>sons</u>,	
And purges his people's land.	and make expiation for his people's land.		and He will cleanse the land of His people
		he will purge the land of his people.	

The comparison of the four reconstructions shows that there is no consensus, neither regarding the question whether the Qumran version with six lines is the older *Vorlage*, nor as to how to translate כל אלהים or if כל מלאכי אלהים[38] or כל בני אלהים[39] originally were in the text. Furthermore, there is no agreement with respect to the interpretation of דם עבדיו or דם בניו. Only in the original of שמים unity seems to prevail, although this term is not always expressed in the same way. These differences show the complexity of the issue of the original *Vorlage*. The eight-line version of the LXX is explained in different ways: through conflations, the inclusion of Ps 96(97):7; harmonization, a deliberately constructed parallelism based on verse 41; or it is the original. It is also argued that Ps 96(97):7 was influenced by Deut 32:43.

It cannot be decided which the correct reconstruction is. It is quite possible that none of the three versions is the original. This variety makes it clear that not only were there different coexisting versions of Deut 32:43, but that all of these versions were equally accepted. The same should probably also apply to all proposed reconstructions that are founded on good arguments and ultimately serve only to demonstrate that our knowledge about the possible *Vorlage* is limited.

Crucial to the wider context in view of Hebrews is the second line of LXX Deut 32:43: καὶ προσκυνησάτωσαν αὐτῷ πάντες υἱοὶ θεοῦ. But the "LXX witnesses testify to two traditions: those that read υἱοὶ θεοῦ and those that read ἄγγελοι θεοῦ."[40] The first tradition is testified in P. Fouad. Inv 266 (Rahlfs 848), the oldest extant witness (middle of the first century BCE). This leaves out πάντες after αὐτῷ (comp. Codex B) and reads αὐτῷ υἱοὶ θ]εο[ῦ.[41] The second tradition is the version of the Song of Moses in Ode 2. It belongs to a group of selected odes, hymns, and prayers, which follow in Codex A immediately after the psalms. Gert J. Steyn

---

38. As disputed by Pakkala.
39. This position is represented, e.g., by Bogaert and Skehan.
40. Gert J. Steyn, *A Quest for the Assumed LXX Vorlage of the Explicit Quotations in Hebrews*, FRLANT 235 (Göttingen: Vandenhoeck & Ruprecht, 2011), 65. See also Steyn, "A Quest for the Vorlage of the 'Song of Moses' (Deut 32): Quotations in Hebrews," *Neot* 34 (2000): 263–72.
41. See Steyn, *Quest*, 64–65.

assumes that the "inclusion of the *Canticum Mosis* in this Greek Psalter, is probably an indication of the liturgical significance it had, a significance which ran through the history of the temple and continued in the early church."[42]

3. Heb 1:6 and the Quest for a Possible Source

In Heb 1:5–13, the author explicitly points out the outstanding position of the Son in a series of seven quotations. Here the Son is juxtaposed to a type corresponding to and surpassing the angels in order to postulate his otherness, uniqueness, and supremacy. In this series, Heb 1:6 is the third quotation. As a possible *Vorlage* for the quotation, several proposals have been made in Hebrews research: Ps 96(97):7; a conflation from Ps 96(97):7 and LXX Deut 32:43; Deut 32:43 and Ode 2:43.[43]

LXX Deut 32:43	Ode 2:43 (LXX^A)	Ps 96(97):7	Heb 1:6b
εὐφράνθητε οὐρανοί ἅμα αὐτῷ	εὐφράνθητε οὐρανοί ἅμα αὐτῷ		
καὶ προσκυνησάτωσαν αὐτῷ πάντες <u>υἱοὶ θεοῦ</u>	καὶ προσκυνησάτωσαν αὐτῷ πάντες <u>οἱ ἄγγελοι θεοῦ</u>	<u>προσκυνήσατε</u> αὐτῷ πάντες <u>οἱ ἄγγελοι αὐτοῦ</u>	καὶ <u>προσκυνησάτωσαν</u> αὐτῷ πάντες <u>ἄγγελοι θεοῦ</u>
εὐφράνθητε ἔθνη μετὰ τοῦ λαοῦ αὐτοῦ καὶ ἐνισχυσάτωσαν αὐτῷ πάντες <u>ἄγγελοι θεοῦ</u>	εὐφράνθητε ἔθνη μετὰ τοῦ λαοῦ αὐτου καὶ ἐνισχυσάτωσαν αὐτῷ πάντες <u>υἱοὶ θεοῦ</u>		

---

42. Steyn, *Quest*, 65.

43. For recent detailed treatments of Deut 32:43 // Ode 2:43 and Heb 1:6, see the discussion of Wolfgang Kraus, "Die Septuaginta als Brückenschlag zwischen Altem und Neuem Testament? Dtn 32 (Odae 2) als Fallbeispiel," in *Im Brennpunkt—die Septuaginta: Band 3: Studien zur Theologie, Anthropologie, Ekklesiologie, Eschatologie und Liturgie der Griechischen Bibel*, ed. Heinz-Josef Fabry and Dieter Böhler, BWANT 174 (Stuttgart: Kohlhammer, 2007), 266–90. Joshua Jipp suggests a conflation from Deut 32:43 and Deut 32:8. He says this "is the most likely source of the quotation," but does not discuss any reasons. This is not convincing to me. Cf. Joshua W. Jipp, "The Son's Entrance into the Heavenly World: The Soteriological Necessity of the Scriptural Catena in Hebrews 1.5–14," *NTS* 56 (2010): 562.

3.2. The Possible *Vorlage* of Heb 1:6

3.2.1. Heb 1:6 and Ps 96(97):7

When comparing Heb 1:6 with Ps 96(97):7 several differences appear: In Ps 96(97):7 καί is missing; the verb form is imperative aorist active 2.P and not 3.P; in front of ἄγγελοι is an article and instead of θεοῦ is αὐτοῦ. These are too many variations to postulate a dependency. The changes must in fact be attributed to the author, and there is no evidence for such a process. Suspicion of a conflation of Ps 96(97):7 and LXX Deut 32:43 complicates the situation unnecessarily and is easily explained on the basis of LXX Deut 32:43, specifically the second and fourth line.[44] It seems to me that Ps 96(97):7 is basically seen as the basis of the quotation because this verse is often viewed as part of LXX Deut 32:43. This view is particularly influenced by the thesis of Skehan.[45] Yet, he does not take into consideration that the text of Ps 96(97):7, as Steyn has properly exposed, "is probably already evidence of either such a conflation, or of *homoioteleuton*, by the composer of the Psalm."[46] All items that meet in Heb 1:6, are available in LXX Deut 32:43. "At the same time, we note that the text of Heb 1:6 also does not clearly support the longer OG text in Deuteronomy 32:43 either."[47] Therefore Tim Mclay rightly asks: "Why should we presume the combination of two separate texts when we require the use of only one?"[48]

3.2. Heb 1:6 and LXX Deut 32:43 // Ode 2:43

When comparing Heb 1:6 with Deut 32:43 // Ode 2:43 it is obvious that the quotation in Hebrews is closer to the text of Ode 2:43 since this reads ἄγγελοι θεοῦ (although without article), while Deut 32:43 reads υἱοὶ θεοῦ.[49] In lines two and

---

44. Hans-Friedrich Weiß, *Der Brief an die Hebräer*, KEK 13 (Göttingen: Vandenhoeck & Ruprecht, 1991), 161; Riggenbach, *Hebräer*, 20; Gerd Schunack, *Der Hebräerbrief*, ZBK 14 (Zürich: Theologischer Verlag, 2002), 27, e.g., argue for a conflation.
45. Skehan, "Fragment," 14. For him, v. 43b is "an exact verbal counterpart of Ps 97:7."
46. Steyn, *Quest*, 67.
47. R. Timothy McLay, *The Use of the Septuagint in New Testament Research* (Grand Rapids: Eerdmans, 2003), 109.
48. McLay, *Use*, 110. Angela Rascher, *Schriftauslegung und Christologie im Hebräerbrief*, BZNW 153 (Berlin: de Gruyter, 2007), 51; George H. Guthrie, *Hebrews*, The NIV Application Commentary 15 (Grand Rapids: Zondervan, 2009), 69, e.g., argue for Ps 96(97):7 as possible source.
49. Herbert Braun, *An die Hebräer*, HNT 14 (Tübingen: Mohr Siebeck, 1984), 353; Otto Michel, *Der Brief an die Hebräer*, KEK 13 (Göttingen: Vandenhoeck & Ruprecht, 1984), 111–12; Erich Gräßer, *An die Hebräer*, EKK 17.1 (Zürich: Benzinger Verlag, 1990), 77, e.g., suggest Deut 32:43 as the only source.

four, Ode 2 provides an inverted version of the terms ἄγγελοι / υἱοὶ θεοῦ of Deut 32:43.⁵⁰ That means that there is a possibility that "either Heb 1:6 is dependent upon the same tradition of OG Deut 32:43 as the Odes—that is, they are independent witnesses to a slightly different text—or one of the writers of Heb 1:6 or Odes 2:43 borrowed from the other."⁵¹ The second possibility, however, creates more difficulty due to the fact that the Odes are only attested from the fifth century by Codex Alexandrinus. This does not mean that the Song of Moses in the slightly different version that is witnessed in Ode 2 had not been in circulation earlier as a liturgical text and that there had probably been two originals.⁵² Therefore, it is entirely possible that the author of Hebrews has used another source than LXX Deut 32:43, a source that read ἄγγελοι θεοῦ in the second line, just like in the Odes.⁵³

Gareth Lee Cockerill has already tried to prove this plausibly in an essay in 1999.⁵⁴ His key question here was: "Which of these terms [ἄγγελοι / υἱοὶ θεοῦ] is the more likely translation of this word in light of the way אֱלֹהִים is translated elsewhere in the LXX?"⁵⁵ It is clear that nowhere in the LXX is the term אלהים translated as υἱοὶ θεοῦ, but as ἄγγελοι (Pss 8:6; 96[97]:7; 137[138]:1). The reading ἄγγελοι has been a conscious choice of the Greek translator, which is based on the theological necessity to distinguish exactly between "dem einzigartigen Gott

---

50. The Göttingen edition reads with A and miniscule 55 ἄγγελοι, while MS R has υἱοί (so B A and others at Deut 32:43b). In v. 43d, the same is to be found. MSS A and 55 read υἱοί and R reads ἄγγελοι. Rahlfs uses the manuscripts A, R, T and 55 for his reconstruction of the book of Odes and omits others. Cf. Marcus Sigismund, "Anmerkungen zur antiochenischen Textform der LXX-Zitatvorlage im Neuen Testament: XXVI.: Oden, 4/2011," http://isbtf.de/wp-content/uploads/2015/01/26_Ant-in-Oden.pdf.

51. R. Timothy McLay, "Biblical Texts and the Scriptures for the New Testament Church," in *Hearing the Old Testament in the New Testament*, ed. Stanley E. Porter (Grand Rapids: Eerdmans 2006), 54. McLay confuses the Odes with the Odes of Salomon, which leads to incorrect dating. The Odes are thought to date back to 500 CE. Cf. McLay, *Use*, 110.

52. LXX itself points to Odes as a type of text. In 3 Kgdms 8:53, it says: γέγραπται ἐν βιβλίῳ τῆς ᾠδῆς. The second Ode of Moses was very well known and was read, divided into 6 parts, as a psalm in the temple. Philo quotes it very often and 4 Maccabees (18:18–19, for example) references it. Cf. Heinrich, Schneider, "Die biblischen Oden im christlichen Altertum," *Bib* 30 (1949): 30–31.

53. See McLay, *Use*, 110.

54. Gareth Lee Cockerill, "Hebrews 1:6: Source and Significance," *BBR* 9 (1999): 51–64. Allen, *Deuteronomy*, 49–51.

55. Cockerill, "Source," 57.

Israels und untergeordneten göttlichen Wesen."[56] This is not the standard translation for אלהים, which is θεός.[57] The translation of the LXX psalm leads Cockerill to postulate ἄγγελοι θεοῦ as the original reading. Υἱοί as a translation for the various Hebrew expressions אלהים and בנים from 4QDeut^q is highly unlikely in his opinion because the contrast between the two expressions would be lost.[58] He attributes the origin of υἱοὶ θεοῦ to various factors:

(1) The original reading must have been בני אלהים.[59]

(2) This compound is usually translated as ἄγγελοι θεοῦ especially when referring to supernal / supernatural beings and as υἱοὶ θεοῦ, when the beings are human. There are instances when υἱοὶ θεοῦ is also used for supernal / supernatural beings.[60]

(3) Owing to the translation of υἱοὶ θεοῦ in Deut 32:43d, the contrast to the following verse is lost.[61]

(4) Υἱοὶ θεοῦ in Deut 32:43b and ἄγγελοι θεοῦ in Deut 32:43d could also be a simple scribal error.[62]

There is a parallelism between the first and second as well as between the third and fourth lines which becomes apparent by the changed order in Ode 2:43: ἄγγελοι θεοῦ are parallel to οὐρανοί and υἱοὶ θεοῦ to ἔθνη / τοῦ λαοῦ αὐτοῦ or rather to τῶν υἱῶν in line five. "The heavens and the angels precede the nations and His sons (people). The logic behind this sequence is even more convincing if the interpolator thought of the angels as the representatives of the nations."[63]

Although David M. Allen does point out that Cockerill's line of argument can be inversed,[64] it seems more convincing that the angels of God are the sons of God, as Robert Hanhart shows[65] using Deut 32:8 und 43 in his discussion of these

---

56. Adrian Schenker, "Götter und Engel im Septuaginta-Psalter: Text- und religionsgeschichtliche Ergebnisse aus drei textkritischen Untersuchungen," in *Der Septuaginta-Psalter: Sprachliche und theologische Aspekte*, ed. Erich Zenger, HBS 32 (Freiburg: Herder, 2001), 193. See also the discussion of Markus-Liborius Hermann, *Die "hermeneutische Stunde" des Hebräerbriefs: Schriftauslegung in Spannungsfeldern*, HBS 72 (Freiburg: Herder, 2013), 254–55.

57. This supports Arie van der Kooij's thesis.

58. Cf. Cockerill, "Source," 58.

59. Cf. Cockerill, "Source," 59.

60. Cf. Cockerill, "Source," 59.

61. Cf. Cockerill, "Source," 59. He seems to speculate if עבדיו in MT is preferable to that of 4QDeut^q even though he is taking the supremacy of the Qumran text into account.

62. Cf. Cockerill, "Source," 60.

63. Cockerill, "Source," 60. He follows Skehan, "Structure," 158–59.

64. Cf. Allen, *Deuteronomy*, 49.

65. Robert Hanhart, "Die Söhne Israels, die Söhne Gottes und die Engel in der Masora, in Qumran und der Septuaginta: Ein letztes Kapitel aus ‚Israel in hellenistischer Zeit'," in *Vergegenwärtigung des Alten Testaments: Beiträge zur biblischen Hermeneutik*,

expressions. He supports the originality of ἀγγέλων θεοῦ and agrees with Bogaert that the long version of LXX is based on a Hebrew source.[66] The verses Deut 32:8 and 43 clearly correspond and, according to Pakkala, are corrected in such a manner that all hints to foreign Gods or divine creatures are erased.[67] The translation of אלהים as ἄγγελοι (Pss 8:6; 96[97]:7; 137[138]:8) in the LXX Psalter further corroborates Pakkala's opinion. Therefore, it is not necessary to note that lines two and four in 4QDeut^q originally read כל בני אלהים. It is not impossible, but there is no proof for this assumption. It could well be a conscious allusion to 4QDeut^j. It is established that there is no Hebrew source for lines three and four of the LXX and this leaves room for speculation. The present material leads to the following considerations: The superiority of the one God is expressed by the proclamation "bow down, all you gods, before him" in 4QDeut^q. In LXX Deut 32:43 // Ode 2:43 the "sons of God" of Deut 32:8 are interpreted as "angels" and אלהים afterwards are understood not as "strange gods" but as "sons of God = angels."[68] These organize the people and therefore belong to the noble area of the one God.[69] While in Deut 32:43b the "sons of God" fall down in front of him (God), proskynesis in Ode 2:43b is completely limited to the "angels." "Das Zeugnis der LXX sagt, daß die Engel als Geschöpfe von Israels Gott nichts, restlos nichts, zu tun haben mit Gottheiten neben dem einen Gott Israels. Das ist das Wesen der LXX als Interpretation."[70] This approach provides a clarity that can also be found in Heb 1:6, following a superior *Vorlage*. I find it highly unlikely that the author changed the text on his own accord. One can speculate, however, whether the author thought ἄγγελοι / υἱοί θεοῦ in Deut 32:43bd expressed the same thing, and

---

Festschrift Rudolf Smend zum 70. Geburtstag, ed. Christoph Bultmann *et al.* (Göttingen: Vandenhoeck & Ruprecht, 2002), 171–72.

66. See Hanhart, "Die Söhne Israels," 175 n. 7.

67. See Pakkala, *Word*, 185–91; Martin Karrer, *Der Brief an die Hebräer: Kapitel 1,1–5,10*, ÖTK 20.1 (Gütersloh: Gütersloher Verlagshaus, 2002), 135.

68. See Karrer, *Hebräer*, 1:135. This discussion can also be found in several manuscripts. In Deut 32:8, Rahlfs reads ἀγγέλων / ἀγγέλον θεοῦ instead of υἱῶν θεοῦ, which is probably based on a Hebrew source בני אל or בני אלהים (4QDeut^j) and preferable to the Masoretic reading בני ישראל (υἱοί Ἰσραήλ) as this is a later version. Cf. Eduard Nielsen, *Deuteronomium*, HAT 1/6 (Tübingen: Mohr Siebeck, 1995), 288–89. See also Pakkala, *Word*, 185–87. Hanhart thinks John William Wever's reconstruction is based on a conjecture. Cf. Hanhart, "Söhne," 171.

69. Cf. Hanhart, "Söhne," 172–73, followed by Cornelius den Hertog, "Deuteronomium 32," in *Genesis bis Makkabäer*, vol. 1 of *Septuaginta Deutsch: Erläuterungen und Kommentare*, ed. Martin Karrer and Wolfgang Kraus (Stuttgart: Deutsche Bibelgesellschaft, 2011), 593–98.

70. Hanhart, "Söhne," 178.

used the term ἄγγελοι from Deut 32:43d in order to provide a contrast between the sons of God and the one and only Son.[71]

Hanhart agrees and demonstrates with Deut 32:8, 43 that the angels of God are the sons of God.[72] He traces the long version of the LXX back to a Hebrew original in accordance with Bogaert.[73] The Old Testament witness did not differentiate between the "sons of Israel," the "angels" and the "sons of God" in his opinion, but between the sons of Israel, the angels and the Son, which will be reflected in Heb 1:6.[74] That the author deliberately altered the text without regard to any other source is not likely. In its original context Deut 32:43 // Ode 2:43 "has reference to the worship or homage due to God. But the writer to the Hebrews understands the text as a prophetic oracle concerning the Son at his exaltation."[75] Quoting from the Song of Moses, the author emphasizes not only the vast superiority of the Son, who, like his father, experiences the proskynesis of the peoples' angels, but also "den universalen Horizont [ab], in dem sich die Leserinnen und Leser des Hebr aus den Völkern vorfinden."[76]

3.3. THE FUNCTION OF DEUT 32:43 // ODE 2:43 IN HEB 1:6

It is difficult to determine the moment of εἰσαγάγῃ τὸν πρωτότοκον εἰς τὴν οἰκουμένην in Heb 1:6a. Wilfried Eisele differentiates between the following possibilities: the beginning of creation, the incarnation, the exaltation of Christ on the

---

71. There is room for speculation that the author quotes from memory and mixes up the expressions. I think that is highly unlikely considering the accuracy of his quotes.

72. Cf. Hanhart, "Söhne," 171–72.

73. Cf. Hanhart, "Söhne," 175 n. 7.

74. Cf. Hanhart, "Söhne," 177: "Der Zeuge des Hebräerbriefs begründet diese Aussage mit dem Schriftbeweis des nur in LXX und Qumran erhaltenen Verses Dtn 32,43— es ist seine älteste Aufnahme als Berufung auf vorgegebenes Zeugnis—in der ursprünglichen Form der LXX: προσκυνησάτωσαν αὐτῷ πάντες ἄγγελοι θεοῦ (Hebr 1,6)."

75. William L. Lane, *Hebrews 1–8: Commentary on Hebrews*, WBC 47A (Dallas: World, 1991), 26. Kraus, "Septuaginta," 279; Karrer, *Hebräer*, 1:134–35; Cockerill, *Hebrews*, 105–8; Lane, *Hebrews*, 1:28; Steyn, *Quest*, 59–72, e.g., argue for Deut 32:43 // Ode 2:43 as possible source. Cf. also Craig R. Koester, *Hebrews: A New Translation with Introduction and Commentary*, AB 36 (New York: Doubleday, 2001), 193.

76. Karrer, *Hebräer*, 1:135. In addition, see Karrer, "Gottes Reden, der Weltkreis und Christus, der Hohepriester: Blicke auf die Schriftrezeption des Hebräerbriefs," in *Frühjudentum und Neues Testament im Horizont Biblischer Theologie*, ed. Wolfgang Kraus and Karl-Wilhelm Niebuhr, WUNT 162 (Tübingen: Mohr Siebeck, 2003), 151–79; and Karrer, "The Epistle to the Hebrews and the Septuagint," in *Septuagint Research: Issues and Challenges in the Study of the Greek Jewish Scriptures*, ed. Wolfgang Kraus and R. Glenn Wooden, SCS 53 (Atlanta: Society of Biblical Literature; 2006), 335–53.

cross, the resurrection and ascension, or the return in the Parousia.⁷⁷ In order to determine which possibility is the most likely, all the details of Heb 1:6 have to be semantically, syntactically and contextually analyzed. Especially the interpretation of πάλιν and ἡ οἰκουμένη harbors clues as to a possible date. Πάλιν could either refer to the beginning of the quote ὅταν δέ or the following verb εἰσάγω. There is evidence for the first possibility in the same usage in Heb 1:5; 2:13; 4:5; and 10:30. However, πάλιν always occurs together with καί. It is different with Heb 4:7; 5:12; 6:1, 6; in these passages, πάλιν is connected to the nearest following verb.⁷⁸ In the New Testament, πάλιν can often be found with verbs describing movement or referring back to a former condition or recurring action.⁷⁹ If it is interpreted as an adverbial of time, Parousia is a likely meaning.⁸⁰ The setting of the event in this case would be οἰκουμένη. If πάλιν is understood to be an introductory phrase, however, the meaning indicates exaltation or enthronement.

Hans-Friedrich Weiß justifies his decision for the Son's exaltation with his interpretation of πάλιν as an introductory phrasing analogous to Heb 1:5, not referring to the second coming (= Parousia) in Heb 9:28. Furthermore, the entire phrase εἰσαγάγῃ τὸν πρωτότοκον εἰς τὴν οἰκουμένην cannot be understood as analogous to Heb 10:5 (εἰσερχόμενος εἰς τὸν κόσμον), in his opinion. Rather, it is a characteristic typology for the epistle, based on three terms πρωτότοκος-εἰσάγειν-οἰκουμένη and forming a structural motif with Heb 1:5.⁸¹ As a matter of fact, entirely different terminology is used in Heb 1:6 and 9:28, achieving a fractional difference between two different topoi.⁸² Πάλιν εἰσαγάγῃ does not say anything about the second coming, but about the movement that can be understood "als

---

77. Cf. Wilfried Eisele, *Ein unerschütterliches Reich: Die mittelplatonische Umformung des Parusiegedankens im Hebräerbrief*, BZNW 116 (Berlin: de Gruyter, 2003), 50. See also the discussion of Lukas Stolz, "Das Einführen des Erstgeborenen in die οἰκουμένη (Hebr 1,6a)," *Bib* 95 (2014): 405–23.

78. See Braun, *Hebräer*, 36.

79. Cf. Horst Balz, "πάλιν," in *Exegetisches Wörterbuch zum Neuen Testament*, ed. Horst Balz and Gerhard Schneider, vol. 3, 2nd ed. (Stuttgart: Kohlhammer, 1992), 20.

80. Riggenbach, *Hebräer*, 19–20; Braun, *Hebräer*, 36; Michel, *Hebräer*, 113, i.e, argue for Parousia. Karrer presents various options: "Momente des Geschehenen … und des Kommenden (2,5 u.ö.) bis hin zur Parusie dürfen Raum behalten (vgl. 9,28). Doch weil sie in der Höhe Gottes grundgelegt sind und das Wort sie vergegenwärtigt, bestimmten nicht die irdischen Tempora die Blickwinkel, sondern der Aktionsmodus." Karrer, *Hebräer*, 1:141. He does state in a previous passage that it is about presenting Christ to the world (cf. 1:140).

81. Cf. Weiß, *Hebräer*, 162–63. Lane focuses only on πρωτότοκος and οἰκουμένη. Cf. Lane, *Hebrews*, 1:26. Contrarily Schunack, *Hebräerbrief*, 27. Exaltation means to him: "eine unzutreffend eingeschränkte Deutung." On the topic πρωτότοκος cf. Walter Michaelis, "πρωτότοκος, πρωτοτοκεῖα," *TWNT* 6:872–82.

82. See also Gräßer, *Hebräer*, 1:78.

nochmalige Bewegung in dieselbe Richtung ... oder als Bewegung in die gegenteilige Richtung bezüglich einer zuvor ausgeführten Bewegung."[83]

The verb εἰσάγειν occurs in Hebrews in this passage only. The subjunctive aorist ὅτε and the particle ἄν, indicating a temporal clause which either describes a future action or an iterative, a recurring event.[84] In the LXX, there is a combination of the phrase εἰσάγειν εἰς τὴν γῆν and the conjunctions ὅταν / ἐάν / ὡς ἄν / ὅπως (cf. Exod 13:5, 11; 23:20; Deut 6:10; 7:1; 11:29),[85] when the passage is about leading Israel into the promised land. In any case, the verb does only occur in this context, especially as the expression εἰσάγειν εἰς τὴν γῆν.[86] As the author subsequently quotes from Deut 32:43 // Ode 2:43 and the theme of the promised land (see the passage about the wilderness wandering in 3:7-4:13 and 11:9) is important to him, it can be safely assumed that this is the starting point for his deliberations.[87]

The term οἰκουμένη occurs just in Heb 1:6 and 2:5, whereas only in the second passage is there a specification: ἡ οἰκουμένη ἡ μέλλουσα. The future world is not the same as the created world, a disparity the author stresses through his usage of the different terms. This is not to say, however, that οἰκουμένη in both passages has the same meaning.[88] It is a fact that in Hebrews the inhabited, populated earth

---

83. Eisele, *Reich*, 51. Gräßer writes about his return to "ihm angestammten (2,10) oder zugewiesenen Ort." Gräßer, *Hebräer*, 1:78.

84. See Eisele, *Reich*, 52; Heinrich von Siebenthal, *Griechische Grammatik zum Neuen Testament* (Gießen: Brunnen, 2011), § 276a. It is not correct that all interpretations exclude an iterative process as Eisele claims. Cf. Karrer, *Hebräer*, 1:140–41.

85. See also Deut 6:23 with ἵνα.

86. Cf. Eisele, *Reich*, 53; Karrer, *Hebräer*, 1:140.

87. In Hebrews, one can find εἰσέρχομαι often (17x to be precise), especially in connection with entering God's rest and the heavenly sanctuary. In Heb 13:20, ἀνάγω is used for the resurrection of Christ. Cf. Koester, *Hebrews*, 192.

88. There is something to be said for that, especially because of περὶ ἧς λαλοῦμεν (2:5). However, Flender and Coenen interpret the expression in different ways. In Heb 1:6, they read it as "bewohnte Welt" where Christ is or will be sent as the Firstborn. In Heb 2:5, they understand it as the coming or future world, no longer under the rule of the angels or Jesus. See Otto Flender and Lothar Coenen, "οἰκουμένη," in *Theologisches Begriffslexikon zum Neuen Testament*, ed. Lothar Coenen and Klaus Haacker (Wuppertal: Brockhaus; Neukirchen-Vluyn: Neukirchener Verlag, 2000), 2:1899. Concerning the οἰκουμένη, Balz believes Heb 1:6 speaks about Parousia and the motif of judgement. In his opinion, Heb 2:5 refers back to Heb 1:6 and relates to the coming rule of Christ and his final victory over all enemies. Cf. Horst Balz, "οἰκουμένη," in *Exegetisches Wörterbuch zum Neuen Testament*, ed. Horst Balz and Gerhard Schneider, 2nd ed. (Stuttgart: Kohlhammer, 1992), 2:1232–33. See also Stolz, "Einführen," 418–20.

of the present is described as κόσμος[89] (= created world).[90] It is utterly striking that, in the New Testament, the term οἰκουμένη is very rare (15x) whereas by contrast κόσμος is used very often.[91] Remarkably, the first of these two terms is almost entirely missing in passages where κόσμος occurs. Horst Balz thinks the reason for this is that οἰκουμένη was often used in Roman times in the context of the adulation of the emperor, thus losing its original theological connotation. By contrast, κόσμος evolved into a theological term used by Hellenistic Judaism and thus Early Christianity in late antiquity.[92] In the LXX, οἰκουμένη is the preferred term in the Psalter (17x) and Isaiah (15x).[93] Κόσμος is much rarer[94] and is only used more often in the later writings of the LXX: Wisdom, 2 Maccabees, and Sirach. In its basic meaning, οἰκουμένη describes the entire earth including its inhabitants and empires, which was created by God and will be judged by Him (cf., amongst others, Pss 9:9; 92[93]:1; 95[96]:13).[95] Whenever the author hints at exaltation, οἰκουμένη must mean the heavenly world: "The context requires that οἰκουμένη be understood as the heavenly world of eschatological salvation into which the Son entered at his ascension."[96] For Harold W. Attridge, however, evidence supporting this interpretation is lacking and he interprets the term as incarnation.[97] In the context of Heb 1, where the main focus lies on the supremacy of the Son, his identity with God and especially his eternal dwelling at the right hand of God, the act of εἰσαγάγῃ τὸν πρωτότοκον εἰς τὴν οἰκουμένην clearly hints at exaltation. "Die Himmelswelt, die Hebr auch sonst gern mit soziomorpher (der Gesellschaftswelt entlehnter) Begrifflichkeit umschreibt (vgl. bes. 2,5), stellt also jene Oikumene, den einzig wirklich und dauerhaft bewohnbaren Weltkreis, dar, in die Christus nach seiner Heilstat als Weltenherrscher zurückkehrt."[98] In order to emphasize the

---

89. See Heb 4:3; 9:26; 10:5; 11:7, 38.
90. Cf. Heb 9:1: κοσμικόν. For a definition of the term, see Michael Wolter, "κόσμος," in *Theologisches Begriffslexikon zum Neuen Testament*, ed. Lothar Coenen and Klaus Haacker (Wuppertal: Brockhaus; Neukirchen-Vluyn: Neukirchener Verlag, 2000), 2:1891–98. In Exod 16:35, οἰκουμένη means the promised land, which the author thinks is used in reference to the coming world in Heb 4:1–11. See Koester, *Hebrews*, 193.
91. For general information cf. Johnston George, "Οἰκουμένη and κόσμος in the New Testament," *NTS* 10 (1964): 352–60.
92. Cf. Balz, "οἰκουμένη," 1230. See also Karrer, *Hebräer*, 1:140.
93. According to BibleWorks, the term occurs 44x without Apocrypha, 48x with Apocrypha (50x including Bar 1:61 und Dan^Th 3:45). In the Psalms, κόσμος does not occur.
94. According to BibleWorks: 28x, with Apokrypha: 71x.
95. Cf. Balz, "οἰκουμένη," 1230; Flender and Coenen, "οἰκουμένη," 1898.
96. Lane, *Hebrews*, 1:27. So also Koester, *Hebrews*, 193; Gräßer, *Hebräer*, 1:78
97. Harold W. Attridge, *The Epistle to the Hebrews: A Commentary on the Epistle to the Hebrews*, Hermeneia (Philadelphia: Fortress Press, 1989), 56.
98. Knut Backhaus, *Der Hebräerbrief*, RNT (Regensburg: Pustet, 2009), 97. Koester, *Hebrews*, 192; Lane, *Hebrews*, 26–27; Gareth Lee Cockerill, *The Epistle to the Hebrews*,

dignity of the Son, the angels fall to their knees to worship him. The proskynesis, formerly God's sole prerogative, is now transferred to the Son (cf. Deut 32:43 // Ode 2:43).[99] Accordingly, οἰκουμένη describes the promised land, which the Son has already entered and where his brothers and sisters will follow him (Heb 2:11). Thus, the future world in Heb 2:5 must be interpreted in the same way: "Weltkreis (οἰκουμένη) meint in diesem Fall wohl nicht die irdische Welt, den Kosmos, sondern die himmlische Welt, die οἰκουμένην μέλλουσα, wie in Hebr 2,5."[100]

4. SUMMARY

Until recently, the LXX and Hebrews were neglected and were dealt with only at the margins of theological discourse. Fortunately, this has changed. The quotation from the Song of Moses is taken out of context and interpreted by the author as christological, stressing the superior dignity of the Son as compared to the angels. According to Deut 32:43 // Ode 2:43, the proskynesis is reserved for God alone, and in Heb 1:6 it is transferred to the Son. At the same time, a universal horizon is opened. The angels who are superior to the people in the Song of Moses and now fall down before the Son, "bekunden indirekt die Unterwerfung der Völker unter den Sohn."[101]

What has not changed so far is that such important works as *Novum Testamentum Graece* (now in its 28th edition), in their margin of Heb 1:6, still refer to Deut 32:43 and Ps 96(97):7 without mentioning Ode 2:43, which is also a part of the LXX. There also is no correction of the view of what is now largely obsolete in Hebrews research, that Heb 1:6 was affected by Ps 96(97):7. It is about time to encourage scholars to further their studies in this direction.

NICNT (Grand Rapids: Eerdmans, 2012), 104 also argue for exaltation. Karrer indicates, that the language used here is politically influenced. Cf. Karrer, *Hebräer*, 1:140. See Schunack, *Hebräerbrief*, 27.

99. Cf. Karrer, *Hebräer*, 1:134–35.
100. Kraus, "Septuaginta," 279–80.
101. Karrer, *Hebräer*, 1:135.

Three Elders: Onias III, Eleazar and Razis as the Embodiment of Judaism in 2 Maccabees

Eugene Coetzer

Abstract: The study of 2 Maccabees has seen exhaustive research on the roles of specific characters. No doubt these characters are utilized as vehicles for advancing a specific ideology and narrative plan. Yet, an aspect which has been overlooked is the unified significance of three principal male characters. Each of these three, the high priest Onias III, the greatly aged scribe Eleazar, and the war veteran Razis, features at a critical point in the text of 2 Maccabees. Each reacts to a specific threat. The respective reactions are, however, dissimilar. The mood seems to develop from a calm, passive, and inclusive attitude into an active resistant stance and exclusive opposition. Such a differentiation is problematic when aiming to determine a desired epistemic practice: which of the three responses should the reader adopt? This paper argues that, behind this apparent development, there lies a consistent communicative strategy, namely, a unified portrayal of the nature of Judaism. In this manner, each of the three elders becomes an embodiment of Judaism.

1. INTRODUCTION

Ancient literature has certainly allowed a place for the wise father figure amongst the heroes of the narrative world. A variety of texts demonstrate the power of employing such a character as ambassador, role model, teacher, philosopher, and in some cases, even as sage. In this context, one sees the Pentateuch proclaim Abraham as the father of nations, whereas the writings of Plato and Xenophon herald Socrates as the father of ethics and epistemology.

The actions of these figures are not only noted because of their remarkable nature, but also because of their rhetorical value. The image of the wise and magnanimous elder can easily be viewed as a character who demands respect, sympathy, and loyalty, thus embodying a desired epistemic practice.

In 2 Maccabees, we find three such characters: the calm and patient high priest, Onias; the unquestionably loyal scribe, Eleazar; and the vigorous elder, Razis. Amongst the scholarly contributions to the study of 2 Maccabees, some aspect of each of these figures has already been well highlighted. Take, for example, Jan Willem Van Henten, who focuses on the second and third elders, Eleazar and Razis in his seminal book *The Maccabean Martyrs as Saviours of the Jewish People*. Here, Van Henten explores the centrality of each martyr's role to the plan of the narrative.[1] Also consider Erich S. Gruen, who, in his well-known article "The Origins and Objectives of Onias' Temple," specifically highlights Onias's role as high priest and his influence on temple practice.[2] Again, Christine Schams shows the likelihood of Eleazar being a Near Eastern Jewish type of scribe/sage as described in Ben Sira.[3]

All of these excellent studies, however, solely focus on the textually implied role of each character: the implications of Onias's office as high priest, the scribal attributes of Eleazar, or the martyrdom of Razis. An aspect which has been overlooked is the combined rhetorical significance of the accounts of all three male characters apropos their key placement within the text of 2 Maccabees. Similar to the three temple scenes in 2 Maccabees, already successfully shown by Pierre J. Jordaan to serve a unified strategic purpose,[4] the author has allotted the beginning, middle, and end of the narrative for each of these three specific characters, respectively.

Each character is placed in a scenario where the author describes a specific threat and a respective, albeit, appropriate Jewish response. At first glance, the significance of these three characters might seem to lie in their similarities. For example, each of these figures is:

- a public figure
- central to the narrative
- a true patriot
- described as noble from birth
- a respected citizen
- completely selfless
- described as flawless/righteous

---

1. Jan Willem van Henten, *The Maccabean Martyrs as Saviours of the Jewish People* (Leiden: Brill, 1997).
2. Erich S. Gruen, "The Origins and Objectives of Onias' Temple," *SCI* 16 (1997): 48–57.
3. Christine Schams, *Jewish Scribes in the Second-Temple Period* (Sheffield: Sheffield Academic, 1998), 314.
4. Pierre J. Jordaan "The Temple in 2 Maccabees: Dynamics and Episodes," *JSem* 24 (2015): 352–65.

However, the premise will be explored that an investigation into the differences between these characters will yield more important results for the study of 2 Maccabees. Each character is described within a uniquely designed context. The threat and response applicable to each of these men is different. There exists a development on various levels between each scenario. With each of the three cases, there seems to exist a progression in:

- active participation
- personal communication
- reference to life after death
- exclusionist attitude
- relationship to God

Consequently, this study will investigate each scenario on a syntactical, semantic and pragmatic level in order to:

- stabilize the text
- investigate both inter- and intratextual relationships
- highlight stylistic traits
- determine development in the specific scenes concerning Onias, Eleazar, and Razis

Lastly, this development will be conceptualized in terms of congruency in order to maintain a consistent proposition and narrative plan.

2. Key Sections

2.1. Onias

The first of the three elders to be mentioned in 2 Maccabees is the high priest Onias. As an aside, four high priests share this name. Two of these lived in the fourth and third centuries BCE and are therefore eliminated. Josephus reports that an Onias, son of Onias, immigrated down to Egypt and established a temple there about a generation after the time of Antiochus IV Epiphanes (i.e., when the Onias mentioned in 2 Maccabees was murdered in Antioch). This implies that the Onias of 2 Maccabees is most likely Onias III.[5]

The priestly figure features at the start of the narrative in 2 Macc 3. In 3:1–3, the reader gets a glimpse of a scenario where all is well with Jerusalem. The holy city dwells amid complete peace (3:1), the nations honor both the city and the temple (3:2), and the financial system of the temple is healthy (3:3). This ideal situation is

---

5. Cf. Daniel R. Schwartz, *2 Maccabees*, CEJL (Berlin: de Gruyter, 2008), 187; and James C. VanderKam, *From Joshua to Caiaphas: High Priests after the Exile* (Minneapolis: Fortress, 2004), 188–97, 204–8.

ascribed to the fact that the Mosaic law is being maintained and because of the piety of the high priest Onias and his hatred of evil. In 2 Macc 3:2 we read:

συνέβαινεν καὶ αὐτοὺς τοὺς βασιλεῖς τιμᾶν τὸν τόπον καὶ τὸ ἱερὸν ἀποστολαῖς ταῖς κρατίσταις δοξάζειν

The term συνέβαινω is used here impersonally and, as confirmed by Takamitsu Muraoka, could have the meaning "to come to pass/to result or follow."[6] The verb is employed to make a transition from the broader context to the specific scenario. Here, however, the description in 3:2 is still part of the general context. It seems that the author suggests a link between the proper following of the law and the honoring of the temple, the latter being a consequence of the obedience to/enforcement of the law. The use of τόπος ("place") in 3:3 in order to refer to the temple is scarce in the LXX. This specific use of the term is also found in 3 Macc 1:9, but is not present prior to 2 Maccabees. In biblical and cognate literature, the term is, however, frequently employed when referring to temples.[7] The reason that is provided by the text for the current situation of peace in Jerusalem is a key in understanding the aim of the rest of the book. Although expressed as an ideal, in the greater part of the narrative, there is, in fact, no peace and no functioning temple. Since the piety of the city is the basis for the current peaceful circumstances, the intended reader would surely know what elements are missing when the peace subsides. Through this description of the *status quo ante,* the prominence of the first elderly male character is established.

This peace is briefly interrupted by the threat posed by the Seleucid government's sanctioned audit of the temple funds. The scene unfolds in 2 Macc 3:14–23 and is most carefully phrased in order to incite the desired emotional response from the intended reader. The clear intention here is to encourage the reader to feel compassion towards the high priest and the whole of the city. In 2 Macc 3:14 we read:

ταξάμενος δὲ ἡμέραν εἰσῄει τὴν περὶ τούτων ἐπίσκεψιν οἰκονομήσων ἦν δὲ οὐ μικρὰ καθ' ὅλην τὴν πόλιν ἀγωνία

Here, the ingressive function of the imperfect verb εἴσειμι ("I go into") heightens the feeling of anticipation. In addition, a valid translation for the term ἐπίσκεψις is "audit."[8] This corresponds with the meaning of "numbering" when ἐπίσκεψις is

---

6. *GELS*, s.v. "συνέβαινω."

7. David Vanderhooft, "Dwelling beneath the Sacred Place: A Proposal for Reading 2 Samuel 7:10," *JBL* 118 (1999): 628–30.

8. C. Bradford Welles, *Royal Correspondence in the Hellenistic Period: A Study in Greek Epigraphy* (New Haven: Yale University Press, 1934), 321; Arno Mauersberger,

employed elsewhere in the LXX (i.e., Num 1:21; 1 Chr 21:5; 23:34) as this is a specific investigation of the funds in the temple. In 3:14, the author uses litotes (the double negative) to underscore the emotional intensity of the scene. This device is also linked with the crisis scenario mentioned in 2 Macc 15:19:

ἦν δὲ καὶ τοῖς ἐν τῇ πόλει κατειλημμένοις οὐ πάρεργος ἀγωνία ταρασσομένοις τῆς ἐν ὑπαίθρῳ προσβολῆς

As Robert Doran has pointed out, litotes is employed nine times in 2 Maccabees as compared to its total absence in 1 Maccabees.[9]

In 2 Macc 3:14b–20 the scene is initiated by the anguish of the whole city and then subdivided into categories of various types of people in anguish: the high priest and other priests (3:15–17), men (3:18), married women (3:19a), and unmarried women (3:19b–20). In this section (3:14–23), a balance is maintained through a linkage between 3:15 and 3:22:

2 Macc 3:15 οἱ δὲ ἱερεῖς πρὸ τοῦ θυσιαστηρίου ἐν ταῖς ἱερατικαῖς στολαῖς ῥίψαντες ἑαυτοὺς ἐπεκαλοῦντο εἰς οὐρανὸν τὸν περὶ παρακαταθήκης νομοθετήσαντα τοῖς παρακαταθεμένοις ταῦτα σῶα διαφυλάξαι προσδοκίαν

2 Macc 3:22 οἱ μὲν οὖν ἐπεκαλοῦντο τὸν παγκρατῆ κύριον τὰ πεπιστευμένα τοῖς πεπιστευκόσιν σῶα διαφυλάσσειν μετὰ πάσης ἀσφαλείας

Notice that verse 22 employs a similar phraseology (πεπιστευμένα τοῖς πεπιστευκόσιν) as is found in verse 15 (παρακαταθήκης ... τοῖς παρακαταθεμένοις). In addition, both verses have the same form of the verb ἐπικαλέω ("I call on/appeal to") and both have some form of the verb διαφυλάσσω ("I preserve/maintain").

The role of the women gathering at the doorways and peeking through the windows (3:19) leads Doran to assume that the view of the author is that the unmarried women should not be present in public.[10] However, such a strategy on the part of the author will be difficult to pinpoint. In this case, it is not evident whether the author is in agreement with the circumstances of the scene as depicted. The text could merely be keeping to the contemporary setting.

Second Maccabees 3:23–24 read:

ὁ δὲ Ἡλιόδωρος τὸ διεγνωσμένον ἐπετέλει. αὐτόθι δὲ αὐτοῦ σὺν τοῖς δορυφόροις κατὰ τὸ γαζοφυλάκιον ἤδη παρόντος ὁ τῶν πνευμάτων καὶ πάσης ἐξουσίας

Polibios-Lexikon (Berlin: Akademie Verlag, 1956), 2.952; and Elias J. Bickerman, *Studies in Jewish and Christian History*, vol. 2 (Leiden: Brill, 1986), 171.

9. Robert Doran, *Temple Propaganda: The Purpose and Character of 2 Maccabees* (Washington: Catholic Biblical Association, 1981), 42.

10. Robert Doran, *2 Maccabees: A Critical Commentary*, Hermeneia (Minneapolis: Fortress, 2012), 85.

δυνάστης ἐπιφάνειαν μεγάλην ἐποίησεν ὥστε πάντας τοὺς κατατολμήσαντας συνελθεῖν καταπλαγέντας τὴν τοῦ θεοῦ δύναμιν εἰς ἔκλυσιν καὶ δειλίαν τραπῆναι

In verse 23, the function of the imperfect form of the verb ἐπιτελέω ("I accomplish") is classified by Doran as conative ("attempting to accomplish"), emphasizing the attempted action.[11] This may be a correct interpretation, but an ingressive function ("beginning to accomplish") seems to be more fitting. The verse that follows (3:24) confirms that the action of Heliodorus may be classified as the attempt to accomplish what had been determined. At this juncture, Heliodorus was already near the treasury. The fact that he was on his way to enter the treasury signifies the first step in achieving what has been planned.

The use of a threat and its appropriated response is of particular significance to this investigation. Any situation of conflict presents an opportunity where the text could describe the correct manner of reacting in such a scenario. This suggests a desired outcome to the reader, who is encouraged to embrace a supportive attitude towards the noble character. Here, in 2 Macc 3, the temple's sanctity is vulnerable and Onias reacts in specific ways. In this regard, the reader is informed that Onias:

- hates evil (3:1)
- is not overcome (3:5)
- welcomes graciously (3:9)
- gives a plain account of the temple funds (3:10)
- displays signs of grief and horror (3:17)
- makes a sacrifice (3:31–34)[12]

These reactions clearly indicate the nonconfrontational nature of Onias's actions. He does not engage with the elements of the threat in any direct way; his actions are reactive rather than proactive. The text demonstrates the importance of depicting Onias as a calm, stable and peaceful character. Furthermore, not much space is allocated to Onias's personal communication. In fact, only indirect references are made to the high priest's speeches; he quarrels with Simon (3:4); welcomes the Seleucid delegates (3:9); and explains the situation of the temple funds (3:10–12). This is odd in a narrative where the rhetorical value of speeches is normally acknowledged and employed. Significantly, even the task of warning Heliodorus in 3:33–34 is given solely to the heavenly figures (as representatives of the divine) and not to the high priest Onias. Lastly, the attitude of Onias towards the imminent enemy is ironically accommodating and inclusive. Even though the text presents

---

11. Doran, *2 Maccabees*, 86.

12. This evidences a Jewish Hellenistic point of view, namely, that prayer is the main category, and one of the ways to pray is to bring a sacrifice. Cf. Schwartz, *2 Maccabees*, 203. This view is also reflected in 2 Macc 12:44; Wis 18:21–22; and Philo, *Life of Moses*, 2.5.

this account as a type of diplomatic dialectic, at no time does the high priest show contempt towards Heliodorus and his men. His dealing with the Seleucids speaks of cooperation and peace. This, taken together with both the author's Hellenistic writing style and the temple's setting described within an international arena in 3:2, seems to support the interpretation that, at this stage, the text proposes the possibility of a peaceful coexistence between Jew and gentile.

2.2. Eleazar

The next elder mentioned in 2 Maccabees is the scribe Eleazar. As was the case with Onias in 2 Maccabees 3, the text of 2 Macc 6 prioritizes a thorough description of the scribe's character.

Firstly, in 6:18, Eleazar is referred to as man of "beautiful and honorable appearance" (τὴν πρόσοψιντοῦ προσώπου κάλλιστος). Here, the term κάλλιστος ("most beautiful") has the connotation of both beautiful and honorable. This type of description of a godly man is also employed by Josephus (*A.J.* 2.224, 231–232). Ludwig Bieler has shown such a reference to beauty to be an important facet in demonstrating the closeness of certain individuals to God.[13] A sense of honor is also depicted by the author in the way that he describes the choice that is set before Eleazar. The old man has to choose between a long life marred by "pollution" or death with "honor" (6:19). Such a choice is paralleled in the story of Achilles (Homer, *Il.* 9.410–416) and depictions of heroes by Aeschylus (*Cho.* 349) and Sophocles (*Aj.* 465). This quest for honor idealizes the typical hero who is, in this case, Eleazar.

Secondly, in 6:18 and 23, Eleazar is described as a man already advanced in years (ἀνὴρ ἤδη προβεβηκὼς τὴν ἡλικίαν). He is also described as being both a Jewish scribe/official (γραμματεύς), as well as a man of honorable conduct from the time of his childhood. Schams has successfully demonstrated that there are a range of meanings (referring to Jewish officials) that may be ascribed to the term γραμματεύς.[14] She further concludes that, despite these possibilities, it is highly likely that Eleazar was a scribe.[15] However, since there is no reference to Eleazar's ability to write, it seems safer to adopt the broader meaning of "official."

Thirdly, in 6:21–22, Eleazar is given a chance by his friends to escape death. This account heightens the emotive appeal of the elderly character and has a dual emotional effect. The reader may well see a chance for the beautiful and honorable old man to free himself. In addition, the fact that the author has Eleazar's friends, and not his enemy, encourage him to seek life and safety, makes the tempting

---

13. Ludwig Bieler, *Theos anēr: Das Bild des "göttlichen Menshen" in Spätantike und Frühchristentum* (Darmstadt: Wissenschaftliche Buchgesellschaft, 1976), 51–54.
14. Schams, *Jewish Scribes*, 314.
15. Schams, *Jewish Scribes*, 314.

offer so much harder to turn down. Tessa Rajak rightly notes that this account is reminiscent of that associated with the death of Socrates.[16]

In sharp contradistinction to the account given of Onias, the text now provides munificent space for the direct communication of Eleazar. The scribe's speeches are prominent. In 6:24–28a, the wise old man provides a detailed, righteous motivation for his brave actions. In the statement, some elements of a worldview become apparent. Firstly, the term παντοκράτωρ ("all-powerful") is employed together with the notion of punishment and reward after death.[17] In this manner, the speech portrays a reality where the all-powerful God of the Jews will deal with individuals after their deaths in a manner that is befitting their actions on earth. These ideas and terminology are not isolated. The term παντοκράτωρ also occurs in 2 Macc 5:20 and in the succeeding martyrology in 2 Macc 7:35–38, which deals with the mother and her seven sons. Furthermore, the same ideas regarding punishment and reward are also evident in the succeeding martyrology.

Another development is the difference in attitude between Onias and Eleazar. The latter takes up a slightly more hostile position towards the antagonists. He declares that they should conduct him into Hades (6:23), refutes the enemy's notions (6:24–28) and still manages to deliver didactic teachings whilst under extreme torture (6:30). Regarding the circumstances under which Eleazar had to eat pig's meat (6:18), there exist different manuscript traditions and emendations (La^{LXVP} Armenian, V La^{BM} Syriac Achminic, L' 46–52 58 311, Peter Katz's emendation[18]). These variants can be divided into two versions of the story, one where Eleazar is forced to open his mouth and one where he is forced to eat, but nothing is said about the actual opening of his mouth. Thus, what is important here, is that the eating of pig's meat was to be met with considerable resistance.

Significantly, even the description of Eleazar's death is orchestrated around his active participation. In 6:27, the reader is informed that the scribe "will therefore courageously exchange this life" (διόπερ ἀνδρείως μὲν νῦν διαλλάξας τὸν βίον).[19] In 6:31, Eleazar "exchanged this life for another" (μετήλλαξεν) and also

---

16. Tessa Rajak, "Dying for the Law: The Martyr's Portrait in Jewish-Greek Literature," in *Portraits: Biographical Representation in the Greek and Latin Literature of the Roman Empire*, ed. Mark J. Edwards and Simon Swain (Oxford: Clarendon, 1997), 41–42.

17. This notion of punishment or reward after death is clear through Eleazar's insistence that he cannot escape from the Almighty either dead or alive. Cf. Doran, *2 Maccabees*, 153.

18. Peter Katz, "Eleazar's Martyrdom in 2 Maccabees: The Latin Evidence for a Point of the Story," *Studia Patristica* 4 (1961): 118–24.

19. The description in 6:27 and 28 are isolated references to death. The phrase διαλλάξας τὸν βίον ("leave this life") and the term ἀπευθανατίζω ("I die well") are not otherwise attested. Cf. Carl Ludwig Wilibald Grimm, *Das erste Buch der Maccabäer* (Leipzig: Hirzel, 1853).

"left behind his own death" (τὸν ἑαυτοῦ θάνατον ... καταλιπών). In the latter pericope, Eleazar is the subject of each verb.

2.3. RAZIS

In 2 Macc 14:37–46, the reader is introduced to a third elder and a new example of what constitutes a righteous ambassador for Judaism. As was implied in the accounts of Eleazar and the mother with her seven sons (2 Macc 6:9b–7:42), the reader is again reminded that there is no price too high for the sake of Judaism and the maintenance of the Jewish way of life. In 14:37–46, Razis is said to have risked "both body and soul for the sake of Judaism" (καὶ σῶμα καὶ ψυχὴν ὑπὲρ τοῦ Ἰουδαϊσμοῦ). The author ensures that the character of Razis is presented as an ideal. Razis is described as one who has goodwill (εὔνοιαν) towards his people, is a "father of the Jews" (πατὴρ τῶν Ἰουδαίων) and who is a "lover of his fellow citizens" (φιλοπολίτης). The latter quality was well-known as a noble characteristic of leaders (Plutarch, *Flam.* 13.8; *Lyc.* 20.4). Through this term (φιλοπολίτης), the hero, Razis, is unified with the other heroes of 2 Maccabees. In 4:5, Onias was also concerned with the best interests of the entire nation, as was Judas towards his men in 2 Macc 12:25. Second Maccabees 14:37–46 contrasts Razis with the two self-serving villains, Menelaus (4:50) and Alcimus (14:8), who, despite their words, did not consider their people at all. Van Henten has shown the Roman influence of the phrase "father of the Jews" (πατὴρ τῶν Ἰουδαίων) through titles such as *parens, pater patriae, parens plebis Romanae, parens omnium civium,* and *parens reipublicae*.[20] David Noy also notes that later inscriptions employ the phrase πατὴρ καὶ πάτρων τῆς πόλεως ("father and patron of the city") or πάτρων τῆς πόλεως ("patron of the city").[21]

In 2 Macc 14:38, we read:

ἦν γὰρ ἐν τοῖς ἔμπροσθεν χρόνοις τῆς ἀμειξίας κρίσιν εἰσενηνεγμένος Ἰουδαϊσμοῦ καὶ σῶμα καὶ ψυχὴν ὑπὲρ τοῦ Ἰουδαϊσμοῦ παραβεβλημένος μετὰ πάσης ἐκτενίας

Here, certain scholars, such as Félix-Marie Abel, Jonathan A Goldstein, and Christian Habicht interpret the participle εἰσενηνεγμένος as passive.[22] Carl Ludwig Wilibald Grimm, however, convincingly argues for the middle use of the verb through referencing the employment of the verb εἰσφέρεσθαι by Polybius.[23] Here,

---

20. Van Henten, *Maccabean Martyrs*, 206–7.
21. David Noy, *Jewish Inscriptions of Western Europe*, 2 vols. (Cambridge: Cambridge University Press, 1993), 114.
22. Félix-Marie Abel, *Les Livres des Maccabées* (Paris: Gabalda, 1949); Jonathan A. Goldstein, *II Maccabees* (Garden City: Doubleday, 1983); Christian Habicht, *2. Makkabäerbuch* (Gütersloh: Mohn, 1976).
23. Grimm, *Maccabäer*; Cf. Polybius, *Hist.* 5.74.9; 11.10.2, 5; and 21.29.12.

the middle tense has the meaning of "to bring forward publicly." Accordingly, Doran rightly translates the verb as "pronounce."[24]

In 14:39, Nikanor sends "over five hundred soldiers" (στρατιώτας ὑπὲρ τοὺς πεντακοσίους) to seize Razis and thus aims to bring "misfortune" (συμφορά) to the Jews (14:40). The number of soldiers sent, although seemingly exaggerated, makes sense, since this may well have been necessary either to make a public display and/or as precautionary method for a public rebellion.

The mention of Nikanor's forces setting fire to the doors in 14:41 serves a dual purpose. Firstly, since fire was not necessary (as the forces were already able to break through the outer door), it serves as support for the depiction of Nikanor's men as a (nameless) mob (τῶν ... πληθῶν). Secondly, the vivid picture of fire heightens the intensity of the situation and the suspense of the reader.

In 14:42, the term ὑποχείριος ("under the control") reminds the reader of Judas's encouragement in 13:11 to pray to the Lord that he would not put the people "under the control" of the abusive gentiles.[25] Through that instance, the reader knows the value of Jewish independence. The author exploits the emotional value of Razis's death through prolongation of the death scene. Doran notes that the author employs various techniques to place the events of 14:45-46 in one sentence: two participles ὑπάρχων καὶ πεπυρωμένος ("breathing and enflamed") are followed by an asyndetic participle ἐξαναστάς ("he stood up"), two genitive absolute participles φερομένων ... ὄντων ("going forth ... being") and another asyndetic participle διελθών ("went through").[26] Before resolving into the main verb ἐνσείω ("I drive into"), there is yet another participle, two asyndetic participles and another participle phrase. In this manner, the actions are tightly bound together in order to maintain an intensity and to portray the most vivid picture of Razis's death. This effort to highlight the death and fully utilize emotion demonstrates the importance of Razis's perseverance.

Once again, as in the case of Onias and Eleazar, one finds a threat and response. Here, the reader is informed that Razis:

- enjoins on himself the sword (14:41)
- runs onto the wall (14:43)
- throws himself headlong into the crowd (14:43)
- becomes emotionally fever pitched (14:45)
- runs through the crowd (14:45)
- exposes his entrails (14:46)
- takes his entrails and hurls them at the crowd (14:46)
- calls on the Master of life (14:46)

---

24. Doran, *2 Maccabees*, 282.
25. Doran, *2 Maccabees*, 283.
26. Doran, *2 Maccabees*, 282.

This list of actions can clearly be distinguished from those attributed to Onias and even the slightly more demonstrative Eleazar. The text portrays Razis as being overtly proactively responsive, exclusive and antithetical. This happens both on a syntactical and semantic level. Like the other two elders, Razis is a firm and steady character. However, unlike the other two elders, Razis's actions actually impede that of the enemy. His actions aggressively clash with those of the enemy and no opportunity is created for a settlement.

3. Development and Context

Through the abovementioned investigation, it has become apparent that there exists a significant development in the attitude and actions of each of the three wise figures as depicted in 2 Maccabees. This progression can be seen in terms of each character's active participation, personal communication and inclusivity/opposition. Furthermore, the threat becomes increasingly personal. Onias faces only the possibility of a desecrated temple, Eleazar is forced to eat swine flesh and Razis is personally hunted down to be captured.

Each character is employed to present a tailored response to a specific threat. This is important since the responses of these protagonists guide the reader to adopt the same attitude towards similar threats. These responses are, however, very different. So what is the text trying to teach the implicit reader? Are there conflicting messages? What is the desired epistemic practice? Should the reader adopt an attitude of

- A – diplomacy, calm exchange of information and inward anguish like Onias?
- B – brave acceptance of death through torture and vocal expression of principles like Eleazar?
- C – direct, active and aggressive confrontation, hostile opposition and refusal of submission like Razis?

Through this deviated line of response, the text seems to communicate a confusing desired epistemic practice. This is, however, only true when overlooking the development in the threat imposed in each case as well. The threat and response presented in each scenario make a series of finely balanced pairs. Each pair develops from a nonhostile diplomatic setting into an eventual antagonist and hostile context. With Onias, the Seleucid delegates arrive with a somewhat diplomatic approach. The goal is to inspect and report. With Eleazar, although more hostile, the possibility of freedom is offered if "mere" principles are discarded. Mention is made of a friendship between the Seleucids and the old man and a plan is devised (albeit not acceptable to Eleazar) for a peaceful resolution. With Razis, no option for a peaceful resolution is countenanced. More than five hundred men are sent to violently seize the old man. They burn the gates and the ill intent of Nikanor is made immediately clear.

This demonstrates an equal progression in both response and threat. With such an equal development it becomes apparent that the three elder characters do not represent a deviation of the text's proposition, but a consistent one. Onias, Eleazar, and Razis signify one and the same desired epistemic practice. The practice moves and changes to accompany that which imposes a threat to its existence. Thus, the proposition is not one of decreasing tolerance and inclusion of outsiders and increasing violence and opposition. It is, rather, a scenario where the three accounts each present Judaism as being consistently noble, righteous, firm, and resolute, where its levels of resistance are always commensurate with the degree of any opposing force. Through the accounts of these three elders, the text establishes Judaism as fully resilient. The stronger the threat, the more severe the response.

No wonder then, that at the height of the proposition's demonstration, in the description of Razis's reaction, a densely referenced presence for Judaism is evident. The collective factor is brought forward in this active and averse scene in 2 Macc 14:

- ἀπὸ Ἱεροσολύμων ("from Jerusalem," 14:37)
- ἀνὴρ φιλοπολίτης ("a man who loved his fellow citizens," 14:37)
- πατὴρ τῶν Ἰουδαίων ("father of the Jews," 14:37)
- Ἰουδαϊσμοῦ ("Judaism," 14:38)
- καὶ σῶμα καὶ ψυχὴν ὑπὲρ τοῦ Ἰουδαϊσμοῦ παραβεβλημένος ("had risked both body and soul for the sake of Judaism," 14:38)
- τοὺς Ἰουδαίους ("the Jews," 14:39)
- τῆς ἰδίας εὐγενείας ("of his own nobility," 14:42)

The high priest, the scribe, and the father of the Jews become the embodiment of Judaism. The three elder figures become one static principled figure, with each of the three scenes demarcating the limits of the tolerance of this way of life. The scene subsequent to that of Razis settles the resilience of Judaism in the minds of the implicit reader. When the threat becomes too severe, the ambassadors of Judaism will always be divinely empowered to completely destroy the threat and restore the balance. Through these three embodiments of the cause, the text enforces confidence in the implicit reader and establishes the immovable nature of Judaism.

4. Conclusion

This analysis reasserts the need for investigations into larger patterns within the text of 2 Maccabees. This would not only improve our understanding of the narrative's aim and larger communicative strategies, but also reestablish the vital role of apocryphal literature in conceptualizing suffering and change in Jewish experience. Through combining a structural and pragmatic analysis, 2 Maccabees is reestablished as a text which demonstrates the creative process of providing solutions to the questions arising from the oppression and abuse of the Jews. Through the accounts of Onias, Eleazar, and Razis the text celebrates the unwavering strength of Judaism and the victory of the Jews.

Demetrius and the Early Reception of the Septuagint

Gunnar M. Eidsvåg

Abstract: The Jews in Ptolemaic Egypt lived in a rich cultural and religious environment. Epigraphic material shows signs of influence from Greek and Egyptian culture and of mixed marriages. It was into this reality that the Torah was translated. In this paper, I look at how Demetrius, a member of this society, points to the Torah as a reference for Jewish identity. My contention is that Demetrius's texts indicate that it was not enough to translate the Torah into Greek in order to secure its place in the Jewish societies in Egypt. The Torah had to be commended.

The Jews of Ptolemaic Egypt lived in a rich cultural and religious landscape. The ancient Egyptian myths were viable and the presence of the Greek-Macedonian pantheon was strong due to the new rulers.[1] The Ptolemies used the rich religious traditions as a governmental instrument, creating the hybrid cult of Sarapis.[2] Jewish orientations in this landscape were probably varied and manifold.[3]

In Egypt, Jews had different occupations. The state control of land ownership and commercial activity limited the possibilities substantially.[4] Many Jews were soldiers or farmers. The mercenary Jews folded into military settlements named by the ethnicity of the group forming the larger part at the establishment of the settlement. The mercenary Jews of Alexandria, for instance, settled into the "Macedonian" military settlement and could therefore refer to themselves as "Macedonians" (Josephus, *B.J.* 2.487; *A.J.* 12.8; *C. Ap.* 2.35).[5] The mercenaries

---

1. Peter M. Fraser, *Ptolemaic Alexandria* (Oxford: Clarendon, 1972), 1:189–301.
2. Fraser, *Ptolemaic Alexandria*, 1:116–17.
3. John J. Collins, *Between Athens and Jerusalem* (Grand Rapids: Eerdmans, 2000), 5.
4. Victor A. Tcherikover and Alexander Fuks, *Corpus Papyrorum Judaicarum*, vol. 1 (Cambridge: Harvard University Press, 1957), 15–16.
5. Tcherikover and Fuks, *Corpus*, 13–14. See also fragment no. 5 in James M. S. Cowey and Klaus Maresch, ed., *Urkunden des Politeuma der Juden von Herakleopolis (144/3–133/2 v. Chr.) (P.Polit.Iud.): Papyri aus den Sammlungen von Heidelberg, Köln,*

were landholders, receiving their piece of land as lease from the king in order to have a sustainable income. Therefore, there were close connections between farmers and mercenaries. Many of the soldiers did not work their land themselves, but hired men to do the job.[6]

Jews on a lower level in the Ptolemaic society could be "king's peasants," field hands, vinedressers, shepherds, et cetera.[7] Interestingly, it appears from the papyri fragments that several Jewish shepherds were called by Egyptian names.[8] Jews were probably artisans, although the evidence from the papyri is scant.[9]

Epigraphic material shows that Jews were spread throughout the whole country.[10] From the second century, we have evidence of the organization of Jewish communities. Especially the papyri from Heracleopolis (143–131 BCE), which attest to a Jewish *politeuma*,[11] are important. These make the existence of a Jewish *politeuma* in Alexandria mentioned in the Letter of Aristeas more likely.[12] Sometime in the late 160's, a member of the high priestly family, the Oniads, formed a military colony with a temple in Leontopolis in the nome of Heliopolis. This community was probably also a *politeuma*.[13] These are only the *politeumata* we have evidence of; there might have been more.[14]

The papyri from Heracleopolis show evidence of a Jewish law court. The phrase they use, "paternal law" (πάτριος νόμος), is ambiguous, but seems to be

---

München und Wien (Wiesbaden: Westdeutscher Verlag, 2001).

6. Tcherikover and Fuks, *Corpus*, 15.

7. Tcherikover and Fuks, *Corpus*, 15.

8. Tcherikover and Fuks, *Corpus*, 16. See also fragment no. 38 (p. 185). There are also fragments showing that Jewish peasants and potters were given Egyptian names, cf. fragment no. 44 and 46 (p. 189–91). See also the list of names in Cowey and Maresch, *Urkunden*, 30–32.

9. Tcherikover and Fuks, *Corpus*, 16–17.

10. Much epigraphic material is accessible in William Horbury and David Noy, *Jewish Inscriptions of Graeco-Roman Egypt* (Cambridge: Cambridge University Press, 1992). Joseph M. Modrzejewski comments and discusses several of these texts. Joseph M. Modrzejewski, *The Jews of Egypt* (Princeton: Princeton University Press, 1995), 73–98. See also Louis H. Feldman, "The Orthodoxy of the Jews in Hellenistic Egypt," *JSS* 22 (1960): 215–37. John M. Barclay, *Jews in the Mediterranean Diaspora* (Berkeley: University of California Press, 1996), 103–24; and James K. Aitken, *No Stone Unturned: Greek Inscriptions and Septuagint Vocabulary* (Winona Lake: Eisenbrauns, 2014).

11. Cowey and Maresch, *Urkunden*; Tcherikover and Fuks, *Corpus*, 6.

12. Erich S. Gruen, *Diaspora: Jews amidst Greeks and Romans* (Cambridge: Harvard University Press, 2002), 75. Sylvie Honigman, *The Septuagint and Homeric Scholarship in Alexandria* (London: Routledge, 2003), 98–101. The Talmud mentions a בית דין in Alexandria (*Toseftha Ketuboth* 3.1 and 2.26d).

13. Cowey and Maresch, *Urkunden*, 5–6.

14. See Cowey and Maresch, *Urkunden*, 4–9; Tcherikover and Fuks, *Corpus*, 6–10.

used in the sense "customs" rather than to the Mosaic law.[15] The papyri from Heracleopolis and other locations indicate that in legal matters Jews concurred with the common laws of the Greeks in Egypt, even in disputes among themselves.[16] Furthermore, the epigraphic material shows signs of interaction with both Greek and Egyptian culture.[17] Mixed marriages are likely evident in the papyri fragments of the remaining documents.[18] Moreover, Jews lent money to other Jews, charging an interest.[19]

The literary works that remain from Jews of this era presumably stem from the higher classes of the Jewish societies.[20] The learning required for these literary achievements is impressive. The writers not only knew their ancestral traditions, but were also well acquainted with Greek literature. In his seminal work on Jewish papyri fragments from antiquity, Victor A. Tcherikover suggested that privileged Jews in Alexandria and the other larger Greek cities probably sought education at the gymnasium. This education was required of those who aspired to be granted citizenship. Education was also necessary for those aspiring to be employed in the Ptolemaic administrative hierarchy.[21]

Many scholars have described this mode of attraction to, and delineation from, the dominant culture.[22] Tessa Rajak has surveyed the manner in which these literary works interacts with the Torah.[23] However, also among the privileged, one may question what part the Torah played as an identity marker.[24] The Ptolemies preferred to use non-natives in, at least part of, the administrative positions. This

---

15. Reinhard G. Kratz, *Historical and Biblical Israel: The History, Tradition, and Archives of Israel and Judah*, trans. Paul Michael Kurtz (Oxford: Oxford University Press 2015), 189 n. 120. Cowey and Maresch, however, do not dismiss the influence of the Mosaic law. In their discussion of papyrus no. 4 (*Urkunden*, 56–60, see also 28), they underline the similarities between the divorce letter required in the petition and the law in Deut 24:1–4.

16. Tcherikover and Fuks, *Corpus*, 33, 147–78; Cowey and Maresch, *Urkunden*, 23–29.

17. Cowey and Maresch, *Urkunden*, 30–32.

18. Tcherikover and Fuks, *Corpus*, no. 128, 236–38.

19. For instances no. 23 and 24 in Tcherikover and Fuks, *Corpus*, 162–67; and no. 8 in Cowey and Maresch, *Urkunden*, 93–102.

20. Tessa Rajak, *Translation and Survival* (Oxford: Oxford University Press, 2009), 237.

21. Tcherikover and Fuks, *Corpus*, 38.

22. For example, Barclay, *Jews*; Elias J. Bickerman, *The Jews in the Greek Age* (Cambridge: Harvard University Press, 1988); Collins, *Athens*; Erich S. Gruen, *Heritage and Hellenism: The Reinvention of Jewish Tradition* (Berkeley: University of California Press, 1998); Gruen, *Diaspora*; Honigman, *Septuagint*; Modrzejewski, *Jews*; Maren Niehoff, *Jewish Exegesis and Homeric Scholarship in Alexandria* (Cambridge: Cambridge Univeristy Press, 2011); Rajak, *Translation*.

23. Rajak, *Translation*, 227–38.

24. Kratz convincingly demonstrates how the scriptural element of the Judaite religion gradually became more important among the different strands of Judeans (*Historical and Biblical Israel*, 133–96).

opened the possibility for Jews to make a career. A possibility that might have tempted some to leave their ancestral traditions.[25]

In this article, I will look at what remains of one writer from the third century BCE, Demetrius. He probably lived in the second part of the century and is the earliest author known to us using the LXX in his writings. I will look at how Demetrius argues for the Torah's position as central for Jewish identity. My contention is: the texts of Demetrius indicate that it was not enough to translate the Torah into Greek in order to secure it a prominent place among Jews. The place of the Torah had to be argued for.

There are several characterizations of Demetrius's texts. Some call them apologetic,[26] others call them exegetic,[27] yet others call them historic.[28] All designations are in their ways suiting. The first characteristic is debated, because apologetic is often understood as directed against outsiders. This is not the case with Demetrius's texts.[29] I will investigate which parts of the text can be said to be apologetic. I will argue why it is likely that Demetrius wrote for Jews, and I will discuss what Demetrius might have attempted to achieve with his writings.

Demetrius

Demetrius most probably resided in Alexandria.[30] Scholars have given him the name "the Chronographer" because of his special approach to writing history. I will return to this issue later in the article. No contemporary sources mention Demetrius and his work is preserved only in quotations found in other sources.[31] The Greek-Roman[32] historian Alexander Polyhistor cites Demetrius in his work Περὶ

---

25. 3 Macc 1 mentions Dositheus who was born a Jew, "but had left his ancestral faith"; see Collins, *Athens*, 67; Modrzejewski, *Jews*, 56–65.

26. Nikolaus Walter, "Demetrius," *JSHRZ* 3.2 (1980): 282; J. Hanson, "Demetrius the Chronographer," *OTP* 2:845; Modrzejewski, *Jews*, 67.

27. Niehoff, *Exegesis*, 51; Nikolaus Walter, "Jewish-Greek Literature of the Greek Period," in *The Hellenistic Age*, ed. William David Davies and Louis Finkelstein, CHJ 2 (Cambridge: Cambridge University Press, 1989), 387.

28. Bickerman, *Jews*, 222; Carl R. Holladay, *Historians*, vol. 1 of *Fragments from Hellenistic Jewish Authors* (Chico: Scholars Press, 1983), 53.

29. Against Fraser, *Alexandria*, 693.

30. We do not know for certain where Demetrius lived, but Alexandria seems most likely. See Gregory Sterling, *Historiography and Self-Definition* (Leiden: Brill, 1992), 153–54; and Holladay, *Fragments*, 51–52.

31. Sterling, *Historiography*, 153.

32. Alexander Polyhistor was from Miletus in Asia Minor but was taken captive by the Romans during the Mithridatic Wars and made a slave. After his release, he continued to live in Rome. He wrote in Greek.

Ἰουδαίων from the first century BCE.³³ This work is also lost, except for quotations in yet later sources. Eusebius (260/265–339/340 CE) had access to Alexander Polyhistor and thereby to Demetrius. Clement of Alexandria also cites Demetrius's work, but it is difficult to say where he got the citation from.³⁴

We have the following texts preserved from Demetrius:³⁵

Eusebius	
Pr. Ev. 9.19.4	Abraham's sacrifice of Isaac
Pr. Ev. 9.21.1–19	Events from Jacob's escape to Charan, to Amram, Moses's father dies.
Pr. Ev. 9.29.1–3	Moses in Midian
Pr. Ev. 9.29.15a	The Israelites arrive at Elim
Pr. Ev. 9.29.16b	The manner in which the Israelites got their weapons in the wilderness
Clement of Alexandria	The number of years between Sennacherib,
Strom. 1.21.141	Nebuchadnezzar and Ptolemy IV

Josephus probably refers to Demetrius in *C. Ap* 1.217–218.

The texts from Eusebius deal with events related in the Pentateuch. The text from Clement has a different content. It refers to Sennacherib, Nebuchadnezzar, and Ptolemy IV. Maren Niehoff argues that these differences are so significant that the fragments must stem from two different authors.³⁶

This is not a necessary conclusion. The divergences can also be explained as different works from the same author.³⁷ It is worth noticing that Clement of Alexandria calls Demetrius's work, "On the Kings of Judaea." It is not certain that the excerpts preserved by Eusebius belong to the same work.³⁸ Furthermore, we should notice that Demetrius's most important method, chronography, characterizes the fragments in both Eusebius and Clement.

---

33. Probably the middle of the century; William Adler, "Alexander Polyhistor's *Peri Ioudaion* and Literary Culture in Republican Rome," in *Reconsidering Eusebius: Collected Papers on Literary, Historical, and Theological Issues*, ed. Sabrina Inowlocki and Claudio Zamagni (Leiden: Brill, 2011), 237; and Sterling, *Historiography*, 149.

34. Emil Schürer, *The History of the Jewish People in the Age of Jesus Christ: 175 B.C.–A.D. 135*, rev. and ed. Geza Vermes, Fergus Millar and Martin Goodman, vol. 3.2 (Edinburg: T&T Clark, 2000), 515; Walter, "Literature," 280.

35. Two of the fragments Eusebius quotes (9.19.4 and 9.29.16b) do not mention Demetrius explicitly as the author. They have, nevertheless, been commonly ascribed to him. Niehoff (*Exegesis*, 39) and Sterling (*Historiography*, 155) express doubts concerning these two fragments, but firm footing is hard to find.

36. Niehoff, *Exegesis*, 55.

37. Walter, "Demetrius," 280.

38. Sterling, *Historiography*, 156–57; Collins, *Athens*, 33; Holladay, *Fragments*, 51; Schürer, *History*, 513. Philo uses βασιλεύς for Moses (*Mos* 2.3–6).

The excerpts that are preserved span over a time frame from Adam to Ptolemy IV Philopater. The latter reference has been the basis for dating Demetrius's text to Philopater's reign, that is, 221–205 BCE.[39] To be fair, this reference can only serve as a *terminus post quem*. A later dating is not impossible. At the time of Philopater, the LXX probably had existed some decades.[40]

The question of the LXX's reliability as a source for Jewish history and customs can explain much of Demetrius's work. Demetrius used several means to show this reliability. The most prominent is the use of genres. Even though Demetrius wrote to Jews concerning the excellence of the Torah, he used genres that originated from Greek authors, that is, "genealogies" and "questions and solutions."[41]

Genealogies

Demetrius is named "the Chronographer" because he was concerned with dating the life of persons and events. The backbone of his account was genealogies, which he found in the Torah. Demetrius did not only use the genealogies to explain kinship, but also as clues for the story's chronology. Greek historians commonly used this technique.[42] Demetrius was not satisfied with placing persons and events in chronological order; he noted the durations of every event and summed up the number of years while relating the story. Let me illustrate by the following example (*Pr. Ev.* 9.21.2–3a):[43]

> Jacob therefore set out for Charran in Mesopotamia, having left his father Isaac a hundred and thirty-seven years of age, and being himself seventy-seven years old. So after spending seven years there he married two daughters of his uncle Laban, Leah and Rachel, when he was eighty-four years old: and in seven years more there were born to him twelve sons; in the eighth year and tenth month Reuben, and in the ninth year and eighth month Symeon ...

---

39. See Sterling, *Historiography*, 153. Niehoff challenges this date on the basis of a distinction between Eusebius's Demetrius and Clement's. She dates the latter to the third century BCE, while the first to the second century BCE (Niehoff, *Exegesis*, 55). On the other hand, if the dating to Philopater's reign is correct, it may throw an interesting light over Demetrius's work. During Philopater's reign, Egyptians rebelled against the new rulers (Sterling, *Historiography*, 162–66). However, we do not find any references to the rebellion in the fragments we have from Demetrius.

40. Jennifer M. Dines, *The Septuagint* (London: T&T Clark, 2004), 41. See also Karen H. Jobes and Moisés Silva, *Invitation to the Septuagint* (Grand Rapids: Baker Academic, 2000), 33–37.

41. Bickerman, *Jews*, 221; Niehoff, *Exegesis*, 38–57; Sterling, *Historiography*, 160–62.

42. Bickerman, *Jews*, 221.

43. Translation from Holladay, *Fragments*.

Demetrius continues, year by year with new children, and after that, new events which he accurately fits into the chronology. And the numbers add up. Jacob was 20 years in Laban's household, then he went to Sikima, where he lived 10 years before the rape of Dinah and the subsequent revenge led them to Luz in Bethel. Jacob was now 107 years old, Demetrius summarizes. From Luz they left for Ephratha, where Rachel died after 23 years of marriage with Jacob. After that, they arrived at Mamre, where Isaac lived. Joseph, who at this point had reached the age of 17, was now sold to Egypt. In Egypt, he spent 13 years in prison, which meant that he was 30 when Pharaoh released him (*Pr. Ev.* 9.21.3b–11).

In this manner, Demetrius's story turns into a massive calculation that he regularly sums up. We should notice that for Demetrius, the order of the numbers is not insignificant. The order is rather more important than the grand total. The purpose of the account is to place events and persons in the correct chronology, and the numbers are just a means to show that the account is accurate. When the numbers add up, the story must be considered trustworthy.

SUMMARIES

Demetrius summarized the story at a remarkable point, which is when Jacob arrives in Egypt (*Pr. Ev.* 9.21.16). Apparently, Demetrius regarded this as such a significant turning point that he found it natural to make a pause in the story. We do not have enough material preserved to know whether Demetrius had several of these summaries, but it is not unreasonable to suggest that he did. At least, we know that the summary departs from three other important events. Demetrius started with Adam and wrote that from Adam to Jacob's entry into Egypt, there were 3624 years. The next point of departure is the deluge. From the deluge to Jacob's entry there were 1360 years. The last departure is the choosing of Abraham. From this event, 215 years passed before Jacob entered Egypt.

By this summary, it seems that Demetrius attempts to determine that Jews had ancient roots. We know of several authors who made similar claims on their nation's behalf.[44] Being able to account for a long and distinguished past was important for asserting a people's national and cultural preeminence.[45] With his calculations, Demetrius joined the competition.

We should notice that a similar tendency to increase the Israelites' age already existed in the Septuagint. Gregory Sterling has computed that the genealogies of Gen 5 and 11 in the MT will amount to 1948 years from Adam to Abraham, while the same lists in the Septuagint amounts to 3314 years.[46] It is the lists in the Septuagint Demetrius used in his summary.

---

44. Sterling, *Historiography*, 163–64.
45. Modrzejewski, *Jews*, 62.
46. Sterling, *Historiography*, 165.

Furthermore, it is likely that the summary point when Jacob enters Egypt has to do with Demetrius's location in Egypt. Precisely in what way is more difficult to say. It is possible that Demetrius may have related to ideas concerning the Jews' origins. Demetrius did not refer to divergent explanations, but this does not mean that they did not exist. It is worth mentioning Hecataeus of Abdera, who wrote early in the third century that the Jews originated from a group of foreigners who were driven out of Egypt. Some of them settled in Greece, but most settled in Canaan. In this account, Hecataeus associated the Jews with Egypt, but he was not specific concerning the Jews' origins. We find another diffuse account in Manetho's *Aigyptiaka*. Manetho wrote about a group called "Hyksos" who came from the east and conquered Egypt. Later, the group was driven out of the country and settled in Jerusalem. Josephus was not in doubt that Manetho here referred to Jews, and if he was right, this accounts for another example of a narrative of the uncertain origins of the Jews.[47]

STYLE

Demetrius did not recount all the events that are related in the Pentateuch, and the episodes he included are briefly told. For instance, Demetrius restricted the story of Jacob and Esau to a few lines as part of the explanation why Jacob left for Harran (*Pr. Ev.* 9.21.1), and the story of how Joseph ended up as a slave in Egypt is mentioned in a subordinate clause (*Pr. Ev.* 9.21.11). The story of Abraham's sacrifice of Isaac is somewhat longer (*Pr. Ev.* 9.19.4), but again, Demetrius focused on the events. The drama therein has to be read between the lines.

Even more eye-catching is how dry and brief Demetrius recounted Sychem's rape of Dinah (*Pr. Ev.* 9.21.9a):

> Now Israel dwelt beside Emmor ten years; and Israel's daughter Dinah was defiled by Sychem the son of Emmor, she being sixteen years and four months old. And Israel's sons Symeon being twenty-one years and four months old, and Levi twenty years and six months, rushed forth and slew both Emmor and his son Sychem, and all their males, because of the defilement of Dinah: and at that time Jacob was a hundred and seven years old.

Demetrius in this manner chose a very compressed style in order to emphasize the chronology.

---

47. It is not certain that this interpretation may be ascribed to Manetho, because the interpretation is dependent on Josephus's reading of the text in a secondary context. Josephus had probably not direct access to Manetho's work. See Gruen, *Heritage*, 55–56; Collins, *Athens*, 9–10; Menahem Stern, *Greek and Latin Authors on Jews and Judaism* (Jerusalem: The Israel Academy of Sciences and Humanities, 1976), 62.

Demetrius mentioned Jacob's fight with the angel while he is on his way back to Canaan (*Pr. Ev.* 9.21.7). Demetrius probably told this episode because it was the reason why Jews did not eat the sinew of the thigh of cattle. What importance he ascribed to this and other dietary regulations, we do not know. We may observe that the dietary laws have been differently handled by other Jewish authors. The author of the Letter of Aristeas wrote extensively about the dietary laws. Apparently, he had no qualms letting the translators dine with the Ptolemaic king. To the contrary, the author described the many days' long banquet elaborately. Furthermore, he proposed an allegorical interpretation of the dietary laws by the mouth of Eleazar, the high priest (§128–170). It is not clear, however, that this allegorization is meant as a moderation of the laws. The answer Eleazar gives is rather an explanation of the laws in accordance with contemporary presuppositions, and here we should notice points of contact with Hellenistic philosophy. Eleazar's explanation departs from questions concerning what constitutes a good life. To him, a good life is a life in fulfilment of the Mosaic laws (§127). Eleazar elaborates this when he justifies the dietary laws. He says that man will be ruined and miserable if he turns to evil, while he corrects his life by turning to the law. The Mosaic law describes a path to a pious life, and God will in his omnipresence punish all those who trespass against it.

Demetrius did not resort to such explanations of the dietary laws when he paraphrased the story of Jacob's wrestle with the angel. He wrote that because an angel touched Jacob on the patriarch's thigh and marked him for life, Jews do not eat this part of cattle. Demetrius's justification does not rest on a philosophical argument, like we find in the Letter of Aristeas. Demetrius let the story in Genesis speak for itself.

CONCLUSION

Demetrius emphasized the genealogies. Demetrius's work on the Torah is not a retelling, which is meant to replace the Torah, such as the book of Jubilees. It is rather a commentary that explains how the events are connected. In other words, Demetrius attempted to underline and substantiate the Torah.

QUESTIONS AND SOLUTIONS

Commentary characteristics are apparent in a couple of passages where Demetrius made some digressions. At these occasions, Demetrius made use of a different genre, which was also common among scholars in Alexandria and that Aristotle described in *Aporemata Homerica*.[48] It is characterized by questions and solutions.[49] The author referred to a critical question, which he thereafter answered.

---

48. Niehoff, *Exegesis*, 38, 41.
49. Collins, *Athens*, 34; Sterling, *Historiography*, 156, 160.

In this manner, Demetrius explained issues that his audience was presumably concerned with.

SOLUTION WHICH SHOWED THAT THE TORAH DID NOT CONTRADICT ITSELF

A matter which Demetrius made an effort to explain (*Pr. Ev.* 9.29.16b) was how the Israelites could have weapons to wage war against the Amalekites (Exod 17:8–9), even though they left Egypt without any weapons (Exod 5:3).[50] Demetrius explained that the answer lies in a detail that the text does not mention explicitly, namely that the people took weapons from the Egyptians who drowned in the Red Sea. Although Exod 14:28 tells that all the Egyptians drowned with chariots and horses, it does not mention what happened to the weapons. Herein lies the opportunity to explain the two seemingly conflicting verses.

SOLUTIONS WHICH EXPLAINED THE ACTIONS OF THE CHARACTERS

Demetrius spent several lines explaining why Joseph, while he was a high-ranking public official in Egypt, did not send for his family immediately but waited until they came by their own choice, driven by famine (*Pr. Ev.* 9.21.13). The reason, according to Demetrius, was to be found in the text. Jacob and his sons were shepherds, a way of living the Egyptians disliked (Gen 46:34). Joseph refrained from gathering his family to Egypt because the Egyptians would not have received them well.

Demetrius furthermore explained why Joseph discriminated between his brothers when he allotted Benjamin five times as much food and five times as many clothes as his brothers (*Pr. Ev.* 9.21.14). This sounds unjust, but Demetrius had an explanation. The reason is, Demetrius wrote, that Leah's seven sons received one portion each, while Rachel only had Joseph and Benjamin. Joseph took two portions and gave Benjamin five. The distribution was then equal between the two sisters: Leah's sons got seven portions, the same as Rachel's.

SOLUTION WHICH DEFINED JEWISH IDENTITY

Marriage is another subject Demetrius engaged in (*Pr. Ev.* 9.29.1–3). Here he was again concerned with genealogies. Demetrius mentioned the genealogy of Moses when he recounted Jacob's arrival in Egypt and when Moses leaves Egypt. Moses's marriage to Zipporah caused Demetrius to investigate her lineage. The question that lies behind the investigation seems to be how Moses could marry a woman from Midian. Keeping marriages within the nation was, in other words,

---

50. Niehoff, *Exegesis*, 40.

one of Demetrius's concerns.[51] He therefore had to explain why Moses, the lawgiver, apparently could allow himself a foreign wife. By closer investigation of the genealogies, however, Demetrius argued that Zipporah was not foreign after all.

The starting point for Demetrius's investigation was Exod 2:15–22. Here, we read that Moses fled to Midian and that he married Zipporah, the daughter of Re'uel.[52] In the Hebrew text, these verses make no explicit mention of Zipporah's lineage and nationality, but the designation of Re'uel as the "Priest of Midian" (Exod 2:16) and the etymology Moses used for his son, Gershom (Exod 2:22), "I have been an alien residing in a foreign land," might be taken as hints. The text, however, does not problematize Zipporah's lineage. In Num 12, Miriam and Aaron complain over Moses's marriage to an Ethiopian woman. Whether they refer to Zipporah is not certain, but it is clear that they consider Moses's marriage as problematic.

Demetrius found it necessary to deal with these uncertainties. He attempted to show that Zipporah was of acceptable lineage for Moses. Demetrius listed up her genealogy in the following manner: Zipporah was the daughter of Re'uel, Re'uel was the son of Dedan, Dedan was the son of Jokshan, who was a son of Abraham and Keturah. In other words, Zipporah was a descendant of Abraham and, therefore, a suiting wife for Moses.

We do not find the genealogy Demetrius used in the MT. The MT does not mention Re'uel among the descendants of Abraham and Keturah (Gen 25). In the MT, we find Re'uel in the list of Esau's descendants in Gen 36. This list mentions Re'uel as Esau's son with Basemat. The LXX version of this list also mentions Re'uel.

The LXX, however, introduces Re'uel already in the genealogy in Gen 25 and this is the genealogy Demetrius used. In LXX Gen 25, we find the following genealogy of Abraham's children with Keturah:

> Now Abraam again took a wife, whose name was Chettoura. And she bore him Zembran and Iexan and Madan and Madiam and Iesbok and Soye. And Iexan was the father of Saba and Thaiman and Daidan. And the sons of Daidan were Ragouel [Re'uel] and Nabdeel and Assourieim and Latouiseim and Loomieim.[53]

---

51. See Gruen, *Heritage*, 114, n. 18; Sterling, *Historiography*, 160; Collins, *Athens*, 34; and Magnar Kartveit, *The Origin of the Samaritans* (Leiden: Brill, 2009), 121. Niehoff does not think that this is about marriage with a gentile woman, because she claims that mixed marriages were not considered problematic at the time of Demetrius (*Exegesis*, 54 n. 47). Against Niehoff, it should be noted that Ezra 9:2 seems to warn against mixed marriages.

52. We find the spelling "Raguel" in the LXX. For the sake of simplicity, I will use Re'uel, also when the reference to him stems from the LXX.

53. Albert Pietersma and Benjamin G. Wright, ed., *A New English Translation of the Septuagint* (Oxford: Oxford University Press, 2007), 21.

In his commentary on this genealogy, John W. Wevers writes that the reason for this confusion of genealogies is unclear.[54] In light of what we can read in Demetrius's work, it appears that the introduction of Re'uel in Gen 25 is connected to Moses's marriage to Zipporah. It is beyond the scope of this article to discuss the origin of this list in the LXX. The question I will discuss is why it was important for Demetrius to connect Zipporah to this genealogy and not to the one where Re'uel is among Esau's sons (Gen 36). In the latter list, Re'uel is just as closely related to Abraham, that is, great grandchild, as in the list we find in LXX Gen 25. Several reasons are possible. These reasons do not mutually exclude each other.

(1) Being concerned with chronology, it was important for Demetrius to demonstrate how likely it was that Moses and Zipporah lived at the same time and were in an appropriate age for marriage. Moses, Demetrius wrote, was in the seventh generation from Abraham, while Zipporah was in the sixth. Demetrius explained this by pointing out that Moses descended from Isaac, Abraham's son with Sarah. Isaac was born when Abraham was 100 years old. Abraham married Keturah when he was 140, according to Demetrius, and she gave birth to Jokshan, Zipporah's patriarch, when Abraham was 142. Demetrius explained the difference of the generations between Moses and Zipporah by the difference in Isaac's and Jokshan's age. The list in Gen 25 allows for such an explanation, while the list in Gen 36, where Re'uel, and thereby Zipporah, are the descendants of Isaac, does not.

(2) Demetrius explained why Abraham's children with Keturah now lived in Midian by reference to Scripture (*Pr. Ev.* 9.29.3). That precisely Midian was the home of Re'uel and Zipporah can be connected to the genealogy in Gen 25. According to Demetrius, the city was named after Midian, Abraham's son. The connection between Abraham, Midian and Re'uel is present in the LXX version of Gen 25. Demetrius used the notion that Abraham's children with Keturah were supposed to travel east (Gen 25:6) to explain Miriam and Aaron's accusations concerning Moses's marriage to an Ethiopian woman. It appears as a misunderstanding that travelling east to Midian, which is situated on the Arabian Peninsula, could explain why Zipporah was accused of being Ethiopian. But Demetrius possibly thought that Ethiopians lived in Midian. We find such an assumption in Ezekiel's *Exagoge*. This is a work that renders the Exodus story by the genre of a Greek tragedy. It was probably written in Alexandria in the second or first century BCE. The *Exagoge* also mentions Moses's marriage with Zipporah. In the episode where Moses meets Zipporah at the well, Zipporah explains that Ethiopians inhabit the area.[55] Whether Ezekiel's *Exagoge* also presented a genealogy, like the

---

54. John W. Wevers, *Notes on the Greek text of Genesis*, SCS 35 (Atlanta: Scholars Press, 1993), 378–79.

55. See Howard Jacobsen, *The Exagoge of Ezekiel* (Cambridge: Cambridge University Press, 1983), 55.

one Demetrius refers to, we do not know.[56] It is noteworthy, however, that Demetrius appeared to have the same idea of who inhabited Midian.

(3) Even though Esau was the grandchild of Abraham, he was considered to be the patriarch of a new nation, the Edomites. Despite the common origins, Israelites were not allowed to marry Edomites (Deut 23:7–8). When Zipporah was placed among Keturah's descendants, she could not be counted as an Edomite, and was therefore a better-suited wife for Moses.

Demetrius also mentioned three other marriages: Jacob's with Leah and Rachel (*Pr. Ev.* 9.21.3), and Joseph's with Asenath (*Pr. Ev.* 9.21.12). That Jacob married Leah and Rachel is not a problem; they were his cousins, daughters of Jacob's uncle, Laban. But it is striking that Demetrius did not address Joseph's marriage with Asenath. Demetrius mentioned that Joseph governed in Egypt for seven years, and that he, during these seven years, married Asenath, the daughter of Pentephres, a priest in Heliopolis. Why Demetrius did not comment on this is hard to explain. In a later work of a different author, which is named *Joseph and Asenath* by modern scholars, Asenath converts before she marries Joseph. Whether Demetrius had similar thoughts, we do not know, but it is striking that he leaves Joseph's marriage with Asenath without a comment.

SUMMARY AND CONCLUSION

By using the genre "question and answer," Demetrius explained and underlined the credibility of the Torah. The answer to the question concerning how the Israelites could find weapons to wage war against the Amalekites underlined the text's inner coherence. The answers concerning Joseph's behavior towards his brothers explained Joseph's actions. These answers also demonstrated the inner coherence of the text, because Demetrius found the answers in other parts of the text. Demetrius did not refer to external sources but let the text speak for itself.

The issues Demetrius chose to explain indicate that he wrote for Jews. The questions concerning the inner logic of the Torah, the dietary laws, Joseph's motives for his behavior, and Moses's marriage are more likely to come from a Jewish context than a gentile. It is not likely that these issues should worry a non-Jew.

WHAT DID DEMETRIUS SEEK TO ACHIEVE WITH HIS TEXTS?

This question is not easy to answer. It is nevertheless part of the text analysis. I mentioned in the introduction that Demetrius attempted to promote the Torah as

---

56. Jacobsen, *Exagoge*, 34.

an important text for Jewish identity. In the present paragraph, I will point at further arguments for this suggestion. In order to do so, I will bring in some aspects related to the concept of identity.

The concept of identity is often used to refer to individuals and their self-definition. However, it can also be used with reference to groups and their common values. The latter, often called "social identity," emphasizes the social context's role in individual behavior. In an exposition of the approach, Dominic Abrams writes that common assumptions and opinions are more important than direct interpersonal influence and material interests for an individual's behavior.[57] What group a person associates with determines how that person behaves, because he or she would like to follow the norms and rules that are constituent of the group. What norms and rules are constituent for the group will be an issue of deliberation and in such a deliberation, it is beneficial to be able to back up one's arguments with reference to an authority.

In order to study a group's self-definition, it is important to analyze how this group relates to a wider social structure where other groups are involved.[58] As part of the wish to preserve a positive understanding of oneself, the evaluation of the self-understanding is affected by how the group judges other groups in the larger society.[59]

In other words, identity can be connected to groups and be defined by the group's values. At the same time, the group's identity is delimited by its relation to other groups. These values and delimitations are affected by the basic structures of the larger society, but they can also be changed and reformulated so that new ideas can flourish. In this manner, we may say that identity can be constructed.

I have attempted to show that Demetrius underlined the credibility of the Torah with the help of the genres "genealogies" and "questions and solutions." In the questions Demetrius dealt with, he never looked for answers outside of the text, but found explanations within the textual corpus. He was faithful towards the content of the text but had no qualms about using Greek language and Greek manners of interpretation to shed light on it. By this approach, Demetrius sought to secure the Torah's position as an important text for the Jews of Alexandria. In the text, he also found arguments to demarcate the Jews from other groups in the society.

---

57. Dominic Abrams, "Social Identity and Groups," in *Group Processes*, ed. John M. Levine (New York: Psychology Press, 2012), 269. See Collins, *Athens*, 2 for a similar approach.

58. Henri Tajfel, "Social Identity and Intergroup Behaviour," *SSI* 13 (1974): 65–93; Henri Tajfel and John Turner, "An Integrative Theory of Intergroup Conflict," in *The Social Psychology of Intergroup Relations*, ed. William G. Austin and Stephen Worchel; (Monterey: Brooks-Cole, 1979), 33–47; Abrams, "Social Identity," 270.

59. Abrams, "Social Identity," 270.

Demetrius's summary of Jacob's entry into Egypt can be interpreted as such a delimitation. Demetrius underlined that Jews originated outside of Egypt by focusing especially on this event. Even though the Israelites' exodus from Egypt under Moses's leadership was important for the Jews, it did not mean that the Israelites, and thereby also the Jews, originated in Egypt. Before the Exodus, the Israelites had been foreigners in Egypt, just like the Jews were foreigners in Egypt at the time of Demetrius.

Demetrius's explanation of Zipporah's lineage can be interpreted as a similar delimitation. Demetrius made efforts to explain that Zipporah descended from Abraham. In light of the epigraphic material, which likely indicate that mixed marriages were not uncommon, this can be read as an argument against marriages with non-Jews.

Another issue in Demetrius's work, which can be characterized as an important value and a demarcation, is his explanation of the dietary laws. Demetrius made no attempt to explain it allegorically or philosophically, like we find later Alexandrian authors did. Demetrius was satisfied with telling the incident that explained the law. Scripture was the justification for the dietary laws.

The final point that we may read out of Demetrius's work, is his emphasis on the Jews' ancient origins. It was probably important for the people to be able to trace their roots far back in time in order to promote their status in competition with other nations. That Demetrius demonstrated the ancient origins of the Jews may be interpreted as a part of their identity construction. Demetrius again used the Torah for this purpose.

In light of these conclusions, it is worthwhile to look briefly at the Septuagint's reception in Alexandria after Demetrius.

Demetrius and the Septuagint's Early Reception in Alexandria

Josephus refers to Demetrius in the following paragraph (*C. Ap.* 1.217–218):

> The majority of these authors [Greek writers] have misrepresented the facts of our sacred books; but all concur in testifying to our antiquity, and that is the point with which I am at present concerned. Demetrius Phalerus, the elder Philo, and Eupolemus are exceptional in their approximation to the truth, and (their errors) may be excused on the ground of their inability to follow quite accurately the meaning of our records.[60]

Josephus lauded Demetrius, here mistakenly confused with Demetrius of Phalerum,[61] for his record of the "earliest times." However, Josephus demurred

---

60. The translation is quoted from Henry St. J. Thackeray, *Josephus: The Life, Against Apion*, LCL 186 (Cambridge: Harvard University Press, 1926).

61. Demetrius of Phalerum was a Greek philosopher at the court of Ptolemy I Soter

somewhat, because Demetrius did not know Hebrew. Josephus therefore hesitated in his praise.[62]

Josephus is probably correct in his assumption that Demetrius did not use Hebrew texts of the Torah. Sterling mentions three points which substantiate the presumption: (1) Demetrius transcribed Hebrew personal names and toponyms in the same manner as the LXX; (2) Demetrius used the same vocabulary as the LXX; (3) Demetrius's work agrees with the LXX wherever the LXX deviates from the Hebrew text.[63]

It does not seem to worry Demetrius that he did not use Hebrew texts. We do not know whether challenges concerning the process of translation were an issue for him at all. We only know that he unhesitatingly used the LXX as the basis for promoting the Torah's credibility.

This use of the LXX may have paved the way for later Jewish writers in Alexandria. Aristobulus and the author of the Letter of Aristeas, who both wrote in the second century BCE, show a deep trust in the translations. Indeed, Aristobulus, who claimed that the translation of the Torah predated Plato, wrote that the translation was a prerequisite for Plato's philosophy. The author of the Letter of Aristeas apparently promoted a similar confidence in a situation where the authority of the translation was questioned. It is therefore interesting to see how this author substantiated the credibility of the translation by recounting a story of how the source text of the translation was brought from Jerusalem and that the finished work was approved by the Jewish community in Alexandria. What this reference to Jerusalem indicates, that is, whether it is an expression of greater confidence in the quality of the texts that originated in the temple, is hard to tell,[64] but it is not unwarranted to assume that there was a consciousness regarding textual matters and that the quality of different texts was discussed. In such a light, the Letter of Aristeas' authorization of the translations is noteworthy.[65]

(306/4–283/2 BCE). Ptolemy I ruled as satrap in Egypt from 323–306 BCE. See Günther Hölb, *A History of the Ptolemaic Empire* (London: Routledge, 2000), 14–34. The *Letter of Aristeas* erroneously places Demetrius of Phalerum in the reign of Ptolemy II Philadelphus (282–246 BCE) and gives him an important role in the story of the origin of the Septuagint. That Josephus, in the quotation above, mistakenly ascribes the writings of Demetrius the Chronographer to Demetrius of Phalerum is likely because the latter probably never wrote anything about Jews or used the Jewish scriptures as a source in his writings.

62. Daniel R. Schwarz, "Josephus on his Jewish Forerunners (*Contra Apionem* 1,218)," in *Studies in Josephus and the Varieties of Ancient Judaism: Louis H. Feldman Jubilee Volume*, ed. Shaye J. D. Cohen and Joshua J. Schwartz (Leiden: Brill, 2007), 202.

63. Sterling, *Historiography*, 158–59.

64. See Emanuel Tov, "The Text of the Hebrew/Aramaic and Greek Bible Used in the Ancient Synagogues," in *Hebrew Bible, Greek Bible and Qumran*, ed. Emanuel Tov, TSAJ 121 (Tübingen: Mohr Siebeck, 2008), 171–88.

65. See §310 in the Letter of Aristeas. The scholars at the Museion in Alexandria were

Summary and Conclusion

In this article, I have attempted to show which traits of Demetrius's work may be characterized as apologetic. I have pointed out Demetrius's promotion of the Torah's credibility as such a trait. Demetrius achieved this by mixing two genres that were common among contemporary Greek authors.

Demetrius interrupted his own condensed style several times. He did this in order to answer questions that he experienced as important for his audience. These questions fit a Jewish context, which indicates that Demetrius's readers were Jewish.

The question concerning what Demetrius sought to achieve by his work, I have approached by two categories from the "social-identity" theory. Demetrius emphasized the ancient origins of the nation as an asset for the Jews and delimited them from other groups by regulating their dietary customs and their choice of partner for marriage. It is therefore reasonable to state that the texts of Demetrius are a voice in the deliberation of Jewish identity in his time.

---

prominent students of textual criticism of the text of Homer. Niehoff suggests that the author of the Letter of Aristeas warns against a similar form of textual criticism on the Septuagint (*Exegesis*, 19–37).

Was the Earth Invisible (LXX Gen 1:2)? A Response to Pieter W. van der Horst

Robert J. V. Hiebert

Abstract: In an article in the *Journal of Septuagint and Cognate Studies* 48 (2015): 5–7, Pieter van der Horst argues that ἀόρατος does not mean "invisible" as it has been rendered in recent translations of LXX Gen 1:2 but "hideous" or "unsightly." In response to that article, this paper will assess the validity of the author's contentions in the light of various philological considerations.

Gen 1:2
והארץ היתה תהו ובהו
the earth was a formless void (NRSV)

ἡ δὲ γῆ ἦν ἀόρατος καὶ ἀκατασκεύαστος
Yet the earth was invisible and unformed (NETS)
Die Erde aber war *unsichtbar* und *ungestaltet* (LXX.D)
Or la terre était invisible et inorganisée (BdA)

In his 2015 article in the *Journal of Septuagint and Cognate Studies*,[1] Pieter van der Horst observes that the phrase והארץ היתה תהו ובהו in Gen 1:2 is rendered ἡ δὲ γῆ ἦν ἀόρατος καὶ ἀκατασκεύαστος in the Septuagint, and that all modern translations of this Greek text agree in understanding the meaning of ἀόρατος to be "invisible." Thus, for example, in LXX.D the word is "unsichtbar" and in BdA it is "invisible." He points out as well that the rendering "invisible" is supported by Takamitsu Muraoka in his *Greek-English Lexicon of the Septuagint* (*GELS*) and

---

[1]. Pieter W. van der Horst, "Was the Earth 'Invisible'? A Note on ἀόρατος in Genesis 1:2 LXX," *JSCS* 48 (2015): 5–7.

by John Wevers in his *Notes on the Greek Text of Genesis*.² Then he asks: "But does this translation make sense?"³

In the ensuing discussion, van der Horst states that semantic range of the Hebrew term תהו "includes the elements of desolation, trackless waste, lifelessness, worthlessness, and futility," but not the concept of invisibility. He maintains that if "the Three" non-Septuagintal Greek translators could come up with "more or less satisfactory translations," then it is unlikely that the Septuagint translators would have been "hampered by unfamiliarity with the meaning" of תהו.⁴ As for "the widely held theory that the translators chose this rendition under the influence of Platonic cosmology," he acknowledges that it is not impossible but then asserts that this "does not solve the problem"—presumably meaning the problem he sees with regard to a translation that makes sense—and he goes on to say that the possibility of Platonic influence seems to him "to be less likely in this case."⁵

The passage in Plato that is typically compared to Gen 1:2 is found in *Timaeus*:

Plato, *Tim.* 50c–d, 51a–b
For the present, then, we must conceive of three kinds [γένη]—the Becoming [τὸ μὲν γιγνόμενον], that "Wherein" it becomes [τὸ δ' ἐν ᾧ γίγνεται], and the source "Wherefrom" the Becoming is copied and produced [τὸ δ' ὅθεν ἀφομοιούμενον φύεται τὸ γιγνόμενον]. Moreover, it is proper to liken the Recipient to the Mother, the Source to the Father, and what is engendered between these two to the Offspring; and also to perceive that, if the stamped copy is to assume diverse appearances of all sorts [ἐκτυπώματος ἔσεσθαι μέλλοντος ἰδεῖν ποικίλου πάσας ποικιλίας], that substance wherein it is set and stamped [τοῦτ' αὐτὸ ἐν ᾧ ἐκτυπούμενον ἐνίσταται] could not possibly be suited to its purpose [παρεσκευασμένον εὖ] unless it were itself devoid of all those forms [ἄμορφον ὂν ἐκείνων ἁπασῶν τῶν ἰδεῶν] which it is about to receive from any quarter.... So likewise it is right that the substance which is to be fitted to receive frequently over its whole extent the copies of all things intelligible and eternal should itself, of its own nature, be void of all the forms [τῶν εἰδῶν]. Wherefore, let us not speak of her that is the Mother and Receptacle of this generated world, which is perceptible by sight and all the senses [τοῦ γεγονότος ὁρατοῦ καὶ πάντως αἰσθητοῦ], by the name of earth [γῆν] or air or fire or water, or any aggregates or constituents

---

2. John William Wevers, *Notes on the Greek Text of Genesis*, SCS 35 (Atlanta: Scholars Press, 1993), 1–2.

3. Van der Horst, "Was the Earth 'Invisible'?," 5.

4. Mistakenly, he includes κενόν "empty, fruitless, void" (LSJ), which I can find nowhere in Wevers's critical edition, along with κένωμα (Aquila) "empty space, nonexistence" (LSJ) and ἀργόν (Symmachus) "lying idle, lying fallow, unwrought, left undone" (LSJ) among his list of satisfactory translations. He does not, however, mention Theodotion's θὲν καὶ οὐθέν, the neologistic counterpart to the rhythmic pair תהו ובהו (Van der Horst, "Was the Earth 'Invisible'?," 5).

5. Van der Horst, "Was the Earth 'Invisible'?," 5.

thereof: rather, if we describe her as a Kind invisible and unshaped [ἀνόρατον εἶδός τι καὶ ἄμορφον], all-receptive, and in some most perplexing and most baffling way partaking of the intelligible.[6]

Van der Horst points out that Plato is employing ἀόρατος in his discussion of "the incorporeal world of the Ideas"[7] ἰδέαι—more precisely, "ideal forms" or "archetypes" (LSJ)—rather than of the earth. As noted above, he does admit that "it can never be ruled out completely that perhaps the translator drew upon Plato's terminology without drawing upon his ideas," but he does "not agree with this explanation."[8] Instead, he agrees with Martin Hengel in *Judentum und Hellenismus* that "in keinem Falle handelt es sich jedoch um bewußte Anspielungen,"[9] and with David Runia in his commentary on Philo's work entitled *On the Creation of the Cosmos according to Moses* "that the hypothesis that the LXX translators themselves were influenced by Plato 'lacks all plausibility.'"[10]

Two matters need to be distinguished in regard to the present discussion concerning the presence of ἀόρατος in LXX Gen 1:2: (1) What does it mean? (2) Did the translator choose this term as a counterpart to תהו as a result of Platonic influence? It strikes me that the second of these questions is somewhat analogous to the one that has often been discussed in relation to the matter of how, if at all, the Hebrew authors/editors of Gen 1–11 were influenced by antecedent Mesopotamian stories about the primeval world. In that discussion, the general consensus amongst scholars would likely be that, while there are undeniable comparabilities between Mesopotamian and Hebrew traditions, it is doubtful that Hebrew tradents or scribes consulted copies of *Enuma Elish* or the *Atrahasis* or *Gilgamesh* epics directly as they crafted their versions of a primeval narrative. Instead, they lived in a world in which the imagery and vocabulary of these traditions were part of the warp and woof of their culture, and they felt constrained to shape the raw materials provided by those traditions into a new form that was informed by the revolutionary encounter they and their forebears had had with Yahweh, the God of Abraham, Isaac, and Jacob.[11] In like manner, and as Van der Horst somewhat grudgingly allows to be a possibility, Platonic terminology that was part of the cultural and literary matrix in which the LXX translators lived could well have

---

6. Roger Gregg Bury, ed., *Timaeus; Critias; Cleitophon; Menexenus; Epistles*, Plato IX, LCL (Cambridge: Harvard University Press, 1929).
7. Van der Horst, "Was the Earth 'Invisible'?," 6.
8. Van der Horst, "Was the Earth 'Invisible'?," 6.
9. Van der Horst, "Was the Earth 'Invisible'?," 6. Martin Hengel, *Judentum und Hellenismus* (Tübingen: Mohr Siebeck 1969), 294–95 n. 361.
10. Van der Horst, "Was the Earth 'Invisible'?," 6; David T. Runia, trans., *On the Creation of the Cosmos according to Moses* (Leiden: Brill, 2001), 165.
11. See, for example, Gordon J. Wenham, *Genesis 1–15*, WBC 1 (Grand Rapids: Zondervan, 1987), xxxix–xli, xlvi–l, 8–9.

been drawn upon by them without them having to resort to the famed Alexandrian library to consult a copy of *Timaeus*.

This seems to me to be the direction in which Martin Hengel is, in fact, pointing in the larger context of the line that van der Horst quotes. Hengel is talking there about

> the first known Jewish "philosopher of religion", Aristobulus [of Alexandria], about 170 BC, who refers to Prov. 8.22ff. and perhaps already presupposes that it has been translated. As Aristobulus expressly stresses that Plato knew Moses' account of creation, even the *Timaeus*, which has the closest contacts with Gen. 1, will not have been unknown to him [Aristobulus]. Whether and how far the translator of Proverbs knew the *Timaeus* is hard to say. The analogies cited, of course, are in no way sufficient to demonstrate literary dependence; nevertheless we can see how Jewish wisdom speculation and the doctrine of creation grew increasingly close to analogous Greek conceptions. This can be seen for the first time in Aristobulus.[12]

In comparing *Timaeus* to LXX Gen 1, Hengel goes on to say:

> There are already certain echoes in the LXX translation of Gen. 1, cf. the rendering of *tōhū wābōhū* by ἀόρατος καὶ ἀκατασκεύαστος, and the formlessness of Platonic matter, *Tim*. 51a, 7: ἀνόρατον ... καὶ ἄμορφον or 30a.5: εἰς τάξιν ἤγαγεν ἐκ τῆς ἀταξίας.... However, in no case do we have deliberate allusions; in part they were also suggested by the original text.... More important than this supposed philosophical borrowing by the translator of the Pentateuch before the middle of the third century BC ... were the later effects of these points of contact, for it could be argued from them that Plato had known the work of Moses.[13]

Thus, on the one hand, Hengel acknowledges the presence of "certain echoes" of *Timaeus* in LXX Gen 1, but on the other hand he asserts that there were no "deliberate allusions," and further that these echoes are suggested by the original text. I assume by "original text" he must mean תהו ובהו, though he does not elaborate. In any case, those echoes would only seem to have been possible if the kind of thinking and vocabulary generated by Plato were already part of the world of ideas familiar to the LXX translators. He points out as well that subsequent interpreters and commentators made such connections between LXX Gen 1:2 and Platonic cosmogony.

Some commentators have pointed to a connection between the Greek text of verse 2 ἡ δὲ γῆ ἦν ἀόρατος "yet the earth was invisible" and that of verse 9 καὶ

---

12. Martin Hengel, *Judaism and Hellenism: Studies in Their Encounter in Palestine during the Early Hellenistic Period*, trans. John Bowden, vol. 1 (London: SCM, 1974), 163.

13. Hengel, *Judaism and Hellenism*, 2:105 n. 372.

ὤφθη ἡ ξηρά "and the dry land appeared."[14] Could this be an indication that what the Greek translator had in mind in describing the earth as invisible was simply the fact that, prior to the separation of land from water on the third day of creation, it was covered by water?[15] That is, of course, a possibility to consider, though it should be noted that two distinct entities are specified in these verses, namely ἡ γῆ "the earth" (v. 2) and ἡ ξηρά "the dry land" (v. 9). Thus, it cannot be assumed that the implied lack of visibility in the latter case fully accounts for the choice of ἀόρατος in verse 2. Furthermore, the fact that this term is paired with ἀκατασκεύαστος "unformed" here to describe the state of the earth prior to the completion of the Creator's activity is striking in view of the fact that, in the *Timaeus* excerpts cited above, Plato uses both παρεσκευασμένον "prepared" and ἀνόρατον "invisible" (as well as ἄμορφον "formless") to describe the substance that receives the stamp or impress of the ἰδέαι "ideal forms" and thereby takes on the shape of the present material world.

If, as I maintain, the employment of ἀόρατος in speculation about cosmic origins is part of the legacy of ideas articulated by Plato that literate Greek speakers inherited, it should not be all that surprising that it might show up in the work of the Septuagint translators when they rendered Hebrew accounts of creation into Greek. That they were not averse to dipping into the well of Greek mythology in recounting the days of yore is indicated elsewhere in Genesis, for example, in the decision to use γίγαντες "giants" as the counterpart to both the נפלים "Nephilim" and the גברים "heroes" in identifying the offspring of the unions between "the sons of God" and "the daughters of humans" in Gen 6:4, not to mention the רפאים "Rephaim" in Gen 14:5. Οἱ γίγαντες were, of course, featured in the tales that had been told by the likes of Homer and Hesiod about the warrior descendants of the gods who were associated with the deterioration of the primeval world.

Homer, *Od.* 7.56–59
Nausithous at the first was born from the earth-shaker Poseidon and Periboea, the comeliest of women, youngest daughter of great-hearted Eurymedon, who once was king over the insolent Giants [ὑπερθύμοισι Γιγάντεσσιν].[16]

Homer, *Od.* 7.199–200, 204–206
But if he is one of the immortals come down from heaven, then is this some new thing which the gods are planning.... If one of us as a lone wayfarer meets them,

---

14. William P. Brown, *Structure, Role, and Ideology in the Hebrew and Greek Texts of Genesis 1:1–2:3*, SBLDS 132 (Atlanta: Scholars Press, 1993), 48 n. 33; Marguerite Harl, *La Genèse*, 2nd ed., BdA (Paris: Éditions du Cerf, 1994), 90.

15. See, for example, Theophilus, *Ad Autolycum* 2.13.40–45; Hippolytus, *Fragmenta in Genesim* 2.1–8; Basil the Great, *Hexaemeron* 2.3.13–14, 20–34.

16. A. T. Murray, ed., *Odyssey I*, LCL (Cambridge: Harvard University Press, 1919).

they use no concealment, for we are of near kin to them, as are the Cyclopes and the wild tribes of the Giants [ἄγρια φῦλα Γιγάντων].[17]

Homer, *Od.* 10.118–120
the mighty Laestrygonians came thronging from all sides, a host past counting, not like men but like the Giants [Γίγασιν].[18]

Hesiod, *Th.* 36–38, 44–47, 50–51
Come thou, let us begin with the Muses who gladden the great spirit of their father Zeus in Olympus with their songs, telling of things that are and that shall be and that were aforetime.... They ... celebrate in song first of all the reverend race of the gods from the beginning [ἐξ ἀρχῆς], those whom Earth and wide Heaven begot [οὓς Γαῖα καὶ Οὐρανὸς εὐρὺς ἔτικτεν], and the gods sprung of these, givers of good things. Then next, the goddesses sing of Zeus, the father of gods and men.... And again, they chant the race of men and strong giants [κρατερῶν τε Γιγάντων].[19]

Hesiod, *Th.* 176–178, 184–186
[A]nd Heaven [Οὐρανός] came, bringing on night and longing for love, and he lay about Earth [Γαίη] spreading himself full upon her.... And as the seasons moved round she bore the strong Erinyes and the great Giants [μεγάλους τε Γίγαντας] with gleaming armour.[20]

The question that now remains to be addressed in this response to van der Horst is what ἀόρατος means in Gen 1:2. The LSJ and *GELS* lexica leave no doubt as to what their compilers adduced it to mean, given the glosses "invisible, unseen" that are provided in conjunction with various passages in Plato (*Phaedo* 85e, *Soph.* 246a, *Theaet.* 155e). Van der Horst argues, however, that in Gen 1:2, it has a meaning that does not appear in the lexica but that, like "many Greek words beginning with an *alpha privativum*," it should be understood to mean essentially what its counterpart that begins with the prefix δυσ- does, that is, δυσόρατος "not to be looked at, unsightly ... hideous,"[21] "ill to look on, horrible" (LSJ). He looks for further support for his thesis to 2 Macc 9:5, where the author says that God struck Antiochus IV ἀνιάτῳ καὶ ἀοράτῳ πληγῇ "with an incurable and invisible blow" (NETS). Van der Horst comments that, in the verses that follow, it is made clear that the disease with which Antiochus was afflicted "was anything but invisible" since, among other things, worms issued from his body (v. 9). He then

---

17. Murray, *Odyssey I*.
18. Murray, *Odyssey I*.
19. Hugh G. Evelyn-White, ed., *Hesiod: The Homeric Hymns and Homerica*, LCL (London: Heinemann; New York: Macmillan, 1914).
20. Evelyn-White, *Hesiod*.
21. Van der Horst, "Was the Earth 'Invisible'?," 6–7.

concludes that it seems "the solution lies in the fact that ἀόρατος can mean 'hideous, unsightly.'"[22]

Is he right? I think not, for several reasons.

First, it should be noted that Herbert Weir Smyth, in his *Greek Grammar*, describes the *alpha privative* as having "a negative force like Lat. *in-*, Eng. *un-* (or *-less*)"[23] whereas the δυσ- prefix, which is to be juxtaposed to εὖ *well*, signifies "*ill, un-, mis-*, denoting something *difficult, bad,* or *unfortunate.*"[24] Smyth goes on to state that "many possessive compounds begin with ἀ(ν)- negative or δυσ- *ill.*"[25] So, there is typically a semantic distinction to be made between words with these prefixes.

Second, a survey of the ἀ- and δυσ- prefixed terms that Van der Horst cites in support of his contention that they are virtually synonymous reveals that, in some cases at least, this is something of an oversimplification, if the definitions given in LSJ are any indication. For example, compare ἄνελπις "without hope" and δύσελπις "hardly hoping, despondent" (Do they really both mean "without hope, desperate" as Van der Horst states?); ἀκαρτέρητος "insupportable ... lacking in endurance" and δυσκαρτέρητος "hard to endure" (Do these both mean "unbearable, hard to endure" as Van der Horst states, and, for that matter, do "unbearable" and "hard to endure" mean the same thing?).

Third, with regard to his appeal to 2 Macc 9:5, while it is true that the *effects* of the πληγή ("blow, stroke" [LSJ]; "blow, stroke, wound, plague, misfortune" [BDAG]) received by Antiochus were clearly visible, what the text in fact says is that the πληγή *itself* was ἀνίατος καὶ ἀόρατος "incurable and invisible." Hence, this text provides no convincing argument against translating ἀόρατος as "invisible" in Gen 1:2.

Fourth, it is relevant for a discussion of this issue to determine how early interpreters understood this passage.

Josephus, *A.J.* 1.27
In the beginning God created [ἔκτισεν] the heaven and the earth. The earth had not come into sight [ὑπ' ὄψιν οὐκ ἐρχομένης], but was hidden in thick darkness [ἀλλὰ βαθεῖ μὲν κρυπτομένης σκότει].[26]

Although ἀόρατος does not appear in this passage, the description of the state of the earth by means of the phrase ὑπ' ὄψιν οὐκ ἐρχομένης "had not come into sight"

---

22. Van der Horst, "Was the Earth 'Invisible'?," 7.
23. Herbert Weir Smyth, *Greek Grammar*, rev. Gordon M. Messing (Cambridge: Harvard University Press, 1956) §885.1.
24. Smyth, *Greek Grammar*, §885.3.
25. Smyth, *Greek Grammar*, §898.c.
26. Henry St. J. Thackeray, ed., *Josephus, Jewish Antiquities*, vol. 1, LCL (Cambridge: Harvard University Press, 1930).

makes it clear that Josephus understands it to be invisibility, presumably because it was hidden in darkness before the creation of light.

> Philo, *Opif.* 29
> First, then, the Maker made an incorporeal heaven [οὐρανὸν ἀσώματον], and an invisible earth [γῆν ἀόρατον], and the essential form of air and void.[27]

Philo does employ the lexeme ἀόρατος that appears in Gen 1:2 in describing the earth, γῆν ἀόρατον, and this word pair in turn parallels οὐρανὸν ἀσώματον "incorporeal heaven." The parallel *alpha privative* forms make it clear that they correspond semantically in the sense of conveying negative force (incorporeal and invisible) rather than that which is "difficult, bad, unfortunate" (or "hideously corporeal" and "hideous looking," if one were to follow Van der Horst's trajectory).

> Irenaeus, *Adv. haer.* 1.11.1.6–12
> Moses, then, they declare, by his mode of beginning the account of the creation, has at the commencement pointed out the mother of all things when he says, "In the beginning God created the heaven and the earth."... Indicating also its invisible and hidden nature [ἀόρατον δὲ καὶ τὸν ἀπόκρυφον αὐτῆς], he said, "Now the earth was invisible and unformed [ἀόρατος καὶ ἀκατασκεύαστος]."[28]

Irenaeus's paralleling of ἀπόκρυφον "hidden" with ἀόρατον makes it clear that he understands the latter term to have to do with visibility rather than appearance.

> Theophilus, *Ad Aut.* 2.13.40–45
> God, through His Word, next caused the waters to be collected into one collection, and the dry land to become visible, which formerly had been invisible [καὶ ὁρατὴν γενηθῆναι τὴν ξηράν, πρότερον γεγονυῖαν αὐτὴν ἀόρατον]. The earth thus becoming visible [ὁρατή], was yet without form [ἀκατασκεύαστος]. God therefore formed [κατεσκεύασεν] and adorned [κατεκόσμησεν] it with all kinds of herbs, and seeds and plants.[29]

Theophilus's contrasting of the adjectives ὁρατός and ἀόρατος in his description of the earth makes it clear that visibility versus invisibility are what he has in mind, rather than beauty versus ugliness.

> Clement of Alexandria, *Strom.* 5.14.93.5.2–5.14.94.2.1
> For "in the beginning," it is said, "God made the heaven and the earth; and the earth was invisible [ἀόρατος]." And it is added, "And God said, Let there be light;

---

27. Francis Henry Colson and George Herbert Whitaker, *Philo, On the Creation; Allegorical Interpretation of Genesis 2 and 3*, LCL (Cambridge: Harvard University Press, 1929).
28. Trans. Alexander Roberts and James Donaldson, *ANF* 18:903.
29. Trans. Marcus Dods, *ANF* 2:210.

and there was light." And in the material cosmogony He creates a solid heaven (and what is solid is capable of being perceived by sense [αἰσθητόν]), and a visible earth [γῆν τε ὁρατήν, and a light that is seen [φῶς βλεπόμενον].[30]

Again the original invisibility (ἀόρατος) of the earth is contrasted by its subsequent visibility (ὁρατός).

> Hippolytus, *Frag.* 2.1–8
> As the excessive volume of water bore along over the face of the earth, the earth was by reason thereof "invisible" [ἀόρατος] and "formless [ἀκατασκεύαστος]." When the Lord of all designed to make the invisible visible [ὁρατὸν τὸ ἀόρατον ποιῆσαι], He fixed then a third part of the waters in the midst; and another third part He set by itself on high, raising it together with the firmament by His own power; and the remaining third He left beneath, for the use and benefit of men.[31]

Once again, the invisibility (ἀόρατος) and visibility (ὁρατός) of the earth are juxtaposed.

> Basil the Great, *Hex.* 2.3.13–14, 20–34
> *"The earth was invisible and unfinished."*... Thus, we are not told of the creation of water; but, as we are told that the earth was invisible [ἀόρατος], ask yourself what could have covered it [τίνι παραπετάσματι καλυπτομένη], and prevented it from being seen [οὐκ ἐξεφαίνετο]? Fire could not conceal it. Fire brightens all about it, and spreads light rather than darkness around. No more was it air that enveloped the earth. Air by nature is of little density and transparent [διαφανής]. It receives all kinds of visible object [πάντα τὰ εἴδη τῶν ὁρατῶν], and transmits them to the spectators [ταῖς τῶν ὁρώντων ὄψεσι παραπέμπουσα]. Only one supposition remains; that which floated on the surface of the earth was water—the fluid essence which had not yet been confined to its own place. Thus the earth was not only invisible [ἀόρατος]; it was still incomplete [ἀκατασκεύαστος]. Even today excessive damp is a hindrance to the productiveness of the earth. The same cause at the same time prevents it from being seen [τοῦ μὴ ὁρᾶσθαι], and from being complete [τοῦ ἀκατασκεύαστον εἶναι].[32]

Basil, like Theophilus and Hippolytus, attributes the invisible state of the earth to its being covered by water. Furthermore, he, like all the others in the preceding survey of early Jewish and Christian interpreters of Gen 1:2, understands the issue to be lack of visibility rather than unsightly appearance.

One final matter in Van der Horst's article should be addressed. In one of his footnotes, Van der Horst comments: "Note that the καί connecting the two adjectives here is possibly a case of καί *explicativum*: the earth was hideous *because* it

---

30. Trans. William Wilson, *ANF* 2:986.
31. Trans. S. D. F. Salmond, *ANF* 5:414.
32. Trans. Blomfield Jackson, *NPNF* 2/8:60.

was in a state of disorder. This is an often overlooked function of καί."[33] In my judgment, this analysis is implausible. Καί is the default rendering of the Hebrew conjunction ו and there is no contextual indicator that it should be understood in any other way but its normal conjunctive sense, that is, "the earth was invisible *and* unformed."

To conclude, then, in the light of various lexical, morphological, and literary considerations, the contention by Van der Horst that ἀόρατος in Gen 1:2 does not mean "invisible" but "unsightly" or "hideous" does not seem likely.

---

33. Van der Horst, "Was the Earth 'Invisible'?," 7 n. 11.

A Semiotic Approach to Analyzing the Widows and Orphans as an *Index* in 2 Maccabees 3:10

Pierre J. Jordaan

Abstract: This article posits that the mentioning of χηρῶν τε καὶ ὀρφανῶν in 2 Macc 3:10 serves as an important marker and is possibly much more than just a combination of two words. From a semiotic perspective, these words may well serve as an index. The author attempts to show that in 2 Macc 3, God intervenes on behalf of such people as the widows and orphans in his holy temple. In this regard, he becomes a father to the orphans and a judge for the widows and will bring justice to people like them.

1. Introduction

The narrative in 2 Macc 3 tells the story of Heliodorus, an emissary of Seleucus, the king of Asia,[1] who visits the temple in Jerusalem with the ultimate intention of confiscating the money from the treasury and presenting it to his master. This occurred after Seleucus had been tipped off by Apollonius (i.e., the governor of Coele-Syria and Phoenicia) apropos certain claims made by a Jewish priest and Seleucid sympathizer named Simon, namely, incalculable amounts of money lied stored up in the Jerusalem temple. When asked about this money, the high priest Onias explained that the amount of money is not as vast as Simon had claimed and also, inter alia, "this money is designated to the widows and orphans." However, these facts do not deter Heliodorus from attempting to steal the money. Consequently, Onias, in unison with the whole Jewish nation, passively resists Heliodorus's attempts to gain access to the treasury. Onias and the faithful appeal

---

For the purposes of this article, the author made use of the Greek text as found in Alfred Rahlfs, *Septuaginta: Id est Vetus Testamentum graece iuxta LXX interpretes* (Stuttgart: Deutsche Bibelgesellschaft, 2006).
1. Normally assumed to be Seleucus IV Philopator (ca. 187–175 BCE).

to God to protect the money and ensure that it is employed for its rightful purposes. Subsequently, as Heliodorus and his men approach the treasury, they are miraculously neutralized by means of a divine epiphany. This takes the form of a rider on a horse, as well as two youths who appear to the left and right of Heliodorus. According to 2 Macc 3:26, they "scourged him continuously, inflicting many blows on him." Heliodorus almost dies in this attack. Indeed, he is only saved after Onias makes a sacrifice on his behalf. Heliodorus is then instructed to thank Onias for what he has done. The outcome of all of this is that Heliodorus has to return to his king empty-handed.

2. The Problem

This narrative displays various difficulties when scrutinized solely from a historical-critical point of view.

Firstly, commentators like Victor A. Tcherikover, Elias J. Bickerman, and Daniel R. Schwartz concur that this story only displays traces of historical accuracy and, as Schwartz expresses it, this tale is nothing more than a "floating legend."[2] Various accounts from Hellenistic stories might have been used to create this narrative. For example, Erich S. Gruen points out that this is a narrative of a patron deity defending his/her sanctuary, similar to those typically found in Greco-Roman literature.[3] In the same vein, Bickerman again reminds us that a horse mostly remained a foreign concept for the Jews at this time.[4] In biblical literature, neither God nor his angels ever mounted a horse. He goes further and claims that the account of the epiphany was most likely concocted from two different extrabiblical sources and further, that the "epiphany" story was probably not accepted by the Jews.

Secondly, what poses another problem is the question of whether or not the Seleucid king had the legal right to audit the surplus money called διαφόρον by Simon in 2 Macc 3:6. If it was indeed διαφόρον, then it follows that it was money previously donated by the Seleucid king for sacrificial purposes. In this context, according to Werner Dommershausen and Bickerman, money not spent by the priesthood in Jerusalem could be reclaimed by the king.[5] However, Robert Doranand Schwartz have a contrary view; the money involved here was not διαφόρον.

---

2. Victor A. Tcherikover, *Hellenistic Civilization and the Jews* (New York: Antheneum, 1982), 158; Elias J. Bickerman, *Studies in Jewish and Christian History*, vol. 1 (Leiden: Brill, 2011), 447–48; Daniel R. Schwartz, *2 Maccabees*, CEJL (Berlin: de Gruyter, 2008), 185.

3. Erich S. Gruen, *Diaspora: Jews amidst Greeks and Romans* (Cambridge: Harvard University Press, 2002), 177.

4. Bickerman, *Studies*, 449.

5. Werner Dommershausen, *1 Makkabäer, 2 Makkabäer* (Würzburg: Echter-Verlag, 1985), 118; Bickerman, *Studies*, 444.

Rather, it was income accumulated from private deposits. Accordingly, the king had no right to it.[6] My question here is: Why did the author bring in this allocation of the money to the widows and orphans (χηρῶν τε καὶ ὀρφανῶν) at this point in 2 Macc 3:10? Is there any special significance in mentioning χηρῶν τε καὶ ὀρφανῶν?

Most commentators do not discuss this problem in much depth. Dommershausen explains: "Für Witwen und Waisen zu sorgen war für den Juden ein wichtiges Gebot," whilst Schwartz refers merely to other sources that focus on the inheritance by widowers.[7] He says nothing about widows or orphans. Doran, however, discusses possibilities of the phrase χηρῶν τε καὶ ὀρφανῶν as either being an objective genitive (i.e., deposits "on behalf" of widows and orphans), or a subjective genitive denoting deposits made "by" widows and orphans.[8] He then goes on to say that if it was a subjective genitive (like the last-mentioned instance), it might be a "rhetorical ploy" made by the author. This would have been done in order to show how heinous the act of confiscating the funds from the temple would have been. Furthermore, it emphasizes that this would surely be an action that would be avenged by God. Doran uses texts like Exod 22:22–24, Deut 10:18, and Ps 68:5 to substantiate his argument. However, the mention of the subjective genitive deposits made "by" widows and orphans as being a rhetorical ploy to inculcate God's involvement may well require Doran to force the text somewhat. In my view, it is really not about χηρῶν τε καὶ ὀρφανῶν being either a subjective or objective genitive. Indeed, it can be either "on behalf of" or "by" the widows and orphans. What is more important here is the fact that *widows and orphans* are specifically mentioned. In this regard, Doran seems to miss the significance of their very reference in the text, even though there are various clues in other texts like Ps 68:5 (LXX 67:6) as a possible context for 2 Macc 3, both as intertext and as possible socioeconomic background. For example, "Uphold the rights of the orphan; defend the cause of the widow" (Isa 1:17).

This paper sets out to explore these tantalizing possibilities. I wish to explore the use of χηρῶν τε καὶ ὀρφανῶν. As Doran indicates, the possible "rhetorical ploy" the author might have employed shows that God punishes people who mistreat widows and orphans. Until now, this issue has not been the main focus of studies on 2 Macc 3. Various other approaches have been used to scrutinize this chapter. In this context, the following examples of previous research are pertinent:

---

6. Robert Doran, *2 Maccabees: A Critical Commentary*, Hermeneia (Minneapolis: Fortress Press, 2012), 81; Schwartz, *2 Maccabees*, 192.

7. Dommershausen, *Makkabäer*, 119; Schwartz, *2 Maccabees*, 194.

8. Doran, *2 Maccabees*, 82.

- James Moffat concentrates mainly on grammar and different textual versions.[9]
- Bickerman focuses on the internal strife amongst the Jews.[10]
- Doran sees 2 Macc 3 as part of temple propaganda.[11]
- Jan Willem Van Henten and Gruen see 2 Macc 3 as an example of a patron-deity defending his/her temple.[12]
- Schwartz and Dommershausen read 2 Macc 3 as an idyllic *status quo ante* where the Jews, Jerusalem and its temple lived in peace with pagan rulers in a mutually respectful coexistence between Judaism and benevolent foreign rule.[13]
- Pierre J. Jordaan even attempted to read 2 Macc 3 as a therapeutic narrative, demonstrating how the author wishes to create an equilibrium between the Jews themselves and their relationship with foreign rulers.[14]

In short, there have been various attempts to interpret 2 Macc 3 and to arrive at some credible understanding. However, reading 2 Macc 3 with special focus on the significance of the very mention of χηρῶν τε καὶ ὀρφανῶν has not been undertaken. Furthermore, the possibility exists that χηρῶν τε καὶ ὀρφανῶν signifies a larger dynamic within the narrative that has not been explored yet. As already stated, Doran[15] believes that the mention of χηρῶν τε καὶ ὀρφανῶν is a "rhetorical ploy" and even alludes to some significant intertexts, but does not venture much further with this line of enquiry. This paper will attempt to remedy this situation by exploring and displaying some new possibilities in understanding 2 Macc 3. In this context, the following questions will need to be addressed:

1. What would be a plausible method that might best give greater clarity to the term(s) χηρῶν τε καὶ ὀρφανῶν in 2 Macc 3:10 and, for that matter, the whole of chapter 3?
2. If one accepts that χηρῶν τε καὶ ὀρφανῶν is a social construct, what does the commentator say about the prevailing circumstances, not only in Jerusalem, but also in the rest of Judea?
3. What conclusion(s) might be drawn from (1) and (2) above?

---

9. James Moffat, "2 Maccabees," in *The Apocrypha and Pseudepigrapha of the Old Testament*, ed. Robert H. Charles, vol. 1 (Berkeley: Apocryphile Press, 1913), 135–36.

10. Elias J. Bickerman, *The God of the Maccabees: Studies in the Meaning and Origin of the Maccabean Revolt* (Leiden: Brill, 1979), 38–39.

11. Robert Doran, *Temple Propaganda: The Purpose and Character of 2 Maccabees* (Washington: Catholic Biblical Association of America, 1981).

12. Jan Willem Van Henten, *The Maccabean Martyrs as Saviours of the Jewish People*, JSJSup 57 (Leiden: Brill, 1979), 34; Gruen, *Diaspora*, 177.

13. Schwartz, *2 Maccabees*, 184; Dommershausen, *Makkabäer*, 117.

14. Pierre J. Jordaan, "Suffering Bodies in 2 Maccabees 3," *In Luce Verbi* 50.4 (2016): 6–7.

15. Doran, *2 Maccabees*, 82.

3. Exposition on Method

The method I wish to propose for looking at χηρῶν τε καὶ ὀρφανῶν is a specific semiotic method once employed by Umberto Eco.[16] As a result of the limitations of space, I will only discuss certain aspects of his approach more broadly. Eco sees all texts as signs. He identifies three categories of signs: icons, indices, and symbols. Each of these needs to be decoded by the reader, listener, or onlooker (interpreter). All of these signs convey a valued message to a lesser or greater extent.

An *icon* as sign is well known to an interpreter and therefore does not need much interpretation. The dragon or snake in Bel and the Dragon is an example of this. The dragon is deliberately depicted as if it were the Babylonians' actual and living deity. In short, they do not only worship the dragon, but they also need to feed it. Thus, this deity is not presented as an abstract and/or heavenly concept. Rather, it is depicted as though it were a real living entity.[17] By employing this icon, the interpreter is encouraged to come to the conclusion that the Babylonians are foolish, as they must first sustain their deity before they can worship it.

An *index* is a little more complicated and occupies the middle ground when interpreting texts. An index is like one's index finger. It "points" in a particular direction and requires a bit more interpretation in order to arrive at its implied meaning. Indices in texts are usually characteristic of larger problems. The index "heart" (καρδία) in 2 Macc 1:3–4 does not refer literally to a human organ that pumps blood, but with the adjective "big" (μεγάλη) it denotes "commitment."[18] In this example, the index points to a deeper problem involving a corrupt priest who is also a Seleucid sympathizer. The index helps the interpreter to realize that the priest lacks genuine commitment towards God and the Jerusalem temple.

Finally, a *symbol* as sign requires a great deal of interpretation. For example, the sign "Assyrian" in the book of Judith may be seen as a symbol. How do Assyrians suddenly surface after four hundred years of absence? The Assyrians in the book of Judith refer to a cruel, violent and immoral threat to the Jews. To make this connection, the interpreter of the sign may well also need a substantial knowledge of history.[19]

---

16. Cf. Umberto Eco, *Semiotics and the Philosophy of Language* (Bloomington: Indiana University Press, 1986).

17. Joseph J. de Bruyn and Pierre J. Jordaan, "Constructing Realities: Bel and the Dragon: Identifying Some Research Lacunae," *OTE* 27.3 (2014): 855.

18. Pierre J. Jordaan, "Body, Space and Narrative in 2 Macc 1:1–10a," *BN* 168 (2016): 97–98.

19. Pierre J. Jordaan and Risimati S. Hobyane, "Writing and Reading War: Rhetoric, Gender and Ethics in Judith," *Ekklesiastikos Pharos* 91.20 (2009): 239.

Textual evidence, that is, intratextual (within a book), intertextual evidence (within a corpus of books), and extratextual evidence (factors like politics, economics and sociology) usually support the interpretation of a sign. For instance, the Babylonians are furious after Daniel kills their deity. Their actual god (icon) was murdered. Thus, they remain without insight and want to retaliate against Daniel.

The same can be said about indices. In subsequent chapters, 2 Maccabees presents Jason and other Seleucid sympathizers as being aberrant, whilst the anti-Seleucid priests are portrayed as being righteous. Thus, as indices, Jason and the priests are depicted as "pointing" towards nonrighteousness. Jason and the priests, without context do not signify anything, however within context the deduction can be made that they are straying from orthodoxy.

Lastly, in Judith, the Assyrians emerge as a symbol of violence, immorality, and cruelty. Their general, Holofernes, it transpires, as drunkard and philanderer, is also part and parcel of this unscrupulous culture.

The key for decoding the signs in each instance is held by the interpreter. However, this should never be done randomly, but as transparently and with as much textual support as possible. This is quite a difficult task as the modern reader has to interpret the text after a gap of over two millennia and still try to establish whether signs within the texts should be considered as icons, indices, or symbols. Having said this, let us now return to the interpretation of χηρῶν τε καὶ ὀρφανῶν in the context of 2 Macc 3. In this regard, I also wish to align the known historical contexts apropos Judea, Jerusalem, and the temple with the time this text might have been written and/or redacted.

4. The Circumstances in and around Jerusalem and Judea (Extratextual Evidence)

Tcherikover vividly describes the prevailing circumstances in Jerusalem during the Maccabean period as not being very favorable for the lower classes.[20] He clearly states why:

> The key to an understanding of the events of the entire period has to be sought not in inter-family quarrels among the aristocracy, but in the conflict of interests between the aristocracy and people, interpreted as the broad section of the lower urban populace, composed of craftsmen, day-laborers, shopkeepers, petty vendors and the rest.... The *plebs urbana* of Jerusalem, if we may use this Roman terminology, was interested neither in diplomatic relations with the Hellenistic world, nor in the conduct of high policy at the royal court of Antioch, nor even the development of commercial relations with other states. It knew one thing

---

20. Tcherikover, *Hellenistic Civilization*, 197–203.

clearly, that as a result of the Hellenistic reform all the affairs of the city were gathered in the hands of the rich and well-connected.[21]

If we take this description of what happened in Jerusalem seriously, it is only natural that in circumstances like these, the poor would suffer the most. This obviously includes the widows and the orphans. They were the people who had to rely on other people for their survival. However, if the people they relied on were disenfranchised and forced outside of Jerusalem, they had real problems. They were literally the lowest of the low and amongst the poorest of the poor. In this regard, Samuel L. Adams specifically refers to widows and orphans as being extremely vulnerable.[22] This would not only make them a nuisance, but also easy victims for exploitation by the wealthy and/or powerful. From an extra-textual point of view (politics, economics and sociology), widows and orphans seem to be significant. If this story is a floating legend, as claimed by Schwartz, the question remains: What is the significance of the χηρῶν τε καὶ ὀρφανῶν in this narrative?

5. INTERTEXTUAL EVIDENCE

In order to establish the significance of χηρῶν τε καὶ ὀρφανῶν in this narrative as a "rhetorical ploy" (i.e., as originally suggested by Doran), I wish to use LXX Ps 67:6[23] as intertext:

τοῦ πατρὸς τῶν ὀρφανῶν καὶ κριτοῦ τῶν χηρῶν ὁ θεὸς ἐν τόπῳ ἁγίῳ αὐτοῦ
... father for orphans and judge for widows in his holy place[24]

LXX Ps 67:6 seems to be important as intertextual background for understanding 2 Macc 3, seeing as different elements in both texts concur. Firstly, the mentioning of orphans and widows. Secondly, the locality which is stated as "in his holy place." "Holy place" is also what the temple is called in 2 Maccabees.

The author of 2 Macc 3 might have had knowledge of LXX Ps 67:6. The difference, however, between these two texts is that LXX Ps 67:6 states certain facts, whereas 2 Macc 3 seems to apply them. In this sense, 2 Macc 3 is LXX Ps 67:6 in action. Furthermore, 2 Macc 3 (in its entirety) may be seen as a reinterpretation of LXX Ps 67:6. In 2 Macc 3, God becomes a father for orphans and a

---

21. Tcherikover, *Hellenistic Civilization*, 192.

22. Samuel L. Adams, *Social and Economic Life in Second Temple Judea* (Louisville: Westminster John Knox, 2014), 58.

23. It should be noted that Doran does not refer specifically to Ps 67:6 but rather the English version which reads the same. I.e., Doran refers to Robert Hanhart's version of the Septuagint (i.e., Ps 67:6). Cf. Doran, *2 Maccabees*, xxi, 82.

24. This is my English translation of the Greek as found in Rahlfs, *Septuaginta*, 68.

judge for widows as he defends their money in the temple. So what happens if one sees the combination χηρῶν τε καὶ ὀρφανῶν in 2 Macc 3:10? The answer is that God will act as judge for widows and become a father to the orphans. This is the possible dynamic that lies behind this sign as an index.

In this way, the combination χηρῶν τε καὶ ὀρφανῶν might be better classified as an index in 2 Macc 3. However, the sign needs some interpretation, but not too much. This sign shows that if there is trouble in his holy place, especially concerning widows and orphans, one need not despair; God will rectify the situation for his widows and orphans who technically reside in his house (holy place).[25] In this sense, there is a dynamic linked to χηρῶν τε καὶ ὀρφανῶν. God will surely come into action if his widows and orphans and their special needs are threatened in the temple.

6. Conclusion

There can be no doubt that the mentioning of χηρῶν τε καὶ ὀρφανῶν in 2 Macc 3:10 serves as an important marker. It is much more than just a combination of two words. From a semiotic perspective, these words serve as an *index*. This index at the beginning of 2 Maccabees signifies that something terrible had gone wrong with the population of Jerusalem. The poorest of poor and lower classes were discounted by the ruling clergy. The clergy were not at all concerned with people like widows and orphans, but only interested in their own affairs. However, if we take LXX Ps 67:6 as a valid intertext, then the phrase χηρῶν τε καὶ ὀρφανῶν also signifies action. God is the one who intervenes on behalf of such people in his holy temple. He becomes a father to the orphans and a judge for the widows. He will bring justice to people like them. Doran is thus correct when he says that the mentioning of χηρῶν τε καὶ ὀρφανῶν is a "rhetorical ploy" that shows that God avenges widows and orphans. As early as in 2 Macc 3, the author already shows a division of people into two groups. On the one hand, there are those who treat people like widows and orphans with contempt, like Simon. On the other hand, one also finds Onias and the faithful, who sincerely care about widows and orphans. God will intervene on their behalf. Until now, nobody has looked at 2 Macc 3 in this way.

---

25. LXX Ps 67:6: τοῦ πατρὸς τῶν ὀρφανῶν καὶ κριτοῦ τῶν χηρῶν ὁ θεὸς ἐν **τόπῳ ἁγίῳ** αὐτοῦ.

Just Like Puericide: The Greek Translation and Interpretation of a Debated Hebrew Phrase in Lamentations 1:20

Gideon R. Kotzé

Abstract: Modern interpreters continue to debate the meaning of בבית כמות in MT Lam 1:20c. They have either proposed grammatical or philological solutions to the perceived problem, or they have resorted to conjectural emendations. The Septuagint, Vulgate, and Targum of Lamentations, however, follow the MT and interpret כמות as a prepositional phrase that expresses a comparison to death. The studies that treat כמות in the MT as a secondary reading do not explore the meaningfulness of these ancient translations or explain how כמות would have developed out of the supposed "correct" readings. With the limitations of the emendations and reinterpretations in mind, this study, first, analyses the similarities and differences between the Greek and Hebrew versions of Lam 1:20 and examines how LXX Lamentations presents the subject matter of the verse's final colon. Secondly, this study explores how data regarding the ancient Near Eastern cultural environment of Lamentations may contribute to a meaningful interpretation of Lam 1:20c. It is argued that the readings in the MT and LXX versions of Lam 1:20c are intelligible, that the emendation of the Hebrew wording is unnecessary, and that the Greek translation, complemented by information on portrayals of Death as a figure responsible for the loss of children and youths in ancient Near Eastern texts, can help the text-critic to make sense of the extant Hebrew wording of the colon.

MT Lam 1:20 and Interpretations of the Debated Final Colon

The final colon of the *resh*-stanza in the Hebrew text of Lam 1 has been a headache for many modern readers of the poem. Different attempts have been made to understand בבית כמות, but no consensus regarding its interpretation has been reached. The meaning of the colon, therefore, remains debated. The Septuagint translation (LXX Lam), the Vulgate, and both the Western and Yemenite versions of the Targum of Lamentations present their own unique renderings of the colon, but, like the vocalized Masoretic text (MT), these ancient translations interpreted כמות as a prepositional phrase that indicates a comparison involving death.[1] The rendering of the colon in the Peshitta differs from these Greek, Latin, and Aramaic translations and does not contain such a comparison. In cases of problematic passages in his Hebrew *Vorlage*, the Syriac translator of Lamentations seems to have generally opted for an intelligible rendering, rather than a literal translation that would remain unclear.[2] The reading ܘܒܒܝܬܐ ܡܘܬܐ ("and in the house is death") in the Peshitta wording of Lam 1:20c appears to be an example of this translation approach and should not necessarily be taken as a witness to a Hebrew source text that did not contain כ before מות.[3] Nevertheless, on the basis of the reading in the

---

1. For the wording of LXX Lam, see below. The Vulgate has the clause *et domi mors similis est* ("and in the house it is like death"). Robert Weber, *Biblia Sacra iuxta Vulgatam Versionem* (Stuttgart: Deutsche Bibelgesellschaft, 2007), 1249. The wordings of the two versions of the targum are similar: ומלגיו חרגת כפנא כמלאכא מחבלא דממני על מותא, "and inside is the agony of starvation like the destroying angel who is appointed over death" (Western recension; the wording is that of Codex Urbanates Ebr. 1, slightly emended to read חרגת instead of תרגת [cf. Christian M. M. Brady, *Targum Lamentations' Reading of the Book of Lamentations* (PhD diss., Oxford University, 1999), 88–89]); ומלגיו חרגת כפנא כמלאך דממונא על מותא, "and inside is the agony of starvation like the angel who is appointed over death" (Yemenite recension; Albert van der Heide, *The Yemenite Tradition of the Targum of Lamentations* [Leiden: Brill, 1981], 12*). Jacob Levy, *Wörterbuch über die Talmudim und Midraschim*, vol. 2 (Darmstadt: Wissenschaftliche Buchgesellschaft, 1963), 106, gives the meaning of חרגא as "Angst; Beängstigung," while Marcus Jastrow, *Dictionary of the Targumim, the Talmud Babli and Yerushalmi, and the Midrashic Literature* (Peabody: Hendrickson, 2005), 498, suggests "dying agony." According to Philip S. Alexander, *The Targum of Lamentations*, ArBib 17B (Collegeville: Liturgical Press, 2008), 125 n. 81, Jastrow's suggestion is "highly speculative" and he cautiously suggests an emendation of the text to read הרג כפנא, "famine slays."

2. Bertil Albrektson, *Studies in the Text and Theology of the Book of Lamentations with a Critical Edition of the Peshitta Text* (Lund: CWK Gleerup, 1963), 211.

3. For the wording of P Lam 1:20, see Albrektson, *Studies*, 43. Albrektson argues that the Syriac translator "prefers a clear and readable rendering to a literal but obscure translation of the Hebrew text, and P's text is exactly the sort of translation we should expect of a difficult passage" (81). See also Rolf Schäfer, "Lamentations," in *General Introduction and Megilloth*, ed. Adrian Schenker *et al.*, BHQ 18 (Stuttgart: Deutsche Bibelgesellschaft, 2004), 119*.

Syriac text, some scholars suggest that the *kaph* of כמות should be deleted.[4] Scholars also delete the *kaph* without reference to the reading in the Peshitta.[5] Other conjectural emendations of כמות that have been proposed by scholars are more radical. According to J. Dyserinck, the wording of the colon should read בבית תך מות ("binnenshuis is het geweld des doods"), but Arnold B. Ehrlich maintains that the correct reading of the final phrase is אך מות ("lauter Pest").[6] Delbert R. Hillers emends כמות into כפנות/כפן ("hunger; famine") on the basis of Ezek 7:15, where the words "sword," "pestilence," and "famine" are collocated, and Jer 14:18, where "sword" and "famine" appear in parallel bicola. He also mentions a few lines from the Lamentation over the Destruction of Sumer and Ur (LSUr) and Deut 32:25 in connection with the emendation.[7] In view of the pair חרב ("sword") and אימה ("terror") in this passage from Deuteronomy, Frank Moore Cross suggests that כמות should be replaced with אימות.[8]

A number of scholars do not emend כמות, but put forward a grammatical explanation of the supposed textual difficulty. Bertil Albrektson, for example, notes that a preposition is omitted when it follows ב and proposes that this is the case with כמות.[9] Accordingly, the latter can be read as though it is a combination

---

4. See, e.g., the comment in the textual apparatus of *BHK*, 1231, as well as the note in Max Haller, *Die fünf Megilloth*, HAT (Tübingen: Mohr Siebeck, 1940), 98.

5. See Karl Budde, Alfred Bertholet, and D. Gerrit Wildeboer, *Die Fünf Megillot: Das Hohelied, das Buch Ruth, Die Klagelieder, Der Prediger, Das Buch Esther*, KHAT (Tübingen: Mohr Siebeck, 1898), 84. According to Hans-Joachim Kraus, *Klagelieder (Threni)*, BKAT 20, 4th ed. (Neukirchen-Vluyn: Neukirchen Verlag, 1983), 23, the only possibility of making sense of the colon is to delete the *kaph*.

6. J. Dyserinck, "De Klaaglideren uit het Hebreeuwsch Opnieuw Vertaald," *ThT* 26 (1892): 365; Arnold B. Ehrlich, *Randglossen zur hebräischen Bibel: Textkritisches, Sprachliches und Sachliches*, vol. 7 (Leipzig: Hinrichs, 1914), 34.

7. Delbert R. Hillers, *Lamentations: A New Translation with Introduction and Commentary*, AB 7 (New York: Doubleday, 1992), 77. The lines that Hillers quotes from *ANET* are lines 399–401 in the composite text of LSUr in the edition of Piotr Michalowski, *The Lamentation over the Destruction of Sumer and Ur* (Winona Lake: Eisenbrauns, 1989), 60, 61: uris$_5^{ki}$-ma šà-bi nam-ús-àm bar-bi nam-ús-àm / šà-bi-a níg-šà-gar-ra-ka i-im-til-le-dè-en-dè-en / bar-bi-a ^{giš}tukul elam^{ki}-ma-ka ga-nam-ba-[e-til-l]e-en-dè-en, "Ur—inside it there is death, outside it there is death, / Inside it we are being finished off by famine, / Outside it we are being finished off by Elamite weapons."

8. Frank Moore Cross, "Studies in the Structure of Hebrew Verse: The Prosody of Lamentations 1:1–22," in *The Word of the Lord Shall Go Forth: Essays in Honor of David Noel Freedman*, ed. Carol L. Meyers and Michael O'Connor (Winona Lake: Eisenbrauns, 1983), 150.

9. Albrektson, *Studies*, 82. Concerning the omission of other prepositions after the preposition ב, see *IBHS* §11.2.9c; JM §133h; and Ernst Jenni, *Die Präposition Kaph*, vol.

of the preposition כ and the prepositional phrase במות. On this interpretation, "death" can be understood as referring to the realm of Sheol.[10] This interpretation has not garnered much support from other scholars.[11] Robert Gordis provides a different solution. He is of the opinion that the *kaph* of כמות is best understood as an emphatic particle (asseverative *kaph*), rather than a preposition that introduces a comparison.[12] Although this interpretation has proved to be quite popular,[13] it has not convinced everyone.[14]

Finally, Felix Perles turns to comparative philology to solve the perceived difficulty of the MT reading. In order to find an appropriate counterpart for חרב in the first colon of verse 20c, he suggests that the problematic word in the parallel colon should be vocalized as כְּמוּת in view of the Akkadian word *kamûtu* ("state of being a captive").[15] The Hebrew word would be a loan from Akkadian, but Perles does not give any evidence to support this possibility.

Judging from these emendations and interpretations of כמות, scholars see the comparison to death in the MT wording as problematic. The emendations and interpretations eliminate the supposed problem, but the scholars who advocate these solutions do not always explain how the reading in the MT would have developed from the suggested "correct" reading. They also do not account for the intelligibility of the wordings of the ancient translations, such as LXX Lamentations, which also contain clauses where a comparison involving death is made. Therefore, from the perspective of textual criticism, which is concerned with how

---

2 of *Die hebräischen Präpositionen* (Stuttgart: Kohlhammer, 1994), 33–34. In his semantic classification of the preposition of כמות, Jenni notes that the text is uncertain (41).

10. Albrektson, *Studies*, 82.

11. Klaus Koenen, *Klagelieder (Threni)*, BKAT 20 (Neukirchen-Vluyn: Neukirchener Verlag, 2015), 15*, 88 also favors this interpretation.

12. Robert Gordis, "Asseverative Kaph in Hebrew and Ugaritic," *JAOS* 63 (1943): 178; Gordis, *The Song of Songs and Lamentations*, rev. ed. (New York: KTAV, 1974), 159.

13. See Adele Berlin, *Lamentations: A Commentary*, OTL (Louisville: Westminster John Knox, 2002), 47; Johan Renkema, *Lamentations*, HCOT (Leuven: Peeters, 1998), 192; Mitchell Dahood, "New Readings in Lamentations," *Bib* 59 (1978): 179; Hans Gottlieb, *A Study on the Text of Lamentations* (Århus: Det Laerde Selskab, 1978), 20; Thomas F. McDaniel, "Philological Studies in Lamentations II," *Bib* 49 (1968): 211–12.

14. See Ulrich Berges, *Klagelieder*, HThKAT (Freiberg: Herder, 2002), 90, who notes that the preposition retains an element of comparison. In this regard, he refers to the discussion of the so-called *kaph veritatis* in GKC §118x.

15. Felix Perles, "Was bedeutet כמות Threni 1,20?," *OLZ* 23 (1920): 157–58; Perles, *Analekten zur Textkritik des Alten Testaments: Neue Folge* (Leipzig: Gustav Engel, 1922), 57. Regarding the meanings attributed to *kamûtu* in passages where it is used, see *CAD* 8, 134. This suggestion is noted in the critical apparatus of *BHS*, 1357, and supported by Wilhelm Rudolph, *Das Buch Ruth; Das Hohe Lied; Die Klagelieder* (Gerd Mohn: Gütersloher Verlagshaus, 1962), 208.

readings in the available textual representatives were probably created, were possibly related, and were potentially meaningful, the abovementioned emendations and interpretations of כמות in Lam 1:20 are not completely convincing. With this in mind, this study singles out the rendering of כמות in LXX Lam 1:20 for closer examination. It briefly considers how the Greek translation represents the subject matter of the three bicola of the verse and subsequently indicates that the Greek text's interpretation of the final colon's wording is in keeping with ideas that was transmitted in the larger cultural environment in which the Hebrew text of Lam 1 circulated. The understanding of כמות exemplified by the Greek translation, which is intelligible within the Hebrew text's cultural setting, allows it to be interpreted as a comparative phrase and makes an emendation thereof unnecessary.

LXX Lam 1:20 and Its Interpretation of the Final Colon

MT Lam 1:20[16]

ראה יהוה כי צר לי מעי חמרמרו
נהפך לבי בקרבי כי מרו מרית
מחוץ שכלה חרב בבית כמות

See O YHWH that I am in distress, my innards have been twisted;
My heart has been turned upside down inside me, because I have wantonly rebelled.
Outdoors the sword made childless, indoors (it made childless) in the same way as Death.

LXX Lam 1:20[17]

ἰδέ, κύριε, ὅτι θλίβομαι· ἡ κοιλία μου ἐταράχθη,
ἡ καρδία μου ἐστράφη ἐν ἐμοί, ὅτι παραπικραίνουσα παρεπίκρανα·
ἔξωθεν ἠτέκνωσέν με μάχαιρα ὥσπερ θάνατος ἐν οἴκῳ

See O Lord, that I was hard-pressed. My belly was troubled;
My heart was turned in me, because I have wantonly rebelled.
Outdoors, a sword made me childless, just like Death did indoors.

The Greek translation of Lam 1:20 exhibits a number of noteworthy interpretations when it is compared with the MT. In both the Hebrew and Greek versions of the verse, the deity is directed to perceive the negative emotional effects that

---

16. Schäfer, "Lamentations," 58.
17. This wording of the Greek text is based on the editions of Joseph Ziegler, ed., *Jeremias, Baruch, Threni, Epistula Jeremiae*, SVTG 15, 3rd ed. (Göttingen: Vandenhoeck & Ruprecht, 2006), 472; and Alfred Rahlfs, *Septuaginta: Id est Vetus Testamentum graece iuxta LXX interpretes* (Stuttgart: Deutsche Bibelgesellschaft, 2006), 758.

past events have had on the first-person speaker. Evidently, according to the verse's opening colon, the speaker is distressed. In the Hebrew text, the speaker is personified Jerusalem and she expresses this negative emotion with a spatial image, צר לי (lit., "it was narrow for me"). Whereas this type of Hebrew phrase relates distress to experiences of confinement, being surrounded, being trapped in narrow spaces, or restricted freedom of movement,[18] the Greek translation equivalent of צר לי, θλίβομαι ("I was hard-pressed"), communicates the distress with an image of the speaker under pressure.[19]

In the next two cola of the verse, personified Jerusalem elaborates on her negative emotion with the use of body part imagery.[20] LXX Lamentations follows its Hebrew counterpart in associating the distress of the speaker with the internal organs.[21] In the first image that describes the physical effects of the speaker's distress on the internal organs, the precise sense of the Hebrew *poalal* verb, חמרמרו,

---

18. Philip D. King, *Surrounded by Bitterness: Image Schemas and Metaphors for Conceptualizing Distress in Classical Hebrew* (Eugene: Pickwick, 2012), 147, notes that the combination of the verb צרר with an impersonal, third-person subject and a prepositional phrase with ל "conceptualizes distress as an Agonist desiring freedom but being restricted by something external."

19. Θλίβομαι is the first example in this verse where the translator did not represent each constituent of a Hebrew phrase's consonantal wording by an individual, literal Greek equivalent. Other examples include the renderings of בקרבי by ἐν ἐμοί and מחוץ by ἔξωθεν. Furthermore, the object of the verb in the sentence ἔξωθεν ἠτέκνωσέν με μάχαιρα is a plus when compared to the MT. Although Ziegler, *Jeremias, Baruch, Threni, Epistula Jeremiae*, 472, omitted the personal pronoun from his eclectic version of the Greek text, Rahlfs, *Septuaginta*, 758, included it in his edition. Codex Vaticanus is the main witness for the reading without με, but the weight of the other textual representatives weigh in favor of regarding the plus as part of the original translation. This plus in the translation makes implicit information in the source text explicit. These features, together with the word order adjustments (see below), create the impression that the Greek translator endeavored to create an intelligible Greek version of the verse's subject matter and did not simply reproduce the formal elements of the Hebrew *Vorlage*'s wording.

20. Concerning the striking body part images in Lamentations (especially Lam 1) and their connection to emotions, see the comments of Christian Frevel, *Die Klagelieder*, NSKAT 20.1 (Stuttgart: Katholisches Bibelwerk, 2017), 20–21.

21. Mark S. Smith, "The Heart and Innards in Israelite Emotional Expressions: Notes from Anthropology and Psychobiology," *JBL* 117 (1998): 434 suggests that the emotion might have been associated with internal organs, because this is the place in the body where distress was physically experienced: "In distressful situations stomach contractions and the movement of blood are felt as a physical experience of anxiety (cf. English 'stomach tied up in knots' and 'butterflies in the stomach'). The biblical use of 'innards' for distress apparently fits these symptoms of the sympathetic nervous system. In short, as with the nose and mouth for anger, the heart for a range of emotions, and the innards for distress, biblical prayer reflects an ancient association of emotions with body parts where these emotions are felt."

as it relates to מעים, is not clear and scholars have put forward different interpretations of the metaphor.²² Irrespective of whether personified Jerusalem says that her innards "fermented," "burned," or "have been twisted," according to the Hebrew text, the Greek translation's use of ταράσσω to render חמר results in a slightly different image. According to this version, the speaker experienced stomach disturbance and draws the Lord's attention to this symptom of distress. "Heart" in the Hebrew and Greek texts of Lam 1:20bα could be understood as a metonym for internal organs, in which case, it would be an appropriate parallel for "innards / belly" in verse 20aβ.

In the Hebrew version of the passage, personified Jerusalem presents her own perspective on the cause of her distress to YHWH and attributes it to her rebellion (מרו מריתי). She declares that she has rebelled and the infinitive absolute specifies the intensity of this action ("I have wantonly rebelled").²³ This sense is conveyed in the Greek translation by a participle followed by a finite verb of the same stem (παραπικραίνουσα παρεπίκρανα).²⁴

---

22. See, e.g., Sara Kipfer, "Angst, Furcht und Schrecken: Eine Kognitiv-Linguistische Untersuchung einer Emotion im biblischen Hebräisch," *JNSL* 42 (2016): 41–42; Angela Thomas, *Anatomical Idiom and Emotional Expression: A Comparison of the Hebrew Bible and the Septuagint*, HBM 53 (Sheffield: Sheffield Phoenix, 2014), 39; Godfrey Rolles Driver, "Hebrew Notes on 'Song of Songs' and 'Lamentations,'" in *Festschrift Alfred Bertholet zum 80. Geburtstag*, ed. Walter Baumgartner et al. (Tübingen: Mohr Siebeck, 1950), 137.

23. See, e.g., Frevel, *Klagelieder*, 138; Koenen, *Klagelieder (Threni)*, 87; Scott N. Callaham, *Modality and the Biblical Hebrew Infinitive Absolute*, AKM 17 (Wiesbaden: Harrassowitz, 2010), 120 identifies Lam 1:20 as an example where the infinitive absolute expresses habitual modality. In such cases in the Hebrew Bible writings, speakers apparently "assert that a proposition is true in a general, non-specific way" (20). Lam 1:20's infinitive absolute construction, however, appears in a non-modal context and, in such contexts, the infinitive absolute often specifies the intense or extreme nature of the action conveyed by the accompanying verb. Cf. Christo H. J. van der Merwe, "The Infinitive Absolute Reconsidered: Review Article," *JNSL* 39 (2013): 78–79.

24. See Takamitsu Muraoka, *A Syntax of Septuagint Greek* (Leuven: Peeters, 2016), 383–85. The *qatal* form מריתי, which appears in the Hebrew wordings of Lam 1:18 and 20, was probably related to מר ("bitter," "bitterness") during the translation process. This would account for the use of a compound form of the Greek verb πικραίνω ("to make bitter," "embitter") to render the Hebrew verb in both verses. Παραπικραίνω acquired the sense "to rebel" by functioning as a translation equivalent of מרה. In this regard, see the discussion of Peter Walters, *The Text of the Septuagint: Its Corruptions and Their Emendation* (Cambridge: Cambridge University Press, 1973), 150–54. From this perspective, LXX Lam does not support the proposal that a different reading from the one represented by the MT circulated in the Hebrew manuscripts on which some of the ancient translations were based.

Although the word order of sentences in the Greek translation of Lam 1:20 generally agree with that of the Hebrew text used for comparison, it deviates in two instances. In the rendering of נהפך לבי בקרבי ("my heart has been turned upside down in my inward part"), the verb ἐστράφη was positioned after its subject, ἡ καρδία μου, while in the final colon, ἐν οἴκῳ, which translates the first prepositional phrase in the Hebrew text, follows after ὥσπερ θάνατος, the translation equivalent of the second Hebrew prepositional phrase. In the case of ἡ καρδία μου ἐστράφη ἐν ἐμοί ("my heart was turned upside down in me"), the result of the changed organization of words was that the sentence resembled the word order of its parallel sentence, ἡ κοιλία μου ἐταράχθη ("my belly was troubled"). In the case of the final colon, the arrangement of constituents in the Greek translation was affected by the choice to render the preposition of כמות with ὥσπερ, a conjunction that introduces a subordinate sentence. The difference in word order between the LXX and MT versions of Lam 1:20c, therefore, need not be attributed to a variant in the Greek translation's Hebrew *Vorlage*. Robin B. Salters mentions the possibility that the Greek translation adjusted the word order to facilitate an understanding of the Hebrew wording according to which the verb שכלה does "double duty" (i.e., there is ellipsis of the verb in the second colon of the strophe).[25] On this interpretation, the speaker laments that the sword causes bereavement of children outdoors in the same way as death does indoors. Indeed, the conjunction ὥσπερ implies that the event involving θάνατος is similar to the one expressed by the preceding main clause, ἔξωθεν ἠτέκνωσέν με μάχαιρα ("outside, a sword made me childless"). Although the verb ἠτέκνωσέν is not repeated, it should be understood as implicit in the subordinate sentence. The nominative θάνατος can be taken as the subject of the omitted verb and is, therefore, presented as a personified figure who is guilty of puericide. This interpretation of כמות in LXX Lam 1:20, wherein death is portrayed as an acting character who causes childlessness, presents an understanding of the wording of the colon that is compatible with ideas about death that were transmitted within the Hebrew text's larger cultural environment. In a number of ancient Near Eastern literary compositions, the figure of Death, as an active, sometimes divine, entity, is explicitly associated with the bereavement of children and youths. A few selected passages from diverse geographical locations (Egypt, the southern Levant, Ugarit, and Mesopotamia), dating to the second and first millennia BCE and written in different languages, will suffice to illustrate this point.

The first passage that bears mentioning is an instruction on the importance of preparing a tomb in the New Kingdom Egyptian didactic text, The Instruction of

---

For this proposal, see Choon-Leong Seow, "A Textual Note on Lamentations 1:20," *CBQ* 47 (1985): 416–19.

25. Robin B. Salters, *Lamentations*, ICC (London: T&T Clark, 2010), 99.

Ani (17.11–18.4).²⁶ In this section of his teaching, the sage, Ani, directs his son, Khonshotep, to have his final resting place prepared so that when the "envoy" (*ipwty*), Death, comes to fetch him, he will be ready. Ani insinuates that it is never too early to be concerned with this important matter, because, so he argues, the figure of Death comes indiscriminately and unexpectedly to young children and to the aged (18.2–4):²⁷

m ir ḏd tw.i m rnn r ṯȝ y.k
iw b(w) rḫ.k pȝ y.k mwt
iw pȝ mwt ḥ<n>p.f pȝ nḫn
pȝ nty m ḳny mwt.f
mi pȝ nty iry.f iȝ wt

Do not say, "I am too young for you to take",
you do not know your death.
When Death comes, he steals the infant,
the one who is in his mother's arms,
just like the one who reached old age.

The second passage appears in Combination II of the plaster inscription from Deir ʿAllā, written in a Northwest Semitic dialect that resists an easy classification as either Canaanite or Aramaic.²⁸ The text was probably penned during the late ninth

---

26. Regarding the date of The Instruction of Ani, Émile Suys, *La Sagesse D'Ani: Texte, Traduction et Commentaire*, AO 11 (Rome: Pontifical Biblical Institute, 1935), viii suggests that the work can be dated at least to the Twentieth Dynasty, while Miriam Lichtheim, *Ancient Egyptian Literature*, vol. 2: *The New Kingdom* (Berkeley: University of California Press, 2006), 135 and Aksel Volten, *Studien zum Weisheitsbuch des Anii* (Copenhagen: Levin & Munksgaard, 1937), 61–62 maintain that it probably came into being during the Eighteenth Dynasty. Joachim Friedrich Quack, *Die Lehren des Ani: Ein neuägyptischer Weisheitstext in seinem kulturellen Umfeld*, OBO 141 (Freiburg: Universitätsverlag; Göttingen: Vandenhoeck & Ruprecht, 1994), 61–62, however, argues in favor of a date in the early Nineteenth Dynasty. Like other didactic texts, it was composed in the literary form of a father instructing his son. The section 17.11–18.4 forms a thematic unit that is flanked by a warning not to overindulge in the drinking of beer (17.6–11) and a subheading that mentions the benefits of obedience to Ani's counsels (18.4–5).

27. The transliteration is based on the hieroglyphic transcription prepared by Quack and follows his emendation of the reading *ḥ<n>p.f*. See. Quack, *Lehren*, 98, 292.

28. Regarding the dialect of the Deir ʿAllā text, see, e.g., Naʿama Pat-El, and Aren Wilson-Wright, "Deir ʿAllā as a Canaanite Dialect: A Vindication of Hackett," in *Epigraphy, Philology, and the Hebrew Bible: Methodological Perspectives on Philological and Comparative Study of the Hebrew Bible in Honor of Jo Ann Hackett*, ed. Jeremy M. Hutton, and Aaron D. Rubin, ANEM 12 (Atlanta: SBL Press, 2015), 13–23; Gary A. Rendsburg,

or eighth century BCE.[29] The fragmentary surface of Combination II is damaged and it is not easy to make sense of the broken wording. It is, therefore, not surprising that scholars have suggested different reconstructions and interpretations of the text. The following words from line 13 are based on Jo Ann Hackett's transcription of Combination II:[30]

> *bm yqḥ . mwt . 'l . rḥm . w 'l* [   ]
>
> Why will Death take the infant of the womb and the infant [   ]

Jacob Hoftijzer argues that the difficult phrase *'l rḥm* denotes an unborn fetus, whereas *w 'l* indicates a child who has already been born.[31] Hackett, however, suggests that the construct phrase "could refer to the suckling child *just out* of the womb, i.e., a newborn child."[32] This suggestion is related to her interpretation of the context of Combination II as that of child sacrifice.[33] Some scholars see in this passage a reference to the god Mot, "the personification of death."[34] Although it

---

"The Dialect of the Deir 'Alla Inscription," *BO* 3.4 (1993): 309–29; P. Kyle McCarter, "The Dialect of the Deir 'Alla Texts," in *The Balaam Text from Deir 'Alla Re-evaluated*, ed. Jacob Hoftijzer, and Gerrit van der Kooij (Leiden: Brill, 1991), 87–99; John Huehnergard, "Remarks on the Classification of the Northwest Semitic Languages," in *The Balaam Text from Deir 'Alla Re-evaluated*, ed. Jacob Hoftijzer, and Gerrit van der Kooij (Leiden: Brill, 1991), 282–93; Jo Ann Hackett, *The Balaam Text from Deir 'Allā*, HSM 31 (Chico: Scholars Press, 1984), 109–24; Jacob Hoftijzer and Gerrit van der Kooij, *Aramaic Texts from Deir 'Alla* (Leiden: Brill, 1976), 300–2.

29. Cf. the comments of Shmuel Aḥituv, *Echoes from the Past: Hebrew and Cognate Inscriptions from the Biblical Period* (Jerusalem: Carta, 2008), 434; Hackett, *Balaam Text*, 18–19.

30. Hackett, *Balaam Text*, 26.

31. Hoftijzer and Van der Kooij, *Aramaic Texts*, 239. If the interpretation of *'l rḥm* as a designation for a fetus is followed, the sentence seems to be a lament over miscarriages. So Hans-Peter Müller, "Die aramäische Inschrift von Deir 'Allā und die älteren Bileamsprüche," *ZAW* 94 (1982): 236.

32. Hackett, *Balaam Text*, 70.

33. Hackett, *Balaam Text*, 80–85. For other interpretations of Combination II, see Erhard Blum, "'Verstehst du dich nicht auf die Schreibkunst …?' Ein weisheitlicher Dialog über Vergänglichkeit und Verantwortung: Kombination II der Wandinschrift vom Tell Deir 'Alla," in *Was ist der Mensch, dass du seiner gedenkst? (Psalm 8,5): Festschrift für Bernd Janowski zum 65. Geburtstag*, ed. Michaela Bauks, Kathrin Liess and Peter Riede (Neukirchen-Vluyn: Neukirchener Verlag, 2008), 40. He argues that it is a sapiential text that presents a dialogue between a teacher/master and an advanced student (33–51). See also Erhard Blum, "Die altaramäischen Wandinschriften vom Tell Deir 'Alla und ihr institutioneller Kontext," in *Metatexte: Erzählungen von schrifttragenden Artefakten in der alttestamentlichen und mittelalterlichen Literatur*, ed. Friedrich-Emanuel Focken and Michael R. Ott, Materiale Textkulturen 15 (Berlin: de Gruyter, 2016), 21–52.

34. Meindert Dijkstra, "Is Balaam also among the Prophets?" *JBL* 114 (1995): 61.

is not certain that *mwt* is a deity here, it seems clear that the figure of Death is "an active personality"[35] who is said to be responsible for the loss of children.

A third noteworthy example is found in a text from Ugarit that combines ritual and myth:

> KTU 1.23.8–11
>
> *mt . w šr . yṯb .*
> *bdh . ḥṭ . ṯkl .*
> *bdh ḥṭ . ulmn .*
> *yzbrnn . zbrm . gpn*
> *yṣmdnn . ṣmdm . gpn .*
> *yšql . šdmth km gpn*
>
> Death-and-Ruler sits enthroned.
> In his hand (is) a sceptre of childlessness.
> In his hand (is) a sceptre of widowhood.
> Those who prune the vine prune him.
> Those who bind the vine bind him.
> He fell to the terrace like a vine.

These lines, in which the figure of Death, in this case, the god Mot,[36] appears, is "a ritual recitation (one sort of ritual action) performed within the context of the ritual that opens in lines 1–7."[37] The setting of the ritual is the period of the grape harvest, that time of the year in late summer/early autumn when the dry season, the dominion of Mot, gives way to the rainy season.[38] The pruning, binding, and felling of Mot described in lines 9–11 of the ritual serve to facilitate this transition of seasons. The ritual act that marks the end of Mot's time of rule is preceded by

---

35. Hoftijzer and Van der Kooij, *Aramaic Texts*, 239.

36. For the identification of *mt w šr* with the god Mot, see, e.g., Stefanie Ulrike Gulde, *Der Tod als Herrscher in Ugarit und Israel*, FAT 2/22 (Tübingen: Mohr Siebeck, 2007), 97–98 n. 96; Mark S. Smith, *The Rituals and Myths of the Feast of the Goodly Gods KTU/CAT 1.23: Royal Constructions of Opposition, Intersection, Integration, and Domination*, RBS 51 (Atlanta: Society of Biblical Literature, 2006), 40–42; John C. L. Gibson, "The Ugaritic Literary Texts," in *Handbook of Ugaritic Studies*, ed. Wilfred G. E. Watson, and Nicolas Wyatt, HdO 39 (Leiden: Brill, 1999), 200; Herbert Niehr, *Religionen in Israels Umwelt* (Würzburg: Echter Verlag, 1998), 36; John F. Healy, "Mot מות," in *DDD*, 600; David T. Tsumura, "An Ugaritic God MT-W-ŠR and His Two Weapons (UT 52:8–11)," *UF* 6 (1974): 409–10. Wyatt advocates a different view according to which *mt w šr* refers to El. See, e.g., Nicolas Wyatt, *Religious Texts from Ugarit*, 2nd ed. (Sheffield: Sheffield Academic, 2002), 326 n. 10; Wyatt, "The Identity of *Mt-w-Šr*," *UF* 9 (1977): 379–81.

37. Smith, *Rituals and Myths*, 48.

38. See Gulde, *Tod als Herrscher*, 96–97; Smith, *Rituals and Myths*, 47–48.

a depiction of the deity of death in the image of a king (lines 8–9). He is given a compound name, "Death-and Ruler,"[39] he sits enthroned and he holds scepters that symbolize his power and rule.[40] These symbols of power and rule are identified as *ṯkl* ("sterility, loss of children")[41] and *ulmn* ("widowhood"). This royal picture implies that Mot exercises his might and dominion especially through the destruction of life that adversely affects families and households. With regard to *ḥṭ ṯkl*, Stefanie Ulrike Gulde is of the opinion that this "sceptre of childlessness" shows Mot as a god who not only destroys life, but also as a god of unfruitfulness who prevents the conception of life.[42] *ṯkl*, however, does not only have the sense of sterility but can also express bereavement of children, who have already been born, by death.[43]

In the Standard Babylonian Version of the Gilgamesh epic, Gilgamesh undertakes a long and arduous journey in search of the immortal Utanapishtim, after his beloved friend, Enkidu, died an unheroic death and he came to realize that a similar fate might befall him. Utanapishtim received immortality from the gods when he survived the great Flood, but Gilgamesh goes to him with the intention of wresting the secret of eternal life from him through battle. Upon meeting the old man, Gilgamesh explains his wretched appearance as caused by sorrow over the loss of Enkidu and the fear of his own death. This is also the reason why he crossed lands, mountains, and seas in relentless pursuit of his goal, to find Utanapishtim and an end to his grief. In his reply, Utanapishtim points out to Gilgamesh that his strength sapping journey only hastens the end of his life. It belongs to the divinely decreed human condition that it is impermanent and the gods do not disclose the time of one's demise.[44] Invisibly, silently, and without forewarning, Death "takes men and women off in the prime of life, like an enemy raiding party seizing people from their homes":[45]

---

39 On the binomial name, especially the interpretation of *šr* as "ruler, prince," see Smith, *Rituals and Myths*, 40, as well as Gulde, *Tod als Herrscher*, 97 n. 96.

40. See the line in an Old Babylonian letter (TCL 17:29, 17) in which *mūtu*, personified death, who snatches children, is called the lord of people: *mu-tum be-lí nišī māriašu itbal*, "Death, the lord of people, took his son." The text is quoted in *CAD* 10.2:317.

41. See *DULAT*, 903.

42. Gulde, *Tod als Herrscher*, 113.

43. See Tsumura, "Ugaritic God MT-W-ŠR," 409.

44. According to Utanapishtim (Tablet X, line 322), the great gods established death and life, but "the day of death they did not reveal (*šá mu-ti ul ud-du-ú ūmī[u$_4$]^{meš}-šú*)." Andrew R. George, *The Babylonian Gilgamesh Epic: Introduction, Critical Edition and Cuneiform Texts*, vol. 1 (Oxford: Oxford University Press, 2003), 698–99.

45. George, *Babylonian Gilgamesh Epic*, 506. The transliteration and the translation of Tablet X, lines 30–307 are quoted from the same volume (George, *Babylonian Gilgamesh Epic*, 696–97).

Tablet X, lines 301–307

a-me-lu-tum šá kīma(gim) *qanê*(gi) *a-pi ḫa-ṣi-pi šùm-šu*
eṭ-la dam-qa ardata(ki.sikil)*ᵗᵃ da-me-eq-tum*:
ur-[ru-ḫiš? ...]-šú-nu-ma i-šal-lal mu-ti
ʾ*ul maʾ-am-ma mu-ú-tu im-mar*:
ul ma-am-m[a ša mu-ti i]m-ʾmarʾ pa-ni-šú
ʾ*ul ma-am-maʾ ša mu-ti rig-ʾma-šúʾ [i-šem-me]*
ag-gu ʾmu-tumʾ ḫa-ṣi-pi amēlu(lú)*-ut-tim*

Man is one whose progeny is snapped off like a reed in the canebrake:
the comely young man, the pretty young woman,
all [*too soon in*] their very [*prime*] death abducts (them).
No one sees death,
no one sees the face [of death,]
no one [hears] the voice of death:
(yet) savage death is the one who hacks man down.

In view of the unpredictability of Death, who cuts off even young people, Gilgamesh's search for immortality is unmasked as a fool's errand, because it is not only doomed to fail (it is the unchangeable decision of the gods that humans must die), but it also achieves the opposite of its desired goal by shortening the uncertain time of Gilgamesh's life.

These passages from the Instruction of Ani, the Deir ʿAllā plaster inscription, the Ugaritic ritual text, and the Gilgamesh epic, where Death is said to be responsible for the loss of children and youths in various rhetorical contexts, imply that this figure was widely known over a long period of time and in different geographical areas of the ancient Near East. It also appears in the book of Jeremiah in a divine oracle of doom that foresees the dead lying everywhere, both inside and outside of Jerusalem:[46]

MT Jer 9:20[47]

כי־עלה מות בחלונינו בא בארמנותינו
להכרית עולל מחוץ בחורים מרחבות

---

46. On the figure of Death in the Hebrew Bible, see Stefanie U. Gulde, "Der Tod als Figur im Alten Testament: Ein alttestamentlicher Motivkomplex und seine Wurzeln," in *Tod und Jenseits im alten Israel und in seiner Umwelt: Theologische, religionsgeschichtliche, archäologische und ikonographische Aspekte*, ed. Angelika Berlejung and Bernd Janowski, FAT 64 (Tübingen: Mohr Siebeck, 2009), 67–85, and regarding the Jeremiah passage, see Gulde, *Tod als Herrscher*, 158–81; and Mark S. Smith, "Death in Jeremiah ix, 20," *UF* 19 (1987): 287–93.

47. The Hebrew text of the passage is quoted from the *BHS* edition.

> For Death climbed into our windows; he entered our palaces
> to cut off the child from the street, the young men from the squares.

Death is portrayed here as an intruder who infiltrated buildings (including fortified ones) with the purpose of destroying children and young men from the public spaces (irrespective of the youths' age or innocence). This image of the figure of מות implies that people inside the city are powerless to keep Death at bay and that there is no deterrent or defense against him. It is complemented by the reference in the next verse to human corpses outside the city that will be as manure in the field and cut grain behind a reaper.

The wide circulation of the representation of Death as a figure who takes the lives of small children and youths in its larger cultural environment, including another Hebrew literary composition, raises the possibility that it also makes an appearance in Lam 1. To be sure, LXX Lamentations exemplifies how the Hebrew wording of the second colon of 1:20c can make sense when the noun in the prepositional phrase כמות is interpreted as a personification of death. This does not mean, however, that the Greek translation and the extant Hebrew version of Lam 1:20c convey exactly the same information. In the Greek text, the speaker claims that a sword made childless outdoors just like Death did indoors. According to the MT wording, personified Jerusalem seems to say that a sword bereaved her of children outside and that it has done so inside the house in a way similar to Death. The idea might be that the sword (a metonym for the wielders of the weapon) killed as indiscriminately, indefensibly, and inescapably inside the house as Death does when he takes the lives of children.

Final Remarks

Attempts to deal with the debated Hebrew wording of MT Lam 1:20's final colon illustrate that conjectural emendations, grammar, and comparative philology are some of the tools text-critics can employ to illuminate or eliminate a textual difficulty. Inventing new readings, unattested in the available textual representatives, searching for grammatical solutions, and supporting a suggested meaning for Hebrew words with evidence from cognate languages are indeed viable options for text-critics to investigate when they endeavor to fashion appropriate meanings for problematic passages. Nevertheless, they should neither fail to explain how the seemingly difficult Hebrew readings developed from the proposed pristine ones through processes of scribal transmission, nor simply ignore or disregard the renderings of the debated readings in the ancient translations. They can also attempt to make sense of debated readings by exploring their communicative potential through the lens of the concepts and themes that circulated in the text's larger ancient Near Eastern environment. For this purpose, text-critics can consult a variety of literary and visual sources from the ancient Near East that served as media for communicating the peoples' ideas and worldviews. It is not only sources that are strictly contemporaneous with a Hebrew composition like Lam 1's purported period of origin that can be enlightening in this regard, but also sources in various languages from different times and locations that provide evidence for the long-term and widespread dissemination of ideas and themes.

In the case of Lam 1:20, the process of translating the Hebrew text into Greek produced a felicitous interpretation of the subject matter of the *Vorlage*, whose wording seems to have been close to that of the MT. The rendering of the reading כמות in the Greek translation is not only intelligible, but the idea it expresses is also comparable to literary portrayals of Death as a figure responsible for the loss of children and youths in various ancient Near Eastern texts. Therefore, the interpretation of the debated Hebrew phrase in LXX Lam 1:20c, coupled with the relevant passages from other ancient Near Eastern texts, provides the text-critic with an avenue along which to make sense of the verse's final bicolon within its broader cultural context. This line of interpretation, according to which there is ellipsis of the verb שכלה in the second colon and מות is understood as a personified figure, has the benefit of obviating the need to change the consonants or vocalization of the MT reading or to avoid the comparison to Death it expresses.

Ps 40(39):7–9 in the Hebrew Bible and in the Septuagint, with Its Reception in the New Testament (Heb 10:5–10)

Wolfgang Kraus

Abstract: The Hebrew and Greek text forms of Ps 40 (LXX Ps 39) exhibit significant differences, especially in verse 7. The Göttingen and Rahlfs/Hanhart editions correct the LXX readings in the manuscripts (inter alia, B, A, and S) towards the Hebrew text. This contribution tackles the question to what extent this is justified, and asks whether another solution to the problem is possible. It examines the citation of the psalm in Heb 10:5–10, and indicates that the Greek readings that differ from the MT were not created by the author of Hebrews. They were part of the LXX text tradition. The passage in Hebrews continues the idea in LXX Ps 39 that obedience is better than sacrifice and interprets it christologically.

The interpreters of Ps 40 traditionally had difficulties to make sense of the disposition of the psalm. After the heading in the first verse, the psalm contains three parts: verses 2–5, a report about an experience of salvation; verses 6–12, a hymn of thanksgiving; and verses 13–18, a lament.[1] It is striking that the third part, verses 13–18, reappears in the book of Psalms without verse 13, forming a psalm of its own, namely, Ps 70. Why is there this salvation report first (vv. 2–5), then the new hymn of thanksgiving (vv. 6–12), then the lament at the end (vv. 13–18), which—on top of that—seems to be completely independent in Ps 70?

The following paper was delivered at the IOSCS Conference 2016 in Stellenbosch. An expanded German version was given at the Septuagint Conference 2016 in Wuppertal. For help with the translation into English, I thank Ulrike Peisker. For discussions of several issues of the paper, I thank Christian Lustig, Saarbrücken, and Martin Rösel, Rostock.

1. Klaus Seybold, *Die Psalmen*, HAT 1.15 (Tübingen: Mohr Siebeck, 1996), 166. Hans-Joachim Kraus is in favor of another division: vv. 2–12, "Dankpsalm bzw. Dankliturgie"; vv. 13–18, "individuelles Klagelied." Hans-Joachim Kraus, *Psalmen I*, BKAT 15.1, 4th ed. (Neukirchen-Vluyn: Neukirchener Verlag, 1972), 306–7.

A solution to this problem might look like this: The statement in verse 8b, "in the מגלת ספר is written of me," refers to a practice of placing a piece of writing at the temple as a votive gift in the form of a scroll. On it, it says what the praying person needs. After the help of YHWH, the community is told what God did; that would be verses 10–11. Then, verses 12–18 could be understood as the former petitionary prayer with which the praying person begged God for help in their hardship.[2]

The custom to place a מגלת ספר at a sanctuary in ancient times is well attested and may be compared to a custom that nowadays still exists: at the so-called Western or Wailing Wall in Jerusalem, sheets with prayers are placed by visitors, petitionary prayers and prayers of thanksgiving. People put down in words what they hope for from God or what they thank Him for. Even the Pope did it, when he visited the Holy Land.[3] A similar practice seems to underlie verse 8 in MT Ps 40, which for long has been difficult to interpret.

My paper consists of three paragraphs. In the first paragraph, we will have a look at MT Ps 40:7–9 in the Hebrew text. The second paragraph is dedicated to Ps 39:7–9 in the LXX version. In the third paragraph, we will look at the quote from Ps 39 LXX in Heb 10:5–10.

1. Ps 40:7–9 in the Hebrew Text

1.1. Form

Psalm 40 is—as mentioned before—a tripartite psalm: report of an experience of salvation (vv. 2–5), thanksgiving prayer (vv. 6–12), and lament (vv. 13–18). This division into three parts, as done by Klaus Seybold, presupposes that the psalm in its present form is a coherent whole instead of consisting of two, originally independent units that had nothing to do with each other. Other divisions, such as the division into two parts, verses 2–12 and verses 13–18, make it difficult to understand the psalm as a whole. The verses 13–18 are then seen as independent and perhaps as added later.[4] According to Seybold, with whom I agree, here the former psalm of lament, in which the praying person had begged for the liberation from his suffering in verse 13ff., is added to the thanksgiving hymn.[5] The song of praise in front of the community (announced in v. 4, conducted in vv. 6–12) is continued

---

2. Seybold, *Psalmen*, 167.
3. See Hans Hermann Henrix and Wolfgang Kraus, ed., *Die Kirchen und das Judentum II: Dokumente von 1986–2000* (Gütersloh: Gütersloher Verlagshaus, 2001), 161: Dokument K.I 48: Vergebungsbitte am 26. März 2000.
4. Kraus, *Psalmen I*, 307.
5. Seybold, *Psalmen*, 167.

with the dedication of the answered prayer of lament, written on a scroll as a votive gift.[6]

1.2. The Understanding of Verse 8

The understanding of verse 8 in the aforementioned sense dates back to a work of Günter Bornkamm.[7] He tried to show that מגלת ספר, as used in verse 8, cannot refer to the Torah[8] or prophetic writings.

This was and still is not uncontroversial. According to Erich Zenger, מגלת ספר is to be understood as a real metaphor for words inspired by God ("Realmetapher für von Gott eingegebene Worte"). To argue this, he names Jer 36:4, 32; 51:63 and Ezek 2:9 as parallel passages. The term מגלת ספר allegedly alludes to phrasings such as ספר הברית or ספר התורה. The expression כתוב עלי ("written on me"), according to Zenger, relates to the wording in Jer 31:33: על-לבם אכתבנה ("I will write it [the Torah] onto their hearts").[9] The scroll may be inscribed within the praying person. This sense of verse 8 is supposed to be supported by verse 9.

The parallels given by Zenger and also the understanding of verse 8 have been rejected as unconvincing by Bornkamm, already in 1964. The term מגלת ספר occurs in Jer 36:2, 4, 6 and more often as a term for the scroll on which Baruch was supposed to write the words of Jeremiah. According to Ezek 2:9; 3:1–3, Ezekiel has to eat the message of God in the form of a scroll (cf. Rev 10:9–10). In Zech 5:1–2, we hear about a flying scroll. None of these passages have a direct reference to the Torah. מגלת ספר is rather an expression for a piece of writing in the form of a scroll.

The subsequent realization of Bornkamm was that such pieces of writing were placed at temples by praying people as a votive gift in ancient times. Such a votive practice was widely spread in ancient times. Not only pieces of writing have been placed at temples, but also votive steles with which, according to a common ancient cultural custom, the person healed or saved by the deity glorified the marvels they experienced by their god.[10]

---

6. Seybold, *Psalmen*, 167, 169: "Dedikation des erhörten Klagegebets, geschrieben auf einer Schriftrolle (8) als Votivgabe."

7. Günter Bornkamm, "Bekenntnis, Lobpreis und Opfer: Eine alttestamentliche Studie," in *Geschichte und Glaube I*, ed. Günter Bornkamm, BEvTh 48 (München: Kaiser, 1968), 122–39.

8. See, e.g., Kraus, *Psalmen I*, 309; also Zenger; see the following note.

9. Frank-Lothar Hossfeld and Erich Zenger, *Die Psalmen I (Ps 1–50)*, NEB 29 (Würzburg: Echter-Verlag, 1993), 256.

10. Bornkamm, "Lobpreis," 133: "entspricht verbreitetem antiken Kultbrauch ... der von der Gottheit Geheilte oder Gerettete ... die ihm widerfahrenen Wundertaten seines Gottes verherrlichen"; see 132–34. See also the commentaries on Hebrews of Martin Karrer, *Der Brief an die Hebräer. 2. Kapitel 5,11–13,25*, ÖTK 20.2 (Gütersloh: Gütersloher Verlagshaus, 2008), 184; Erich Gräßer, *An die Hebräer II*, EKK 17.2 (Zürich Benziger;

Furthermore, Bornkamm assumed that the scroll means the thanksgiving hymn of the psalmist himself.[11] This seems to be only *one* possibility to understand the verse, though. It seems more likely to understand the מגלת ספר, like Seybold did, as the former prayer of lament that now is placed at the temple as a votive gift. This prayer of lament appears as an independent psalm in Ps 70. Consequently, this is an example of a reuse of a votive text.[12]

1.3. CONCERNING THE CRITICISM OF SACRIFICES IN PS 40

In the interpretation of Ps 40, it is highly debated whether verses 6–9 are a case of cult criticism. Bornkamm compared the verses to other passages from the psalms that harbored cult criticism (Ps 50:7ff.; 69:31ff.) and argued that those are not examples of a general rejection of sacrifices as in the sense of, for example, 1 Sam 15:22 ("obedience is better than sacrifice"). This kind of criticism is possible because this passage is not about statutory, common temple sacrifices, but rather about the sacrifices and offerings of thanks that are not generally regulated by the law and which were offered according to one's respective situation and fortune. The offering of the thanksgiving hymn and the praise of God takes the place of these sacrifices by serving as a sacrifice itself.[13]

Hans-Joachim Kraus accentuates a different aspect. In his opinion, prophetic criticism of the sacrifices continues to have an effect on the mentioned texts (Pss 40:7; 50:13; 51:18).[14] He considers Amos 5:22; Isa 1:11; Jer 6:20; and also 1 Sam

---

Neukirchen-Vluyn: Neukirchener Verlag, 1993), 215; see also Georg Gäbel, *Die Kulttheologie des Hebräerbriefes: Eine exegetisch-religionsgeschichtliche Studie*, WUNT 212 (Tübingen: Mohr Siebeck, 2006), 187. Those who visit places of pilgrimage such as Altötting or Lourdes will recognize some parallels. There, votive gifts from people who experienced help or healing can be found in the church and the cloister; handwritten or printed pieces of writing include thanksgiving to God or Mary or Jesus. But there can also be found artificial limbs, sticks, fabrics and many other things as a testimonial of the experience of help.

11. Bornkamm, "Lobpreis," 133: "das Danklied des Psalmisten selbst"; see also Gäbel, *Kulttheologie*, 187.

12. Seybold, *Psalmen*, 271: "ein Beispiel für die Weiterverwendung eines Votivtextes." This was also true if Ps 70 was the older version and Ps 40:14–18 the younger text; cf. Seybold, *Psalmen*, 169–70.

13. Bornkamm, "Lobpreis," 130: "nicht um gesetzlich vorgeschriebene, allgemeine gottesdienstliche Opfer handelt, sondern um die vom Gesetz nicht generell regulierten Opfer und Dankopfer, die je nach Lage und Vermögen dargebracht wurden. An deren Stelle tritt die Darbringung des Dankliedes und des Lobpreises Gottes als Opfer."

14. Kraus, *Psalmen I*, 309, against Mowinckel, who found only another accentuation, namely from sacrifice to song ("vom Opfer auf das Lied"). This is also the case in Bernd Janowski, "Auf dem Weg zur Buchreligion: Transformationen des Kultischen im Psalter,"

15:22 to be forming the background. But—and this is another important aspect—according to verse 9, the obedience opposed to the sacrifice is explicitly applied to the Torah. This is why Kraus assigns the postexilic Torah devoutness to the statements. In the context of this Torah devoutness, particularly Deuteronomy and the prophecy of Jeremiah should then have taken a special role (Deut 6:6; 30:11ff.; Jer 31:31–41; cf. Ps 19:8): the declaration of obedience takes the place of the sacrifices.

How may it come to such an opposition of "obedience instead of sacrifice"? Seybold stresses that, regarding his views that the cultic facilities were ineffective, the praying person refers to a "special inspiration": in verse 7, it says that God had opened his ears for this insight.[15] Allegedly, the inspiration in Job 4:12ff., which is also about a special insight that is expressed by means of the *metaphor of the ear* and experienced by Job, is comparable. So, the praying person, by a special divine inspiration, comes to the conclusion that sacrifices, meat, incense, and sin offerings are inadequate in his situation—that obedience to the Torah is rather what God wants from him (v. 9). He is prepared to do so since he has the Torah in his heart. This attitude can indeed refer to postexilic Torah devoutness, but it is initiated by a special inspiration that the praying person received.

2. LXX Ps 39:7–9

2.1. General Structure

The overall structure of LXX Ps 39 mainly coincides with the Hebrew text. After verse 1 as an introduction, three parts can be distinguished. The division must be done differently, though: verses 2–5; verses 6–11; verses 12–18. The finishing of the second part, which in MT Ps 40 is done in verse 12, in the LXX is done in verse 11, already, by stating that the praying person has not kept silent the mercy of God and his truth in the grand assembly.

Verse 12 then continues with an adversative σὺ δέ, κύριε. God is begged not to withdraw his sympathy from the praying person.

By the means of ὅτι, verse 13 relates back to verse 12 and stresses the vast number of miseries that the praying person was captured by, which is why he needs the help of God. So, verses 12 and 13 are much closer connected in the LXX than they are in the MT. Thus, the division must be done after verse 11.

2.2. Differences to the MT in Verses 7–9

The translation of Ps 40:7–9 in the LXX mainly matches the Hebrew text. There are only three differences that are relevant in terms of contents in verse 7.

---

in *Trägerkreise in den Psalmen*, ed. Frank-Lother Hossfeld, Johannes Bremer and Till Magnus Steiner, BBB 178 (Göttingen: Vandenhoeck & Ruprecht, 2017), 244.

15. Seybold, *Psalmen*, 169.

2.2.1. The first difference concerns the verb in verse 7a. In the MT, it says that God "does not derive pleasure" (לא חפצת) from the sacrificial meal (זבח) and gift offering (מנחה). The LXX translates that God did *not want* (θέλω) sacrifices (θυσία) and offerings (προσφορά).

2.2.2. In verse 7c, the text of both critical editions (Göttingen and Rahlfs/Hanhart) and the MT read the singular ὁλοκαύτωμα. A couple of LXX manuscripts such as the P. Bod. 24 give the plural ὁλοκαυτώματα[16] though, coinciding with the quote from the psalm in Heb 10.

2.2.3. The most important difference is to be found in verse 7b. There, the MT says: "ears you dug me." According to the Göttingen edition or rather Rahlfs or Rahlfs/Hanhart, the LXX translates: "ears you have *prepared/fashioned* for me," thus changing only the verb. But this way of reading of the critical editions is most questionable.

The citation in Heb 10:7 offers "a *body* you have prepared for me" in the quote from LXX Ps 39. This means that it not only has a different verb but also σῶμα instead of ὠτία. The noun σῶμα is attested by all main manuscript of the LXX, and also by P. Bod. 24. The editor of the critical text, Alfred Rahlfs, and his successors assumed that the reading of "body" from the epistle to the Hebrews penetrated into the text of the psalm and thus, they decided not to follow the main manuscripts of the LXX, which all read "body." Therefore, they wrote, in accordance with the MT and some late LXX witnesses, "ears."[17] We have to admit, however, that at the time of Alfred Rahlfs, P. Bod. 24 was not known yet.

Several attempts have been made to solve the problem by the assumption of a writing mistake, homophony, or a theological intention in the Hebrews quote, but none has led to a scholarly consensus.[18] Most commentators of Hebrews are

---

16. See on this Gert J. Steyn, *A Quest for the Assumed LXX Vorlage of the Explicit Quotations in Hebrews*, FRLANT 235 (Göttingen: Vandenhoeck & Ruprecht, 2011), 287. Instead of the verb ᾔτησας in v. 7 (fin), P. Bod. 24 reads the verb ηὐπόκησας, several manuscripts read εὐδόκησας.

17. For details cf. Steyn, *Quest*, 284–87; Martin Karrer, "LXX Psalm 39:7–10 in Hebrews 10:5–7," in *Psalms and Hebrews: Studies in Reception*, ed. Dirk J. Human and Gert J. Steyn (New York: T&T Clark, 2010), 137–43. The criteria of the Rahlfs edition are analyzed by Siegfried Kreuzer in the proceedings of the Septuaginta Conference, Wuppertal 2016 (to appear in WUNT).

18. See Karen H. Jobes, "Rhetorical Achievement in the Hebrews 10 'Misquote' of Psalm 40," *Bib* 72 (1991): 387–96; Jobes, "The Function of the Paronomasia in Hebrews 10:5–7," *TJ* 13 (1992): 181–91; Christian-B. Amphoux and Gilles Dorival, "'Des oreilles, tu m'as creusées' ou, 'un corps, tu m'as ajusté'? À propos du Psaume 39 (40 TM), 7," *Philologia* 35 (2006): 315–27. See also Karrer, "LXX Ps 39," 144, 142; Gäbel, *Kulttheologie*, 189 n. 66.

of the opinion that the *Vorlage* of Hebrews already read σῶμα.¹⁹ If we look at other citations in Hebrews, we can observe that the author is rather reluctant concerning textual changes compared to his *Vorlage*.

But does this also mean that the text of LXX Ps 39 has to be changed? Martin Karrer clearly states: "we must correct the critical text of LXX Ps 39:7 against Rahlfs. Σῶμα is the better text."²⁰ The compromise offered by Karrer, according to which σῶμα should *at least* be mentioned as a very well-testified way of reading in the upper text of the critical editions, does not seem necessary after renewed examination of Gert Steyn: "There are, however, no thorough text critical reasons to accept the reading of Rahlfs."²¹ Thus, in LXX Ps 39:7, according to Steyn, it should be read: "A body you have prepared for me." Therefore, both substantive and verb would differ from the MT.

But, as Christian B. Amphoux and Gilles Dorival have worked out, we have evidence for both, σῶμα and ὠτία, even in patristic writings from the second to the fifth century.²² So it seems to me that the difference between MT and several LXX witnesses is part of the LXX text tradition and is not due to the author of Hebrews. The reason why this difference came into being could be twofold: "The most likely explanation of the discrepancy is that, within the LXX tradition, ΗΘΕΛΗΣΑΣΩΤΙΑ was misread as ΗΘΕΛΗΣΑΣ(Σ)ΩΜΑ…. Alternatively, σῶμα may be a free translation or 'interpretive paraphrase of the MT' …, based on the idea of the listening ear as *pars pro toto*, the whole being the obedient person (cf. on this Is. 40:4f)."²³

The differences between singular and plural forms, as they later also appear in Heb 10, can be found in several LXX manuscripts such as Codex Alexandrinus and the Lucianic text, too.

The translation of מגלת ספר with κεφαλὶς βιβλίου in the LXX is also of importance. The term only occurs again in Ezek 2:9, where it refers to a papyrus scroll.²⁴ In Ezek 3:1–3, it only says κεφαλίς (without βιβλίου; cf. 2 Esdr 6:2). From

---

19. So, e.g., Harold Attridge, *The Epistle to the Hebrews*, Hermeneia (Philadelphia: Fortress, 1989), 274; Paul Ellingworth, *The Epistle to the Hebrews: A Commentary on the Greek Text*, NIGTC (Grand Rapids: Eerdmans; Carlisle: Paternoster, 1993), 500; William L. Lane, *Hebrews 9–13*, WBC 47b (Dallas: Word, 1991), 255.

20. Karrer, "LXX Ps 39," 143.

21. Steyn, *Quest*, 286.

22. "Le mot 'oreilles' est présent, au IIᵉ s., chéz Irénée, au IVᵉ s., chéz Eusèbe de Césarée, Diodore de Tarse, Didyme d'Aleandrie, au Vᵉ s., chéz Théodore de Mopsueste. Les témoins du mot 'corp' sont un peu plus nombreux, mais pas beaucoup: Origène au IIIᵉ s., Eusèbe de Césarée et Didyme d'Alexandrie au IVᵉ s., les deux Hésychius, le Pseudo-Athanase et Théodoret de Cyr au Vᵉ s." Amphoux and Dorival, "Des oreilles," 324.

23. Ellingworth, *Hebrews*, 500 (with citation of William Lane; italics by Ellingworth).

24. Natalie Siffer-Wiederholt, "Ps 39 (40)," in *Psalmen bis Daniel*, vol. 2 of *Septuaginta Deutsch: Erläuterungen und Kommentare*, ed. Martin Karrer and Wolfgang Kraus (Stuttgart: Deutsche Bibelgesellschaft, 2011), 1611, or more specifically "Anfang einer

the context, it becomes clear that each time, a piece of writing is meant. Neither here nor there it refers to the Torah.

2.3. Criticism of Sacrifices in LXX Ps 39

The criticism of sacrifices in LXX Ps 39 does not fundamentally differ from the one in the Hebrew text. If the text-critical decision to read σῶμα instead of ὠτία was right, the statement of the LXX in verse 7 would gain a different accentuation, though. The phraseology according to which God "dug ears" pointed to a God-given insight in MT Ps 40:7 based on which the praying person came to a rejection of sacrifices. Now, this understanding in LXX Ps 39 was not possible anymore. God "prepared a body." If the translator took "ears" as *pars pro toto* and wrote "body," this would mean that a human being, in their whole existence, is called to fulfil God's will. "The body which was 'prepared' for the speaker by God is given back to God as a 'living sacrifice', to be employed in obedient service to him."[25]

The Greek translation did—as Georg Gäbel indicates—adequately grasp the intention of the MT, but it also sharpened and intensified it. For only now the physically practiced and practical obedience forms an explicit opposite to cultic sacrifice.[26] This accentuation is stressed by the introduction of δέ in verse 7b. This accentuation perfectly matches verse 9, according to which the praying person intends to carry out the will of God and for that carries the nomos in the midst of his heart or belly.

The use of οὐκ ἠθέλησας in verse 7 for לא חפצת in the MT also stresses this accentuation. If it was the case that the plural ὁλοκαυτώματα, as stated in P. Bod. 24, was also the original version, a generalizing aspect would already become perceptible in the LXX text (and not only in Heb 10): all types of sacrifices are rejected.[27]

Buchrolle bzw. eines Textes"; so Hermut Löhr, "Ezechiel 1–19," in *Psalmen bis Daniel*, vol. 2 of *Septuaginta Deutsch: Erläuterungen und Kommentare*, ed. Martin Karrer and Wolfgang Kraus (Stuttgart: Deutsche Bibelgesellschaft, 2011), 2863.

25. Frederik F. Bruce, *The Epistle to the Hebrews*, NICNT (Grand Rapids: Eerdmans 1964), 232; see also Gäbel, *Kulttheologie*, 190.

26. Gäbel, *Kulttheologie*, 190: The Septuaginta had "die Intention des MT zutreffend erfasst, aber auch zugespitzt und verstärkt. Denn erst hier kommt der leiblich vollzogene, lebenspraktische Gehorsam nun in ausdrücklichen Gegensatz zum Opferkult zu stehen."

27. Gäbel, *Kulttheologie*, 190. According to Gräßer, *Hebräer*, 2:216: "Alle Arten von Opfer werden abgelehnt."

3. The Quote from LXX Ps 39 in Heb 10

3.1. The Context

Before we come to the quotation itself, we need to have a short look at the context. In 6:20, the author of Hebrews says that Jesus went ahead of "us" into the Holy of Holies, that is, behind the curtain, as a high priest according to the order of Melchizedek.[28] This, in 7:1–10:18, is followed by a closed line of argumentation in different steps without a parenetic interruption.[29]

Hebrews 7 picks up the thesis of 6:20 and elaborates on Jesus as the high priest in opposition to the earthly priesthood against the background of Gen 14 and LXX Ps 109.[30] In chapter 8, the author introduces his main argument: κεφάλαιον δὲ ἐπὶ τοῖς λεγομένοις. According to this, Jesus is such a high priest who (according to LXX Ps 109:1) has seated himself at the right hand of the throne of the majesty, as a servant of the truly heavenly tabernacle erected by God, not a human being. The installation of Jesus is understood as realization of the announced new διαθήκη. This new and better order is based on better promises.[31]

In Heb 9, this main argument is expounded in comparison to determinations of the first διαθήκη, especially by taking into account Lev 16 and Exod 24. Jesus is μεσίτης of the new διαθήκη (Heb 9:15).[32] He offered himself as a sacrifice to

---

28. According to Gerd Schunack, *Der Hebräerbrief*, ZBK (Zürich: Theologischer Verlag, 2002), 74, Heb 5:11–6:20 has to be seen as a "metakommunikatives Zwischenstück." Karrer, *Hebräer II*, 19, calls it: "Appell zur Aufmerksamkeit." Hans-Friedrich Weiß, *Der Brief an die Hebräer*, KEK 13 (Göttingen: Vandenhoeck & Ruprecht, 1991), 327, speaks of: "Vorbereitung der Rede für die 'Vollkommenen.'"

29. The outline of Heb 7:1–10:18 has been analysed in Wolfgang Kraus, "Zur Aufnahme von Ex 24f. im Hebräerbrief," in *Heiliger Raum: Exegese und Rezeption der Heiligtumstexte in Ex 24–40*, ed. Matthias Hopf, Wolfgang Oswald, and Stefan Seiler, Theologische Akzente 8 (Stuttgart: Kohlhammer, 2016), 94–99.

30. The impact of Gen 14:18–20 and LXX Ps 109:1 on the argument of Hebrews has been analyzed in Wolfgang Kraus, "Zur Aufnahme und Funktion von Gen 14,18–20 und Ps 109 LXX im Hebräerbrief," in *Text—Textgeschichte—Textwirkung: Festschrift zum 65. Geburtstag von Siegfried Kreuzer*, ed. Thomas Wagner, Jonathan M. Robker and Frank Ueberschaer, AOAT 419 (Münster: Ugarit-Verlag, 2014), 459–74.

31. The understanding of διαθήκη in Hebrews has been analysed in Wolfgang Kraus, "Die Bedeutung von Διαθήκη im Hebräerbrief," in *The Reception of Septuagint Words*, ed. Eberhard Bons, Ralph Brucker and Jan Joosten, WUNT 367 (Tübingen: Mohr Siebeck, 2014), 67–83. The counting of evidence on p. 72 has to be corrected. It must read: "Zu den 17 expliziten Belegen ist διαθήκη noch viermal implizit zu ergänzen (8,7.13; 9,1.18). Damit ist eine Gesamtzahl von 21 erreicht."

32. The understanding of μεσίτης in Hebrews has been analysed in Wolfgang Kraus, "Jesus als 'Mittler' im Hebräerbrief," in *Vermittelte Gegenwart: Konzeptionen der*

God through the eternal spirit (9:14). Through his blood, the way into the Holy of Holies was consecrated (9:23). Hebrews 10 then offers the sum of the main arguments,[33] divided into two parts. Part 1: 10:1–10: The opposite of the sanctification through Christ to the earthly sacrificial cult.[34] Part 2: 10:11–18: The highness of Christ and the finality of the new διαθήκη. In Heb 10, central themes opened up in Heb 1:3c–d are brought to completion.[35] The third main part of the λόγος παρακλήσεως (again marked by parenesis) then begins with Heb 10:19.

3.2. The Closer Context

Our paragraph, Heb 10:1–10, can be subdivided into two subsections: 10:1–4; 10:5–10.[36] In 10:1–4, the context of the יום הכיפורים is still present. This suggests the mentioning of the blood of bulls and goats. The verses objectively repeat the thoughts of 9:6–10. Thereby, the thoughts on the earthly cult in 9:1–10 are taken up again.

The cultic law is merely like a shadow of the goods to come, not their actual nature.[37] Thus, it is soteriologically insufficient.[38] The awareness of sins is still present (v. 2). Instead of bringing forgiveness, the yearly sacrifices represent a constant "reminder" of the sins (v. 3). Verse 4 summarizes harshly and unambiguously: The blood of bulls and goats cannot take away sins.

In verse 5, the quote from LXX Ps 39 follows, introduced by διό. It is seen as a *statement of Jesus* at his entering into the cosmos and includes the verses 6–7.

The verses 8 and 9 again contain two fragments of the quote from the psalm. The first fragment is introduced by "above, he says": God did not want sacrifices and they did not please him either. Afterwards, the author interjects as an explanation: "Where they (the sacrifices) are still offered according to the law." In verse 9, the second fragment appears: "afterwards, he says, behold, I come to carry out your will." Regarding this, it is explained that the first (order) is annulled and the second (order) is put in place. Verse 10 finishes this train of thought in that it states that "we" are sanctified in this will through the sacrificing of the body of Christ.

Gottespräsenz von der Zeit des Zweiten Tempels bis Anfang des 2. Jh. n.Chr., ed. Andrea Taschl-Erber and Irmtraud Fischer, WUNT 367 (Tübingen: Mohr Siebeck, 2016), 293–315.

33. Karrer, *Hebräer II*, 183: "die Summa des Hauptarguments."

34. With two parts: 10:1–4, 5–10; Heb 10:10 picks up 9:28.

35. Karrer, *Hebräer II*, 183: In Heb 10 "gelangen zentrale Motive des großen in 1,3c–d eröffneten Zusammenhanges zum Abschluss." But Karrer is in favor of another division for Hebrews: The second main part, in his view, contains Heb 4:14–10:31, and does not close already in 10:18. But cf. Kraus, "Aufnahme von Ex 24f," 94–99.

36. See for the following, Gäbel, *Kulttheologie*, 185–202.

37. For the meaning and function of σκιά, and εἰκών in Hebrews cf. Kraus, "Aufnahme von Ex 24f," 100–102.

38. Gäbel, *Kulttheologie*, 186.

3.3. The Quote in Heb 10:5–7

The quote in Hebrews differs from the MT and the critical editions of the LXX but coincides with MS 2013—that is, the Upper Egyptian text version.[39] If we leave aside the use of σῶμα instead of ὠτία in the critical LXX editions for a moment, then there are three differences of importance between the LXX text and the Hebrews quote.[40]

3.3.1. In verse 6, the author of Hebrews writes the plural ὁλοκαυτώματα instead of the singular ὁλοκαύτωμα in the LXX text. This alteration can have different explanations: Either the author of Hebrews takes the plural because his text is based on a different source text than the reconstructed critical text. Or he willingly changed the number to stress the multitude of the sacrifices. P. Bod. 24 (= MS 2110) gives the plural also for the text of the psalm. Thus, it is possible that a text like this has been the *Vorlage* for Hebrews.

3.3.2. Instead of the verb ᾔτησας in verse 6, Hebrews reads εὐδόκησας. The verb ᾔτησας in LXX Ps 39 is substantiated by Codex Vaticanus, whereas Sinaiticus and Alexandrinus read ἐζήτησας.[41] P. Bod. 24 also reads εὐδόκησας in LXX Ps 39.[42] This matches LXX Ps 50:18. Thus, it should not be assumed that this is a case of an intentional correction by the author.[43] The *Vorlage* could have looked like this as well. The similarity of LXX Ps 39 and 50 could represent an inner harmonization within the LXX. What this adds up to is that the verb εὐδοκέω is not a favorite word of the author of Hebrews but only occurs in quotes.[44]

3.3.3. The most important difference to the psalm is to be found in the closing line of the quote. There, the syntax has been changed and the end of the psalm verse is left out. While in verse 9 it says: "To carry out your will, my God, is what I wanted, and your law is within me," Hebrews omitted both the verb ἐβουλήθην and the end "your law is within me." Thereby, the part of the verse "to carry out your will, God," which in the psalm is dependent on ἐβουλήθην, is now related to

---

39. Gäbel, *Kulttheologie*, 188 n. 63; see Ulrich Rüsen-Weinhold, *Der Septuagintapsalter im Neuen Testament: Eine textgeschichtliche Untersuchung* (Neukirchen-Vluyn: Neukirchener Verlag, 2004), 203.

40. For details, cf. Steyn, *Quest*, 287–91.

41. Rahlfs notes in the apparatus that εὐδόκησας in some of the LXX manuscripts comes from Heb 10:6.

42. See Karrer, *Hebräer*, 2:195.

43. See Steyn, *Quest*, 291; diff. Gäbel, *Kulttheologie*, 191.

44. Karrer, *Hebräer*, 2:196: "eine innere Abstimmung innerhalb der LXX."

the finite verb "I come" at the beginning of the verse as an infinitive. This alteration seems to be an intentional variation by the author of Hebrews that enabled him to use the quote from the psalm christologically.

3.4. THEOLOGICAL ACCENTUATION IN THE PSALM-QUOTE

We begin with the observation that the quote from LXX Ps 39 varyingly reappears in fragments in verses 8–9. These sentences from LXX Ps 39 should be the ones that particularly mattered to the author. In this second quotation, the passage with ὠτία or σῶμα is left out. What is opposed to each other as first and second statement is rather: "Sacrifices and offerings and burnt offerings and sin offerings you did not want and you do not derive pleasure from them." In opposition to this stands: "Behold, I come to carry out your will." At first glance, the question whether it is supposed to be "body" or "ears" does not matter here.[45] But, in the following verse, we read: "By this will we have been sanctified through the offering of the body of Jesus Christ once and for all." The reference to the "body" seems to be the reason why LXX Ps 39, which before Hebrews has no reception history in Jewish or Christian writings, has been cited here.[46]

While the MT deals with obedience as opposed to the sacrifices based on a special inspiration of the praying person of the psalm, the LXX continues this thought by opposing physical obedience to the sacrificial cult. The author of Hebrews, for his part, continued this line and amplified it christologically. The body offered the possibility to actively carry out the will of God in the psalm text as well. So, the σῶμα and thus, the carrying out of the will of God, takes the place of sacrifices and burnt offerings.[47] This is continued in Hebrews and related to the heavenly reality. Here, not the sacrificial cult and the carrying out of God's will is still in opposition, but rather the earthly cult and Christ's heavenly offering.

The quote from the psalm is spoken by Christ himself, who enters the world, not by the dying Jesus. He quotes the psalm because of the aforementioned insufficiency of the earthly cult (10:1–4). This is why the link with διό in verse 5 raises the expectation of something that, as a new *earthly* event, brings the solution: This happened through Jesus. The adoption of the body when entering the world is the first step to accomplish the will of God. Its culmination lies in the "offering" of the "body" of Jesus. The earthly death of Jesus is at the same time understood as a heavenly event. The key point could be described like this: The devoutness of

---

45. This could be a further argument that the author of Hebrews is not responsible for the alteration of "ears" into "body" in the psalm text. Instead, he already found "body" in his *Vorlage*.

46. Steyn, *Quest*, 284, 292.

47. Gäbel, *Kulttheologie*, 192: "So tritt σῶμα das und damit das Tun des Willens Gottes an die Stelle von Schlacht- und Brandopfern." But this is only true for LXX Ps 39 and not for Hebrews.

Jesus is called προσφορά in Heb 10:10–14—analogous to the sacrifices in verses 5 and 8. The term προσφορά originally is a cultic one. It does not appear often in the LXX—only in late LXX books, and in the Psalms only here. Σῶμα occurs in Hebrews only in 10:5 and 10:10. It is not a cultic term for sacrifices or matters of sacrifice. It is rather about the physical existence. When in Heb 10:10, the προσφορά is newly determined by the term σῶμα, then this is about the physical self-giving, which is expressed in sacrificial terminology without itself being an earthly sacrifice.[48] The self-giving is a surpassing and a substitution of the sacrificial cult, but at the same time it is what the sacrificial cult hinted at – without being able to achieve it itself.[49] The author of Hebrews interprets the earthly self-giving of Jesus as a heavenly προσφορά. Therefore he also surpasses the argumentation of the psalm christologically.

To sum up:

(1) Hebrews brings to completion a position that began in MT Ps 40, which was continued in LXX Ps 39 (obedience is better than sacrifice) and again continued and interpreted christologically in Heb 10: The obedient earthly death of Jesus is understood as a heavenly event.

(2) Hebrews combines its priestly theology with the idea of a new διαθήκη from Heb 8:6 onwards, quoting LXX Jer 38:31–34. In Heb 10:16–17, the quote from LXX Jer 38 reoccurs. This is about the laws that are written onto the heart and about the forgiveness of sins as the epitome of the new διαθήκη.[50] The sacrificial cult formed the first διαθήκη. It is surpassed and annulled by the second one.[51] LXX Ps 39 and LXX Jer 38, just as Ezek 36:26ff. are in close correlation to each other and form prerequisites for the argumentation in Hebrews.[52]

(3) What primarily matters for Hebrews is not criticism of the cult, but the remission of sins, predicted in LXX Jer 38. Through the self-giving of Jesus, the new διαθήκη becomes reality. Now, the entrance to the Holy of Holies is open, which could not have been achieved by the earthly sacrificial cult, but only by the obedient death of the Son of God as a προσφορά τοῦ σώματος ἐφάπαξ.

---

48. Gäbel, *Kulttheologie*, 194; Karrer, *Hebräer*, 2:197.

49. Gäbel, *Kulttheologie*, 195. I do not think, in the New Testament, Rom 12:1–2 is comparable to Heb 10:10 (*pace* Gäbel, *Kulttheologie*, 195 with reference to Berger, Stegemann, Siegert und Seidensticker).

50. It is not "the Torah," but οἵ νόμοι which are written onto the heart. On this, see Wolfgang Kraus, "Die Rezeption von Jer 38,31–34 (LXX) in Hebräer 8–10 und dessen Funktion in der Argumentation des Hebräerbriefes," in *Text-Critical and Hermeneutical Studies in the Septuagint*, ed. Johann Cook and Hermann-Josef Stipp, VTSup 157 (Leiden: Brill, 2012), 447–62.

51. Gäbel, *Kulttheologie*, 195.

52. Kraus, *Psalmen*, 1:462; Gäbel, *Kulttheologie*, 196 n. 96.

Samaria's Downfall in the Versions: The Masoretic Text, Vaticanus, and the So-Called Lucianic Recension

Jonathan M. Robker

Abstract: Second Kings (= 4 Reigns) 17 presents one of the most theologically poignant chapters within Reigns and even within Deuteronomistic literature. Yet, this chapter does not exist as an unchanging monolith; the relevant versions of this text in Hebrew and Greek attest significant variants. This paper will consider distinctions in the Greek tradition, with particular attention to the so-called Antiochene text (traditionally identified with some Lucianic Recension), and their relationships to the development of the (proto-)Masoretic text. This examination of the witnesses will aid in sketching the profile of the various textual traditions, their recensional characteristics, and their relationship to each other.

The problems within the text history of Kings are both manifold and well-known. Yet, it remains imperative to address text-critical and text-historical issues in Kings to shore up the foundation of subsequent literary-historical and redaction-critical models for the composition of Kings, the Deuteronomistic History, or the Enneateuch. At the same time, such critical reflection about the attested variants in manuscripts may provide some hints about how earlier scribes dealt with the texts they transmitted. To this end, one must consider the characteristics of the textual witnesses for Kings, especially within the Greek textual tradition and its relationship to the Masoretic tradition. It is particularly useful to concentrate on a single pericope to discuss the various text-critical issues, even more so on one that attests a number of differences and theological poignancy. To fulfill these criteria, this paper focuses on 2 Kgs 17 (= 4 Kgdms / Reigns 17) in Hebrew and in its two primary Greek text types. The first is the kaige text of Vaticanus (B; generally this is identical with the Rahlfs text [Ra.]) and the second is the so-called Luicianic recension (also known as the Antiochene text = Ant.).[1] The Greek versions

---

1. B's folios 468–471 were consulted via the DigiVatLab Greek manuscript 1209 online facsimile edition; cf. http://digi.vatlib.it/view/MSS_Vat.gr.1209. Other than the

remain distinct from each other and from the Masoretic text (MT) in many cases. This paper presents some examples of this, defining, expounding, and evaluating them to identify some idiosyncrasies of each textual tradition. Other relevant witnesses—like the *Vetus Latina*, Alexandrinus, and Origen—serve as important aids for reflecting on Kings' textual history. This discussion of the relationship of the Greek witnesses to each other and to MT occurs of course in the wake of the observations of Henry St. J. Thackeray, Dominique Barthélemy, and Siegfried Kreuzer (among others) about the precise boundaries of the translational units in Samuel and Kings, the characteristics of the kaige recension, and the potential for identifying Old Greek (OG) readings within Ant.[2] Ultimately, this paper suggests that neither of the Greek text types purely attests the OG and that scribes probably edited MT in a few stages after the initial translation of Kings into Greek. In other words, while each of the textual traditions for Kings may evince elements of an older version of the book, none of the witnesses exclusively attests the oldest readings. I will attempt to demonstrate this thesis' probability by considering a few theologically and ideologically characteristic verses from the chapter.

---

abbreviations for divine names and καί and ν at the end of a line, the few relevant differences between Ra. and B will be noted here. Most of them probably resulted from simple errors. Abbreviations for divine names appear in vv. 2, 7–9, 11–13, 16–21, 23, 25–26, 27–28, 32–36, 39, and 41. The phrase θεοι ετεροι etc. is not abbreviated. The final ν or καί of a line is abbreviated in vv. 4, 6, 10, 11, 13–19, 21, 23–24, 26, 28–30, 32–35, 39, and 41. The Ra. text is of course the *Handausgabe*, Alfred Rahlfs and Robert Hanhart, *Septuaginta. Editio Altera* (Stuttgart: Deutsche Bibelgesellschaft, 2006). The consulted edition of Ant. is Natalio Fernández Marcos and José Ramón Busto Saiz, *1–2 Reyes*, El texto antioqueno del Biblia Griega, vol. 2 (Madrid: Instituto de Filología del CSIC, Departmento de Filología Bíblica y de Oriente Antiguo, 1992).

2. For Thackeray's observations about the distinct translational units in Reigns, cf. Henry St. J Thackeray, "The Greek Translators of the Four Books of Kings," *JTS* 8 (1907): 262–78. For Barthélemy, cf. Dominique Barthélemy, *Les devanciers d'Aquila*, VTSup 10 (Leiden: Brill, 1963). For an overview of the relevance of Ant. for the text history of Samuel-Kings, cf. Natalio Fernández Marcos, "The Antiochene Edition in the Text History of the Greek Bible," in *Der Antiochenische Text der Septuaginta in seiner Bezeugung und seiner Bedeutung*, ed. Siegfried Kreuzer and Marcus Sigismund (Göttingen: Vandenhoeck & Ruprecht, 2013), 57–73. For a summary of Kreuzer's work and a bibliography, cf. Siegfried Kreuzer, "Der Antiochenische Text der Septuaginta. Forschungsgeschichte und eine neue Perspektive," in *Der Antiochenische Text der Septuaginta in seiner Bezeugung und seiner Bedeutung*, ed. Siegfried Kreuzer and Marcus Sigismund (Göttingen: Vandenhoeck & Ruprecht, 2013), 23–56. Cf., also for a position more consistent with that proffered here, Natalio Fernández Marcos, "The Lucianic Text in the Books of Kingdoms: From Lagarde to the Textual Pluralism," in *De Septuaginta: Studies in Honour of John William Wevers on His Sixty-Fifth Birthday*, ed. Albert Pietersma and Claude Cox (Mississauga: Benben Publications, 1984), 161–74.

2 Kgs // 4 Kgdms 17:1

V.	MT	Ra.	Ant.
1	בִּשְׁנַת שְׁתֵּים עֶשְׂרֵה לְאָחָז מֶלֶךְ יְהוּדָה מָלַךְ הוֹשֵׁעַ בֶּן־אֵלָה בְשֹׁמְרוֹן עַל־יִשְׂרָאֵל תֵּשַׁע שָׁנִים	ἐν ἔτει δωδεκάτῳ τῷ Αχαζ βασιλεῖ Ιουδα ἐβασίλευσεν Ωσηε υἱὸς Ηλα ἐν Σαμαρείᾳ ἐπὶ Ισραηλ ἐννέα ἔτη	ἐν ἔτει δωδεκάτῳ Ἀχαζ βασιλέως Ἰούδα ἐβασίλευσεν Ὡσῆε υἱὸς Ἠλὰ ἐν Σαμαρείᾳ ἐπὶ Ἰσραὴλ ἐννέα ἔτη.

The best place to begin this survey is the opening verse of the chapter. The first verse of 4 Kgdms 17 presents two exiguous differences in the Greek traditions. One notes the additional dative article τῷ in Ra. (= B) when contrasted with Ant. This additional article matches the dative βασιλεῖ attested in Ra. This in turn demonstrates that Ra. is closer to MT than Ant. is; Ant. attests the more syntactically adequate genitive βασιλέως, whereas the dative in Ra. matches the use of the ל in MT. However, in this case Ra. ≠ B. Instead, B has the curious combination of the dative article τῷ with the genitive noun βασιλέως. Rather than transmit the text of B in this case, Rahlfs relied on Alexandrinus (A) and Venetus (N, = Basilo-Vaticanus), as well as a number of minuscules, in reconstructing his OG version. More likely, these later majuscules and minuscules present secondary correctives to an OG corrupted in transmission. In this instance, the direction of corruption can be explained readily, in my opinion: the OG (or an earlier stage of the Greek, at least) either looked like Ant. or included the genitive object τοῦ, but this reading was corrupted through dittography. Vaticanus itself attests precisely this dittography: the dative article here came about through the duplication of the last two letters of the number δωδεκάτῳ, perhaps replacing the genitive article or supplying an otherwise absent article. Later, this apparent grammatical error was corrected in the fashion attested by A, N, and the various minuscules, which—at the same time—had the happy benefit of correcting the text toward proto-MT. The OG favored the genitive in these framing elements in Kingdoms, as attested throughout Ant. and in the nonkaige portions of B, but usually—though not always—with the article.[3] Should the OG have included an article here, it must have been the matching genitive, as generally preserved in the nonkaige frames of Kingdoms. Were that the case, that could imply that B recorded it incorrectly

---

3. Ant. has the article in 3 Kgdms 15:9, 25, 28, 33; 16:23; 22:52; 4 Kgdms 1:19; 8:25; 13:1, 11; 14:1; 15:1, 13, 17, 23, 27, 32; 16:1; 17:1; and 18:1; Ant. does not have the article in 3 Kgdms 16:6, 15, 38; 4 Kgdms 9:29; 14:23; 15:8. B matches this usage in 15:9, 25, 33; 16:6; 4 Kgdms 9:29; 14:23; and 15:23 [references in 16:15 and 38 absent in B]. 3 Kgdms 22:41 in B uses the dative article, but the genitive noun, probably in a case of dittography, just like in 4 Kgdms 17:1. In 3 Kgdms 16:29 Ant. = 16:28a B, both have the genitive article, but have no noun.

under the influence of the preceding -τω and Ant. must have deleted it. Thus, it seems probable that neither of these Greek versions perfectly delivers the OG, but using both of them permits us to reconstruct a likely OG version.

2 Kgs // 4 Kgdms 17:2

V.	MT	Ra.	Ant.
2	וַיַּעַשׂ הָרַע בְּעֵינֵי יְהוָה רַק לֹא כְּמַלְכֵי יִשְׂרָאֵל אֲשֶׁר הָיוּ לְפָנָיו	καὶ ἐποίησεν τὸ πονηρὸν ἐν ὀφθαλμοῖς κυρίου πλὴν οὐχ ὡς οἱ βασιλεῖς Ισραηλ οἱ ἦσαν ἔμπροσθεν αὐτοῦ	καὶ ἐποίησε τὸ πονηρὸν ἐνώπιον Κυρίου παρὰ πάντας τοὺς γενομένους ἔμπροσθεν αὐτοῦ.

The second verse of 4 Kgdms in B demonstrates elements typical to kaige. First, it demonstrates an essentially perfect superficial translation of each morphosyntactical element of MT. Secondly—and more importantly—B (= Ra.) uses the phrase ἐν ὀφθαλμοῖς as a translation for the Hebrew בעיני. Kaige editors favored this standard equivalence in Kings, particularly in the evaluative notices about a king's reign.[4] On the other hand, Ant. reads ἐνώπιον, the equivalent attested throughout the nonkaige portions of Kingdoms and almost ubiquitously in these evaluative framing elements in Ant.[5] And the distinctions between these versions go beyond the superficial use of equivalents. The Antiochene text views Hoshea more negatively than either B or MT. Regarded in the greater context, Ant. implies that Hoshea thus impacts Israel's downfall more substantially. So, which version of Hoshea is older?

Probably the Antiochene version of Hoshea.[6] Two factors commend this interpretation. First, the negative Ant. Hoshea presents a narratological apex of wickedness before the destruction and resettling of the north. More importantly, the extant *Vetus Latina* manuscripts all attest this reading, either as *et fecit malignum in conspectu Domini prae omnes qui fuerant* (pluperfect) *ante eum* (MSS 91–95) or as *et fecit male in conspectu Domini super omnes qui fuerunt* (perfect) *ante eum* (MS 115 = Vindobonensis). The Greek attested in Ant., παρὰ

---

4. Ἐν ὀφθαλμοῖς κυρίου = בעיני יהוה: 1 Kgs 22:43; 2 Kgs 1:13–14; 3:2, 18; 10:5, 30; 13:2, 11; 14:3; 15:3, 9, 18, 24, 28; 16:2; 17:2, 17; 18:3; 20:3; 21:2, 6, 9, 15–16, 20; 22:2; 23:32, 37; and 24:9. Ἐνώπιον κυρίου = בעיני יהוה: 1 Kgs 11:8; 14:22; 15:5, 11, 26, 34; 16:7, 19, 25, 28[b] (// 22:43 MT), 30; 20:20[G], 25[G]; 2 Kgs 1:18[b] (// 3:2 MT); 8:18, 27; 12:3; 14:24; and 24:19. No nonkaige text in B attests ἐνώπιον κυρίου for בעיני יהוה.

5. Exceptions in 4 Kgdms 15:18; 16:2.

6. While Jürgen Werlitz and Siegfried Kreuzer note the differences in the traditions, they make no comment on the priority of the variants. Jürgen Werlitz and Siegfried Kreuzer, "Basileion IV. Das vierte Buch der Königtümer / das zweite Buch der Könige. Nach dem antiochenischen Text," in *Genesis bis Makkabäer*, vol. 1 of *Septuaginta Deutsch: Erläuterungen und Kommentare*, ed. Martin Karrer and Wolfgang Kraus (Stuttgart: Deutsche Bibelgesellschaft, 2011), 964

πάντας τοὺς γενομένους ἔποσθεν αὐτοῦ, strikingly reminds the reader of the evaluations of both Omri (3 Kgdms 16:25) and Ahab (16:30 B = 16:39 Ant.); only the adverb ὑπέρ instead of παρά distinguishes the two.[7] With these factors in mind, it seems more likely that Ant. presents something closer to OG, if not OG, than B. This in turn implies that OG favored a *Vorlage* distinct from MT. This supposed *Vorlage* must have been edited to be something closer to what we currently find in MT. Vaticanus matches MT, suggesting that someone edited an older Greek version to be more consistent with its contemporary Hebrew reference text. The translation technique attested in this verse and the vocabulary of ἐν ὀφθαλμοῖς commend identifying this person or these persons with some editor or editors in the kaige tradition.

2 KGS // 4 KGDMS 17:4

V.	MT	Ra.	Ant.
4	וַיִּמְצָא מֶלֶךְ־אַשּׁוּר בְּהוֹשֵׁעַ קֶשֶׁר אֲשֶׁר שָׁלַח מַלְאָכִים אֶל־סוֹא מֶלֶךְ־מִצְרַיִם וְלֹא־הֶעֱלָה מִנְחָה לְמֶלֶךְ אַשּׁוּר כְּשָׁנָה בְשָׁנָה וַיַּעַצְרֵהוּ מֶלֶךְ אַשּׁוּר וַיַּאַסְרֵהוּ בֵּית כֶּלֶא	καὶ εὗρεν βασιλεὺς Ἀσσυρίων ἐν τῷ Ὡσηε ἀδικίαν ὅτι ἀπέστειλεν ἀγγέλους πρὸς Σηγωρ βασιλέα Αἰγύπτου καὶ οὐκ ἤνεγκεν μαναα τῷ βασιλεῖ Ἀσσυρίων ἐν τῷ ἐνιαυτῷ ἐκείνῳ καὶ ἐπολιόρκησεν αὐτὸν ὁ βασιλεὺς Ἀσσυρίων καὶ ἔδησεν αὐτὸν ἐν οἴκῳ φυλακῆς.	καὶ εὗρεν βασιλεὺς ἀσσυρίων ἐν Ὡσῆε ἐπιβουλήν, διότι ἀπέστειλεν ἀγγέλους πρὸς Ἀδραμέλεχ τὸν Αἰθίοπα τὸν κατοικοῦντα ἐν Αἰγύπτῳ. καὶ ἦν Ὡσῆε φέρων δῶρα τῷ βασιλεῖ ἀσσυρίων ἐνιαυτὸν κατ' ἐνιαυτόν, ἐν δὲ τῷ ἐνιαυτῷ οὐκ ἤνεγκεν αὐτῷ μαναά. καὶ ὕβρισε τὸν Ὡσῆε ὁ βασιλεὺς ἀσσυρίων καὶ ἐπολιόρκησεν αὐτὸν καὶ ἔδησεν αὐτὸν ἐν οἴκῳ φυλακῆς.

For 4 Kgdms 17:4, Ra. = B. yet Ant. is substantially longer than B.[8] At first glance, MT = Ra., but with closer inspection, a number of problems become apparent. The article before the proper name Ὡσηε in Ra. does not match any element of MT. This contradicts the typical usage of articles in kaige, which generally have some graphical equivalent in MT, whether the article ה or the marker of the direct object את or some preposition (see above to v. 1), as Kreuzer has satisfactorily demonstrated. Note that Ant. does not have this article, and thus has an appearance ironically more in line with what one would expect from kaige. Thus, since the translation technique regarding articles is inconsistent with kaige,

---

7. In each of these cases Ant. = B.
8. Again, while recognizing the distinctions in this verse, Werlitz and Kreuzer proffer no comment on the priority of any reading ("Basileion IV Ant," 964).

one can regard B as closer to the OG than Ant. is, or B could even be identical with OG for this reading.

Again in the fourth verse, B's translation of קשר with ἀδικία remains otherwise unparalleled in the kaige texts of Kingdoms. For this Hebrew root, kaige tended to favor some verbal or nominal form of the Greek root συστρέφω.[9] On the other hand, kaige favors ἀδικία as a translation for עון, as does Dan-θ′, which regularly uses ἀδικία as a standard equivalent for עון in the Hebrew sections.[10] Nonetheless, ἐπιβουλή—as in Ant.—never appears in Kingdoms at all otherwise, as an equivalent for קשר or any other root, regardless of whether one relies on B or Ant.[11] Statistically speaking, then, it seems unlikely that either of the Greek versions we have of Kings translated the term קשר currently found in MT. At the very least, they must have been inconsistent with their other usages in this one instance. Of the two Greek terms here, B's ἀδικία ("unrighteousness") is clearly more theological than Ant.'s ἐπιβουλή ("plot against"), and even more theological than MT's קשר "revolt."

Superficially at least, it thus seems that Ant. stands closer than B to MT in this case, even if MT and Ant. may not have been identical. This unusual translation in Ant. commends it having read something else, though what it was must remain speculation. Likely the reading was at least similar to MT. Perhaps this presents evidence of genuine Lucianic editing toward a proto-MT that was inconsistent with OG. The Hebrew textual tradition must have been edited sometime after the translation of Kings into Greek, but before the time of Lucian. Since the *Vetus Latina* implies readings similar to the Antiochene text and MT (MS 115: *insidia*; MSS 91–95: *cogitationem adversus eum*), but distinct from B, one can perhaps tentatively date this editing to the decades surrounding the transition between eras. Considered together, this evidence could again suggest preferring B as OG for this reading.

The name recorded for the king of Egypt in 4 Kgdms 17:4 creates substantial problems. For example, B/Ra.'s transcription of the proper name recorded in MT, סוא, with Σηγωρ is surprising; one would expect Σηγωρ to reflect some Hebrew sibilant (צ, ס, שׁ, שׂ) followed by an ע or ג and then a ר.[12] Yet, no such tradition for spelling the name like this exists anywhere, and at best the ס appears to have been shared between MT and B. Perhaps someone confused the ו and ג, as well as א and ר. But as far as I see it, such confusion—particularly for א and ר—is only really conceivable in the paleo-Hebrew script, *a* and *r* respectively.

---

9. Cf. 2 Kgs 14:19; 15:15, and 30, but also 1 Kgs 16:16.

10. Cf. Dan-θ′ 9:13, 16, and 24.

11. The Greek ἐπίβουλος does occur in some cases as an equivalent for שטן; cf. 1 Sam 29:4; 2 Sam 19:23; and 1 Kgs 5:18, but 1 Kgs 11:14, 23, and 25.

12. The Hexapla corrected the reading to match proto-MT, proffering σωα, which A and N followed.

At the same time, the name Adrammelech mentioned in Ant. hardly makes sense here. It cannot have anything to do with the Hebrew סוא. Otherwise, the name Ἀδραμέλεχ is reserved for one of Sennacherib's sons (cf. 2 Kgs 19:37 // Isa 37:38) or a deity (cf. 2 Kgs 17:31). No other text identifies him as an Ethiopian king in Egypt. Thus, it is more likely that someone removed this name as inconsistent with other biblical and extrabiblical data than that someone added it at a later time. Even Rahlfs considered it a pre-Lucianic, Antiochene reading found already in the writings of Theophilus of Antioch.[13] That means that Ant. might attest the OG in this longer reading. Again the *Vetus Latina* adds weight to this thesis. Should this have been the case, someone must have emended the text before the kaige recension read whatever it did (I would suggest something like סגר or סער). Should kaige have read differently from what we now find in MT, we would have to reckon with at least two recensions or transmutations of the Hebrew text of Kings after the OG translation: one to whatever kaige read and one that edited that (or made a mistake) to what we now have in MT. This, combined with some other evidence, aids in identifying Ant.'s longer reading as closer to OG than B is.

Rahlfs regards Ant.'s translation of כשנה בשנה as a corrective toward MT (B translated incorrectly in his opinion). In order to increase the impact of the phrase שנה בשנה, Lucian created a new sentence repeating the main points from MT and B. Evidence for this appears in Lucian's copying of the transliteration μαναα from B, when Lucian otherwise used δωρα.[14] However, Rahlfs overlooked 1 Sam 1:7, a nonkaige text that translates the Hebrew שנה בשנה with ἐνιαυτὸν κατ' ἐνιαυτόν.[15] This equivalency remains identical with that found in 2 Kgs 17:4 Ant. That could imply that Ant. presents an OG reading. Perhaps parablepsis or some other error stands behind this difference. Rahlfs' suggestion that Lucian created a longer reading, copying material from elsewhere in the verse might still be possible; however, one must note that Ant.'s suggested copying does not match Ra. in Ra.'s mentioning the title of the king of Assyria. Lucian would also have to have added the phrase καὶ ὕβρισε τὸν Ὡσῆε ὁ βασιλεὺς ἀσσυρίων, unlike anything in either Ra. or MT. Rahlfs offers no explanation for this addition. Considered together, it

---

13. Cf. Alfred Rahlfs, *Lucians Rezension der Königsbücher* (Göttingen: Vandenhoeck & Ruprecht, 1911), 114–15. He included it in his catalogue of pre-Lucianic readings that could not have resulted from Lucianic editing of OG. Cf. Rahlfs, *Lucians Rezension*, 290.

14. Cf. Rahlfs, *Lucians Rezension*, 208.

15. Franz Winter and Siegfried Kreuzer, "Basileion IV: Das vierte Buch der Königtümer / Das zweite Buch der Könige; Nach dem Text der Handausgabe von Rahlfs," in *Genesis bis Makkabäer*, vol. 1 of *Septuaginta Deutsch: Erläuterungen und Kommentare*, ed. Martin Karrer and Wolfgang Kraus (Stuttgart: Deutsche Bibelgesellschaft, 2011), 100 regard Ra. (which they here identify as "LXX") as a paraphrase of MT, which is perhaps correct. It does surprise the exegete that the kaige version of this phrase remains so distinct from MT.

remains more likely that the kaige text in B was emended to be more like MT than that Ant. was emended in several ways to be less like MT. One other case in 17:4 demonstrates, however, that MT must have been edited again after the recensional work found in kaige.

The term, apparently as a translation for the Hebrew √עצר in 4 Kgdms 17:4, present in both Ant. and Ra. (= B), comes from the Greek πολιορκέω. The equivalency attested here stands uniquely in Kingdoms and thus raises suspicion. Perusing the versions demonstrates that kaige favors πολιορκέω for another Hebrew term: √צור used as a verb;[16] cf. 2 Sam 20:15; 2 Kgs 16:5; 17:5 (!); 18:9; and 24:11. Otherwise the nonkaige translators of Kingdoms favored κάθιζω with either the affixed prepositions περι- or δια- for Hebrew √צור; cf. 2 Sam 11:1; 1 Kgs 15:27: 16:17; 20:1 MT; and 2 Kgs 6:24–25.[17] On the other hand, the translators and even editors of Kingdoms apparently favored the Greek verb ἔχω with either of the attached prefixes ἀπό- or συν- as an equivalent for √עצר; cf. 1 Sam 21:6, 8; 2 Sam 24:21, 25; 1 Kgs 8:35; 21:21 MT; 2 Kgs 4:24; 9:8; and 14:26.[18] It seems likely, then, that 2 Kgs 17:4 originally read וַיַּצְרֵהוּ (without the vowels in its *Vorlage* of course) for MT's וַיַּעַצְרֵהוּ and that the ע currently found in MT resulted from a scribal error or an emendation after the translation of the text into Greek, even after the kaige editing of OG toward MT attested in B. It looks like it may have been what Jerome read when translating the Vulgate (*vinctum* from *vinio*). Considered together, these data suggest that proto-MT changed sometime after the text found in B was edited toward proto-MT and whatever recensional activity Lucian may have undertaken, but before Jerome's translation into Latin.

2 KGS // 4 KGDMS 17:7

V.	MT	Ra.	Ant.
7	וַיְהִי כִּי־חָטְאוּ בְנֵי־יִשְׂרָאֵל לַיהוָה אֱלֹהֵיהֶם הַמַּעֲלֶה אֹתָם מֵאֶרֶץ מִצְרַיִם מִתַּחַת יַד פַּרְעֹה מֶלֶךְ־מִצְרָיִם וַיִּירְאוּ אֱלֹהִים אֲחֵרִים	καὶ ἐγένετο ὅτι ἥμαρτον οἱ υἱοὶ Ισραηλ τῷ κυρίῳ θεῷ αὐτῶν τῷ ἀναγαγόντι αὐτοὺς ἐκ γῆς Αἰγύπτου ὑποκάτωθεν χειρὸς Φαραω βασιλέως Αἰγύπτου καὶ ἐφοβήθησαν θεοὺς ἑτέρους	καὶ ἐγένετο ὀργὴ Κυρίου ἐπὶ τὸν Ἰσραήλ, διότι ἥμαρτον οἱ υἱοὶ Ἰσραὴλ Κυρίῳ τῷ θεῷ αὐτῶν τῷ ἀναγαγόντι αὐτοὺς ἐκ Αἰγύπτου ὑποκάτωθεν χειρὸς Φαραω βασιλέως Αἰγύπτου ἀφ' ἧς ἡμέρας ἀνήγαγεν αὐτοὺς καὶ ἕως τῆς ἡμέρας ταύτης, καὶ ἐφοβήθησαν θεοὺς ἑτέρους,

---

16. This distinguishes the translation from the noun צור.

17. Note that 2 Kgs 5:23 presents no obvious Greek translation for this Hebrew term; MT 1 Kgs 7:15 and 2 Kgs 12:11 each present unique translations (from χωνεύω [probably from יצק] and σφίγγω [otherwise only attested in Prov 5:22], respectively). 1 Sam 23:8 presents the exact reverse situation to that postulated here for 2 Kgs 17:4.

18. The only real exceptions to this trend are 1 Sam 9:7; 1 Kgs 18:44; and the text at hand, 2 Kgs 17:4. Again, this favors the argumentation for the changing text proposed here.

Verse 17:7 presents some interesting theological variants between the Greek traditions. In this case, B once again remains substantially closer to MT than Ant. does, including every graphical element present in the consonantal text. This fact can be seen in its use of the definite articles and in its plus of γῆς when contrasted with Ant. The so-called Lucianic text contains two substantial pluses and two minor variants in this verse.[19] The two minor variants are the reading διότι instead of ὅτι and the transposition of the dative definite article τῷ. Kaige editors only ever rarely kept or used διότι in Kingdoms, suggesting that its removal would be consistent with their editorial technique.[20] The Antiochene text does not use this term overwhelmingly often either (some ten times in Kingdoms mostly in γδ), suggesting that it presents OG in this case. The transposition of the article remains consistent with kaige's technique as well. Taken together, these observations suggest that 2 Kgs 17:7 underwent recensional activity from someone in the kaige school.

As to the more substantial pluses in Ant., each of them makes a significant theological point: the first reflects on YHWH's anger being against Israel, explaining in the context precisely what led to Israel's destruction;[21] the second plus provides a more negative evaluation in Ant. than in the other witnesses in that it reports that the sinning against God continued from the time of the Exodus to the present.[22] While theoretically possible that someone added these phrases at such a late phase of transmission, it seems more likely that their harsh tone caused their removal from the developing MT tradition and its reflection in the kaige text of B. Palimpsestus Vindobonensis also commends the Antiochene reading as old.

2 Kgs // 4 Kgdms 17:19

V.	MT	Ra.	Ant.
19	גַּם־יְהוּדָה לֹא שָׁמַר אֶת־מִצְוֹת יְהוָה אֱלֹהֵיהֶם וַיֵּלְכוּ בְּחֻקּוֹת יִשְׂרָאֵל אֲשֶׁר עָשׂוּ	καί γε Ιουδας οὐκ ἐφύλαξεν τὰς ἐντολὰς κυρίου τοῦ θεοῦ αὐτῶν καὶ ἐπορεύθησαν ἐν τοῖς δικαιώμασιν Ισραηλ οἷς ἐποίησαν	καί γε καὶ 'Ιούδας καὶ αὐτὸς οὐκ ἐφύλαξε τὰς ἐντολὰς Κυρίου τοῦ θεοῦ αὐτοῦ, καὶ ἐπορεύθη ἐν τοῖς δικαιώμασι παντὸς Ἰσραήλ οἷς ἐποίησαν, καὶ ἀπώσαντο τὸν Κύριον ἐξ αὐτῶν ἅπαν τὸ σπέρμα Ἰσραήλ.

---

19. Cf. the observations in Werlitz and Kreuzer, "Basileion IV Ant," 964–65.

20. The only occasions are 2 Sam 13:12; 19:43; and 1 Kgs 22:18.

21. Rahlfs curiously considered it only an expansion so that the Hebrew phrase ויהי כי would have a more satisfactory ending; cf. Rahlfs, *Lucians Rezension*, 278.

22. Again, Rahlfs considered this a Lucianic addition, in this case based on the similar references to the Exodus in 1 Sam 8:8 and 2 Sam 7:6; cf. Rahlfs, *Lucians Rezension*, 254. He did not consider the alternative, that the other witnesses removed it to avoid such a glaringly negative evaluation of Israel.

Verse 19 contains significant distinctions regarding the evaluation of Judah and God's interaction with them. In this verse, it again becomes clear that B essentially matches MT, commending its identification with kaige recensional undertakings. The Antiochene text more explicitly condemns Judah in a few ways. First it identifies it more as a single entity rather than as a group, making Judah "himself" reject the Lord "his God," and not "their God" as in B and MT.[23] The *Vetus Latina* again supports this so-called Lucianic reading as older. At the same time, Ant. includes Judah more explicitly in the sins of the Israelites by noting that they "wandered in the ways of all Israel." Kings rarely used the phrase "all Israel" to refer to the Northern Kingdom, particularly after its recounting of the division of the monarchy. By the end of 1 Kgs 14, the term essentially vanishes; cf. 3 Kgdms 15:33; 16:16; and 4 Kgdms 3:6, but 3 Kgdms 18:19 and 22:17. Terminologically, the Greek translation (and probably its older *Vorlage*) goes to some lengths to distinguish the north from the united monarchy or those faithful to the Lord: "Israel" refers to the north, whereas "all Israel" refers to all of the tribes or all of the faithful. By referencing "all Israel" in this negative evaluation, Ant. essentially lumps Judah and Israel together. It seems more likely that someone at a later date would have emended this text to remove this conglomeration. Adding the adjective "all" seems hardly likely, but its removal makes perfect sense in an ideology that continued to draw or even expand distinctions between southerners and northerners. This all commends understanding Ant. as the OG in these cases, again with support from the *Vetus Latina*.[24]

2 KGS // 4 KGDMS 17:26

V.	MT	Ra.	Ant.
26	וַיֹּאמְרוּ לְמֶלֶךְ אַשּׁוּר לֵאמֹר הַגּוֹיִם אֲשֶׁר הִגְלִיתָ וַתּוֹשֶׁב בְּעָרֵי שֹׁמְרוֹן לֹא יָדְעוּ אֶת־מִשְׁפַּט אֱלֹהֵי הָאָרֶץ וַיְשַׁלַּח־בָּם אֶת־הָאֲרָיוֹת וְהִנָּם מְמִיתִים אוֹתָם כַּאֲשֶׁר אֵינָם יֹדְעִים אֶת־מִשְׁפַּט אֱלֹהֵי הָאָרֶץ	καὶ εἶπον τῷ βασιλεῖ Ἀσσυρίων λέγοντες τὰ ἔθνη ἃ ἀπῴκισας καὶ ἀντεκάθισας ἐν πόλεσιν Σαμαρείας οὐκ ἔγνωσαν τὸ κρίμα τοῦ θεοῦ τῆς γῆς καὶ ἀπέστειλεν εἰς αὐτοὺς τοὺς λέοντας καὶ ἰδού εἰσιν θανατοῦντες αὐτοὺς καθότι οὐκ οἴδασιν τὸ κρίμα τοῦ θεοῦ τῆς γῆς	καὶ εἶπον τῷ βασιλεῖ ἀσσυρίων λέγοντες Τὰ ἔθνη ἃ ἀπῴκισας καὶ κατῴκισας ἐν ταῖς πόλεσι Σαμαρείας, οὐκ ἔγνωσαν τὸν νόμον τοῦ θεοῦ τῆς γῆς, καὶ ἀπέστειλεν εἰς αὐτοὺς λέοντας, καὶ ἰδοὺ εἰσιν θανατοῦντες ἐν αὐτοῖς, καθότι οὐκ οἴδασι τὸ κρίμα τοῦ θεοῦ τῆς γῆς.

---

23. The Septuaginta Deutsch translates incorrectly in these cases; cf. Wolfgang Kraus and Martin Karrer, ed., *Septuaginta Deutsch: Das griechische Alte Testament in deutscher Übersetzung* (Stuttgart: Deutsche Bibelgesellschaft, 2009), 466.

24. Werlitz and Kreuzer, "Basileion IV Ant," 965 reckon with a distinct *Vorlage* for Ant. in the longer conclusion of v. 19 (= v. 20 in Ra. and MT). This supposition is probably accurate.

Turning our attention to verse 26, one notes that B matches MT in terms of the usage of articles. This commends it as a verse revised by kaige. Simultaneously, this ascription remains somewhat difficult for the entirety of the verse, since its translation of וַתּוֹשֶׁב with ἀντεκάθισας is *hapax legomenon* and thus remains both distinct from MT and inconsistent with kaige's translation technique, unless kaige had a distinct *Vorlage*. On the other hand, Ant. does match MT in this case. This makes B's reading, at least in this term, possibly an OG reading. More importantly in this verse, one notices the distinct terminology for the teaching (νόμος) or the judgment (κρίμα) within the Greek traditions. Again in this case, B = MT, whereas Ant. differs from both. The Masoretic tradition and Vaticanus mention that the people addressing the king of Assyria note that those dwelling in the land remain ignorant of the judgment of the God of the land. The so-called Lucianic recension ascribes their difficulties to ignorance of the law of the God of the land. How might one explain this? I would suggest that later scribes editing the text away from something like Ant. holds more plausibility than the other way around. My reasoning is that later scribes may have felt reticence about two matters described in this verse: (1) that the northerners learned the law of the God of the land (i.e., YHWH), and (2) that the law of the God of the land was reintroduced by the king of Assyria. When one recognizes that νόμος presents a standard equivalent for the Hebrew תורה, this becomes all the more likely. Perhaps later editors wanted to refute Torah's existence in the north after Israel's downfall. This could evince tension between these scribes and the people living in Samaria, perhaps during the late Hellenistic or early Roman periods. To this end, they emended the text so that the people living in Samaria were unfamiliar with the judgment (A = "judgments") of the God of the land.

Conclusions

Many more distinctions could be discussed here, like the shorter reading in verses 14–15 in B than in MT or Ant. or the shorter reading in MT than B and Ant. in verse 32, but generally they only serve to support the few observations made here about the textual transmission of Kings / Kingdoms in the various traditions. So, finally, what preliminary conclusions does this brief survey permit? The most important issue remains the inconsistency in the versions. This inconsistency precludes the identification of a single Greek manuscript or even manuscript tradition with the OG. Rather, it seems that these texts must have undergone changes in several stages. For example, the opening of the chapter suggests that an error must have crept into the tradition of Vaticanus at some point. Rahlfs, like some antique scribes, changed the text to make it more grammatically consistent internally, while simultaneously making it more closely match proto-MT. The Deuteronomistic evaluation of Hoshea in verse 2 varies in the witnesses as well. While MT and B reduce Hoshea's wickedness, Ant. has a more unfavorable view of him, describing him in terminology quite similar to Ahab and Omri. The contrast between these versions demonstrates distinct attitudes about the monarch's personal culpability for Israel's destruction. This implies in turn that the text was emended from a version that suggested more personal accountability to one that was more general. Likewise, the distinct names of the Egyptian king in verse 4 suggest that the Hebrew parent tradition could have changed on multiple occasions after the initial translation into Greek. Vaticanus reflects one possible stage in which Adrammelech had been removed, while MT demonstrates another. Most importantly, this survey has advanced three matters: (1) the appreciation of the so-called Lucianic recension. Ant. apparently has much to offer in reconstructing OG readings, as seen in some cases in this selection and contrary to Rahlfs' evaluation of that tradition. The Old Latin translation often supports Ant., demonstrating that these readings must be older than Lucian. At the same time, it would be inappropriate to identify Ant. *in toto* with OG, since it also appears to have undergone minor editing: missing articles, occasionally increasing proximity to MT, et cetera (2) The kaige recension was inconsistently applied to this chapter and presumably to many or any others in Kings. While it becomes clear that the Greek text in Vaticanus has often been emended towards a Hebrew text like MT, this has by no means been carried to its logical and consistent conclusion. (3) Some of the distinctions in the versions demonstrate theological or ideological distinctions, meaning that they must be especially appreciated in their nuances before any general models for the diachronic development of the book can be postulated. One notes, for example, that the Deuteronomistic tenor toward Hoshea varies in the witnesses. That implies that some Deuteronomistic editor or recensor may have added or composed that evaluation, but that other editors—regardless of which version you accept as older—later changed that evaluation. Since redaction-historical models of Kings generally base on such theological language, it becomes paramount to identify which Deuteronomistic version was oldest. (4) The evidence suggests that MT must have been edited on a few occasions after the translation of OG. This becomes apparent from the distinctions between OG, kaige, Lucian, and MT, demonstrating that the Hebrew text continued to morph in some minor ways into the Common Era. Nonetheless, by comparing and contrasting the witnesses we can arrive at older stages of the book of Kings. Only once this has been achieved can one really concentrate on developing literary-critical and redaction-historical models for the development of that narrative.

אולי—Perhaps in the Septuagint

Seppo Sipilä

Abstract: This paper discusses the renderings of the Hebrew adverb אולי in the Septuagint. The adverb appears forty-five times in the Hebrew Bible. We shall discuss the various ways translators have handled the adverb. After consulting tools like Muraoka's Hebrew/Aramaic Index to the Septuagint, one might expect to find the Greek adverb ἴσως as a counterpart for the Hebrew adverb, but this is only rarely the case. In half of the cases, the Greek counterpart for the Hebrew adverb is a future conditional construction. The other half includes various other ways to handle the adverb. Purely literal translations like ἴσως are rare, making our topic worthy of closer investigation.

אולי IN HEBREW

Biblical Hebrew does not contain many adverbs and clausal adverbs are even rarer.[1] אולי belongs to this rare group of Hebrew clausal adverbs.[2] In the standard Hebrew dictionaries, the common translations for אולי are "perhaps," "vielleicht," or "peut-être." Normally, the discussions offered by various dictionaries are limited mainly to a set of recommended translations appearing in certain situations such as in expressions of hope, request or fear. Classical grammars of Hebrew do not normally discuss אולי,[3] but some modern grammars do. Waltke and O'Connor

---

1. Ronald J. Williams, *Hebrew Syntax: An Outline*, 2nd ed. (Toronto: University of Toronto Press, 1976), §377. On Hebrew adverbs in general, see, e.g., *IBHS*, §39.1b.

2. Joshua Blau, *An Adverbial Construction in Hebrew and Arabic: Sentence Adverbials in Frontal Position Separated from the Rest of the Sentence*, Proceedings of Israel Academy of Sciences and Humanities 6.1 (Jerusalem: Israel Academy of Sciences and Humanities, 1977), however, does not discuss אולי.

3. A look at a classical grammar like GKC shows that the discussion is mainly on the morphology of a set of adverbs (§100), but their syntactical treatment is lacking. Waltke and O'Connor (*IBHS*, §39.3.1a) lament that "many grammars of Hebrew in fact pass over the adverbs." They mean that any treatment of the adverbs might be lacking.

define אולי as a disjunct. As such, it modifies the content of a clause, especially its truth conditions.[4] As they say nothing more about the functions of אולי, we need to look closely at the actual usages of אולי.

Our adverb appears forty-five times in the Hebrew Bible, but late authors use it rarely. It appears only in direct discourse, and in various contexts. Two examples may suffice to give us an idea about the differences in the usage of אולי.

In Gen 16:2, Sarah says to Abraham בא נא אל שפחתי אולי אבנה ממנה, "enter in my maid servant, perhaps I will be build up from her" (i.e., perhaps I will have a child from her).

In Hos 8:7, on the other hand, God says through the prophet קמה אין לו צמח בלי יעשה קמח אולי יעשה זרים יבלעהו, "grain has no growth for it, nor will it produce any flour. Perhaps it will produce, strangers will consume it."

We can see that the adverb makes the content of a clause uncertain, but there can be different kinds of uncertainty. In Genesis, the uncertainty links with Sarah's command. Human experience tells us that not every sexual intercourse results into pregnancy. In Hosea, on the other hand, the obvious conflict with the previous statement creates the uncertainty. If there is no harvest, any thoughts about its destiny are by necessity mere speculation.

In principle, uncertainty can have a connection with two different grammatical means. A speaker can indicate uncertainty of an expression by referring to the truth-value of the content of the clause. She or he can also indicate this by referring to the nature of the source of the information behind the clause.[5] These two types have a connection to two different mental processes, because the mechanism on how to evaluate the truth-value of the content and how to deal with the nature of the source are different, even though the results of these two can overlap. We might think further and claim that different mental processes affect the ways a translator handles an issue at stake.

While אולי is a modal adverb, it is useful to ask on what basis the speaker grounds the uncertainty expressed by the Hebrew adverb, because this has a connection to the mental processes of the reader of the text, including the ancient translators. In our reading of the texts, two main reasons cause the uncertainty expressed by the adverb אולי. Sometimes the context signals to us that the case is about a lack of necessary information. In other cases, doubt regarding the results of the previous action causes the uncertainty. This paper claims that these two

---

4. *IBHS*, §39.3.4. The term disjunct is taken from the grammarians of English.

5. Lloyd B. Anderson, "Evidentials, Paths of Change, and Mental Maps: Typologically Regular Asymmetries," in *Evidentiality: The Linguistic Coding of Epistemology*, ed. Wallace Chafe and Johanna Nichols (Ablex: Norwood, 1986), 310–11; Jan Nuyts, *Epistemic Modality, Language, and Conceptualization: A Cognitive-Pragmatic Perspective* (John Benjamins: Amsterdam, 2000), 27; and Raf van Rooy, "The Relevance of Evidentiality for Ancient Greek: Some Explorative Steps through Plato," *Journal of Greek Linguistics* 16 (2016): 5–6.

different types of uncertainty have a link to two different mental processes. In the case of the lack of information, the process concerns screening the encyclopaedic knowledge (what might be missing from the text?), but in case of previous actions the screening concerns the short-term memory and the communicative situation (what did the text just say?).[6] We shall divide the cases with the Hebrew adverb accordingly into two groups. There are twenty-five cases where the previous action causes the uncertainty and twenty cases where the lack of information prompts it.

THE LXX RENDERINGS

The Septuagint translators have reacted to our adverb in several different ways, but this becomes evident only when we study the cases in detail. The Hatch-Redpath Concordance and Muraoka's Hebrew/Aramaic Index create an expectation that the Greek adverb ἴσως would be the rendering for the Hebrew אולי.[7] One finds ἴσως, however, only four times as the rendering for אולי.[8] In twenty-three cases, the rendering is a conditional construction. In ten cases, we can find an adverbial rendering. A final clause appears in eight cases. Two cases are exceptional and twice the Greek translator might not have had the Hebrew adverb in his *Vorlage* at all. Such a variety of cases calls for a deeper analysis.

We will base our analysis of the Greek translations on the usage of the Hebrew adverb and divide the cases according to the two types of uncertainty connected with the Hebrew adverb. First, we shall look at the cases where the uncertainty and the previous action in the text belong together. Thereafter we shall look at the cases where the lack of information seems to cause the uncertainty in the text.[9]

---

6. Nuyts, *Epistemic Modality*, 261–94 identifies two different processes in speakers' minds; the encyclopaedia and the situational model. These two overlap with the two processes we have in mind. He then claims that the epistemic evaluations take place in either of these two. See, esp., Nuyts, *Epistemic Modality*, 293.

7. HRCS, 695; Takamitsu Muraoka, *Hebrew/Aramaic Index to the Septuagint: Keyed to the Hatch-Redpath Concordance* (Grand Rapids: Baker, 1998), 14.

8. All in all, ἴσως appears ten times on the LXX. Three cases appear in 4 Maccabees and three times the Hebrew counterpart is not the adverb אולי: 1 Sam 25:21 (אך); Jer 5:4 (אך); and Dan 4:24 θ' (הן).

9. On the method used in this paper, see Ilmari Soisalon-Soininen "Methodologische Fragen der Erforschung der Septuaginta-Syntax," in *Studies zur Septuaginta-Syntax*, ed. Ilmari Soisalon-Soininen, AASF 237 (Helsinki: Suomalainen tiedeakatemia, 1987), 41–42.

Table: Greek Renderings of the Hebrew Adverb אולי

Greek rendering	previous action	lack of information
ἴσως	4	
μήποτε	3	3
εἰ + ind.fut.	6	4
ἐάν + subjunctive	2	8
εἰ + opt.		2
εἰ μή + ind.aor.		1
Opt.		1
μή		1
ἵνα	2	
ὅπως	6	
Aliter	2	
Total	25	20

אולי IN CONNECTION WITH THE PREVIOUS ACTION

The Septuagint translators employed six different ways to render the Hebrew adverb in contexts where uncertainty is caused by the previous action. I shall exclude two cases from my analysis, because in those cases, the text of the LXX does not have any counterpart for whole clauses in the MT.[10]

A natural Greek counterpart for the Hebrew adverb is—as mentioned earlier—the Greek adverb ἴσως, because the Greek adverb expresses uncertainty in a similar way to the Hebrew adverb.[11] The use of an adverb can be seen as a literal translation and the use of literal translations in the LXX is not uncommon. However, the adverb ἴσως appears only four times in contexts where uncertainty is caused by a previous action. At the same time, these four form all of the occurrences where the Greek adverb is used as a rendering for the Hebrew adverb, irrespective of the cause of uncertainty. The use of an adverb to render a similar kind of an adverb is easy, because the processing effort is minimal.[12]

---

10. The excluded cases are in Isa 47:12b and in Lam 3:29.

11. Ἴσως is not the only possible adverb the translators could have used. Jerker Blomqvist and Poul Ole Jastrup, *Grekisk Grammatik* (Copenhagen: Akademisk forlag, 1991), §264.2b mentions the adverb τάχα as expressing uncertainty, but it is not used by the LXX translators in rendering the Hebrew adverb. See also *GELS*, 346.

12. On the processing effort, see, e.g., Ernst-August Gutt, *Translation and Relevance: Cognition and Context* (Manchester: St. Jerome, 2000), 28. The general claim is that people tend to minimise the processing efforts when interpreting any communication.

Gen 32:21 אכפרה פניו במנחה ההלכת לפני ואחרי כן אראה פניו אוּלַי יִשָּׂא פָנָי
Ἐξιλάσομαι τὸ πρόσωπον αὐτοῦ ἐν τοῖς δώροις τοῖς προπορευομένοις αὐτοῦ, καὶ μετὰ τοῦτο ὄψομαι τὸ πρόσωπον αὐτοῦ· ἴσως γὰρ προσδέξεται τὸ πρόσωπόν μου

Here, Jacob prepares to meet his brother Esau.[13] The previous action that Jacob is about to do is sending gifts to his brother. Maybe the gifts will produce a friendly reaction. In connection with the adverb ἴσως, the translator employed the conjunction γάρ, but this is not a formal rendering for the Hebrew אוּלַי.

The Greek adverb μήποτε also appears as a counterpart for the Hebrew adverb. The Greek adverb originally meant "never" (= μή ποτε), but in later Greek it came to mean "perhaps" and it is therefore a natural counterpart for the Hebrew adverb.[14] Only the translator of Genesis used μήποτε in contexts where uncertainty is related to the previous action in the text.

Gen 24:5 אוּלַי לא תאבה האשה ללכת אחרי אל הארץ הזאת
Μήποτε οὐ βούλεται ἡ γυνὴ πορευθῆναι μετ' ἐμοῦ ὀπίσω εἰς τὴν γῆν ταύτην

This is a reply by the servant of Abraham to the command to go and get a wife for Isaac from Abraham's relatives abroad (vv. 2–4).[15] The previous action is Abraham's command. The servant wants to protect himself and therefore asks for further instruction on what to do in case his master's intention cannot be met when the girl is not willing to accept the invitation.

Gen 27:12 אוּלַי ימשני אבי והייתי בעיניו כמתעתע
μήποτε ψηλαφήσῃ με ὁ πατήρ μου, καὶ ἔσομαι ἐναντίον αὐτοῦ ὡς καταφρονῶν

Jacob expresses doubt that the instructions from Rebekah may not work out. Jacob has a different skin texture than his brother. The father might be blind, but he can feel the difference of skin.

We can classify the translations where the Hebrew adverb is rendered with a corresponding Greek adverb, either ἴσως or μήποτε, as literal translations. Literal translations like these are naturally something that we may expect to find in the LXX. What is perhaps surprising is the low number of translations with a Greek adverb. Even the less literal translators of the LXX have rendered common conjunctions like ו or כי employing literal translations more often than our adverb.[16]

---

13. The other passages with ἴσως are in Jeremiah: 26(33):3, 36(43):3, and 36(43):7.
14. Takamitsu Muraoka, *A Syntax of Septuagint Greek* (Leuven: Peeters, 2016), §29ba iv discusses the construction μήποτε + the subjunctive as expressing apprehension. On Gen 24:5, see also §83cd.
15. Later on, in 24:39, the servant reports on this discussion and there the translator used μήποτε, too.
16. See, e.g., Anneli Aejmelaeus, *Parataxis in the Septuagint*, AASF 31 (Helsinki: Suomalainen tiedeakatemia, 1982), 122–25; and Seppo Sipilä, *Between Literalness and*

Besides the adverbial renderings for the Hebrew adverb, the Greek translators used *conditional constructions* when dealing with it. The conditional constructions are all future cases, when the uncertainty in Hebrew has a link to the previous action. Future conditional constructions are a natural way to express uncertainty, because the future by itself is uncertain. Future conditional cases are not, however, of equal status when it comes to the degree of uncertainty. The interplay between the predicates of the protasis and the apodosis effect the degree of uncertainty.

When the translator decided to use a conditional construction, the logic of the text changed. The uncertainty is not very clearly a result of any previous action, but is rather an opinion of the speaker in question. At the same time, the translator shifted the focus to the apodosis of the construction. This may be because of a general tendency in many languages to avoid focusing on the evaluation of the state of affairs.[17] Accordingly, a conditional construction might have looked like a tempting possibility to our translators.

In the cases where uncertainty is connected with the previous action in the text, the most common conditional construction has the conjunction εἰ and the future indicative in both clauses, both in the protasis and the apodosis.[18] Grammarians classify this type of conditional construction as neutral or real.[19] Here, the uncertainty is present because of the future, but it is not underlined, unlike some other future conditional constructions. The protasis in this neutral case expresses strong feeling and commonly suggests something undesired, feared, or taking place independent of the speaker's will.[20] Often, but not always, the future indicative in Greek matches with *yiqtol* in Hebrew. As this is not always the case, the Hebrew verb form does not alone explain the use of the future in Greek.

Num 23:3 התיצב על עלתך ואלכה אולי יקרה יהוה לקראתי ודבר מה יראני והגדתי לך
Παράστηθι ἐπὶ τῆς θυσίας σου, καὶ πορεύσομαι, εἴ μοι φανεῖται ὁ θεὸς ἐν συναντήσει, καὶ ῥῆμα, ὃ ἐάν μοι δείξῃ, ἀναγγελῶ σοι

The previous action is the command for King Balak to wait. The prophet Balaam is indicating that he does not wish to encounter God. We can interpret this as a very clever translation where the reader is lead to anticipate God's reply to Balak (vv. 7b–10) and Balak's reaction (v. 11) to it. God will not allow the prophet to curse Israel and this is a message that does not please the king.

Freedom, Publication of the Finnish Exegetical Society 75 (Helsinki: Finnish Exegetical Society, 1999), 74–76.

17. Nuyts, *Epistemic Modality*, 259.

18. According to Muraoka, *Syntax of Septuagint Greek*, §89aaa i, the apodosis in the translated texts of the LXX very often has the future indicative.

19. See, e.g., Muraoka, *Syntax of Septuagint Greek*, §89aa.

20. Herbert Weir Smyth, *Greek Grammar* (Cambridge: Harvard University Press, 1956), §2328.

Sometimes the translators strengthen the uncertainty by adding a particle to the protasis. The reason is simple. The neutral conditional construction indicates only a mild form of uncertainty. Thus, the additional particle signals to the reader that the expression enhances the intended uncertainty.

Num 22:11 עתה לכה קבה לי אתו אולי אוכל להלחם בו וגרשתיו
καὶ νῦν δεῦρο ἄρασαί μοι αὐτόν, εἰ ἄρα δυνήσομαι πατάξαι αὐτὸν καὶ ἐκβαλῶ αὐτὸν ἀπὸ τῆς γῆς

The particle ἄρα underlines the improbability of the protasis.[21] The passage is a part of Balaam's answer to God. The prophet reports that King Balak had asked him to curse Israel. The translator made Balaam express this as if King Balak himself would not believe the victory. In this manner, the translator anticipates the future events; Balak was not able to overcome Israel.

2 Sam 14:15 אדברה נא אל המלך אולי יעשה המלך את דבר אמתו
Λαλησάτω δὴ πρὸς τὸν βασιλέα, εἴ πως ποιήσει ὁ βασιλεὺς τὸ ῥῆμα τῆς δούλης αὐτοῦ
εἴ πως] ὅπως L

The adverb πως also underlines the improbability of the protasis.[22] The previous action is an advice to talk to the king. The use of the adverb only enforces the natural expectation that the king might not listen to an ordinary woman, especially when she, with her polite words, criticizes King David concerning his exiled son, Absalom.

Thus, the translators occasionally wanted to emphasize the improbability by using an additional particle. In all cases, the particle fits very well with the text and helps the reader to realize the intended uncertainty.

The use of a construction with ἐάν in the protasis also indicates uncertainty, but in case of the future constructions, the nuance is that the author sees the protasis as plausible or prominent.[23] The uncertainty then seems to be milder than in the previous cases.

Num 22:6 ועתה לכה נא ארה לי את העם הזה ... אולי אוכל נכה בו ואגרשנו מן הארץ
καὶ νῦν δεῦρο ἄρασαί μοι τὸν λαὸν τοῦτον, ... ἐὰν δυνώμεθα πατάξαι ἐξ αὐτῶν, καὶ ἐκβαλῶ αὐτοὺς ἐκ τῆς γῆς

---

21. John Dewar Denniston, *The Greek Particles*, 2nd ed. (Oxford: Clarendon, 1954), 38; Smyth, *Greek Grammar*, §2796. See also Van Rooy, "Relevance of Evidentiality," 14: "it [ἄρα] suggests a lower degree of epistemic certainty on the speaker's part about the contents of the proposition."

22. See LSJ, 1562. The other case with πως is in Jer 51(28):8.

23. Smyth, *Greek Grammar*, §2322–23; and Muraoka, *Syntax of Septuagint Greek*, §89ab.

This case relates to Num 22:11 discussed earlier. Verse 6 is part of the original request of King Balak. The previous action is the request to curse Israel. As these are the words of King Balak, it is only natural that the uncertainty is played down. Unlike the prophet, the king hardly doubts his success in overcoming Israel with the help of the curse. In verse 11, the prophet expresses the same by indicating the uncertainty.

Hos 8:7 קמה אין לו צמח בלי יעשה קמח אולי יעשה זרים יבלעהו
δράγμα οὐκ ἔχον ἰσχὺν τοῦ ποιῆσαι ἄλευρον· ἐὰν δὲ καὶ ποιήσῃ, ἀλλότριοι καταφάγονται αὐτό

The uncertainty in Hebrew is created by the obvious contradiction of the previous statement that the grain does not produce harvest. The translator seems to put the contradiction out of focus. The conjunction δέ creates a contrast to the previous clause and therefore directs the reader to keep the two separate. The Greek text seems to say that in case there would be a harvest, it is very probable that the enemy would consume it, not the farmers themselves.

The conditional constructions offered translators several possibilities to add nuances to the uncertainty connected with the previous action in the text. They could, therefore, indicate their own interpretation of the text more accurately than by using an adverb to express the uncertainty. Since the use of conditional construction requires considerations of the context of the Hebrew adverb, they cannot be seen as literal translations, but free and suitable ones.

As the Hebrew adverb is rare and only occasionally appears in later texts, there is a possibility that the translators sought help from Aramaic אילו in understanding it.[24] This fact may have directed them to use the conditional constructions as often as they do. Even when this would be possible, the adequate handling of the construction was rather demanding when compared with the use of a Greek adverb.

Finally, one finds several cases where the Hebrew adverb is rendered by using a *final conjunction* ὅπως or ἵνα. This is surprising because the use of a final clause downplays the overall uncertainty indicated by the Hebrew adverb. Only the translators of the Pentateuch used ἵνα. Others used ὅπως.

Gen 16:2 בא נא אל שפחתי אולי אבנה ממנה
εἴσελθε οὖν πρὸς τὴν παιδίσκην μου, ἵνα τεκνοποιήσῃς ἐξ αὐτῆς

Sarai's confidence in Greek that she will get a child is premature according to the normal human experience, but in the text of Genesis it is not.[25] Indeed, the boy is born. The translator indicates this to the reader by using a final construction.

---

24. Jan Joosten kindly pointed out the possibility of the Aramaic influence to me.

25. The other case in Exod 32:30 is similar. There Moses is confident that he will succeed in atoning the sins of the people.

1 Sam 6:5 ונתתם לאלהי ישראל כבוד אולי יקל את ידו מעליכם
καὶ δώσετε τῷ κυρίῳ δόξαν, <u>ὅπως</u> κουφίσῃ τὴν χεῖρα αὐτοῦ ἀφ' ὑμῶν

While, in Hebrew, it is not certain that honoring the God of Israel would help, in the Greek there is no doubt about it.[26] This might be a theological interpretation by the translator.[27] Perhaps it was difficult for the translator to indicate that honoring God might not bring a positive outcome. The continuation of the story does not reveal if God did react on the action after all or not.

Ezek 12:3 וגלית ממקומך אל מקום אחר לעיניהם אולי יראו כי בית מרי המה
καὶ αἰχμαλωτευθήσῃ ἐκ τοῦ τόπου σου εἰς ἕτερον ἐνώπιον αὐτῶν, <u>ὅπως</u> ἴδωσιν, διότι οἶκος παραπικραίνων ἐστί

In the Hebrew, God is in doubt whether the people will notice the symbolic act of the prophet and react accordingly. After all, they are rebellious, blind, and deaf (v. 2). The Greek text does not hint at the uncertainty, but sets out the issue as neutral and straightforward. Maybe this has to do with the theological interpretation of the text. Perhaps it was difficult for the translators to let God express any doubts at all.

The translators used final clauses in cases where their interpretation demanded setting the uncertainty in the background. In the Pentateuch, this happened only twice. Outside of the Pentateuch, expectations concerning God and his will might have triggered the use of the final clauses, because, in all cases, the uncertainty is connected to the act of God.

אולי IN CONNECTION WITH THE LACK OF INFORMATION

In the cases discussed so far, the uncertainty links with the previous action in the text. However, in some instances this is not the case. Sometimes the uncertainty is based on a missing piece of information. The Septuagint translators employed six different ways to render the Hebrew adverb in contexts where the uncertainty is caused by the lack of necessary information.

When the uncertainty is caused by a lack of information, the Hebrew adverb is rendered with a *Greek adverb* only three times and in all of the cases with μήποτε. It is the only literal rendering used in contexts where the uncertainty is created by the lack of information. The use of an adverb is easy for the translator, because it requires a minimal amount of processing effort.

---

26. The cases in 1 Sam 9:6, Amos 5:15, Jonah 1:6, and Zeph 2:3 are similar.
27. On the theological interpretations in the LXX in general, see Anneli Aejmelaeus, "What We Talk about When We Talk about Translation Technique," in *X Congress of the International Organization for Septuagint and Cognate Studies, Oslo, 1998*, ed. Bernard A. Taylor, SCS 51 (Atlanta: Society of Biblical Literature, 2001), 547–52.

Gen 43:12 ואת הכסף המושב בפי אמתחתיכם תשיבו בידכם אולי משגה הוא
τὸ ἀργύριον τὸ ἀποστραφὲν ἐν τοῖς μαρσίπποις ὑμῶν ἀποστρέψατε μεθ᾽ ὑμῶν·
<u>μήποτε</u> ἀγνόημά ἐστιν

The text does not state the actual error. It was, of course, that the servants of Joseph returned the payment to the brothers. Thus, the μήποτε clause merely expresses apprehension.[28]

1 Kgs 18:27 כי שיח וכי שיג לו וכי דרך לו אולי ישן הוא ויקץ
ὅτι ἀδολεσχία αὐτῷ ἐστιν, καὶ ἅμα μήποτε χρηματίζει αὐτός, ἢ <u>μήποτε</u> καθεύδει αὐτός, καὶ ἐξαναστήσεται
ἢ μήποτε] ἢ ποτε L(-19)

This is part of the ironic comment made by Elijah at Carmel. The previous clause also includes μήποτε and it was natural for the translator to use it here too.[29]

Job 1:5 כי אמר איוב אולי חטאו בני וברכו אלהים בלבבם
ἔλεγεν γάρ ᾽Ἰὼβ <u>Μήποτε</u> οἱ υἱοί μου ἐν τῇ διανοίᾳ αὐτῶν κακὰ ἐνενόησαν πρὸς θεόν

Job seems to play a safe game and offers sacrifices just in case the children had sinned. He does not know it, but supposes that they did. We ought to take the verb ברך as an ironic statement.[30] "Blessing God" means actually the contrary. Supposing that we can use the MT as a rough estimate of the Hebrew *Vorlage* of the Old Greek, the translator dealt with his parent text freely. Most notable, the irony in the Hebrew is lost in the Greek translation.

In cases where a previous action causes the uncertainty and also in cases where the lack of information creates the uncertainty, the Greek translators have employed *conditional constructions* to render the Hebrew adverb. A future conditional construction is a suitable way to render the Hebrew adverb, but the logic and the focus in the text changes when the translator used a conditional construction. When the conjunction is εἰ and both clauses include the future indicative, the construction expresses uncertainty only because the future is unknown.

---

28. Muraoka, *Syntax of Septuagint Greek*, §29ba (iv).
29. On the problems connected with the previous part of the verse, see, e.g., Jobst Bösenecker, "Basileion III: Das dritte Buch der Königtümer / das erste Buch der Könige," in *Septuaginta Deutsch: Erläuterungen und Kommentare zum griechischen Alten Testament*, vol. 1, ed. Martin Karrer and Wolfgang Kraus (Stuttgart: Deutsche Bibelgesellschaft, 2011), 937.
30. On the irony, see, e.g., Dominique Barthélemy et al., ed., *Preliminary and Interim Report on the Hebrew Old Testament Text Project*, vol. 3 (New York: United Bible Societies, 1979), 2.

אוּלַי—Perhaps in the Septuagint

Jer 20:10 אוּלַי יְפֻתֶּה וְנוּכְלָה לוֹ וְנִקְחָה נִקְמָתֵנוּ מִמֶּנּוּ
εἰ ἀπατηθήσεται καὶ δυνησόμεθα αὐτῷ καὶ λημψόμεθα τὴν ἐκδίκησιν ἡμῶν ἐξ αὐτοῦ

This is a malicious wish by the friends of the prophet. They do not know whether the prophet will do this or not. The future indicative in the protasis expresses strong feeling.[31] The Greek construction probably indicates that the malicious friends are not in control of the destiny of the prophet.

Jer 21:2 כִּי נְבוּכַדְרֶאצַּר מֶלֶךְ בָּבֶל נִלְחָם עָלֵינוּ אוּלַי יַעֲשֶׂה יְהוָה אוֹתָנוּ כְּכָל נִפְלְאֹתָיו וְיַעֲלֶה מֵעָלֵינוּ
ὅτι βασιλεὺς Βαβυλῶνος ἐφέστηκεν ἐφ' ἡμᾶς, εἰ ποιήσει κύριος κατὰ πάντα τὰ θαυμάσια αὐτοῦ, καὶ ἀπελεύσεται ἀφ' ἡμῶν

In this case, the construction indicates that the king and his companion recognize that the will of God is beyond their power. As such, we may see it as a theological interpretation by the translator.

In two cases, the translators strengthened the uncertainty by using the Greek adverb πως. The Greek adverb is needed to clearly express the uncertainty.

1 Kgs 20(21):31 וְנֵצֵא אֶל מֶלֶךְ יִשְׂרָאֵל אוּלַי יְחַיֶּה אֶת נַפְשֶׁךָ
καὶ ἐξέλθωμεν πρὸς βασιλέα Ἰσραήλ, εἴ πως ζωογονήσει τὰς ψυχὰς ἡμῶν
ἐξέλθωμεν] πορευθῶμεν L

The enemy cannot anticipate a kind reaction by the king of Israel. Perhaps he will let Ben-hadad live, perhaps not. In this case, the apodosis precedes the protasis. The adverb πως probably makes the uncertainty concerning the future acts of the king more explicit.

2 Kgs 19:4 אוּלַי יִשְׁמַע יְהוָה אֱלֹהֶיךָ אֵת כָּל דִּבְרֵי רַב שָׁקֵה ... וְהוֹכִיחַ בַּדְּבָרִים אֲשֶׁר שָׁמַע יְהוָה אֱלֹהֶיךָ
εἴ πως εἰσακούσεται κύριος ὁ θεός σου πάντας τοὺς λόγους Ραψακου, ... καὶ βλασφημεῖν ἐν λόγοις, οἷς ἤκουσεν κύριος ὁ θεός σου, καὶ λήμψῃ προσευχὴν περὶ τοῦ λείμματος

The Greek translator understood the verse differently than the Masoretes. Hezekiah wishes in the Hebrew text that God would rebuke the blasphemy. In the Greek text, however, he asks the prophet to pray for the people in Jerusalem. The Greek adverb probably makes the uncertainty concerning the acts of God more explicit.

In several cases, the protasis includes ἐάν with the subjunctive. These constructions can be seen as expressing the condition as plausible. Six cases belong

---

31. Smyth, *Greek Grammar*, §2328.

to one individual narrative, where Abraham bargains with God over the destruction of Sodom.

Gen 18:24 אוּלַי יֵשׁ חֲמִשִּׁים צַדִּיקִם בְּתוֹךְ הָעִיר הַאַף תִּסְפֶּה
ἐὰν ὦσιν πεντήκοντα δίκαιοι ἐν τῇ πόλει, ἀπολεῖς αὐτούς;

Abraham does not know the number of righteous in Sodom but suggests a hypothetical number.[32] The Greek construction indicates, however, that Abraham is—at least in words—quite certain about the number of righteous. The choice of the construction ἐάν with the subjunctive must be because of the nature of the discussion. The translator, thus, shows good understanding about the text and the information it implies.

Josh 14:12 אוּלַי יְהוָה אוֹתִי וְהוֹרַשְׁתִּים כַּאֲשֶׁר דִּבֶּר יְהוָה
ἐὰν οὖν κύριος μετ' ἐμοῦ ᾖ, ἐξολεθρεύσω αὐτούς, ὃν τρόπον εἶπέν μοι κύριος

The Greek conjunction οὖν is not a part of the formal rendering of the Hebrew adverb, but a free addition for the sake of coherence. The translator also supplied the copula to the protasis. The construction suggests that Caleb holds it quite likely that he is able to drive out the Anakim. After all, that was God's promise. Again, the translation shows a good understanding of the text and its implications.

1 Kgs 18:5 אוּלַי נִמְצָא חָצִיר וּנְחַיֶּה סוּס וָפֶרֶד וְלוֹא נַכְרִית מֵהַבְּהֵמָה
ἐάν πως εὕρωμεν βοτάνην καὶ περιποιησώμεθα ἵππους καὶ ἡμιόνους, καὶ οὐκ ἐξολοθρευθήσονται ἀπὸ τῶν κτηνῶν
ἐάν πως] εἴ πως L + aliq. mss. | ἐξολοθρευθήσονται] ἐξολοθρευθήσεται L

Finding grass for the cattle is not certain, because of the drought. The Greek translator made the destruction of the cattle the main event. The Greek adverb πως increases the improbability, but the vividness of the construction remains; finding grass is indeed extremely important, but not necessarily plausible.

Twice we find the optative in the protasis. This construction is rare in the LXX.[33] When the construction is directed towards the future, the nuance is that the condition is only just possible and, thus, expresses relatively great uncertainty.[34]

---

32. The same is then true for the rest of the cases in Gen 18:28, 29, 30, 31, and 32, even though they include ellipses.

33. See Anwar Tjen, *On Conditionals in the Greek Pentateuch: A Study of Translation Syntax*, LHBOTS 515 (New York: T&T Clark, 2010), 51, where the cases are listed.

34. Muraoka, *Syntax of Septuagint Greek*, §89aa; Smyth, *Greek Grammar*, §2329.

2 Sam 16:12 אוּלַי יראה יהוה בעוני[35] והשיב יהוה לי טובה תחת קללתו
εἴ πως ἴδοι κύριος ἐν τῇ ταπεινώσει μου καὶ ἐπιστρέψει μοι ἀγαθὰ ἀντὶ τῆς κατάρας αὐτοῦ

David cannot know whether God will notice the humiliation or not. The Greek adverb πως underlines the uncertainty.

1 Sam 14:6 לכה ונעברה אל מצב הערלים האלה אוּלַי יעשה יהוה לנו כי אין ליהוה מעצור להושיע
Δεῦρο διαβῶμεν εἰς μεσσαβ τῶν ἀπεριτμήτων τούτων, εἴ τι ποιήσαι ἡμῖν κύριος· ὅτι οὐκ ἔστιν τῷ κυρίῳ συνεχόμενον σῴζειν.

εἴ τι ποιήσαι ἡμῖν κύριος] εἴ πως ποιήσει τι κύριος ἡμῶν L + *aliq.* mss.

The Greek text is exceptional and several scholars have discussed it. The exceptionality has more to do with the content of the expression and its interpretation than with the grammar of the sentence. How does the protasis link with the apodosis? In other words, can the supposed act by God be a condition of the exhortation to climb up in order to meet the enemy, as the present punctuation in our printed texts lead us to believe?[36] Anwar Tjen, in his recent study, rejected this possibility and interpreted the Greek conjunction εἰ as an interrogative, or more likely, a conjunction introducing a final clause.[37]

In this study, however, the Greek text is understood as including a conditional construction. The Greek translators have turned the Hebrew adverb אוּלַי into various kinds of conditional causes, but interrogatives do not appear and the final clauses are introduced either with ἵνα or with ὅπως. Consequently, the translator seems to have started a conditional construction "if the Lord will do something for us, we will succeed" or something similar, without realizing that the continuation cannot act as an apodosis of the construction. Therefore, an exceptional case is created. The subjunctive (διαβῶμεν) in the apodosis is rare, but brings in the uncertainty.[38]

The material includes few free renderings, too. The *optative* alone can express uncertainty in Greek, especially if it appears with the particle ἄν. Such potential optatives express uncertainty by the speaker, and one can therefore use it as a part

---

35. The *qere* is בְּעֵינִי.
36. See Albert Pietersma and Benjamin G. Wright, ed., *A New English Translation of the Septuagint* (Oxford: Oxford University Press, 2007), 257: "Let us go over to Messab of these uncircumcised, if perhaps the Lord may do something for us."
37. Tjen, *Conditionals in the Greek Pentateuch*, 52. See also Muraoka, *Syntax of Septuagint Greek*, §29dc (iii) and §89aaa. See Wolfgang Kraus and Martin Karrer, ed., *Septuaginta Deutsch: Das griechische Alte Testament in deutscher Übersetzung* (Stuttgart: Deutsche Bibelgesellschaft, 2009), 314: "ob der Herr für uns etwas tun wird."
38. Smyth, *Greek Grammar*, §2363.

of a polite expression.[39] Without the particle, the optative is more normally interpreted as a wish.[40] In one case, the optative (without ἄν) appears as the rendering for the Hebrew adverb. As a visible counterpart for the Hebrew adverb is lacking, the translation is free, but in principle suitable. For the translator, the optative is not, however, a demanding option, because the processing effort is not very high. After all, one needs to understand the core of the clause where the Hebrew adverb appears in order to use the optative.

Isa 37:4 אוּלַי ישמע יהוה אלהיך את דברי רב שקה
εἰσακούσαι κύριος ὁ θεός σου τοὺς λόγους Ραψάκου

This is part of a reported speech. The king does not know if God will listen to the prophet or not. The Hebrew text differs somewhat from the Greek in this verse, but not at the beginning of it.[41] This case is parallel to 2 Sam 19:4, where a conditional construction is used to handle the Hebrew adverb. When the translator used the optative, he reduced the uncertainty, because a wish expressed by the optative can be fulfilled.[42] It is possible that the reducing of the uncertainty is connected with God. A faithful believer might not easily express any doubt in his or her faith in God's kindness.

Once, the Greek translation uses a *rare construction* in Greek. Μή with the indicative can express fear, but also concern or doubt.[43] The use of μή with the indicative can be understood as a final clause and, thus, this free rendering relates to the cases with ἵνα and ὅπως discussed earlier. The difference is, however, that the μή-clause does refer to uncertainty, whereas the aforementioned other final clauses do not.

Josh 9:7 אוּלַי בקרבי אתה יושב ואיך אכרות[44] לך ברית
Ὅρα μὴ ἐν ἐμοὶ κατοικεῖς, καὶ πῶς σοι διαθῶμαι διαθήκην;

---

39. Blomqvist, *Grekisk Grammatik*, §264.2b and Muraoka, *Syntax of Septuagint Greek*, §29db ii. According to Muraoka, uncertainty means a theoretical possibility or likelihood that something happens, not any ability or capability by the subject in question.

40. Muraoka, *Syntax of Septuagint Greek*, §29db i.

41. See however, Kraus and Karrer, *Septuaginta Deutsch*, 1260: "*Möge doch* der Herr, dein Gott, hinhören auf deie Worte von Rabsakes."

42. Blomqvist, *Grekisk Grammatik*, §264.2a; and Muraoka, *Syntax of Septuagint Greek*, §29db (i).

43. Raphael Kühner, *Ausführliche Grammatik der griechischen Sprache*, vol. 2: *Satzlehre*, 3rd ed. (Hannover: Hanh, 1904), §553b, esp. sections 5b and 6b. See also Smyth, *Greek Grammar*, §1774. This type of a final clause is missing from Muraoka, *Syntax of Septuagint Greek*, §83ba, where he discusses the uses of μή with the indicative.

44. The *qere* is אֶכְרָת.

The Israelites do not know if they can trust the ambassadors form Gibeon or not. The Greek rendering is surprising and free. It is actually clever, because we can find similar expressions in Greek literature.[45] This case shows the translator's ability to use the full potential of Greek.

Finally, there is a case where the Greek text with a conditional construction does not have a hint of uncertainty. In this case, the conditional construction deals with actions that have taken place earlier.

אוּלַי נטתה מפני כי עתה גם אתכה הרגתי Num 22:33
καὶ εἰ μὴ ἐξέκλινεν, νῦν σὲ μὲν ἀπέκτεινα, ἐκείνην δὲ περιεποιησάμην

Commentators working with this verse commonly suggest an error in the MT.[46] Instead of the adverb אוּלַי, we should perhaps read the unreal condition with לוּלֵי (if the donkey had not turned away). This—so it seems—is a natural way of reading the Hebrew text, because there is no doubt that the donkey turned away.[47] As the translator of Numbers did use conditional constructions to render the Hebrew adverb in some other passages, one cannot exclude the possibility that his parent text here also had the adverb and not the conjunction לוּלֵי. If this was the case, then the use of an unreal conditional construction (μή in the protasis)[48] is an indication that the translator was well aware of the storyline and could react to it while translating.

Conclusions

As we have seen during the discussion of the various renderings, the Greek translators used different kinds of ways to handle the Hebrew adverb אוּלַי. Most of the cases are possible and understandable renderings, because the Greek text expresses uncertainty too. The most striking cases are those where the Greek text does not express uncertainty. I have partly explained this as a solution to a theological problem connected with the will of God. Maybe for some translators uncertainty in connection with the will of God was a problem.

For the LXX translators, literal translations using adverbs ἴσως and μήποτε were easy and safe options, because of the minimal amount of processing information required in using them. It is therefore surprising how seldom they used them. Less literal translations employing conditional constructions are more demanding, because in order to produce a well-formed conditional construction, one

---

45. See also examples in Muraoka, *Syntax of Septuagint Greek*, §67.
46. See, e.g., *HALOT*, 21.
47. It is not self-evident that the MT, as it stands, is corrupt.
48. For the unreal conditional construction with μή with the indicative, see Smyth, *Greek Grammar*, §2286. This passage is an example of an unreal construction without ἄν in the apodosis in Muraoka, *Syntax of Septuagint Greek*, §89ba.

must work with both the protasis and with the apodosis in Greek. This demands a better awareness of the content of the context of אולי than when using a Greek adverb. The same seems to be the case with the rare free renderings with the optative and with μή and the indicative in the final clause.

Because the number of cases is limited, it is difficult or almost impossible to determine meaningful differences between individual translators. It is, however, worth noticing that even the otherwise literal translators, like those of Jeremiah and Ezekiel, are actually using less literal or even free renderings when it comes to the translation of our Hebrew adverb.[49]

---

49. On the translators of Jeremiah and Ezekiel, see the helpful discussion in Raija Sollamo, *Renderings of Hebrew Semiprepositions in the Septuagint*, AASF 19 (Helsinki: Suomalainen tiedeakatemia, 1979), 286–328.

Rethinking the Original Language of the Book of Judith

Satoshi Toda

Abstract: It is generally thought that the book of Judith, transmitted first and foremost in Greek, was originally composed in a Semitic language. The authoritative view of Hanhart is that "Der griechische Text des Buches Iudith ist ein Übersetzungstext. Seine Vorlage war entweder hebräisch oder aramäisch." This view is followed by another specialist, Bogaert, although with some nuances. However, setting the book of Judith against the Hellenistic period in which the importance of Greek-speaking Judaism has been increasingly stressed calls into question whether the problem of the original language has definitively been solved. Is it not possible to think of a different possibility? The purpose of this paper is to rethink the problem with some fresh perspectives. The discussion will be focused on three points. First, the main argument for the Semitic original of the book of Judith seems to be that numerous calques of Hebrew expressions are found in the Greek text of Judith. However, one can argue that such calques are quite possible even in original Greek compositions. Secondly, concerning the generally assumed Hebrew original of the book, the position of the Vulgate needs to be discussed, especially paying attention to what Jerome has to say concerning our problem. In my view, what Jerome says concerning the original language of a document should be regarded with great caution (as in the case of some Egyptian monastic works, like the Letters of Antony, as well as the Rules of Pachomius). Finally, a detailed analysis of Judith's discourse in chapter 11 will be presented, which, in my opinion, is the key for the interpretation of the problem. Thus, this paper intends to show the plausibility of Greek as the language of composition of the book of Judith.

1. STATE OF RESEARCH

Specialists of studies of the Greek Old Testament are doubtless well aware of the fact that, concerning the problem of the original language of the book of Judith, which has been discussed quite intensively during last two decades, the view that the book of Judith was written originally not in a Semitic language but in Greek has been gaining more and more ground. To mention only one recent work, in 2014 a detailed commentary of the book of Judith was published in German by two scholars, Helmut Engel and Barbara Schmitz, and both of them are in favor of the theory of Greek original of Judith.[1]

The turning point of the research is perhaps to be situated in early 1990s, when Engel published an article advocating the theory of Greek as the original language of Judith.[2] Since then, naturally the shift of the opinion of scholars has only been gradual, and needless to say, there are still those who favor the theory of Hebrew (or Semitic) original of Judith today.[3] Thus the *status quaestionis* is still controversial.

---

1. Barbara Schmitz and Helmut Engel, *Judit*, HThKAT (Freiburg: Herder, 2014), especially 40–43. Scholars who clearly favor the theory of Greek as the original language of Judith include, in addition to Engel and Schmitz, Claudia Rakel, *Judit - über Schönheit, Macht und Widerstand im Krieg: Eine feministisch-intertextuelle Lektüre*, BZAW 334 (Berlin: de Gruyter, 2003), 33–40; Jan Joosten, "The Original Language and Historical Milieu of the Book of Judith," *Meghillot* 5–6 (2008): 159*–76*; and Jeremy Corley, "Septuagintalisms, Semitic Interference, and the Original Language of the Book of Judith," in *Studies in the Greek Bible: Essays in Honor of Francis T. Gignac, S.J.*, ed. Jeremy Corley and Vincent T. M. Skemp, CBQMS 44 (Washington: Catholic Biblical Association of America, 2008), 65–96, among others.

2. Helmut Engel, "'Der HERR ist ein Gott, der Kriege zerschlägt': Zur Frage der griechischen Originalsprache und der Struktur des Buches Judit," in *Goldene Äpfel in silbernen Schalen: Collected Communications to the Thirteenth Congress of the International Organization for the Study of the Old Testament, Leuven 1989*, ed. Klaus-Dietrich Schunck and Matthias Augustin, BEATAJ 20 (Frankfurt am Main: Peter Lang, 1992), 155–68. Still earlier, Toni Craven, in her book, *Artistry and Faith in the Book of Judith* (Chico: Scholars Press, 1983), 5, writes "I am no longer convinced that we should assume a Hebrew original on the basis of Hebraisms in the Greek text and Jerome's dubious claims" and thus is strongly leaned toward the theory of Greek original. However, she does not provide concrete arguments in favor of that theory.

3. For instance, Benedikt Otzen, *Tobit and Judith* (London: Sheffield Academic, 2002), 140, after reviewing in great detail earlier studies in various aspects of the book of Judith, still adheres to the theory of Hebrew (or Semitic) original of Judith: "the character of the Greek versions of the book of Judith makes it more than likely that the Greek is a translation from either Hebrew or Aramaic." See, especially, Otzen, *Tobit and Judith*, 81–93 (ch. 13: "History and Topography") and 132–42 (ch. 18: "Date and Authorship," and ch. 19: "Texts, Versions and Canon").

2. Jerome's Testimony on the Translation of the Book of Judith

When discussing our problem, mention has often been made of Jerome's testimony on the translation of the book of Judith. Jerome says that he made his translation of Judith "in one night (*unam lucubratiunculam*)" from a Semitic *Vorlage* (*Prologus Iudith*).[4] Evidently, the problem is whether such a boastful testimony is reliable. This question concerning Jerome's trustworthiness is important, because, if one adopts the theory of Greek original of Judith, it necessarily implies that Jerome's testimony is not trustworthy at all. Is Jerome to be trusted?

At the very least, Jerome is a figure to be treated with great caution. Literarily, he is extremely ambitious, which is evident from the fact that one of his most famous works *De viris illustribus* (*Catalogue of eminent persons*) mentions, in its last chapter (ch. 135), Jerome himself; Jerome styles himself *vir illustris*. The boastful and implausible expression *unam lucubratiunculam* has already been mentioned above.

Furthermore, it would be better to discuss a concrete example in order to illustrate Jerome as a literarily ambitious author or translator. The example concerns Jerome's Latin translation of monastic texts related to Pachomius. Pachomius was an Egyptian monk of the fourth century and he is well known for having successfully established and led one of the oldest monasteries in the world ("monastery" in the modern sense of the term). This Pachomius is said to have set down various rules for his monks, and these rules are preserved most notably by Jerome's Latin translation. The textual situation of the Rules of Pachomius is such that, in some parts, the Rules of Pachomius are preserved not only in Jerome's translation, but also in a Greek version and in Coptic fragments. It is normally assumed that Coptic is the original language of the Rules of Pachomius, since Pachomius himself was an indigenous Egyptian with no higher education. Also, in this case, Jerome writes, as usual in his translation activity, a prologue to his translation, and mentions the existence of the Coptic version, so as to create the impression that he also had this version before him.[5] This, however, is improbable and, in any case, since Jerome

---

4. Robert Weber, *Biblia sacra iuxta Vulgatam versionem*, ed. Roger Gryson, 5th ed. (Stuttgart: Deutsche Bibelgesellschaft, 2007), 691.

5. The wording is as follows: *Qui* [i.e., *Pachomius, Theodorus, et Orsiesius*, ST] *primi per Thebaidem et Aegyptum coenobiorum fundamenta iecerunt iuxta praeceptum Dei et angeli, qui a Deo sub hanc ipsam institutionem missus fuerat. Itaque quia diu tacueram et dolorem meum silentio devoraram, urgebant autem missi ad me ob hanc ipsam causam Leontius presbyter et ceteri cum eo fratres, accito notario, ut erant de aegyptiaca in graecam linguam versa, nostro sermone dictavi, ut et tantis viris imperantibus, ne dicam rogantibus, oboedirem, et bono, ut aiunt, auspicio longum silentium rumperem.* Quoted from Amand Boon, ed., *Pachomiana Latina: Règle et épitres de S. Pachôme, épitre de S. Théodore et "Liber" de S. Orsiesius. Texte latin de S. Jérôme*, Appendice: *La Règle de S. Pachôme. Fragments coptes et excerpta grecs*, ed. L. Th. Lefort, Bibliothèque de la Revue d'Histoire ecclésiastique 7 (Louvain: Bureaux de la Revue, 1932), 4–5.

did not know Coptic, it would have been of no use, even if Jerome had seen the Coptic version himself.

What I want to argue here is the following: one observes some cases in which the Coptic and the Greek versions of the Rules of Pachomius are almost identical, while the Latin version is quite different from both of them. Here are the examples (the underlined words can be considered almost identical):

Praecepta 88:[6]
Coptic: ⲟⲩⲧⲉ <u>ⲛ̄ⲛⲉⲣⲱⲙⲉ ⲧⲱⲟⲩⲛ ⲉⲟⲩⲱⲙ ⲏ̄ ⲥⲱ ⲉ</u>ⲣⲧⲟⲟⲩⲉ ϩⲓⲧⲛ̄ⲛⲏⲥⲧⲓⲁ· ⲙⲛ̄ⲛ̄ⲥⲁⲧⲣⲉϥⲛ̄ⲕⲟⲧⲕ̄ ⲛϥ̄ⲱⲃϣ̄
Greek: <u>Μηδεὶς ἀναστῇ ἐσθίειν καὶ πίνειν</u> εἰς τὴν ἑξῆς νηστείαν, μετὰ τὸ καθεύδειν ἐν τῷ ὑπνῶσαι
Latin: *Postquam obdormierit, si post somnum nocte evigilaverit et sitire coeperit, ieiunii autem instat dies, bibere non audebit*

The Latin expression *nocte evigilaverit et sitire coeperit*, which is explanatory, corresponds to nothing in the Coptic or the Greek.

Praecepta 92:[7]
Coptic: <u>ⲛ̄ⲛⲉⲣⲱⲙⲉ ⲧⲉⲣⲥ̄ⲡⲉϥⲥⲱⲙⲁ ⲧⲏⲣϥ̄ ⲭⲱⲣⲓⲥ ϣⲱⲛⲉ</u>· ⲟⲩⲧⲉ ⲉϫⲱⲕⲙ̄ ⲏ̄ ⲉⲉⲓⲁⲁϥ ⲉⲃⲟⲗ ⲕⲁⲕⲱⲥ ⲡⲁⲣⲁⲑⲉ ⲉⲧⲧⲱϣ ⲛⲁⲩ
Greek: <u>Μηδεὶς ὅλον τὸ σῶμα ἀλείψῃ χωρὶς νόσου</u>· οὔτε λούσεται· οὔτε ἀπονίψεται καθὼς προστέτακται αὐτοῖς
Latin: <u>*Totum*</u> autem <u>*corpus nemo perunget nisi causa infirmitatis, nec lavabitur,*</u> *nec aqua omnino nudo corpore perfundetur, nisi languor perspicuus sit*

The Latin expression *aqua omnino nudo corpore*, which is again explanatory, corresponds to nothing in the Coptic or the Greek, nor does the clause *nisi languor perspicuus est*.

This phenomenon can be interpreted as follows: On the one hand, the fact that the Coptic and the Greek versions are almost identical means that the text thus attested is most probably the original text.[8] On the other hand, the fact that the Latin version differs greatly from both of them means that the Latin version is not

---

6. Coptic: Boon, *Pachomiana Latina*, 155 (reconstructions of Lefort are incorporated); Greek: Boon, *Pachomiana Latina*, 179 (Recension A); Latin: Boon, *Pachomiana Latina*, 39.

7. Coptic: Boon, *Pachomiana Latina*, 156; Greek: Boon, *Pachomiana Latina*, 179 (Recension A); Latin: Boon, *Pachomiana Latina*, 39.

8. This needs to be said in order that one can be sure of the original text of the Rules of Pachomius, because, despite what is said above concerning the normal assumption of the original language of the Rules of Pachomius, in my view, it is not impossible to think that, in cases where the Coptic version differs from the Greek, on the one hand, and the Greek and the Latin are almost identical, on the other, the Greek rather than the Coptic shows the (more) original text. Of course, such a matter should be discussed in its own right elsewhere.

a faithful translation, but rather a free rendering of the *Vorlage*. We see that even in the case where Jerome does not explicitly say that his translation is "translating meaning from meaning rather than word from word,"[9] it can contain some free renderings. Thus, one has to expect that Jerome's translation cannot be held in high esteem for the purposes of textual criticism, especially when he himself says, as in the case of the book of Judith, that the translation is not verbal or literal.[10]

To return to the main discussion of this paper, Robert Hanhart, the authoritative editor of the Greek text of Judith, says that whereas Origen, a Christian author of the third century, had no access to any Semitic version of the book of Judith, Jerome, for his part, knew the Semitic version, according to what he says in the prologue of the Latin translation he made. Hanhart, being a serious and diligent biblical scholar who does not consider Jerome a liar at all, examines details of the Latin translation and argues that the Latin version has high value with regard to the problem of the original language.[11] However, such high evaluation of Jerome's translation cannot be justified.

3. An Additional Argument in Favor of the Greek Original of Judith: Chapter 11

Before continuing the discussion, I have to confess here that I agree with the discussions of those scholars who advocate the theory of Greek original of Judith and I think their discussions are valid in themselves.

Thus, if there still remains something to be added to the discussion that favors the original Greek composition of Judith, then I argue that special attention should be paid to the discourse Judith delivered in chapter 11. Obviously, this discourse is of great importance to the entire story of the book of Judith, since the salvation of not only Betulia but the entire Israel depended on the success, or the failure, of

---

9. This is the expression used in the prologue to Judith. The Latin original reads as follows: *magis sensum e sensu quam ex verbo verbum transferens* (Weber, *Biblia sacra*, 691).

10. It should be clear that here I am not trying to discredit totally the value of Jerome's various testimonies on his various translation activities. Where he is (much) more specific about how he made the translation in question, his testimony can be trusted at face value. Saying this, I am thinking of the case of his translation of a parabiblical text, which is called by modern scholars the Gospel of the Nazarenes. In the case of the Gospel of the Nazarenes, Jerome not only says that he translated the document from "Hebrew" (or "Syro-Chaldaic tongue") into "Greek and Latin," but also mentions some Semitic words used in the *Vorlage* from which Jerome made his translation (Jerome mentions, e.g., the following Semitic words: *Osanna Barrama, Mahar*), and thus it is certain that, in this case at least, Jerome had the Semitic text in question in hand.

11. This is how I understand the following phrase of Hanhart: "Die Textform des Originals kann nur indirekt über das Mittelglied der Vulgata erschlossen warden." Robert Hanhart, *Text und Textgeschichte des Buches Judith*, MSU 14 (Göttingen: Vandenhoeck & Ruprecht, 1979), 10.

this discourse of Judith. And, of course, the story shows that the discourse was a tremendous success, because "her words were pleasing in the sight of Holofernes and of all his servants; and they marveled at her wisdom, and said, 'There is not such a woman from one end of the earth to the other, for beauty of face, and wisdom of words [συνέσει λόγων]'" (Jdt 11:20–21).[12]

However, it does not suffice that the discourse should be praised solely in the text itself; the reader of the text should also appreciate it as a discourse full of "wisdom of words." What, then, was the "wisdom of words," or, to be more precise, what was considered to be the "wisdom of words" in antiquity? I argue that, in antiquity, wisdom of words lay in a sophisticated use of words. To put it differently, in antiquity, a discourse composed of variegated words flowing, as it were, from a rich fountain of vocabulary was regarded as showing "wisdom of words" It is well known, for instance, that Callimachus of Cyrene, one of the most erudite authors in the Hellenistic period or perhaps in the entire antiquity, was fond of rare and unusual things,[13] and this tendency of his was surely reflected in his use of words as well. From this perspective, it appears that Judith's discourse shows a concentrated use of what I call "variegated words."

What I call "variegated words" also includes words that might seem rather normal, but which are in reality relatively rarely used in the Greek Old Testament. Thus, (1) the word κατακολουθέω, which figures in verse 6, is not a special word, but occurs in the Greek Old Testament five times[14] (HRCS, 734a: 1 Esdr 7:1; Jdt 11:6 [this verse]; Jer 17:16 [רעה]; Dan LXX 9:10 [הלך]; and 1 Macc 6:23). Similar words, such as ἀκολουθέω and ἐπακολουθέω, are used more frequently, fourteen and sixteen times respectively (excluding the instances in the translations of Aquila, Symmachus, etc.). Hatch and Redpath quote הלך for Dan LXX 9:10, and רעה for Jer 17:16, but κατακολουθέω and רעה are quite different in meaning and this might suggest that, behind κατακολουθέω, there is no corresponding Hebrew word. A textual search in the *TLG* database shows 703 instances of κατακολουθέω in total. One can, therefore, say that κατακολουθέω is not used infrequently in Greek literature in general.

---

12. The translation quoted here (because of its greater literalness) is that of Arthur E. Cowley, "Judith," in *Apocrypha*, vol. 1 of *The Apocrypha and Pseudepigrapha of the Old Testament in English*, ed. Robert H. Charles (Oxford: Clarendon, 1913), 261, checked of course against the edition of Robert Hanhart, ed., *Iudith*, SVTG 8.4 (Göttingen: Vandenhoeck & Ruprecht, 1979), 120–21.

13. Concerning the language style of Callimachus, the following can be quoted as an example: "Der sprachliche Stil [of Callimachus, ST] ist entgegen dem Epos knapp, aber gerne inkonzinn, figurenreich, auf Wechsel und Buntheit bis hin zum Unterhaltungston bedacht und auf Seltenes und Ungewöhniches erpicht, aber doch so, daß alles noch eben durch Autoritäten gedeckt bleibt." Hans Herter, "Kallimachos," in *Iuppiter-Nasidienus*, vol. 3 of *Der Kleine Pauly: Lexikon der Antike in fünf Bänden*, ed. Konrat Ziegler and Walther Sontheimer (München: Deutscher Taschenbuch Verlag, 1979), col. 77.

14. For the number of occurrences, I refer to HRCS.

(2) Τελείως is used in the same verse 6, occurring four times in the Greek Old Testament (HRCS, 1343a: Jdt 11:6 [this verse]; 2 Macc 12:42; 3 Macc 3:26; 7:22). For these four instances of τελείως, no corresponding Hebrew word is quoted by Hatch and Redpath. Needless to say, τελείως is used very frequently in Greek. The relative scarcity of τελείως in the Greek Old Testament might be interpreted as an indication that many documents are actually translations from Hebrew. However, it is also possible to interpret the scarcity in question as a reflection of the peculiar character of the Greek of the Old Testament. So, the use of τελείως in the book of Judith might suggest that it is an original Greek composition.

(3) Κατόρθωσις in verse 7 occurs three times in the Greek Old Testament (HRCS, 756b: 2 Chr 3:17; Jdt 11:7 [this verse]; and Ps 96[97]:2). It is not evident whether the Hebrew words quoted by Hatch and Redpath (יכין in the case of 2 Chr 3:17: מכון in the case of Ps 96[97]:2) correspond exactly to κατόρθωσις or not. It goes without saying that κατόρθωσις itself is a very common word in Greek literature in general.

(4) Πανούργευμα (meaning "knavish trick, villainy") in verse 8 occurs three times in the Greek Old Testament (HRCS, 1053a: Jdt 11:8 [this verse]; Sir 1:6; 42:18). While Sir 1:6 is absent in the Hebrew version rediscovered at the end of the nineteenth century, Sir 42:18 is present in it, and the Greek expression in question (πανούργευμα αὐτῶν) corresponds to the Hebrew מערומיהם, which seems to be a rare word also in Hebrew.[15] Thus, in this case, the relatively infrequent use of πανούργευμα is matched by the relatively scarce occurrence of מערומיהם. A textual search in *TLG* shows sixty-nine instances of πανούργευμα in total, which are not a lot.

(5) Στράτευμα (meaning "expedition; armament, army") in the same verse, occurs seven times in the Greek Old Testament (HRCS, 1295b: Jdt 11:8 [this verse]; 1 Macc 9:34; 2 Macc 5:24; 8:21; 12:38; 13:13; 4 Macc 5:1); for these seven instances of στράτευμα, no corresponding Hebrew word is quoted by Hatch and Redpath. Among the words of similar meaning, it is στρατιά (meaning "army"; in the Greek Old Testament it is confounded with στρατεία, meaning "expedition") that is more frequently used in the Greek Old Testament (HRCS, 1295c–1296a: 46 or 47 instances in total). A textual search in *TLG* shows 6604 instances of στράτευμα in total.

(6) Ἐκλαλέω in the verse 9 is a *hapax legomenon* in the Greek Old Testament (HRCS, 435a) and no corresponding Hebrew word is quoted by Hatch and Redpath. However, Hatch and Redpath's concordance shows that λαλέω, that is, without

---

15. Pancratius C. Beentjes, ed., *The Book of Ben Sira in Hebrew: A Text Edition of All Extant Hebrew Manuscripts and A Synopsis of All Parallel Hebrew Ben Sira Texts*, VTSup 68 (Leiden: Brill, 1997), 74 (MSS B and M). This word, which apparently derives from the root ערם ("shrewd"), is not found in Jacob Levy, *Neuhebräisches und chaldäisches Wörterbuch über die Talmudim und Midraschim*, 4 vols. (Leipzig: Brockhaus, 1876–1889), BDB or *HALOT*.

prefix, occurs many times (HRCS, 841–46). The Greek Old Testament contains also the instances of ἐπιλαλέω (HRCS, 523c: another *hapax*, Jer 8:17) and συλλαλέω (HRCS, 1301c: 5x, Exod 34:35; 3 Kgdms 12:14; Prov 6:22; Isa 7:6; and Jer 18:20). Thus, the use of λαλέω with prefix might not necessarily suggest the original Greek composition.

(7) Ἔκβολος and (8) ἄπρακτος in verse 11 deserve closer examination. This verse is remarkable, also stylistically, in the sense that it contains a double meaning (ὁ κύριός μου can be interpreted as designating both Holofernes and the Lord of Israel), which apparently functions throughout this entire discourse. Additionally, the use of ἔκβολος and ἄπρακτος seems to be fairly rare.

As for (7) ἔκβολος, which is a *hapax* in the Greek Old Testament (HRCS, 421b), its use is rare even in the entire Greek literature from Homer down to Byzantine period. A textual search in *TLG* shows only twenty-five instances.[16] Used by Euripides, Callimachus, Jdt 11:11 [this verse], Shepherd of Hermas, Lucianus, Iamblichus, et cetera, ἔκβολος seems to be a literarily usable word, so to speak.

(8) Ἄπρακτος is not rare at all in Greek literature in general. A textual search in *TLG* shows 2771 instances of ἄπρακτος in total. In the Greek Old Testament, it occurs three times (HRCS, 150b: Jdt 11:11 [this verse]; 2 Macc 12:18; and 3 Macc 2:22), and no corresponding Hebrew word is quoted by Hatch and Redpath. The problem is how to interpret this fact. In the case of Syriac, in order to express something corresponding to Greek words with α-privative, it suffices to add the negation just before the word which expresses the idea in the positive sense; and I assume that a similar method can also be used in Hebrew. However, in Hatch and Redpath, I have found no word which means the "positive sense of ἄπρακτος," as it were, nor have I found the participial use of the verb πράσσω in such meanings. Thus, the rare use of ἄπρακτος in the Greek Old Testament might suggest the original Greek composition.

(9) Ὁπηνίκα in verse 11 occurs in the Greek Old Testament twice (HRCS, 1001b: Jdt 11:11 [this verse] and 4 Macc 2:21). A textual search in *TLG* shows 2095 instances of ὁπηνίκα in total. Thus, one can say that the use of ὁπηνίκα in the Greek Old Testament is relatively rare, but the reason is not immediately clear.

(10) Ἀτοπία in verse 11 is a *hapax* in the Greek Old Testament (HRCS, 176b), as is (11) παρεκλείπω in verse 12 (HRCS, 1066b). In Greek literature in general, ἀτοπία is not an infrequent word at all. A textual search in *TLG* shows 1729 instances of ἀτοπία in total. Παρεκλείπω, on the other hand, seems indeed to be very rarely used in Greek literature in general: a textual search in *TLG* shows only four instances of παρεκλείπω in total. Used by Jdt 11:12 (this verse), Aelius Aristides, Pseudo-Athanasius of Alexandria, and Photius, παρεκλείπω seems to be a literarily usable word.

---

16. In order to count instances, I have done the textual search by ἔκβολ and ἐκβόλ using the option "diacritics sensitive." This distinction was necessary in order to exclude the declined forms of ἐκβολή from the analysis.

(12) Σπανίζω in verse 12 occurs four times in the Greek Old Testament (HRCS, 1281c: 4 Kgdms 14:26; Jdt 11:12 [this verse]; Job 14:11; and LXX Dan 9:24). In Greek literature in general, the use of σπανίζω is not rare. A textual search in *TLG* shows 573 instances of σπανίζω in total (including twelve instances of ὑποσπανίζω). It is not certain whether four occurrences in the Greek Old Testament should be interpreted as rare or not.

(13) Μετακομίζω in verse 14 is a *hapax* in the Greek Old Testament (this reading is not registered in HRCS), although this reading can be a matter of dispute. Μετακομίζω itself is not a rare word at all. A textual search in *TLG* shows 609 instances of μετακομίζω in total and, furthermore, derivative words such as μετακομιστέον, εὐμετακομιστός, δυσμετακομιστός and μετακόμισις are also used. This suggests that the word μετακομίζω is quite common in use. The reason why μετακομίζω is *hapax* in the Greek Old Testament is not immediately clear.

(14) Προσαναφέρω in verse 18 occurs three times (HRCS, 1212b: Tobit 12:13; Jdt 11:18 [this verse]; and 2 Macc 11:36). A textual search in *TLG* shows ninety instances of προσαναφέρω in total, which are not a lot. However, it is not easy to interpret these data, as there are many verbs which have the compound prefix προσανα- (or προσαν-).

(15) Γρύζω in verse 19 (meaning "grumble, mutter, growl [of a dog], grunt [of a pig]"), which figures in the quotation of Exod 11:7, occurs three times in the Greek Old Testament (HRCS, 278a: Exod 11:7; Josh 10:21; and Jdt 11:19 [this verse]). A textual search in *TLG* shows 141 instances of γρύζω in total (including nine instances of ἀναγρύζω, two instances of ἀντιγρύζω, one instance of ἐπιγρύζω, and twelve instances of ὑπογρύζω [fourteen instances of γογγρύζω are excluded from these statistics]). It is not certain whether 114 instances in the entire Greek literature are many or not.

Finally, (16) πρόγνωσις of the verse 19 occurs twice (HRCS, 1205c: Jdt 9:6 and 11:19 [this verse]). In a certain context (e.g., in medical treatises), πρόγνωσις can be used quite frequently (for example, Galen's works contain hundreds of instances of πρόγνωσις). Its use abounds also in Christian literature, so the word is quite common. However, I think that in the book of Judith, this word, spoken by a woman, could have been regarded as showing "wisdom of words."

Admittedly the analysis is not quite clear-cut, but at least, uses of certain rare, but nonetheless literarily usable, words (such as ἔκβολος, ἄπρακτος, and παρεκλείπω) have been observed.

4. Concluding Remarks

The result of the analysis presented above should be clearly stated here. Arguing simply that rare words are used in the book of Judith does not suffice to demonstrate that its language of composition is Greek; we know that, for example, the book of Sirach, which is known to have been translated from Hebrew, abounds in such rare words.[17] However, in the case of the book of Judith, such rare words figure in a concentrated manner in the discourse delivered by the protagonist of the story, and in the story the discourse is applauded as showing "wisdom of words." Needless to say, such a showing off of the "wisdom" works solely in Greek. Thus, the literary intention of the author, coupled with the concentrated use of rare words such as we have seen above, does strongly suggest, if not demonstrate, that the book of Judith was originally written in Greek.

The main idea presented in this paper came to my mind while attending a class of Biblical Greek given by Reverend Father Pierre-Maurice Bogaert, an eminent specialist of the book of Judith, about twenty years ago in Louvain-la-Neuve. I am not sure if Father Bogaert agrees with my idea or not, but, in any case, the matter is, in my opinion, worthy of specialists' consideration.

---

17. This aspect of Sirach is studied in great detail by: Christian Wagner, *Die Septuaginta-Hapaxlegomena im Buch Jesus Sirach: Untersuchungen zu Wortwahl und Wortbildung unter besonderer Berücksichtigung des textkritischen und übersetzungstechnischen Aspekts*, BZAW 282 (Berlin: de Gruyter, 1999).

Visio Dei in the Septuagint

Michaël N. van der Meer

Abstract: It has often been noted that the Septuagint tries to attenuate the idea that God can be seen directly by humans. Nevertheless, the alternative attitude, to tolerate such statements, can also be observed in the same translations. Thus far, explanations for these phenomena have been sought primarily within Jewish literature. The present contribution to this discussion tries to broaden the horizon by taking into account both the diversity of vision reports in the Hellenistic world and the diversity within Second Temple Judaism. It is argued that beholding the Deity in the Hellenistic world is not seen as impossible or a purely metaphysical cognitive act in the Platonic sense, but first of all a priestly privilege in which lay people can participate under certain circumstances.

1. INTRODUCTION

Discussion of theological themes in the Septuagint between Hebrew Bible and New Testament is both indispensable and problematic. Unlike the writings of Jewish and Christian Scriptures, the books of the Septuagint for the most part do not present genuine compositions, but rather translations of Hebrew scriptural books, often in a very literal manner, and stand therefore apart from the compositions that came to be known as the Jewish and Christian Bibles. On the other hand, New Testament writings and conceptions are unthinkable without the Septuagint as intermediate stage between Hebrew Scripture and Early Christianity. Major Christian concepts such as the notion of God as Lord (κύριος) rather than a Deity with a personal name (יהוה), as Almighty ruler (παντοκράτωρ) rather than captain of the heavenly hosts (צבאות), his anointed redeemer (χριστός/משיח) and his unilateral will or testament (διαθήκη) rather than a bilateral covenant (ברית) all have their roots in the Greek translation and transformation of Hebrew concepts.

Yet, if the Greek translations of Hebrew Scripture did present a sort of *praeparatio evangelica*, as church father Eusebius of Caesarea and, in his wake,

German scholar Georg Bertram have claimed,[1] it was only to a limited extent and most likely not intended. Whereas the Letter of Aristeas goes at great lengths to demonstrate the compatibility of the Greek translation of the Pentateuch with Greek culture, the translation of almost all Greek translations of Jewish Scripture defies an easy accommodation between Jewish and Hellenistic culture. The author of the Letter of Aristeas may have promoted an equation between Israel's God and Zeus via the word-play ὁ Ζήν-τὸ ζῆν, "to live" (§16),[2] and the author of a comparable pseudepigraphic tale about Joseph and Aseneth may have provided a scenario for the marriage between Jewish and Egyptian priestly traditions, the translators of the biblical books were in fact very careful to avoid such syncretisms.[3] For them, the God of Israel was not an ἄναξ, the common title for Zeus, but ὁ κύριος, "the rightful ruler of the world,"[4] his spokesmen (נביאים) were not μάντεις, "diviners," but προφῆται, "official representatives,"[5] and his instruction (תורה) was not διδαχή, "instruction," or θεσμός, "law-code," but rather νόμος, "authoritative tradition." The translation itself often stretches the comprehensibility of those accustomed to elegant Greek style. The perceived messianic outlook of the Pentateuch often says more about the modern Christian interpreters than the

---

A preliminary version of this paper was presented at the seminar on "Seeing God: Visual Perception of the Divine in the Hebrew Bible, the Septuagint, and the New Testament," held on 8 September 2016 during the Stellenbosch 2016 IOSOT Congress. I thank the organizers, professors Jan Joosten and Gert Steyn, for their kind invitation to participate in this session and present my views on the Septuagint part of this theme. I also thank professor Hans Ausloos for his kind criticism of my lecture during the plenary discussion and afterwards. Finally, I thank my former *Doktorvater* Arie van der Kooij for his continuing critical feedback.

1. See Georg Bertram, "Praeparatio evangelica in der Septuaginta," *VT* 7 (1957): 225–49.
2. See also Aristobulus 4 *apud* Eusebius, *Praep. ev* 13.13.6.
3. See, e.g., Folker Siegert, *Zwischen hebräischer Bibel und altem Testament. Eine Einführung in die Septuaginta*, Münsteraner Judaistische Studien 9 (Münster: Lit, 2001), 218–86; and my study "The Greek Translators of the Pentateuch and the Epicureans," in *Torah and Tradition: Papers Read at the Sixteenth Joint Meeting of the Society for Old Testament Study and the Oudtestamentisch Werkgezelschap; Edinburgh 2015*, ed. Klaas Spronk and Hans Barstad, OtSt 70 (Leiden: Brill, 2017), 176–200.
4. See also Charles H. Dodd, *The Bible and the Greeks* (London: Hodder & Stoughton, 1935); Robert Hanhart, "The Translation of the Septuagint in Light of Earlier Tradition and Subsequent Influences," in *Septuagint, Scrolls and Cognate Writings: Papers Presented to the International Symposium on the Septuagint and Its Relations to the Dead Sea Scrolls and Other Writings*, ed. George J. Brooke and Barnabas Lindars, SCS 33 (Atlanta: Society of Biblical Literature, 1992), 339–72.
5. See Erich Fascher, *ΠΡΟΦΗΤΗΣ: Eine sprach- und religionsgeschichtliche Untersuchung* (Gießen: Töpelmann, 1927).

intention of the translators.[6] If the translators did have any intention at all, it was almost always to offer a faithful rendering of the Hebrew original in front of them.

Whereas these observations are sufficient for many scholars to dismiss the idea of a theology of the Septuagint altogether, some scholars have pleaded for a theological approach of the Septuagint. Scholars such as Isac Leo Seeligmann,[7] Arie van der Kooij,[8] Martin Rösel,[9] and Johann Cook,[10] for example, have pointed to recurring patterns of intentional deviations of the Greek translators from their Hebrew source text for discernable theological reasons. Particularly the relatively free translations of the books of Isaiah and Proverbs, but also the Pentateuch, Daniel, and, I might add, Joshua,[11] can be studied as documents of Hellenistic Jewish theology. Hence, the foreseeable future will see both a handbook on the theology of the Septuagint,[12] as well as a full-fledged historical and theological lexicon of the Septuagint.[13]

---

6. See the critical essays on this topic by John J. Collins, Anneli Aejmelaeus, and Albert Pietersma in *Septuagint and Messianism*, ed. Michael A. Knibb, BETL 195 (Leuven: Peeters, 2006).

7. See Isac L. Seeligmann, *The Septuagint Version of Isaiah: A Discussion of Its Problems*, MVEOL 9 (Leiden: Brill, 1948).

8. Arie van der Kooij, *Die alten Textzeugen des Jesajabuches: Ein Beitrag zur Textgeschichte des Alten Testaments*, OBO 35 (Freiburg: Universitätsverlag; Göttingen: Vandenhoeck & Ruprecht, 1981). See my recent overview of his work in "Septuagint Research in the Netherlands," *JSCS* 51 (2018): 21–40.

9. Martin Rösel, "Theo-Logie der griechischen Bibel: Zur Wiedergabe der Gottesaussagen im LXX-Pentateuch," *VT* 48 (1998): 49–62; Rösel, "Towards a 'Theology of the Septuagint,'" in *Septuagint Research: Issues and Challenges in the Study of the Greek Jewish Scriptures*, ed. Wolfgang Kraus and R. Glenn Wooden, SCS 53 (Atlanta: Society of Biblical Literature, 2006), 239–52.

10. Johann Cook, *The Septuagint of Proverbs: Jewish and/or Hellenistic Proverbs? Concerning the Hellenistic Colouring of LXX Proverbs*, VTSup 69 (Leiden: Brill, 1997); Cook, "Towards the Formulation of a Theology of the Septuagint," in *Congress Volume: Ljubljana 2007*, ed. André Lemaire, VTSup 133 (Leiden: Brill, 2010), 621–40.

11. See my overview articles of the Greek Joshua in *T&T Clark Companion to the Septuagint*, ed. James K. Aitken (London: Bloomsbury, 2015), 86–101, and *Textual History of the Bible*, ed. Armin Lange and Emanuel Tov, vol. 1b (Leiden: Brill, 2016), 269–74.

12. Hans Ausloos and Bénédicte Lemmelijn, eds., *Theology of the Septuagint*, Handbuch zur Septuaginta 6 (Gütersloh: Gütersloher, forthcoming).

13. Eberhard Bons and Jan Joosten, eds., *Historical and Theological Lexicon of the Septuagint* 1.A–Γ (Tübingen: Mohr Siebeck, forthcoming), see the prospectus: https://www.mohr.de/en/multi-volume-work/historical-and-theological-lexicon-of-the-septuagint-610100000.

2. Methodology

Nevertheless, it is clear that a strict methodology is required in order to speak meaningfully about Septuagint theology. The caveats and criteria for such an enterprise have been spelled out by Seeligmann, Rösel, Cook, Ausloos, myself and others:[14]

1. The statements have to deal with intentional decisions made by the Greek translators, that is, deal with those places where the Greek version differs from the Hebrew text, either MT or a different Hebrew *Vorlage*.
2. Differences from the Hebrew source text may pertain to ubiquitous Greek calques, for example, κύριος for יהוה, but only where it is clear that a plausible alternative was available (e.g., IAΩ),[15] but rejected. It is useful to remind oneself of the dictum by Theo van der Louw that behind every free translation in the Septuagint, or transformation, as he calls it, stands a literal rendering that has been rejected.[16] Finding out *why* such alternative has been rejected can be the first step towards a theology of the Septuagint.
3. One has to take into account both the diversity and the relative unity of the Greek translations of Hebrew Scripture. The translation process may have taken several centuries (from the early third century BCE for the Pentateuch to the late first

---

14. Seeligmann, *Septuagint Version of Isaiah*, 95–97ff.; Rösel, "Theo-Logie der griechischen Bibel"; Rösel, "Towards a Theology of the Septuagint"; Cook, "Towards the Formulation of a Theology of the Septuagint"; Hans Ausloos, "Sept défis posés à une théologie de la Septante," in *Congress Volume Stellenbosch 2016*, ed. Louis C. Jonker, Gideon R. Kotzé, and Christl M. Maier, VTSup 177 (Leiden: Brill, 2017), 228–50; Michaël N. van der Meer, "Problems and Perspectives in Septuagint Lexicography: The Case of Non-compliance (ἀπειθέω)," in *Septuagint Vocabulary: Pre-history, Usage, Reception*, ed. Eberhard Bons and Jan Joosten, SCS 58 (Atlanta: Society of Biblical Literature, 2011), 65–86.

15. See Frank Shaw, *The Earliest Non-mystical Jewish Use of IAΩ*, CBET 70 (Leuven: Peeters, 2014).

16. Theo van der Louw, *Transformations in the Septuagint. Towards an Interaction of Septuagint Studies and Translation Studies*, CBET 47 (Leuven: Peeters, 2007), 57.

century CE for Ecclesiastes) and do not follow a unified translation policy. Instead, they reflect the interests of Jewish groups over different periods of time[17] and different places.[18]

4. On the other hand, Rösel insists that in order to be able to speak about Septuagint theology, the intentional ideological changes should not be particular to a singular translation unit (e.g., a single biblical book), but overarching phenomena covering a considerable part of the so-called corpus of Septuagintal books.[19]

5. In order to contextualize the theological differences between the Hebrew source text and the Septuagint, many scholars refer to more or less contemporary writings from Hellenistic and early Roman writings. Here too, however, date and setting matter. All too often Hellenism is equated with Platonism and Platonic and Philonic writings, on the one hand, or Jewish apocalyptic writings, on the other hand, are used to explain theological transformations in the Septuagint.[20] Yet, the cultural spectrum of the Hellenistic *Umwelt* of the Septuagint was far

---

17. See, e.g., the relatively free renderings of Isaiah, Daniel, and 1 Esdras possibly from Leontopolis in the mid second century BCE versus the literalistic renderings of the kaige-group, possibly from Palestine, around the turn of the second to first century BCE. This may point to a distinction between a highly educated Jewish establishment at Alexandria and a group of newcomers led by the exiles high priest Onias (IV), as argued by Arie van der Kooij, "The Old Greek of Isaiah and Book III of the Sibylline Oracles: Related Pieces of Jewish Literature in Ptolemaic Egypt," in *Die Septuaginta–Geschichte, Wirkung, Relevanz. 6. Internationale Fachtagung veranstaltet von Septuaginta Deutsch (LXX.D), Wuppertal 21.–24. Juli 2016*, ed. Martin Meiser, Michaela Geiger, Siegfried Kreuzer, and Marcus Sigismund, WUNT 405 (Tübingen: Mohr Siebeck, 2018), 673–84.

18. See the overview of the discussion about Alexandria, Leontopolis, Jerusalem and Antioch as possible places of origin for various Greek translations in Gilles Dorival, Marguerite Harl and Olivier Munnich, *La Bible grecque des Septante. Du judaïsme hellénistique au christianisme ancien* (Paris: Cerf, 1994), 101–9; and further Johann Cook and Arie van der Kooij, *Law, Prophets, Prophets, and Wisdom: On the Provenance of Translators and Their Books in the Septuagint Version*, CBET 68 (Leuven: Peeters, 2012).

19. Already the differences between the large Septuagint codices Vaticanus, Alexandrinus, and Sinaiticus regarding the number of books included in the Old Testament part make it difficult to speak of an Alexandrian canon. For the sake of convenience, the books included in the manual edition of the Septuagint by Rahlfs is taken as the corpus of Septuagintal books.

20. See, e.g., Martin Rösel, *Übersetzung als Vollendung der Auslegung. Studien zur Genesis-Septuaginta*, BZAW 223 (Berlin: de Gruyter, 1994). See my discussion of perceived Middle Platonic dualism on the Greek translation of Genesis in Michaël N. van der Meer, "Anthopology in the Ancient Greek Versions of Genesis 2," in *Dust of the Ground and Breath of Life (Gen 2:7): The Problem of a Dualistic Anthropology in Early Judaism and Christianity*, ed. Jacques T. A. G. M. van Ruiten and George H. van Kooten, TBN 20 (Leiden: Brill, 2016), 37–57.

176   VAN DER MEER

wider than Platonism, which, after all, became prevalent in Alexandria only during the Roman and Byzantine periods.[21] Greek papyri from Hellenistic and early Roman Egypt containing documents, literary and subliterary compositions, contain a wealth of information about the cultural milieu in which the Septuagint came into being.[22] Although the importance of these sources for the study of the Septuagint is often acknowledged, it is still rather seldom that they are really brought to bear in the study of the cultural context of Septuagint theology.

3. THE THEME OF VISIO DEI IN THE SEPTUAGINT

It is here that my contribution to the discussion about Septuagint theology sets in. Many scholars have observed a tendency observable in many books of the Septuagint to attenuate the idea that humans can actually behold God. Whereas several passages in the Hebrew Bible plainly describe patriarchs and prophets beholding God,[23] the Greek translators seem to have modified these statements; see, for example, the *loci classici* in the Pentateuch: Exod 24:9–11, 33:11–13, 17–23, and Num 12:8:

Exod 24:9–11

MT   ויעל משה ואהרן נדב ואביהוא ושבעים מזקני ישראל: ויראו את אלהי ישראל ותחת רגליו כמעשה לבנת הספיר וכעצם השמים לטהור: ואל אצילי בני ישראל לא שלח ידו ויחזו את האלהים ויאכלו וישתו:

Then Moses and Aaron, Nadab, and Abihu [+ Eleazar and Ithamar, 4QpaleoExod^m, SP], and seventy of the elders of Israel went up, and *they saw the*

---

21. See the historical overviews of ancient Greek philosophy, e.g., Friedo Ricken, "Philosophie," in *Einleitung in die griechische Philologie*, ed. Heinz-Günter Nesselrath (Leipzig: Teubner, 1997), 507–60; Keimpe Algra, Jonathan Barnes et al., ed., *The Cambridge History of Hellenistic Philosophy* (Cambridge: Cambridge University Press, 1999). On the Middle Platonism, see John Dillon, *The Middle Platonists: A Study of Platonism 80 B.C. to A.D. 220* (London: Ducksworth, 1977); Troels Engberg-Pedersen, ed., *From Stoicism to Platonism: The Development of Philosophy, 100 BCE–100 CE* (Cambridge: Cambridge University Press, 2017). See further the comprehensive assessment of Martin Hengel, *Judentum und Hellenismus* (Tübingen: Mohr Siebeck, 1973).

22. John A. Lee, *A Lexical Study of the Septuagint Version of the Pentateuch*, SCS 14 (Chico: Scholars, 1983); and more recently his overview article, "The Vocabulary of the Septuagint and Documentary Evidence," in *Die Sprache der Septuaginta*, ed. Eberhard Bons and Jan Joosten, LXX.H 3 (Gütersloh: Gütersloher, 2016), 98–118.

23. There are many studies devoted to this theme in the Hebrew Bible. Some also take into account the Babylonian and Ugaritic parallels; see, e.g., the still useful studies by Friedrich Nötscher, *"Das Angesicht Gottes schauen" nach biblischer und babylonischer Auffassung* in the appendix: Wolf Wilhelm Graf Baudissin, *"Gott schauen" in der alttestamentlichen Religion*, (Darmstadt: Wissenschaftliche Buchgesellschaft, 1968); Joseph Reindl, *Das Angesicht Gottes im Sprachgebrauch des Alten Testaments*, ETS 25 (Leipzig: St. Benno, 1970).

God of Israel. Under his feet there was something like a pavement of sapphire stone, like the very heaven for clearness. God did not lay his hand on the chief men of the people of Israel; also they beheld God, and they ate and drank. (NRSV)

LXX Καὶ ἀνέβη Μωυσῆς καὶ Ἀαρὼν καὶ Ναδὰβ καὶ Ἀβιοὺδ καὶ ἑβδομήκοντα τῆς γερουσίας Ισραηλ, καὶ εἶδον τὸν τόπον, οὗ εἱστήκει ἐκεῖ ὁ θεὸς τοῦ Ισραηλ· καὶ τὰ ὑπὸ τοὺς πόδας αὐτοῦ ὡσεὶ ἔργον πλίνθου σαπφείρου, καὶ ὥσπερ εἶδος στερεώματος τοῦ οὐρανοῦ τῇ καθαριότητι. καὶ τῶν ἐπιλέκτων τοῦ Ισραηλ οὐ διεφώνησεν οὐδὲ εἷς· καὶ ὤφθησαν ἐν τῷ τόπῳ τοῦ θεοῦ, καὶ ἔφαγον καὶ ἔπιον. And Moyses and Aaron and Nadab and Abioud and seventy of the elders' council of Israel went up. *And they saw the place, there where the God of Israel stood,* and that which was beneath his feet, like something made from lapis lazuli brick and like the appearance of the firmament of heaven in purity. And not even one of the chosen of Israel perished. *And they appeared in the place of God* and were eating and drinking. (NETS)

Whereas the Hebrew text boldly states that Moses, Aaron with his sons, and the seventy members of the elders of Israel (מזקני ישראל/γερουσία Ισραηλ) in fact saw the God of Israel and lived to tell it, the Greek translation removes this idea and states that they only saw the place where God stood (καὶ εἶδον τὸν τόπον) and that they were seen (ויחזו read as *niphal* in spite of the Classical Hebrew construction with the object marker את which dictates a *qal* reading of the verb) in the place of God (καὶ ὤφθησαν ἐν τῷ τόπῳ τοῦ θεοῦ).[24] The ancient Hebrew witnesses of this passage (4QpaleoExod^m and SP) do differ from the MT, but only regarding the number of Aaronide sons (and future ancestors of the high-priestly lineage).[25] Later Greek revisers corrected the Old Greek towards MT (α' καὶ εἶδον τὸν θεὸν Ἰσραήλ) but even here with a small adaptation (σ' καὶ εἶδον ὁράματι τὸν θεὸν Ἰσραήλ).

Exod 33:11–13

MT ודבר יהוה אל משה פנים אל פנים כאשר ידבר איש אל רעהו ... ויאמר משה אל יהוה ... הודעני נא את דרכיך ואדעך למען אמצא חן בעיניך ...

Thus the LORD used to speak to Moses face to face, as one speaks to a friend ... Moses said to the LORD, "... show me your ways, so that I may know you and find favor in your sight ..." (NRSV)

---

24. See, e.g., Alain Le Boulluec and Pierre Sandevoir, *L'Exode*, BdA 2 (Paris: Cerf, 1989), 246–47; John W. Wevers, *Notes on the Greek Text of Exodus*, SCS 30 (Atlanta: Scholars Press, 1990), 384–86; Joachim Schaper, "Exodos," in *Septuaginta Deutsch. Erläuterungen und Kommentare zum griechischen Alten Testament*, ed. Martin Karrer and Wolfgang Kraus, vol. 1 (Stuttgart: Deutsche Bibelgesellschaft, 2011), 308: "Eine dogmatische Korr."

25. Almost all modern commentators, including the editors of *BHK* and *BHS*, seem to have missed this variant.

LXX καὶ ἐλάλησεν κύριος πρὸς Μωυσῆν ἐνώπιος ἐνωπίῳ, ὡς εἴ τις λαλήσει πρὸς τὸν ἑαυτοῦ φίλον ... Καὶ εἶπεν Μωυσῆς πρὸς κύριον ... ἐμφάνισόν μοι σεαυτόν· γνωστῶς ἴδω σε, ὅπως ἂν ὦ εὑρηκὼς χάριν ἐναντίον σου ...
And the Lord spoke to Moyses face to face, as if someone should speak to his own friend ... And Moyses said to the Lord, "... disclose yourself to me. Let me see you recognizably in order that I might find favor before you ..." (NETS)

Whereas this passage, both in its Hebrew and Greek versions, starts by stating that Moses and God communicated face to face (פנים אל פנים/ἐνώπιος ἐνωπίῳ), the remainder of the chapter makes clear that things were not that easy for Moses. Hence, Moses asks the favor of seeing God directly. The Hebrew text has twice the *hiphil* form of ידע, whereas the Greek translator offers some unusual Greek renderings for this common Hebrew verb, namely, ἐμφάνισόν μοι σεαυτόν γνωστῶς ἴδω σε, "make yourself visible for me in order that I see you with full knowledge."[26] The remainder of the chapter makes clear that Moses will not see God face-to-face, because no man is allowed to see God directly and remain alive (Exod 33:20 לא תוכל לראת פני כי לא יראני האדם וחי/Οὐ δυνήσῃ ἰδεῖν μου τὸ πρόσωπον οὐ γὰρ μὴ ἴδῃ ἄνθρωπος τὸ πρόσωπόν μου καὶ ζήσεται). Instead, Moses sees God's glory (כבוד/δόξα) from behind (Exod 33:23 וראית את אחרי ופני לא יראו/καὶ τότε ὄψῃ τὰ ὀπίσω μου τὸ δὲ πρόσωπόν μου οὐκ ὀφθήσεταί σοι). Apparently, the roots of attenuation of anthropomorphic statements about God can be found already in the Hebrew Bible itself (cf. also Deut 4:12, 15).

Numbers 12:6–8 makes clear that God does not communicate with Moses through riddles or dreams, as he does with prophets, but directly, from mouth to mouth (פה אל פה/στόμα κατὰ στόμα). Whereas the Hebrew text states that Moses beheld God's form (ותמנת יהוה יביט), the Greek translator attenuated this statement by transforming God's "form" (תמונה) into his "glory" (δόξα) and by employing an aorist form (καὶ τὴν δόξαν κυρίου εἶδεν) for the Hebrew *yiqtol* (יביט) rather than a Greek praesens or imperfect which likewise express regularity. Apparently, for the Greek translator, this statement referred back to the singular event narrated in Exod 33:23.[27]

Num 12:6–8

MT ויאמר שמעו נא דברי אם יהיה נביאכם יהוה במראה אליו אתודע בחלום אדבר בו:
לא כן עבדי משה בכל ביתי נאמן הוא: פה אל פה אדבר בו ומראה ולא בחידת ותמנת יהוה יביט ומדוע לא יראתם לדבר בעבדי במשה:

---

26. See *GELS*, 135a and 230b for the English translations; Schaper, "Exodos," 317–19.
27. See Gilles Dorival, *Les Nombres*, BdA 4 (Paris: Cerf, 1994), 67, 303; John W. Wevers, *Notes on the Greek Text of Numbers*, SCS 46 (Atlanta: Scholars Press, 1998), 187–88; Martin Rösel and Christine Schlund, "Arithmoi," in *Septuaginta Deutsch. Erläuterungen und Kommentare zum griechischen Alten Testament*, ed. Martin Karrer and Wolfgang Kraus, vol. 1 (Stuttgart: Deutsche Bibelgesellschaft, 2011), 463.

And he said, "Hear my words: When there are prophets among you, I the LORD make myself known to them in visions; I speak to them in dreams. Not so with my servant Moses; he is entrusted with all my house. With him I speak face to face—clearly, not in riddles; *and he beholds the form of the LORD*. Why then were you not afraid to speak against my servant Moses?" (NRSV)

LXX καὶ εἶπεν πρὸς αὐτούς Ἀκούσατε τῶν λόγων μου· ἐὰν γένηται προφήτης ὑμῶν κυρίῳ, ἐν ὁράματι αὐτῷ γνωσθήσομαι, καὶ ἐν ὕπνῳ λαλήσω αὐτῷ. οὐχ οὕτως ὁ θεράπων μου Μωυσῆς· ἐν ὅλῳ τῷ οἴκῳ μου πιστός ἐστιν· στόμα κατὰ στόμα λαλήσω αὐτῷ, ἐν εἴδει καὶ οὐ δι' αἰνιγμάτων, *καὶ τὴν δόξαν κυρίου εἶδεν*· καὶ διὰ τί οὐκ ἐφοβήθητε καταλαλῆσαι κατὰ τοῦ θεράποντός μου Μωυσῆ;

And he said to them, "Hear my words: If there is a prophet of you for the Lord, in a vision I will be known to him, and in sleep I will speak to him. Not so my attendant Moyses; in my whole house he is faithful. Mouth to mouth I will speak to him, in visible form and not through riddles. *And he has seen the glory of the Lord*. And why were you not afraid to speak against my attendant Moyses?" (NETS)

Such evasive maneuvers can be found throughout the Septuagint. Particularly the device to read the verb ראה with God as object as a *niphal* instead of a *qal* (see already Exod 24:11) proved to be a convenient solution to statements that apparently embarrassed the Greek translators. An example is provided by Ps 17(16):15. This prayer (תפלה/προσευχή) revolves around hearing and seeing. It opens (v. 2) with the hope that God will look favorably on the psalmist (עיניך תחזינה מישרים), which is subtly transformed by the Greek translator into a wish that the psalmist will see justice (οἱ ὀφθαλμοί μου ἰδέτωσαν εὐθύτητας). The psalm closes with a similar hope of vindication, apparently after a night of trial:[28]

Ps 17(16):15

MT אני בצדק אחזה פניך אשבעה בהקיץ תמונתך
   As for me, I shall behold your face in righteousness; when I awake I shall be satisfied, beholding your likeness. (NRSV)

LXX ἐγὼ δὲ ἐν δικαιοσύνῃ ὀφθήσομαι τῷ προσώπῳ σου, χορτασθήσομαι ἐν τῷ ὀφθῆναι τὴν δόξαν σου.
   But as for me, I shall *appear to* your face in righteousness; I shall be fed when your *glory appears.* (NETS)

Besides the passive rendering of the verb חזה, "to behold (cf. v. 2), the notion of "waking up" (הקיץ) has been adjusted to the same idea of "being seen" (ὀφθήσομαι

---

[28]. See the commentaries on the Psalter, e.g., Charles A. Briggs and Emilie G. Briggs, *A Critical and Exegetical Commentary on the Book of Psalms*, ICC (Edinburgh: T&T Clark, 1906), 127–37; Hans-Joachim Kraus, *Psalmen*, 5th ed., BKAT 15.1 (Neukirchen: Neukirchener, 1978), 271–80.

... ὀφθῆναι). As in Num 12:8, the "form of God" (תמונה) has been transformed into God's "glory" (δόξα).

4. Theological Interpretations

As soon as scholars started to investigate the character of the Old Greek translations of the Hebrew Bible in their own right, these features were noted and described in terms of avoidance of anthropomorphic statements. Thus, already in 1841, Zacharias Frankel noticed these deliberate changes introduced by the Greek translator for theological reasons.[29] According to Abraham Geiger, these adaptations in the Septuagint should be seen as attempts by the Greek translators to avoid offensive statements about Israel's God.[30] A century later, Charles T. Fritsch collected all instances of such anti-anthropomorphic renderings in the Septuagint, which include the following passages (excluding the ones discussed above):[31]

Text	MT	LXX
Gen 32:31	פניאל	Εἶδος θεοῦ
Exod 3:6	כי ירא מהביט אל האלהים	εὐλαβεῖτο γὰρ κατεμβλέψαι ἐνώπιον τοῦ θεοῦ
Exod 19:21	פן יהרסו אל יהוה לראות	μήποτε ἐγγίσωσιν πρὸς τὸν θεὸν κατανοῆσαι
Exod 23:15	לא יראו פני ריקם	οὐκ ὀφθήσῃ ἐνώπιόν μου κενός
Exod 23:17	יראה כל זכורך אל פני ארון יהוה	ὀφθήσεται πᾶν ἀρσενικόν σου ἐνώπιον κυρίου τοῦ θεοῦ σου
Exod 34:20	ולא יראו פני ריקם	οὐκ ὀφθήσῃ ἐνώπιόν μου κενός
Exod 34:23	שלש פעמים בשנה יראה כל זכורך את פני הארן יהוה אלהי ישראל	τρεῖς καιροὺς τοῦ ἐνιαυτοῦ ὀφθήσεται πᾶν ἀρσενικόν σου ἐνώπιον κυρίου τοῦ θεοῦ Ισραηλ
Exod 34:24	בעלותך לראות את פני יהוה אלהיך	ἂν ἀναβαίνῃς ὀφθῆναι ἐναντίον κυρίου τοῦ θεοῦ σου

---

29. Zacharias Frankel, *Über den Einfluß der palästinischen Exegese auf die alexandrinische Hermeneutik* (Leipzig: Barth, 1851), 83–85.

30. Abraham Geiger, *Urschrift und Übersetzungen der Bibel in ihrer Abhängigkeit von der innern Entwicklung des Judenthums* (Breslau: Hainauer, 1857), 337–43.

31. Charles T. Fritsch, *The Anti-Anthropomorphisms of the Greek Pentateuch* (Princeton: Princeton University Press, 1943); Fritsch, "A Study of the Greek Translation of the Hebrew Verbs 'to See', with Deity as Subject or Object," in *Harry M. Orlinksy Volume*, ErIsr 16 (Jerusalem: Israel Exploration Society, 1982), 51*–56*. The theology of anti-anthropomorphism can be traced back already to the third century BCE in the description of Hecataeus of Abdera (*FGH* 6 apud Diodorus of Sicily 40.4: ἄγαλμα δὲ θεῶν τὸ σύνολον οὐ κατασκεύασε διὰ τὸ μὴ νομίζειν ἀνθρωπόμορφην εἶναι τὸν θεόν, "he had no images whatsoever made of them, being of the opinion that God is not in human form," text and trans. Walton, LCL).

Deut 16:16	ולא יראה את פני יהוה ריקם	οὐκ ὀφθήσῃ ἐνώπιον κυρίου τοῦ θεοῦ σου κενός
Deut 31:15	וירא יהוה באהל	καὶ κατέβη κύριος ἐν νεφέλῃ
1 Sam 1:22	ונראה את פני יהוה	καὶ ὀφθήσεται τῷ προσώπῳ κυρίου
1 Sam 3:21	ויסף יהוה להראה בשלה	καὶ προσέθετο κύριος δηλωθῆναι ἐν Σηλωμ
1 Sam 28:13	אלהים ראיתי עלים מן הארץ (God singular)	Θεοὺς ἑόρακα ἀναβαίνοντας ἐκ τῆς γῆς (foreign gods)
Ps 11(10):7b	ישר יחזו פנימו "the upright shall behold his face"	εὐθύτητα εἶδεν τὸ πρόσωπον αὐτοῦ, "his face beheld uprightness"
Ps 34(33):6	הביטו אליו	προσέλθατε πρὸς αὐτὸν
Ps 42(41):3	מתי אבוא ואראה פני אלהים	πότε ἥξω καὶ ὀφθήσομαι τῷ προσώπῳ τοῦ θεοῦ
Ps 63(62):3	בקדש חזיתיך לראות עזך וכבודך	ἐν τῷ ἁγίῳ ὤφθην σοι τοῦ ἰδεῖν τὴν δύναμίν σου καὶ τὴν δόξαν σου
Ps 84(83):8	יראה אל אלהים בציון	ὀφθήσεται ὁ θεὸς τῶν θεῶν ἐν Σιων
Job 19:26	ומבשרי אחזה אלוה "then from my flesh I shall see God"	ταῦτα παρὰ γὰρ κυρίου ταῦτά μοι συνετελέσθη, "for these things have been accomplished on me by the Lord"
Job 19:27	אשר אני אחזה לי ועיני ראו "whom I shall see on my side, and my eyes shall behold"	ἃ ἐγὼ ἐμαυτῷ συνεπίσταμαι ἃ ὁ ὀφθαλμός μου ἑόρακεν, "things I am conscious of in myself, things my eye has seen"
Job 22:14	ולא יראה	καὶ οὐχ ὁραθήσεται
Job 23:9	ולא אחז	καὶ οὐ κατέσχον
Job 33:26	וירא פניו בתרועה "and he sees His face with joy"	εἰσελεύσεται δὲ προσώπῳ καθαρῷ σὺν ἐξηγορίᾳ, "and he will enter with a clean face and with thanks"
Isa 17:7	ביום ההוא ישעה האדם על עשהו	τῇ ἡμέρᾳ ἐκείνῃ πεποιθὼς ἔσται ἄνθρωπος ἐπὶ τῷ ποιήσαντι αὐτόν
Isa 31:1	ולא שעו על קדוש ישראל	καὶ οὐκ ἦσαν πεποιθότες ἐπὶ τὸν ἅγιον τοῦ Ισραηλ
Isa 38:11	לא אראה יה בארץ החיים	οὐκέτι μὴ ἴδω τὸ σωτήριον τοῦ θεοῦ ἐπὶ τῆς γῆς
Zech 9:14	ויהוה עליהם יראה	καὶ κύριος ἔσται ἐπ' αὐτοὺς
2 Chr 26:15	זכריהו המבין בראות האלהים	Ζαχαριου τοῦ συνίοντος ἐν φόβῳ κυρίου (< ביראת)

This list makes clear that the phenomenon is both pervasive and selective. Books such as Genesis, Numbers, Judges, Kings, Psalms, Job, Amos, and Isaiah also contain well-known sections where the protagonists (Jacob, Israel, Samson's parents, Micah, Amos, Isaiah, Job) see God with their own eyes. In these cases, the Greek translators did not alter the diction of the Hebrew texts:³²

Text	MT	LXX
Gen 32:20	ואחרי כן אראה פניו	καὶ μετὰ τοῦτο ὄψομαι τὸ πρόσωπον αὐτοῦ
Gen 32:31	כי ראיתי אלהים פנים אל פנים ותנצל נפשי	εἶδον γὰρ θεὸν πρόσωπον πρὸς πρόσωπον καὶ ἐσώθη μου ἡ ψυχή
Num 14:14	שמעו כי אתה יהוה בקרב העם הזה אשר עין בעין נראה אתה יהוה	ἀκηκόασιν ὅτι σὺ εἶ κύριος ἐν τῷ λαῷ τούτῳ ὅστις ὀφθαλμοῖς κατ' ὀφθαλμοὺς ὀπτάζῃ κύριε
Judg 13:22	מות נמות כי אלהים ראינו	ᴮθανάτῳ ἀποθανούμεθα ὅτι θεὸν εἴδομεν (ᴬἑωράκαμεν)
1 Kgs 22:19	ראיתי את יהוה ישב על כסאו	εἶδον τὸν κύριον θεὸν Ισραηλ καθήμενον ἐπὶ θρόνου αὐτοῦ
Isa 6:1	ואראה את אדני ישב על כסא רם ונשא	εἶδον τὸν κύριον καθήμενον ἐπὶ θρόνου ὑψηλοῦ καὶ ἐπηρμένου
Amos 9:1	ראיתי את אדני נצב על המזבח	εἶδον τὸν κύριον ἐφεστῶτα ἐπὶ τοῦ θυσιαστηρίου
Ps 27(26):8	אמר לבי בקשו פני את פניך יהוה אבקש	σοὶ εἶπεν ἡ καρδία μου Ἐζήτησεν τὸ πρόσωπόν μου· τὸ πρόσωπόν σου, κύριε, ζητήσω.
Job 42:5	ועתה עיני ראתך	νυνὶ δὲ ὁ ὀφθαλμός μου ἑόρακέν σε

In one case (not mentioned by Fritsch) the Greek translator even seems to have introduced the notion of seeing God where there is no warrant for it in the Hebrew text, that is, Exod 25:8:³³

MT ועשו לי מקדש ושכנתי בתוככם
And have them make me a sanctuary, so that I may *dwell* among them. (NRSV)
LXX καὶ ποιήσεις μοι ἁγίασμα καὶ ὀφθήσομαι ἐν ὑμῖν
And you shall make a holy precinct for me, and *I shall appear* among you. (NETS)

---

32. Cf. also passages such as Gen 12:7; 16:3; 17:1; 18:1; 22:14; 26:2, 24; 35:1, 9; 48:3; Exod 3:16; 4:1, 5; 6:3; Lev 9:4; 16:2; Deut 33:16 and 34:10, where the context makes clear that God is seen.

33. The commentaries on LXX Exod 25:8 attribute this change to the Greek translator (Wevers, *Notes on Exodus*, 395), either for reasons of anti-anthropomorphism (thus Schaper, "Exodos," 310) or because the Greek translator would have wanted to avoid the idea that God would settle among the Israelites (Le Boulluec and Sandervoir, *L'Exode*, 252), since the Greek translator of Exodus avoids the notion of שכן with God as subject each time in the Greek Exodus (24:16 καταβαίνω; 29:45–46 ἐπικληθῆναι, 40:35 σκιάζω).

Fritsch simply noticed this incongruity and did not attempt to explain it. In Gen 32:20 and Ps 27(26):8, the formulation is modal, that is, Jacob and the psalmists hope to see God's face. The context of Gen 32 and Judg 13 makes clear that Jacob and Samson's parents in fact had seen an angel of God. In Isaiah and Job, however, we find both statements that seem to avoid ánd acknowledge the possibility of humans to see God. The only Greek translation unit that seems to display a very tight consistent pattern appears to be the Greek Psalter where the whole idea of humans actually seeing God seems to be eradicated completely.

With the release of all the unpublished Dead Sea Scrolls in 1990, many scholars expected to find Hebrew parallels for Septuagint variants as shown already for Samuel and Jeremiah. A fresh examination of the phenomenon of "The Treatment in the LXX of the Theme of Seeing God" by Anthony Hanson, published posthumously,[34] revealed many interesting parallels in the targumim, Philo, and Qumran sectarian literature, but no direct parallels in the Qumran biblical manuscripts. For these and other reasons, Innocent Himbaza concludes that the phenomenon is indicative of the theology of the translator and does not reflect an edition of the Hebrew text prior to MT.[35]

The parallels with nonbiblical Jewish literature of the Second Temple period (Philo, apocalyptic literature) have come to play an important role in the assessment of the theology of the Greek Psalter. Schaper claimed that the Greek Psalter reflects a fully elaborated eschatology distinct from the Hebrew original with a network of messianic references and allusions to the idea of resurrection of the dead.[36] In his view, the Septuagint should be studied within its historical and cultural context rather than strictly within the parameters of linguistic-grammatical translation-technical studies. This claim prompted harsh criticism from the part of Albert Pietersma who insisted upon the Hebrew *Vorlage* as first and foremost

---

34. Anthony T. Hanson, "The Treatment in the LXX of the Theme of Seeing God," in *Septuagint, Scrolls and Cognate Writings: Papers Presented to the International Symposium on the Septuagint and Its Relations to the Dead Sea Scrolls and Other Writings (Manchester, 1990)*, ed. George J. Brooke and Barnabas Lindars, SCS 33 (Atlanta: Scholars Press, 1992), 557–68.

35. Innocent Himbaza, "Voir Dieu: LXX d'Exode contre TM et LXX du Pentateuque," in *L'Écrit et l'Esprit: Études d'histoire du texte et de théologie biblique en homage à Adrian Schenker*, ed. Dieter Böhler, Innocent Himbaza and Philippe Hugo, OBO 214 (Fribourg: Academic Press; Göttingen: Vandenhoeck & Ruprecht, 2005), 100–11. See also the detailed commentary on the theophany passages in the Greek Exodus by Larry Perkins, "The Greek Translator of Exodus: *Interpres* (translator) and *expositor* (interpreter): His Treatment of Theophanies," *JSJ* 44 (2013): 16–56. Perkins comes to similar conclusions as Himbaza (to whom he does not refer).

36. Joachim Schaper, *Eschatology in the Greek Psalter*, WUNT 2/76 (Tübingen: Mohr Siebeck, 1995).

context of the Greek translation.[37] His interlinear model denies any perceived theology of the Septuagint that can be explained in linguistic terms.[38] In an attempt to find a middle course between these maximalist and minimalist positions concerning theology in the Septuagint Psalter, Holger Gzella paid much more attention to linguistic observations in his dissertation about eschatology in the Greek Psalter.[39] Nevertheless, with respect to the theme of seeing God, he maintained that the Greek Psalter (particularly Ps 17[16]:15, discussed above) reflects the eschatological theme of beholding God in the afterlife ("jenseitige Gottesschau"), not unlike the Platonic philosopher who beholds the world of Ideas with his intellect.[40]

The relation between Platonic perception of the divine absolute, the Septuagint, and Philonic exegesis forms the core of a recently published volume on *Gottesschau* and *Gotteserkenntnis* edited by Evangelia Dafni.[41] For Dafni there is no significant distinction between Platonism and the Old Testament, particularly since she believes Plato knew and used the Old Testament.[42] Hence, we are back to the position outlined at the beginning of this paper, where Hellenistic influence upon the Septuagint is all too easily equated with Platonism and where Greek modifications of the Hebrew Pentateuchal text is all too quickly seen through the lens of Philo.

---

37. Albert Pietersma, review of *Eschatology in the Greek Psalter*, by Joachim Schaper, *BO* 54 (1997): 185–90.

38. Albert Pietersma, "A New Paradigm for Addressing Old Questions: The Relevance of the Interlinear Model for the Study of the Septuagint," in *Bible and Computer: The Stellenbosch AIBI-6 Conference*, ed. Johann Cook (Leiden: Brill, 2002), 337–64.

39. Holger Gzella, *Lebenszeit und Ewigkeit: Studien zur Eschatologie und Anthropologie des Septuaginta-Psalters*, BBB 134 (Berlin: Philo, 2002).

40. Gzella, *Lebenszeit und Ewigkeit*, 229–51. Cf. Plato, *Symp.* 211e: αὐτὸ τὸ θεῖον καλὸν δύναιτο μονοειδὲς κατιδεῖν, "to behold the divine beauty itself, in its unique form."

41. Evangelia G. Dafni, ed., *Gottesschau-Gotteserkenntnis: Studien zur Theologie der Septuaginta*, vol. 1, WUNT 387 (Tübingen: Mohr Siebeck, 2017).

42. Evangelia G. Dafni, *Genesis, Plato und Euripides: Drei Studien zum Austausch von griechischem und hebräischem Sprach- und Gedankengut in der Klassik und im Hellenismus*, Biblisch-theologische Studien 108 (Neukirchen: Neukirchener, 2010); Dafni, "Gotteserkenntnis in Platons Theaitetus und in der Septuaginta," in *Gottesschau-Gotteserkenntnis: Studien zur Theologie der Septuaginta*, ed. Evangelia G. Dafni, vol. 1, WUNT 387 (Tübingen: Mohr Siebeck, 2017), 221–55.

5. Religion-Historical Interpretations

The first scholar to broaden the horizon of this discussion beyond the confines of biblical and para-biblical literature is Jan Joosten.[43] He pointed to the Egyptian context, where the notion of "seeing the Deity" was a central element in the native religious tradition. The expression under discussion "to see the god(s)," θεοὺς ἰδεῖν, is attested in Manetho's *Aegyptiaka* (*apud* Josephus, *C. Ap.* 1.232–33), where it is told that pharao Amenophis' wish to behold the gods (θεῶν γενέσθαι θεατήν) could only be fulfilled when he would cleanse the country from the polluted people (i.e., Israelites). The tendency of the Greek translators to avoid the idea of seeing the Deity would then be a polemic against this Egyptian tradition with its polytheism and exclusive privileges for the Egyptian kings and priests. In his view, the two contrasting tendencies observable in the Septuagint, that is, both to attenuate ánd to tolerate the notion of seeing God, could be explained in terms of difference in provenance of the Greek translators: the polemical attitude would be characteristic for a Palestinian provenance, whereas the more tolerant theology would be typical for the Egyptian context.

Joosten tries to support his thesis by pointing to other examples of Egyptian influence on the Greek translation of the Pentateuch, such as the Egyptian loanwords ἄχει, "reeds," (cf. the different Hebrew transcription אחו), θῖβις, "basket, box" (תבה), and οιφι, "ephah" (איפה), as well as similar cases of Jewish-Egyptian polemics observable in Hellenistic-Jewish writings by Artapanus and Demetrius. Interesting as these examples may be, they do not contextuallize the idea of seeing god(s) in the Hellenistic Egyptian and Palestinian settings.

In a recent contribution to this discussion, Martin Rösel points out that in Egyptian religion, "seeing the deity" (Egyptian: *mꜣꜣ nṯr*), was a privilege reserved for the local priesthood.[44] Even the processions during religious festivals may not have exhibited the cult statues, according to Rösel. Furthermore, the tendency to avoid speaking about face-to-face vision of God has a parallel in the tendency to avoid speaking about God's factual dwelling on earth as well as meeting (יעד) God.[45] Hence, seeing the deity in Egyptian religion must have been exceptional and probably something spiritual and intellectual, rather than factual.

---

43. Jan Joosten, "To See God: Conflicting Exegetical Tendencies in the Septuagint," in *Die Septuaginta: Texte, Kontexte, Lebenswelten. Internationale Fachtagung veranstaltet von Septuaginta Deutsch (LXX.D), Wuppertal 20.–23. Juli 2006*, ed. Martin Karrer and Wolfgang Kraus, WUNT 219 (Tübingen: Mohr Siebeck, 2008), 287–99.

44. Martin Rösel, "Wie Gott sich erkennen lässt: Gottesschau und Gotteserkenntnis in der Septuaginta," in *Gottesschau-Gotteserkenntnis: Studien zur Theologie der Septuaginta*, ed. Evangelia G. Dafni, vol. 1, WUNT 387 (Tübingen: Mohr Siebeck, 2017), 163–76.

45. Martin Rösel, "Tempel und Tempellosigkeit: Der Umgang mit dem Heiligtum in der Pentateuch-LXX," in *Die Septuaginta–Texte, Theologien, Einflüsse. 2. Internationale Fachtagung veranstaltet von Septuaginta Deutsch (LXX.D), Wuppertal 23.–27.7.2008*, ed.

6. Dream Visions

To my mind, more could and should be said about the religion-historical background of seeing god(s) in the Hellenistic context. As a matter of fact, a large number of inscriptions and papyri from the Hellenistic world do report a vision of the deity, if only indirectly (through dreams, oracles, or manifestations in natural events). They demonstrate Joosten's point that the expression "seeing God" had a very clear and tangible referent in the Greek-Egyptian and Graeco-Roman cultural context of the early Greek translations of Hebrew Scripture (Pentateuch, Joshua, Isaiah). They almost always occur in the context of temples and a particular priesthood responsible for the proper interpretation. To a certain extent, this supports Rösel's point that seeing God was not a common phenomenon available to every ordinary person. Yet, it does not prove that seeing God in this Hellenistic context was already exclusively or predominantly seen as a metaphysical cognitive enterprise in the Platonic-Philonic sense. In order to demonstrate my points, I will discuss papyri and inscriptions from the Hellenistic world that illustrate the various ways a deity could, under special circumstances, become visible for certain privileged persons.

For instance, the papyri from the temple dedicated to Greek-Egyptian god Sarapis at Memphis from 172–152 BCE (UPZ I 2-105) provide a fascinating insight into the dream oracles recorded by a Macedonian, called Ptolemaios, who lived as a recluse (κάτοχος) among Egyptian priests and officials in a shrine devoted to Astarte in the temple precincts.[46] One of the documents from his discarded archive appears to be a scribal exercise of Ptolemaios's younger brother Apollonios, who drafted a rather inaccurate version of a composition now known as the Dream of King Nectanebo (UPZ I 81).[47] Recently Demotic counterparts of

---

Wolfgang Kraus, Martin Karrer and Martin Meiser, WUNT 252 (Tübingen: Mohr Siebeck, 2010), 447–61.

46. Ulrich Wilcken, *Papyri aus Unterägypten*, vol. 1 of *Urkunden der Ptolemäerzeit (ältere Funde)* (Berlin: de Gruyter, 1927) with extensive introduction and commentary. See also Naphtali Lewis, *Greeks in Ptolemaic Egypt: Case Studies in the Social History of the Hellenistic World* (Oxford: Clarendon, 1986), 69–87.

47. Wilcken, *Urkunden*, 369–74. See also Jörg-Dieter Gauger, "Der 'Traum des Nektanebos'–Die griechische Fassung," in *Ägypten und Apokalyptik. Eine kritische Untersuchung der relevanten Texte aus dem griechisch-römischen Ägypten*, ed. Andreas Blasius and Bernd U. Schipper, OLA 107 (Leuven: Peeters, 2002), 189–219. For a discussion of the parallels between this composition and the Old Greek version of Isaiah, see Arie van der Kooij, "The Old Greek of Isaiah and Other Prophecies Published in Ptolemaic Egypt," in *Die Septuaginta–Texte, Theologien, Einflüsse. 2. Internationale Fachtagung veranstaltet von Septuaginta Deutsch (LXX.D), Wuppertal 23.–27.7.2008*, ed. Wolfgang Kraus, Martin Karrer and Martin Meiser, WUNT 252 (Tübingen: Mohr Siebeck, 2010), 72–84; and my paper "Visions from Memphis and Leontopolis: The Phenomenon of the Vision Reports in the Greek Isaiah in the Light of Contemporary Accounts from Hellenistic

this semi-literary composition have turned up in the Carlsberg archive.[48] The narrative probably belonged to the stories that somewhat later came to be known as the Alexander Romance, early Hellenistic propaganda claiming the rightful rulership of Alexander the Great via his real father, the last native Egyptian king, Nectanebo II. The description thus fits generally accepted early Hellenistic conventions about what to expect from divine encounters. The vision of the gods is described very vividly:

> In the 16th (regal) year of the 21th to the 22nd (day) of the (month) Pharmouthi (= July, 5–6, 343 BCE).... After Nectanebo the king had gone to Memphis and had brought a sacrifice and had prayed to the gods to reveal the future (ἀξιώσαντος τοὺς θεοὺς δηλῶσαι τὰ ἐνεστηκότα), there appeared to him in a dream (ἔδοξεν κατ' ἐνύπνον) a papyrus boat, called in Egyptian *roops*, coming to anchor at Memphis, on which was a great throne (ἐφ' οὗ ἦν θρόνος μέγας); on it was seated the greatly honored, benefactress of fruits and commandress of the gods, Isis (ἐπὶ τε τούτου καθῆσαι τὴν μεγαλώδοξον εὐεργέτειαν καρπῶν ... καὶ θεῶν ἄνασον Ἴσιν), while all the gods of Egypt were standing around her at the right-hand and left-hand side of her (καὶ τοὺς ἐν Ἀγύπτῳ θεοὺς πάντας παραστάναι αὐτῇ ἐγ δεξιὸν καὶ εὐωμένων αὐτῆς). One of them came forward to the middle with the estimated size of 21 feet tall, called in Egyptian Onouris, in Greek however Ares. (UPZ I 81, col. ii, lines 1–16)

Here, as elsewhere, the medium is the dream, not unlike the dream visions found in the Hebrew Bible (e.g., in the book of Daniel). The divine beings in this Greek-Egyptian text are mega-sized, as is their entourage. The recipient of this divine manifestation is no ordinary being, but the pharaoh, but the intermediary (Petesis) could be a person of lower rank. Ptolemaios also recorded his own dreams (UPZ I 77–80), but they deal with human affairs.

This also applies to the priest Hor who lived in approximately the same place and time as the κάτοχος Ptolemaios. Hor, a priest originally from Sebennytos, protested against abuses in the Ibis-cult of Thoth and tried to invigorate his pleas to the Ptolemaic court by means of oracles dealing with the Seleucid occupation of

---

Egypt," in *Isaiah in Context: Studies in Honour of Arie van der Kooij on the Occasion of His Sixty-Fifth Birthday*, ed. Michaël N. van der Meer, Percy van Keulen, Wido van Peursen and Bas ter Haar Romeny, VTSup 138 (Leiden: Brill, 2010), 281–316.

48. P.Carlsberg 562, see Kim Ryholt, "Nectanebo's Dream or The Prophecy of Petesis," in *Ägypten und Apokalyptik. Eine kritische Untersuchung der relevanten Texte aus dem griechisch-römischen Ägypten*, ed. Andreas Blasius and Bernd U. Schipper, OLA 107 (Leuven: Peeters, 2002), 221–41. See also Ryholt, *Narrative Literature from the Tebtunis Temple Library*, The Carlsberg Papyri 10, Carsten Niebuhr Institute Publications 35 (Copenhagen: Museum Tusculanum, 2013), 157–70: "A Sequel to the Prophecy of Petesis (P.Carlsberg 424, P. Carlsberg 499, and P.Carlsberg 559 + PSI inv. D 60 recto."

Egypt (170–168 BCE) under Antiochus IV Epiphanes.[49] One of the fifty-eight preserved Demotic ostraca (O.dem.Hor 1) contains a *vaticinium ex eventu* related to the Seleucid retreat from Egypt in 168 BCE, but actually written in 159 BCE:

> When I came to Heliopolis in Khoiak (day? ..., within) the sanctuary of Osormnevis, I was told in a dream to put this writing before the great men. (I went before?) *Tryn* the prophet of Khons, the scribe of Pharaoh at Memphis ... that which was verified when Antiochus (*ꜣ tyks*) was to the north of *Pr-ꜥ-ꜣ wrys* and Egypt divorced itself. I stood with *Ḥryns* who was the head of the army and the agent of Pharaoh Ptolemy our Lord. I caused him to discover the matters (...) which had come before me, the fortune of the Pharaoh. The Lady of the two lands, Isis, was the one who ordained them, the great god Thoth the one who recorded in connection with them. I was told in a dream: Isis, the great goddess of this portion of Egypt and the land of Syria, is walking upon the face of the water of the Syrian sea. Thoth stands before her (and) takes her hand, (and) she reached the harbor (at) Alexandria. She said: "Alexandria is secure (against the) enemy. (O.dem.Hor 1, lines 5–14; text and trans. Ray)

In this oracle, the deities Isis and Thoth are seen by a local priest, again in a dream vision. The address is the king, but even more important are the higher priestly authorities who apparently have to authorize this vision. Apparently, the *Sitz im Leben* of the *visio Dei* was the temple and was the highest echelon of the priesthood a *conditio sine qua non* for its authority.

Propaganda and royal connections were important for many sanctuaries in the Hellenistic period. The priesthood of Memphis entertained relatively good relations with the Ptolemaic rulers in Alexandria. In return, they received gifts, status, and power over rival sanctuaries.[50] Other sanctuaries engraved the accomplishments of the local deities in stone, thereby enhancing their popularity as pilgrimage site for all kind of people suffering from various illnesses. Especially the temples devoted to Asclepius had a reputetion to maintain. The one on the Greek mainland, Epidaurus, housed stelai with some seventy stories of miraculous cures by Apollo and Asclepius (Ἰάματα τοῦ Ἀπολλῶνος καὶ τοῦ Ἀσκλαπιοῦ, thus

---

49. John D. Ray, *The Archive of Ḥor*, Texts from Excavation 2 (London: Egypt Exploration Society, 1976); see further my "Visions from Memphis and Leontopolis," 308–12.

50. See Werner Huß, *Der makedonische König und die ägyptische Priester. Studien zur Geschichte des ptolemäischen Ägypten*, Historia Einzelschriften 85 (Stuttgart: Steiner, 1994); Dorothy Thompson, *Memphis under the Ptolemies*, 2nd rev. ed. (Princeton: Princeton University Press, 2012), as well as the general histories of the Ptolemaic Empire, e.g., Günter Hölbl, *Geschichte des Ptolemäerreiches: Politik, Ideologie und religiöse Kultur von Alexander der Großen bis zur römischen Eroberung* (Darmstadt: Wissenschaftliche Buchgesellschaft, 1994), trans. *A History of the Ptolemaic Empire* (London: Taylor & Francis, 2000), and Werner Huß, *Ägypten in hellenistischer Zeit* (München: Beck, 2001).

the title of stele 1), dating from the second half of the fourth century BCE.[51] The narratives all follow a more or less similar pattern in which a supplicant (ἱκέτης) came to the temple, received a dream vision during the night while sleeping in the sanctuary (ἐγκαθεύδων δὲ ὄψιν εἶδε) in which it seemed as if the god was present (ἐδόκει οἱ ὁ θεὸς ἐπιστάς), after which the supplicant was cured the following morning. In each of these visions the visitors see the deity, see for example:

> Ambrosia from Athens, blind in one eye. She came as a suppliant to the god [αὕτα ἱκέτις ἦλθε ποὶ τὸν θεόν). Walking about the sanctuary (τὸ ἱαρόν), she ridiculed some of the cures as being unlikely and impossible, the lame and the blind becoming well from only seeing a dream (χωλοὺς καὶ τυφλοὺ[ς] ὑγιεῖς γίνεσθαι ἐνύπνιον ἰδόν[τας μό]νον). Sleeping here, she saw a vision (ἐγκαθεύδουσα δὲ ὄψιν εἶδε). It seemed to her the god came to her (ἐδόκει οἱ ὁ θεὸς ἐπιστάς) and said he would make her well, but she would have to pay a fee by dedicating a silver pig in the sanctuary as a memorial for her ignorance. When he had said these things, he cut her sick eye and poured a medicine over it. When day came she left well. (Stele A, lines 33–41, text A4; text and trans. LiDonnici)

Although the deity was not seen directly, but only in a dream, his presence was real enough for the many visitors. At least that is what the local priesthood promoting the cult of Asclepius wanted their clientele to believe. The temple was accessible for every purified person and not restricted to a priviliged priestly or royal caste.

7. Epiphanies

During the Greco-Roman period, the cult of Asclepius became very popular. In a praise of Asclepius-Imhoutes on a first-second century CE papyrus from Oxyrhynchus (P.Oxy. 11.1381), we find a story about an Egyptian scroll about the deeds of Pharaoh Mencheres and his architect Imhotep of the third dynasty, which was found during the reign of the same Pharaoh Nectanebo II we encountered already in the Serapeum archive discussed above.[52] The cult of Asclepius, so the story goes, had decayed for several years and the priests had abandoned the temple. Thus, the god was compelled to take action. The occasion arose when the writer of the document visited the temple with his ill mother as supplicants and the god demanded a translation of the Egyptian eulogy in return for healing the ill

---

51. See, e.g., Lynn R. LiDonnici, *The Epidaurian Miracle Inscriptions: Text, Translation and Commentary*, TT 36 (Atlanta: Scholars Press, 1995).

52. Bernard P. Grenfell and Arthur S. Hunt, ed., *The Oxyrhynchus Papyri*, part 11 (London: Egypt Exploration Fund, 1915), 221–34; see also Lewis, *Greeks in Ptolemaic Egypt*, 72–74.

mother.[53] Due to the difficulty of the task, the author put off the work for a later period. Hence, the deity had to remind him of his promise:

> Having often begun the translation of the said book in the Greek tongue (ἐγὼ δὲ πολλάκις τῆς ἀ]ὐτῆς βίβλου τὴν ἑρμηνείαν [ἀρ]ξάμενος Ἑλληνίδι γλ[ώ]σσῃ) I learnt at length how to proclaim it ([ἔμ]αθον ὂν αἰῶνι κηρῦξαι), but while I was in the full tide of composition my ardour was restrained by the greatness of the story, because I was about to make it public (δ[ι]ότι ἔξω ἐλεῖν ἔμελλο[ν] αὐτήν); for to gods alone, not to mortals, is it permitted to describe the mighty deeds of the gods (θε[οῖ]ς γὰρ μόνοι[ς] ἀλλ' οὐ [θν]ητοῖς ἐ[[φ]]φικ[[..]]τ[ὸ]ν τὰς θεῶν διηγεῖσθα[ι] δυνάμεις).... Therefore avoiding rashness I was waiting for the favourable occasion afforded by old age, and putting off the fulfillment of my promise ...
>
> But when a period of three years had elapsed, in which I was no longer working, and for three years my mother was distracted by a fever lasting more than three days, He (i.e., the deity) which had seized her, at length having with difficulty comprehended we came as suppliants before the god (ἱκέτ[α]ι παρῆμεν ἐπὶ τὸν θεὸν), entreating him to grant my mother recovery from disease. He, having shown himself favorably, as he is to all, in dreams, cured her by simple remedies (ὁ δ' οἷα καὶ πρὸς πάντας χρηστὸς δι' ὀνειράτων φανεὶς εὐτελέσιν αὐτὴν ἀπήλλαξεν βοηθήμασιν); and we rendered due thanks to our preserver (τῷ σώσαντι) by sacrifices. When I too afterwards was suddenly seized with a pain in my right side, I quickly hastened to the helper of the human race (τὸν βοηθὸν τῆς ἀνθρωπίνης), and he, being again disposed to pity (εἰς ἔλεον), listened to me, and displayed still more effectively his particular clemency (εὐεργεσίαν), which, as I am intending to recount his terrible powers, I will substantiate (ἣν ἐπαληθειῶ μέλλων τὰς αὐτοῦ φρικτὰς δυν[ά]με[ι]ς ἀπαγγέλειν):
>
> It was night, when every living creature was asleep except those in pain, but divinity showed itself the more effectively (τὸ δὲ θεῖον ἐνεργέστερον ἐφαίνετο).... Heavy in the head with my troubles I was lapsing half-conscious into sleep ({ἀ}λήθαργος [ε]ἰς ὕπνον ἐφερόμην), and my mother, as a mother would for her child (and she is by nature affectionate), being extremely grieved at my agonies was sitting without enjoying even a short slumber, when suddenly she perceived—it was no dream or sleep (εἶτ' ἐξαπ[ί]νης ἑώρα—οὔτ' ὄναρ οὔθ' ὕπνος), for her eyes were open immovably, though not seeing clearly, for a divine and terrifying vision came to her (βλέποντες μὲν οὐκ ἀκρειβῶς, θ[[..]]εία γὰρ αὐτὴν μετὰ δέ[ο]υς εἰσῄει φαντασία[[ν]]), easily preventing her from observing the god himself or his servants, whichever it was (καὶ ἀκό[π]ως κατ[ο]πτεύειν κωλύουσα εἴτε αὐτὸν τὸν θεὸν εἴτε αὐτοῦ θεράποντας). In any case there was some one whose height was more than human, clothed in shining raiment and carrying in his left hand a book (πλὴν ἦν τις ὑπερμήκης μὲν ἢ κατ' ἄνθρωπον λαμπ[ρ]αῖς ἠμφιεσμένος ὀθόναις τῇ εὐωνύμῳ χειρὶ φέρων βίβλον), who after merely regarding me two or

---

53. For the phenomenon of incubation, see, e.g., Gil H. Renberg, *Where Dreams May Come: Incubation Sanctuaries in the Greco-Roman World*, RGRW 184.1–2 (Leiden: Brill, 2017).

three times from head to foot disappeared. When she had recovered herself, she tried, still trembling, to wake me, and finding that the fever had left me and that much sweat was pouring off me, did reference to the manifestation of the god (τὴν μὲ[ν] τοῦ θε[ο]ῦ προσεκύνησε[ν] ἐπιφάνειαν), and then wiped me and calmed me. When I spoke with her, she wished to declare the virtue of the god, but I anticipating her told all myself; for everything she saw in the vision appeared to me in dreams (ὅσα [γ]ὰρ δι[ὰ] τῆς ὄψεως εἶδεν ταῦτα ἐγ[ὼ] δι' ὀνειράτων ἐφαντασιώθην).... (P.Oxy. 11.1381.2.32–7.140)

It is not often that we find such an elaborate report in the papyri and inscriptions of a divine vision. The narrative is also exceptional for the circumstance that the deity appears both in dream (to the author) and directly (to his mother). In the latter case, we find an interesting ambiguity between concealment (βλέποντες μὲν οὐκ ἀκρειβῶς) and transparancy (λαμπ[ρ]αῖς ἠμφιεσμένος ὀθόναις). Nevertheless the parallel shows that we should make a sharp distinction between seeing God in a dream and seeing God in a more direct manner. Interesting for Septuagint studies is the fact that the theophany is connected to the translation of ancient authoritative scripture in a time of transition from the ancient constitutions to the Hellenistic period. The vision itself is described in terms of ὄψις, φαντασία and ἐπιφάνεια. Although such visions are not daily routine, they are not deemed impossible for the author and his readership. Nevertheless, the context of a temple seems indispensable in this case too. The deity had to lure the author of the document and his mother to his sanctuary with the aid of diseases. Only in the sacred precincts could he appear both in dreams and in person.

Other famous epiphanies were recorded on a momumental marble stone at the sanctuary of Athena at Lindos at the island of Rhodes compiled by the inhabitants of the city in 99 BCE on the basis of earlier recordings.[54] In a time when the authority of the Lindian temple was declining, the inhibitants of the city made sure to record the gifts granted to Athena both by heroes from the mythical past (e.g., Kadmos, Minos, Herakles) and important historical figures (e.g., King Amasis of Egypt, the Persian general Datis, Alexander the Great, Ptolemy II Philadelphus). Only after the long list of dedications, we find stories about epiphanies that occured at this sanctuary and which saved the city from foreign oppression. The first of these epiphanies relate to the delivery of the city from its siege by King Darius around 494 BCE by means of a miraculous epiphany of the goddess in a storm:[55]

---

54. See, e.g., Christian Blinkenberg, *Die lindische Tempelchronik* (Bonn: Marcus & Weber, 1915); Carolyn Higbie, *The Lindian Chronicle and the Greek Creation of Their Past* (Oxford: Oxford University Press, 2003).

55. See Pausanias, *Descr.* 1.4.4; 10.23.1–2 for a parallel relating storm, earthquake, and avalanche that put off the Gauls from capturing Delphi.

Epiphanies (Ἐπιφάνειαι). When Darius king of the Persians sent out great forces for the enslavement of Greece (Δαρείου τοῦ Περσᾶν βασιλέως ἐπὶ καταδουλώσει τᾶς Ἑλλάδος ἐκπέμψαντος μεγάλας δυνάμεις), his naval expedition landed on this first of the islands. When throughout the land people became terrified at the onset of the Persians, some fled together to the most fortified places, but the majority were gathered at Lindos. The enemy established a siege and besieged them, until, on account of the lack of water, the Lindians, being worn down, were of a mind to surrender the city to the enemy. During this time, the goddess, standing over one of the rulers in his sleep, called upon him to be bold (καθ' ὃν δὴ χρόνον ἁ μὲν θεὸς ἑνὶ τῶν ἀρχόντων ἐπιστᾶσα καθ' ὕπνον παρεκάλει θαρσεῖν), since she was about to ask her father for the much-needed water for them. After he had seen the vision, he announced to the citizens the command of Athena (ὄψιν ἰδὼν ἀνάγγειλε τοῖς πολίταις τὰν ποτίταξιν τᾶς Ἀθάνας). Then, reckoning that they had enough to hold out for five days only, asked only for a truce of that many days from the enemy, saying that Athena had sent away to her own father for help, and if there was nothing forthcoming in the allotted time, they said that they would hand the city over to them. Datis, the admiral for Darius, when he heard this, immediately laughed. But when on the next day a great dark storm cloud settled over the acropolis (ἐπεὶ δὲ ἐν τᾶι ἐχομέναι ἁμέραι γνόφ[ο]υ μείζ<ο>νος περὶ τὰν ἀκρόπολιν συσστάντος) and a big storm rained down across the middle, then, paradoxically, the ones being besieged had abundant water, but the Persian force was in need. The enemy was astounded at the manifestation of the goddess (καταπλαγεὶς ὁ βάρβα[ρος] τὰν τᾶς θεοῦ ἐπιφάνειαν), and took off his own accroutements covering his body; he sent for dedication (εἰσέπεμψε ἀνα[θ]έ[μ]ειν) the mantle and torque.... Datis himself broke up his quarters because of the events aforementioned, made a treaty of friendship with the besieged people, and declared in addition that the gods protect these people (αὐτὸς δ[ὲ] ὁ Δᾶτις ἀνέζευξε ἐπὶ τὰς προκειμέ[ν]ας πράξεις φιλίαν ποτὶ τοὺς πολιορ[κ]ηθέντας συνθέσμενος καὶ ποταποφω[νή]σας, ὅτι τοὺς ἀνθρώπους τούτους θεοὶ φυλάσσουσι).
(Lindian chronicle D, lines 1-47; text and trans. Higbie)

The reliability of this epiphany is further underpinned by references to nine Greek historical works, now lost. The epiphany of the goddess took place in two stages: first in a dream to one of the rulers of the city and then in the miraculous event of rainfall precisely on the acropolis. The narrative is conspicuously anonymous: only the well-known admiral of Darius, Datis, is mentioned. In another (third) narrative from the same Lindian chronicle relating to the siege of Demetrius Poliorcetes (305–304 BCE) we find more specific details about the people involved. Not surprisingly, the protagonist of the story is a priest:

Other (epiphany) (ἄλλα). When the city was besieged by Demetrius, Kallikles, having retired from the priesthood of Athena the Lindian (ὁ ἐεικὼς ἐκ τᾶς ἱερατείας τᾶς Ἀθάνας τᾶς Λινδίας), but still living in Lindos, believed that the goddess stood over him in a sleep (ἔδοξε ... ἐπιστᾶσαν αὐτῶι καθ' ὕπνον τὰν θεόν) to command him to announce to one of the *prytaneis*, Anaxipolis, that he should write to King Ptolemy and should invite [him] to come to the aid of the city ...

The first time that Kallikles saw the vision, he did nothing (τὸ μὲν οὖν πρᾶτον ἰδὼν τὰν ὄψιν ὁ Καλλικλῆς ἡσυχίαν εἶχε). But when the same thing happened to him repeatedely—for six nights in a row standing over his head she made the same command (συνεχῶς γὰρ ἐξ [ν]ύκτας ἐπισταμένα τὰν αὐτὰ[ν] ἐποιεῖτο ποτίταξιν)—then Kallikles, arriving at the city, set forth these things (Lindian chronicle D, lines 94–113; text and trans. Higbie)

Both the narrative sequence (first disbelief, then action) and the vocabulary (ἔδοξε ... ἐπιστᾶσαν αὐτῶι καθ' ὕπνον τὰν θεὸν) is remarkably similar to the dream-vision reports presented in the previous section. Apparently, the notion of seeing the deity had become so common in the Hellenistic world that it had acquired its own stereotyped literary formulations.

In the Greco-Roman world, such epiphanies were not only inscribed in monumental documents, they were also regularly depicted in iconographical form. At the sanctuary of Artemis at Brauron, some 20 km southeast of Athens, several

votive altars have been found depicting an epiphany of Artemis to her worshippers, dating from fourth century BCE. Usually the superhuman size of the deity is accentuated. Of course the donor and his family, here a certain Antiphanes, his wife Aristonike and their household, with their dedications (a bull) to the deity are also presented in full:[56]

---

56. https://commons.wikimedia.org/wiki/File:Brauron_-_Votive_Relief3.jpg. For a discussion see Verity Platt, "Epiphany," in *The Oxford Handbook of Ancient Greek Religion*, ed. Esther Eidiniv and Julia Kindt (Oxford: Oxford University Press, 2015), 491–504. For the biblical-theological context of the term *epiphany*, see—instead of the very meagre treatment in *TWNT*—Elpidus Pax, *ΕΠΙΦΑΝΕΙΑ: Eine religionsgeschichtliche Beitrag zur biblischen Theologie*, Münchener Theologische Studien 1.10 (München: Zink, 1955), and *TLNT* 2:65–68.

8. Processions

In the Greco-Roman world, Hellenistic Egypt in particular, one did not have to be ill or delirious to see the gods. The gods would leave their sanctuaries on a regular basis to be carried around in a procession (Greek πομπή or κωμασία).[57] According to Herodotus (*Hist.* 2.58), the Egyptians preserved a very ancient tradition:

> It would seem too that the Egyptians were the first to establish solemn assemblies, and processions, and services (Πανηγύρις δὲ ἄρα καὶ πομπὰς καὶ προσαγωγὰς); the Greeks learnt all this from them. (text and trans. Godley, LCL)

According to Hecataeus of Abdera who wrote a treatise on the Egyptian customs (Περὶ τῆς Αἰγυπτιῶν φιλοσοφίας, *FGH* 264) at the very beginning of the Ptolemaic age (ca. 300 BCE), the Egyptians

> also set up make such statues and temples to these sacred animals because they do not know the true form of the deity (κατασκευάζειν δὲ καὶ ἀγάλματα τεμένη τῶι μὴ εἰδέναι τὴν του θεοῦ μορφήν). (*FGH* 264.1 *apud* Diogenes Laërtius, *Vitae* 1.10; text and trans. Hicks, LCL)

Of course, the gods needed to be kept at safe distance from the mob, especially when they were riotous such as the locals at Papremis.

> At Papremis sacrifice is offered and rites performed as elsewhere; but when the sun is sinking, while a few of the priests are left to busy themselves with the image (ἄγαλμα), the greater number of them beset the entrance of the temple, with clubs of wood in their hands; they are confronted by more than a thousand men, all performing vows and all carrying wooden clubs like the rest. The image of the god in a little wooden gilt casket, is carried on the day before this from the temple to another sacred chamber (τὸ δὲ ἄγαλμα ἐὸν ἐν νηῷ μικρῷ ξυλίνῳ κατακεχρυσωμένῳ προεκκομίζουσι τῇ προτεραίῃ ἐς ἄλλο οἴκημα ἱρόν). The few who are left with the image draw a four-wheeled cart carrying it in its casket; the other priests stand in the temple porch and prevent its entrance (οἱ μὲν δὴ ὀλίγοι οἱ περὶ τὤγαλμα λελειμμένοι ἕλκουσι τετράκυκλον ἅμαξαν ἄγουσαν τὸν νηόν τε καὶ τὸ ἐν τῷ νηῷ ἐνεὸν ἄγαλμα); the votaries take the part of the god, and smite the priests, who resist. There is hard fighting with clubs, and heads are broken, and as I think (though the Egyptians told me no life was lost), many die of their wounds. (Herodotus, *Hist.* 2.63.2; text and trans. Godley, LCL)

---

57. See, e.g., Walter Burkert, *Griechische Religion der archaischen und klassischen Epoche*, RdM 15 (Stuttgart: Kohlhammer 1977), 163–66; trans. *Greek Religion* (Cambridge: Harvard University Press, 1985), 99–101. Marion True, Jens Daehner, Janet B. Grossman, and Kenneth D. S. Lapatin, "Greek Processions," in *Processions, Sacrifices, Libations, Fumigations, Dedications*, vol. 1 of *Thesaurus cultus et rituum antiquorum*, ed. Vassilis Lambrinoudakis and Jean C. Balty (Los Angeles: Getty Publications, 2004), 1–20.

When the Apis bull died and a new young bull was found to replace him, not every one was allowed to see the procession of the new Apis, according to Hecateaus, yet women were allowed to watch:

> And then, putting it on a state barge fitted out with a gilded cabin, conduct it *as a god* to the sanctuary of Hephaestus at Memphus (ἔπειτ' εἰς θαλαμηγὸν ναῦν οἴκημα κεχρυσωμένον ἔχουσαν ἐμβιβάσαντες ὡς θεὸν ἀνάγουσιν εἰς Μέμφιν εἰς τὸ τοῦ Ἡφαίστου τέμενος). During these forty days only women may *look* at it (ἐν δὲ ταῖς προειρημέναις τετταράκονθ' ἡμέραις μόνον ὁρῶσιν αἱ γυναῖκες); they standing facing it (κατὰ πρόσωπον ἱστάμεναι) and pulling up their garments show their genitals (καὶ δεικνύουσιν ἀνασυράμενοι τὰ ἑαυτῶν γεννητικὰ μόρια), but henceforth they are forever prevented from coming into the presence of this god (τὸν δ' ἄλλον χρόνον ἅπαντα κεκωλυμένον ἐστὶν εἰς ὄψιν αὐτὰς ἔρχεσθαι τούτῳ τῷ θεῷ). (*FGH* 264 F 25 *apud* Diodorus of Sicily 1.85; text and trans. Oldfather, LCL)

The bull is described here as a deity (ὡς θεὸν). The restrictions on his visibility has less to do with the idea that the deity is imperceivable for human senses, but rather with cultural customs.

We find several depictions of Egyptian processions on tomb reliefs, for example, the oracle scene of Amenhotep I (1526–1506 BCE) in the tomb of Amemose, his high priest (Theban Tomb 19).[58] What makes this depiction so special

---

58. Jaroslav Czerny, "Egyptian Oracles," in *A Saite Oracle Papyrus from Thebes in the Brooklyn Museum (Papyrus Brooklyn 47.218.3)*, ed. Richard A. Parker and Jaroslav Czerny (Providence: Brown University Press, 1962), 42. Image: Georges Foucart, *Tombes thébaines: nécropole de Dirâ' Abû'n-Nága: Le tombeau d'Amonmos*, MIFAO 57.3 (Cairo: IFAO, 1935).

is the fact that the hieroglyphic inscription makes clear that we are dealing with an oracle delivered during a solemn procession. Apparently, for the ancient Egyptians a procession was more than the carrying around of a special vessel, but an occasion to face and consult the deity, of course under the appropriate authority of the high priest.

Another depiction of a procession can be found on a papyrus from the Saite period (P.Brookl. 47.218.3) dating from 4 October 651 BCE. It commemorates the oracle given by Amon-Re to the high priest and prophet, Montemhet, to grant his father, Harsiese, leave from the service of Amon for that of Montu-Re Harakhti.[59] The papyrus has not survived fully, but enough remains visible of the cult statue carried by a large number of priests:

Classical Greece had its own traditions of processions. Particularly well known are the Panathenian processions of the twelve Olympic gods from Athens to Eleusis, instituted in 586 BCE, according to tradition, by the same Athenian ruler, Peisistratus, who had the Homeric traditions collected and codified. Although here too, cult personnel played an important role, the direction and protection of the rituals seemed to be in the hands of rulers who were not specifically tied to a particular priesthood. Xenophon, *Hipp*. 3.2–4, describes the role for the cavalry required for the escort of the procession (see also Thucydides, *P.W.* 6.56–58; IG II/III² 334):

> As for the processions (Τὰς μὲν οὖν πομπὰς), I think they would be most acceptable both to the gods and to the spectators (καὶ τοῖς θεοῖς κεχαρισμενωτάτας καὶ τοῖς θεαταῖς εἶναι - mind the alliteration, MNvdM) if they include a gala ride in the market place (εἰ ὅσων ἱερὰ καὶ ἀγάλματα ἐν τῇ ἀγορᾷ ἐστι). The starting point

---

59. Parker and Czerny, *Saite Oracle Papyrus*. Source of the image: https://en.wikipedia.org/wiki/Saite_Oracle_Papyrus#/media/File:Saite_Oracle_Papyrus,_October_4,_651_B.C.E.,_47.218.3a-j.jpg.

would be the Herms; and the cavalry would ride round saluting the gods at their shrines and statues (ταῦτα ἀρξάμενοι ἀπὸ τῶν Ἑρμῶν κύκλῳ περιελαύνοιειν πιμῶντες τοὺς θεούς). So at the Great Dionysia the dance of the choruses forms part of the homage offered to the Twelve and to other gods (καὶ ἐν τοῖς Διονυσίοις δὲ οἱ χοροὶ προσεπιχαρίζονται ἄλλοις τε θεοῖς καὶ τοῖς δώδεκα χορεύοντες). (text and trans. A. E. Marchant, LCL)

This text makes clear that the words for "god" (θεός) and his or her "cult image" (ἄγαλμα) could be used interchangeably and that, once the necessary precautions were taken, the gods would be visible to all spectators (θεαταῖς). Again, a sharp distinction between seeing god in the form of a statue and seeing God in a spiritual, metaphysical, Platonic sense, does not seem to match the ideas and expressions of the people in antiquity.

Of course, over-ambitious rulers would try to add their own image to that of the Olympian deities. In the case of Philip II of Macedonia, this *hybris* coincided with his assassination, as recorded by Diodore of Sicily, *Bib. hist.* 16.92.5–93.1. Here too, the gods were visible to all in the theatre:

> Finally the drinking was over and the start of the games set for the following day. While it was still dark, the multitude of spectators hastened into the theater (εἰς τὸ θέατρον) and at sunrise the procession formed (τῆς πομπῆς γινομένης). Along with lavish display of every sort, Philip included in the procession statues of twelve gods (εἴδωλα τῶν δώδεκα θεῶν ἐπόμπευε) wrought with great artistry and adorned with a dazzling show of wealth to strike awe into the beholder (ταῖς τε δημιουργίαις περιττῶς εἰργασμένα καὶ τῇ λαμπρότητι τοῦ πλούτου θαυμαστῶς κεκοσμημένα), and along with these was conducted a thirteenth statue of himself (σὺν δὲ τούτοις αὐτοῦ τοῦ Φιλίππου τρισκαιδέκατον ἐπόμπευε θεπρεπὲς εἰδώλων), so that the king exhibited himself enthroned among the twelve gods (σύνθρονον ἑαυτὸν ἀποδεικνύντος τοῦ βασιλέως τοῖς δώδεκα θεοῖς). (text and trans. Wells, LCL)

In Hellenistic Egypt, the Greek and Egyptian traditions concerning procession fused. The great pompe held by Ptolemy II Philadelphus, which is described in such great detail by Kallixeinos of Rhodos (*FGH* 627 F 2 = Athenaeus, *Deipn.* 5, 196a–203b),[60] of course included images of the gods, but does not seem to be dominated so pervasively by the priesthood. The Canopus and Memphis decrees (238 BCE and 198 BCE) seem to settle the balance between the powerful and priviliged priesthood at Memphis and the Ptolemaic court at Alexandria.

The Canopus decree (OGIS 56) commemorates the retrieval of the cult images that had been stolen from Egypt by Cambyses (ll. 9–10: τὰ ἐξενεχθέντα ἐκ τῆς χώρας ἱερὰ ἀγάλματα ὑπὸ τῶν Περσῶν), but now retrieved by Ptolemy III Euergetes and restored to their Egyptian sanctuaries. One of the issues settled in this

---

60. E. E. Rice, *The Grand Procession of Ptolemy Philadelphus*, Oxford Classical and Philosophical Monographs (London: Oxford University Press, 1983).

decree (ψήφισμα) is a feast and boat-procession (l. 56: καὶ ἄγουσιν αὐτῇ ἑορτὴν καὶ περίπλουν ἐν πλείοσιν ἱεροῖς) for the deceased daughter of Ptolemy III and his wife Berenice, who went straight to the eternal world as virgin (ll. 47–48: συνέβη ταύτην παρθένον οὖσαν ἐξαίφνης μετελθῶν εἰς τὸν ἀέναον κόσμον).[61] The decree is sanctioned not only by the king and queen (ll. 1–3), but also the entire priestly hierarchy consisting of οἱ ἀρχιερεῖς καὶ προφῆται καὶ οἱ ἄδυτον εἰσπορευόμενοι πρὸς τὸν στολισμὸν τῶν θεῶν καὶ πτεροφόραι καὶ ἱερογραμματεῖς καὶ οἱ ἄλλοι ἱερεῖς οἱ συναντήσαντες ἐκ τῶν κατὰ τὴν χώραν, "the high priests, and the prophets, and those who go into the holy place to array the gods in their ornamental apparel, and the bearers of the feathers, and the sacred scribes, and the other priests who gathered themselves together from the temples throughout the country."[62]

9. Apotheose

This decree also demonstrate a third aspect of the visibility of the gods in the Hellenistic world. Although the deceased princess may no longer be visible as living person, she very much lives on as goddess thanks to her ἀποθέωσις (l. 55). In fact, also her parents are consistently called gods throughout the stele, as are almost all Hellenistic rulers from the third century BCE onwards.[63] When the word θεός occurs in the documentary papyri, it is predominantly with reference to the Ptolemaic kings and the Roman emperors after them. It is well known that Alexander the Great already promoted his own deification (see, e.g., the Alexander Romance), and that his successors adopted titles with godlike connotations, such as "Saviour" (Σωτήρ), "Benefactor" (Εὐεργέτης), or "Divine manifestation" (Ἐπιφανής). Particularly the fourth Seleucid king, Antiochus IV Epiphanes, has gone down into history as adversary of the One God of Israel, according to Jewish tradition.

10. Priestly Authorization

What does this all have to do with the Septuagint? Thus far, we have seen that, in the Hellenistic world, the gods could be seen through dreams, epiphanies in natural phenomenon such as storms, in processions, and in the form of the living

---

61. E. A. Wallis Budge, *The Decrees of Memphis and Canopus*, vols. 1–3 (London: Paul, Trench, Trübner, 1904), books on Egypt and Chaldaea: 17–19.

62. See the still authoritative description of the priestly hierarchy in Hellenistic Egypt by Walter Otto, *Priester und Tempel im hellenistischen Ägypten*, vols. 1–2 (Berlin: Teubner, 1905–1908).

63. See, e.g., Kostas Buraselis and Sophia Aneziri, "Apotheosis," in *Purification; Initation; Heroization; Apotheosis; Banquet; Dance; Cult Images*, vol. 2 of *Thesaurus cultus et rituum antiquorum*, ed. Vassilis Lambrinoudakis and Jean C. Balty (Los Angeles: Getty Publications, 2004), 158–85.

monarchs. None of these meetings was ordinary, but not entirely impossible either. In a time of globalization, acculturation and cultural competition, one could even argue that theo-vision had become commercial business for otherwise outdated sanctuaries. In this regard, I concur with Jan Joosten who argued that the theology of the Septuagint translators in this respect should be seen against the religion-historical background of contemporary Hellenistic Egyptian cultic practices. I find myself also in agreement with Martin Rösel who stressed the fact that seeing God was not a common experience for every ordinary person. What was necessary in almost all of the cases discussed above was the intermediation of priestly authorities. This brings me to an aspect of Septuagint studies that until recently has been neglected, that is, the question of authorship and authorization of the Greek translations of Hebrew Scripture.

It is still widely believed that the Greek translations of Israel's sacred writings were made by lay individuals, dragomen, with the best intentions, but with hardly sufficient comptences to deal with the difficult task at hand. Now, translating ancient writings from an Afro-Asiatic language into an Indo-European one without the modern tools such as dictionaries, grammars, comparative models, was an arduous task, as we have seen in the example provided by P.Oxy. 11.1381, discussed above.[64] Yet, it is not very likely that such a translation could be made without the approval, authorization, manpower, and financial support of the ruling priesthood. As a matter of fact, the Letter of Aristeas acknowledges the importance of the high priest of Jerusalem in the project of translating the Pentateuch. For that reason, Van der Kooij has stressed the role of the Jewish priestly aristocracy in Jerusalem as authorizing authority behind the Greek Pentateuch.[65]

Furthermore, it is clear that what we call "priests" and "priesthood" is in fact rather imprecise terminology for a very elaborate hierarchical system of lower and higher priests. The Jewish hierarchy of the priesthood in Jerusalem or its substitutes (Leontopolis, Qumran, Mount Gerizim?) may not have been as complex as the Egyptian hierarchy described (OGIS 56: Canopus decree ll. 1–3) or depicted

---

64. See also Sebastian P. Brock, "The Phenomenon of the Septuagint," in *The Witness of Tradition: Papers Read at the Joint British-Dutch Old Testament Conference Held at Woudschoten, 1970*, ed. Adam S. Van der Woude, OtSt 17 (Leiden: Brill, 1972), 11–36.

65. See, e.g., Arie van der Kooij, "The Promulgation of the Pentateuch in Greek according to the Letter of Aristeas," in *Scripture in Transition: Essays on Septuagint, Hebrew Bible, and Dead Sea Scrolls in Honour of Raija Sollamo*, ed. Anssi Voitila and Jutta Jokiranta, JSJSup 126 (Leiden: Brill, 2008), 179–91; van der Kooij, "The Pentateuch in Greek and the Authorities of the Jews," in *Text-Critical and Hermeneutical Studies in the Septuagint*, ed. Johann Cook and Hermann-Josef Stipp, VTSup 157 (Leiden: Brill, 2012), 3–20; van der Kooij, "The Septuagint of the Pentateuch," in Van der Kooij and Cook, *Law, Prophets, Wisdom*, 15–62; van der Kooij, "Scholars and Officials in Early Judaism: The Sôfer of Jesus Ben Sira," in *Septuagint, Sages, and Scripture. Studies in Honour of Johann Cook*, ed. Randall X. Gauthier, Gideon R. Kotzé, and Gert J. Steyn, VTSup 172 (Leiden: Brill, 2016), 190–204.

above, but it certainly knew "grades of holiness."⁶⁶ The most detailed description of this hierarchy (עדת קדושים, col. 1 line 16) can be found in the War Scroll, 1QM II, 1–4:⁶⁷

ואת ראשי הכוהנים יסרוכו אחר	- The high priests (cf. οἱ ἀρχιερεῖς) they shall dispose behind
כוהן הראש	- the High Priest
ומשנהו	- and his deputy (i.e., the vice high priest?)
ראשים שנים עשר להיות משרתים בתמיד לפני אל	- twelve high priests shall be serving in the perpetual service (or: daily burnt-offering) before God
וראשי המשמרות ששה ועשרים במשמרות ישרתו	- The heads of the courses, twenty-six, in their courses they shall serve.
ואחריהם ראשי הלויים לשרת תמיד שנים עשר אחד לשבט וראשי משמרות איש במעמדו ישרתו	- After them the heads of the Levites to serve perpetually, twelve, one for each tribe. And the heads of the courses shall each serve in his place
וראשי השבטים ואבות העדה אחריהם להתיצב תמיד בשערי המקדש	- The heads of the tribes and the fathers of the congregation behind them, to stand perpetually at the gates of the sanctuary.

Contemporary Jewish documents (11QT^a 57; Sir 38–39, 1 Maccabees, Josephus, *A.J.* 4) reflect a similar distinction between the highest layer of (high) priests standing closest to God, an inner circle of *intimi*, and a lower and larger layer of priests and Levites, and finally a layer of lay people.

For the priesthood in Jerusalem, seeing the Deity was a privilige and responsibility entrusted to the high priest as *primus inter pares* of this high court of high priests. According to this conception, seeing the Deity was not impossible, but highly imprudent and therefore potentially dangerous. For that reason, the Greek translators did not deny the possibility of humans to appear before God altogether, but rather tried to attenuate the diction of the Hebrew text, where a rereading of the original would allow for such procedure. Important ancestors, such as Abraham, Jacob, Moses and others could appear before God, just as God could be seen by them on special occasions, even though the number of such events was to be kept to a minimum (LXX Num 12:7). This explanation might also apply to the book of Job where the actual *visio Dei* is reserved for the climax of the book (42:1).

---

66. After Philip P. Jenson, *Graded Holiness: A Key to the Priestly Conception of the World*, JSOTSup 106 (Sheffield: JSOT Press, 1992).

67. Text and translation after Yigael Yadin, *The Scroll of the War of the Sons of Light against the Sons of Darkness* (Oxford: Oxford University Press, 1962), 262–65; and Florentino García Martínez and Eibert J. C. Tigchelaar, *The Dead Sea Scrolls Study Edition* (Leiden: Brill, 1997) 1:114–15.

For these priests, the question was not *if* God was visible at all, but *where*?, and most importantly: *for whom*? Even though God may have decided to appear to pious people in the past, the proper place for him to reside was the temple and the proper personnel to serve him was the priesthood. Without the *presentia realis* of God in the temple the whole cultus would be meaningless. Hence the addition of Eleazar and Ithamar in the SP and its precursor 4QpaleoExod^m in Exod 24:9–11. Hence also the changes in the Greek version of Exod 25:8 and 29:45–46, where the notion of God's visibility was deliberately introduced in the text.

This theology may perhaps also explain the differences in the Old Greek of Isaiah, which probably originated in circles around the exiled high priest Onias IV in Leontopolis.[68] Seeing God in the temple by a priestly figure such as Isaiah (Isa 6) may not have been as problematic for the Greek translator as the idea that a king (Hezekiah according to Isa 38:11), military leaders sending messengers to Egypt for aid (31:1), let alone ordinary human beings (17:7) could see God. In Amos 9:1, where the idea of God's visibility has also been maintained in the Greek version, the context is also cultic (see the reference to the מזבח, "altar," θυσιαστήριον in the same verse).

11. Sadducees and Pharisees

Yet, our parameters for charting the diversity within the theology of the Septuagint might require even further calibration beyond the imprecise oppositions between Judaism versus Hellenism, dynamic versus dualistic (Platonic) thinking, Jerusalem versus Alexandria, monotheism versus paganism, and priestly aristocacy versus monarchy. The aftermath of the Sixth Syrian War (170–168 BCE) not only altered the power balance between the Ptolemies and Seleucids, as well as that between the Ptolemaic court and Memphite priesthood, but also that in Jerusalem between the ruling factions. The Oniade house became divided and the non-priestly family of Maccabeans took over the rule of Judea including the institutions of temple and high priesthood. As a result, the religious landscape transformed into the variety of factions known from the New Testament and contemporary Judean writings, namely, that of Maccabeans, Sadduccees, Pharisees, and Essenes.[69]

---

68. See the studies by Seeligmann, Van der Kooij and Van der Meer mentioned above.

69. See the many introductions to and handbooks on Second Temple Judaism, e.g., Emil Schürer, Geza Vermes, Matthew Black, and Alec T. Burkill, *A History of the Jewish People in the Age of Jesus Christ (175 B.C.–A.D. 135)*, vols. 1–3 (Edinburgh: T&T Clark, 1973–1987); and James C. VanderKam, *An Introduction to Early Judaism* (Grand Rapids: Eerdmans, 2001). Although many scholars would now be very hesitant to speak about a Pharisaic movement already in the middle of the second century BCE, I consider the sociological analogy for the onset of Jewish fractions as a result of the drastic changes in society

If Jacob Lauterbach is to be believed, one of the implicit differences between the Sadducee aristocracy and the Pharisaic popular movement pertained to the question whether God could be seen at all.[70] Whereas the Sadducees derived their authority from their priviliged hereditary position as custodians of the temple elected by God to be approached on the Day of Atonement by their *primus inter pares*, the high priest as God's chamberlain, the Pharisees denied the concept that God would be bound to one specific location (the temple) and would be actually visible, even only partially from behind or from below, to the high priest. Although none of the statements in the works of Josephus or the rabbinic writings about the differences between the Pharisees and Sadducees actually mention this distinction,[71] this can be inferred, according to Lauterbach, from the different ways the incense should be brought into the Holy of Holies on the Day of Atonement (Lev 16:12).

Perhaps this difference might explain the more rigid approach to the statements about the *visio Dei* in the Septuagint, particularly the Old Greek Psalter. It has been argued, convincingly to my mind, by Venetz and Van der Kooij among others, that the provenance of the Old Greek Psalter was Palestine, rather than Egypt (Alexandria).[72] There are also reasons to connect the Old Greek Psalter with Palestinian rabbinic traditions as argued already by Barthélemy.[73] Other scholars, such as Schaper, would go even further by describing the Old Greek Psalter as a proto-Pharisaic document.[74] Nevertheless, the consistent denial and transformations of expressions dealing with the visibility of God, as we find in the Old Greek Psalter, accords well with this idea that the Pharisees preferred panentheism over pontifical priviliges: God was accessible for every believer as long as the Torah was studied meticulously and its prescriptions followed in every detail. Perhaps

---

after the Antiochean crisis as outlined by Albert I. Baumgarten, *The Flourishing of Jewish Sects in the Maccabean Era: An Interpretation*, JSJSup 55 (Leiden: Brill, 1997), persuasive.

70. Jacob Z. Lauterbach, "A Significant Controversy between the Sadducees and the Pharisees," *HUCA* 4 (1927): 173–205. See also Louis Finkelstein, *The Pharisees: The Sociological Background of Their Faith* (Philadelphia: Jewish Publication Society of America, 1938), 119–20.

71. See Jacob Neusner, *The Rabbinic Traditions about the Pharisees before 70*, 3 vols. (Leiden: Brill, 1971); Steve Mason, *Flavius Josephus on the Pharisees: A Compostion-Critical Study*, StPB 39 (Leiden: Brill, 1991).

72. Hermann-Josef Venetz, *Die Quinta des Psalteriums: Ein Beitrag zur Septuaginta- und Hexaplaforschung* (Hildesheim: Gerstenberg, 1974); Arie van der Kooij, "On the Place of Origin of the Old Greek of Psalms," *VT* 33 (1983): 67–74. See also my paper, "The Question of the Literary Dependence of the Greek Isaiah upon the Greek Psalter Revisited," in *Die Septuaginta–Texte, Theologien, Einflüsse. 2. Internationale Fachtagung veranstaltet von Septuaginta Deutsch (LXX.D), Wuppertal 23.–27.7.2008*, ed. Wolfgang Kraus, Martin Karrer, and Martin Meiser, WUNT 252 (Tübingen: Mohr Siebeck, 2010), 575–614.

73. Dominique Barthélemy, *Les devanciers d'Aquila*, VTSup 10 (Leiden: Brill), 41–53.

74. Schaper, *Eschatology*, 160–64: "The Greek Psalms as a Document of Proto-Pharisaic Theology."

that would explain why the Greek Psalter does not allow for deviations from the rule that humans can not see God as we still find in the older Greek versions of the Pentateuch, Isaiah, and Job.

12. Concluding Remarks

When the author of the Gospel of John wrote the famous words that no one has ever seen God (1:18 Θεὸν οὐδεὶς ἑώρακεν πώποτε), he did not only distance himself from the pagan traditions of cultic processions, incubations, and epiphanies common in the Greco-Roman world, but also from the traditions preserved and nourished by the priestly Sadducee elite in Jerusalem. These priests may not have disposed of a cult image to carry around on a regular basis,[75] nor may they have been as hospitable to foreigners as their colleagues in the Serapeum of Memphis where the Greek recluse Ptolemaeus lived as a hermit among the local cult personnel, but they did share with their colleagues the idea of the visibility of their Deity, provided that the proper precautions are taken. Like the priesthood of the temple for Athena at Lindos, they claimed the special protection of their god from hostile siege (by Assyrian King Sennacherib or Persian King Darius), special epiphanies in times of distress (2 Macc 3) as well as cures for individuals (Hannah in 1 Sam 1, King Hezekiah in Isa 38; the visitors of the Aclepius temples). Like the priesthood of Memphis, they claimed important political oracles originating at their sanctuary and, more importantly, they claimed the authority over the proper interpretation of such divine messages as described vividly by Hecataeus of Abdera:

---

75. Several scholars have argued that the language of "seeing God" in fact reveals the existence of a cult statue of YHWH in the pre-exilic temple of Jerusalem, see, e.g., Herbert Niehr, "In Search of Yhwh's Cult Statue in the First Temple," in *The Image and the Book: Iconic Cults, Aniconism, and the Rise of Book Religion in Israel and the Ancient Near East*, ed. Karel van der Toorn, CBET 21 (Leuven: Peeters, 1997), 73–96; Christoph Uehlinger, "Anthropomorphic Cult Statuary in Iron Age Palestine and the Search for Yahweh's Cult Images," in *The Image and the Book. Iconic Cults, Aniconism, and the Rise of Book Religion in Israel and the Ancient Near East*, ed. Karel van der Toorn, CBET 21 (Leuven: Peeters, 1997), 97–156. Other scholars argue that the YHWH-cult in the preexilic temple of Jerusalem was aniconic from the beginning, see, e.g., Othmar Keel, *Jahwe-Visionen und Siegelkunst. Eine neue Deutung der Majestätsschilderungen in Jes 6, Ez 1 und Sach 4*, SBS 84-85 (Stuttgart: Katholisches Bibelwerk, 1977); Othmar Keel and Christoph Uehlinger, *Göttinnen, Götter und Gottessynbole*, QD 134 (Freiburg: Herder, 1992); and Tryggve N. D. Mettinger, *No Graven Iamge? Israelite Aniconism in Its Ancient Near Eastern Context*, CB.OT 42 (Stockholm: Almqvist, 1995), to mention only a few landmarks in a long-standing scholarly debate. If there had been a cult statue of YHWH in Jerusalem (or Samaria) at all, it had probably been removed (God-napped by the Assyrians?) before the deuteronomistic movement originated, perhaps by the end of the seventh century BCE.

They (i.e. the Jews) call this man high priest, and believe that he acts as a messenger to them of God's commandments (καὶ νομίζουσιν αὐτοῖς ἄγγελον γίνεσθαι τῶν τοῦ θεοῦ προσταγμάτων). It is he, we are told, who in their assemblies and other gatherings announces what is ordained, and the Jews are so docile in such matters that straight way they fall to the ground and do reverence tot he high priest when he expounds the commandments to them (ὥστε παραχρῆμα πίπτοντας ἐπὶ τὴν γῆν προσκυνεῖν τὸν τούτοις ἑρμενεόντα ἀρχιερέα). (*FGH* 264 6 *apud* Diodorus of Sicily 40.3)

Without intimate knowledge of the religion-historical context of the Septuagint, these theological nuances will easily go unnoticed. As is the case for biblical theology of the Hebrew Bible in general, the alternative *Religionsgeschichte Israels oder Theologie des Alten Testaments*—thus the title of a major contribution to the study of biblical theology[76]—is flawed and should make way for a complementary model.

Thus, the strategy observable in some passages in the Septuagint to attenuate the idea that humans see God, or rather take the initiative to meet God face-to-face, can be explained as a form of reluctance to put the Jewish deity on a par with the pagan gods. The Greek translators of the Pentateuch did not deny the possibility of seeing God, but tried to reserve this privilige for famous ancestors and Moses in particular. To that end, they read *qal* forms of the verb ראה as *niphal* (ὀφθῆναι, LXX Exod 24:11), attenuated its direct meaning with the help of the adverb γνωστῶς (LXX Exod 33:13), or modified the object of that verb into "the place where God stood" (LXX Exod 24:10–11) or "the glory of God" (δόξα LXX Exod 33:23, LXX Num 12:8). To see the gods, as Manetho put it, was not impossible in Hellenistic Egypt, but neither was it a democratic right for every inhabitant of the Greco-Roman world. One might see the deity through dream visions or even more or less directly in the temple, through epiphanies, in the form of a cult statue during processions, or in the form of deified rulers. In almost all cases, a specific cultic context and particularly its cultic personnel, a layer of elite high priests, were necessary for communication and authentication of such visions. In that sense, the *visio Dei* remained restricted to priviliged persons.

Yet, this reluctance does not mean that already during the Ptolemaic and Seleucid periods (300–150 BCE) Platonic philosophy informed the translators. It may be possible that already Pharisaic groups in the Maccebean age objected to the priestly-Sadducean idea that God could only be seen in the temple of Jerusalem, but was to be found everywhere, as Lauterbach has suggested. This might explain the strict approach attested in the Old Greek Psalter.

The idea that the deity can only be perceived through the intellect, from γνόφον to γνῶσις so to speak, finds its first real expression in Jewish thought—as

---

76. *Jahrbuch für biblische Theologie* 10 (1995), 2nd ed. (Neukirchen: Neukirchener, 2001).

far as I can see—in the works of the Jewish Greek philosopher Aristobulus (middle of the second century BCE) in a hymn attributed to Orpheus:

Εἷς ἔστ' αὐτοτελής, αὐτοῦ δ' ὕπο πάντα τελεῖται,
ἐν δ' αὐτοῖς αὐτὸς περινίσσεται, οὐδέ τις αὐτὸν
εἰσορᾷα ψυχὴν θνητῶν, νῷ δ' εἰσοράαται (...)
οὐδέ τίς ἐσθ' ἕτερος. σὺ δέ κεν ῥέα πάντ' ἐσορήσω,
αἴ κεν ἴδῃς αὐτόν· πρὶν δή ποτε δεῦρ' ἐπὶ γαῖαν,
τέκνον ἐμόν, δείξω σοι, ὁπηνίκα {τὰ} δέρκομαι αὐτοῦ
ἴχνια καὶ χεῖρα στιβαρὴν κρατεροῖο θεοῖο.
αὐτὸν δ' οὐχ ὁρόω· περὶ γὰρ νέφος 'στήρικται
λοιπὸν ἐμοί· στᾶσιν δὲ δεκάπτυχον ἀνθρώποισιν.
οὐ γάρ κέν τις ἴδοι θνητῶν μερόπων κραίοντα,
εἰ μὴ μουνογενής τις ἀπορρὼξ φύλου ἄνωθεν Χαλδαίων.

There is one who is complete in himself, but all things are completed by him,
And he himself moves about in them. No mortal
Casts an eye on him; rather, he is beheld by the mind. (...)
And there is no other God. You would easily have a vision of all things
If you saw him at that time, once in the past here on earth.
My child, I will show you when I see his
Footsteps and the strong hand of the mighty God.
But I do not see him, for in my way a residual, encircling cloud has been fixed
And ten layers of obscurity stand over men's vision.
No mortal man would have seen the Lord and ruler
Except a certain person, an only son, by descent an offshoot
Of the Chaldean race (text and trans. Holladay)[77]

Nevertheless, even here do we find the paradox that, on the one hand, God is invisible for mortal eyes, yet seen by a single, only-begotten son, here a reference to Moses as Lawgiver. It is the same ambivalence that we find in the Prologue to the Gospel of John: No one has seen God, yet we behold him in the person of rabbi Jesus of Nazareth. As I see it, it is the continuous interplay between testimony and counter-testimony that characterizes biblical theology.[78] Only when we take into account this diversity, seen against the background of the cultural context into which the biblical traditions were formulated, are we able to get a glimpse of what otherwise remains unseen.

---

77. Carl R. Holladay, *Fragments from Hellenistic Jewish Authors*, TT 39 (Atlanta: Scholars Press, 1995), 166–69.

78. Walter Brueggemann, *Theology of the Old Testament: Testimony, Dispute, Advocacy* (Minneapolis: Fortress, 1997).

Doublets in the Catena of the Paris Psalter: An Analysis of Psalms 1, 3, and 5

Leontien Vanderschelden

Abstract: In the catena of the so-called "Paris Psalter" (*Paris. gr.* 139 = Rahlfs 1133), several excerpts from patristic commentaries are placed together to comment on the text of the Psalms. Surprisingly, some of those excerpts were the (ultimate) source of two similar catena fragments commenting on one and the same psalm verse: a phenomenon that is called "a doublet." One is tempted to link those doublets to the remarkably complex composition of the catena, which combined and completed three earlier catenae on the Psalms. Since different sources are combined, and the overlap between the fragments would not always have been noticeable to the composer, the existence of doublets is not surprising after all.

The so-called Paris Psalter, a name given to the tenth-century manuscript *Parisinus graecus* 139 (Rahlfs 1133), is mostly known for its wonderful miniatures and has been the subject of several art-historical studies,[1] but it also contains a textual commentary on the Psalms in the form of a catena. This type of text consists of a sequence of excerpts, in this case from patristic commentaries on the Psalms. Yet, the text has not been studied as closely as the miniatures.

The composition of the catena as a sequence of exegetical excerpts seems to be random, even more if we take into account that some excerpts occur more than

---

1. See for example Hugo Buchthal, *The Miniatures of the Paris Psalter: A Study in Middle Byzantine Painting*, Studies of the Warburg Institute 2 (London: The Warburg Institute, 1938); Anthony Cutler, *The Aristocratic Psalters in Byzantium*, Bibliothèque des Cahiers archéologiques 13 (Paris: Picard, 1984), 63–71; John Lowden, "Observations on Illustrated Byzantine Psalters," *The Art Bulletin* 70 (1988): 242–60; Kurt Weitzmann, "Der Pariser Psalter Ms. Grec. 139 und die mittelbyzantinische Renaissance," *Jahrbuch für Kunstwissenschaft* 6 (1929): 178–94; and Steven H. Wander, "The Paris Psalter (Paris, Bibliothèque nationale, cod. gr. 139) and the Antiquitates Judaicae of Flavius Josephus," *Word & Image* 30.2 (2014): 90–103.

once in the commentary on one and the same psalm verse, a phenomenon that is called "a doublet."[2] The overlapping excerpts are never fully identical: in most (but not all) of the doublets, the first excerpt is a literal copy of the respective section of the original patristic commentary, while the other excerpt is a paraphrase of that same source text, with or without omissions or additions.

The occurrence of such doublets strikes one as rather odd: there does not seem to be any convincing reason for the presence of both of the fragments in the exegesis of a certain psalm verse. Moreover, it is difficult to state whether the composer of this catena could have noticed their presence. There has never been a study on this topic, so in this article, I want to analyse the methodology of the catena in the light of its tradition and composition. In a comparison between, on the one hand, the source text and the two fragments of the doublets and, on the other hand, the doublet and its surrounding fragments, I will attempt to explain the existence of doublets in Pss 1, 3, and 5.[3]

1. Doublets in the Exegesis of Ps 1

The commentary text of the catena in the Paris Psalter contains forty-three fragments for Ps 1: ten fragments form five doublets, which can each be retraced to the same segment of a commentary by one of the church fathers.

The first doublet, consisting of fragments 5 and 6 of the catena,[4] comments on the first verse of Ps 1. Fragment 5 is attributed to Theodoret, whereas fragment 6 has an abbreviated attribution that can either be Theodoret or Theodore.[5] Their text is based on a fragment of the Psalm commentary by Theodoret of Cyr (PG 80:866b–869a).[6] The first excerpt is a paraphrase of only a small part of the source text (PG 80:868a–b), while the second one literally repeats the commentary on

---

2. This terminology was used by Gilles Dorival in French, see Gilles Dorival, *Les chaînes exégétiques grecques sur les Psaumes: Contribution à l'étude d'une forme littéraire*, vol. 1, Spicilegium Sacrum Lovaniense, Études et documents 43 (Leuven: Peeters, 1986), 236.

3. For each of the cases discussed here, an appendix at the end of this article offers the textual material: the texts of the Psalm under discussion, of the excerpts that form the doublet and of the source. My selection of Pss 1, 3, and 5 is based on earlier selections by Dorival (*Les chaînes exégétiques*, 1:IX–XII) and Mühlenberg (Ekkehard Mühlenberg, *Psalmenkommentare aus der Katenenüberlieferung*, vol. 3, PTS 19 [Berlin: de Gruyter, 1975], 7) and other criteria.

4. This numbering is my own, based on the position of the fragments in the catena. The numbering is continued from Ps 1 to 3 and 5, since Pss 2 and 4 are not included in my selection (cf. n. 3).

5. This faulty attribution is not an isolated case in the *Parisinus*: throughout the exegesis of Ps 1, nearly every excerpt of Theodoret is attributed to Theodore.

6. Theodoret of Cyr, *Interpretatio in Psalmos*, ed. Jacques Paul Migne, PG 80 (Turnhout: Brepols, 1977).

that first verse (PG 80:866b–869a). The second fragment breaks off abruptly because the last Bible citation of Theodoret's commentary has been left out. The literal excerpt offers the reader of the catena more information and even an introduction to Theodoret's commentary of the Psalms as a whole. In the section that follows the one overlapping with the first fragment, it broaches new subjects: the exegesis of the word μακάριος is followed by an explanation of other elements from the Psalter lemma (ἀσεβεῖς, ἁμαρτωλοί, and λοιμοί). The fragments that precede and follow the doublet in the catena discuss the phrase οὐκ ἐπορεύθη ἐν βουλῇ ἀσεβῶν, which is not commented upon in either of the fragments of the doublet. Since the first excerpt is a short summary of only a part of Theodoret's commentary, it is not easy for the composer or the reader to see the parallel between both fragments at first sight.

Both the excerpts that form the second doublet, which is also a commentary on the first verse of Ps 1, overlap less than those of the first doublet, even though they are based on the same passage in the Psalter homilies of Basil of Caesarea (PG 29:220b–224c).[7] Fragments 7 and 9, both correctly attributed to Basil, are separated by an excerpt attributed to Eusebius that does not have anything in common with them, since it deals with another subject, namely, the categories of sinful people (cf. Ps 1:1). In the case of this doublet, the first and shorter excerpt is the literal one: it copies the beginning of Basil's commentary on verse 1 but leaves out one sentence. The second fragment is a paraphrased version of a longer segment of the source text, with the same omission as fragment 7. There is no verbal overlap between both fragments, but the content of the beginning of fragment 9 corresponds with that of fragment 7. Here too, it is difficult to state whether the composer could tell the similarity of content in both fragments.

The next doublet comprises two short excerpts, each attributed to a different author. Fragment 10 is correctly attributed to Asterius, while fragment 15 is attributed to Athanasius. The text of fragment 15 can indeed be found almost completely in PG 27:61a,[8] but its exact text is given by Richard in his edition of the commentary of Asterius Sophista on Ps 1:1.[9] Since Richard's edition is based on a ninth-century manuscript transmitting the first Palestinian catena (cf. infra), I am inclined to prefer his edition over PG 27 and therefore to attribute this fragment to Asterius. Fragment 10 is a paraphrased version of the commentary piece, while fragment 15 reproduces the original text literally. Fragment 15 does not only treat the διδασκαλίας καθέδρα as fragment 10 does, but also the καθέδρα

---

7. Basil of Caesarea, *Homiliae super Psalmos*, ed. Jacques Paul Migne, PG 29 (Paris: Petit-Montrouge, 1857).

8. Athanasius of Alexandria, *Expositiones in Psalmos*, ed. Jacques Paul Migne, PG 27 (Turnhout: Brepols, 1979).

9. Marcel Richard, *Asterii Sophistae Commentariorum in Psalmos quae supersunt. Accedunt aliquot Homiliae anonymae*, Symbolae Osloenses Suppl. 16 (Oslo: Brøgger, 1956), 249.

λοιμῶν, a topic continued in fragment 16, attributed to Hesychius.[10] Although the fragments of the doublet are too short to allow any sound conclusion, it still seems that the overlap is quite obvious, although the fragments are attributed to a different author and are not as close to each other as in the previous doublets.

The fourth doublet consists of fragment 12 and 18 attributed to Eusebius, two fragments almost identical in their content. They are both based on Eusebius of Caesarea's commentary on the second verse of Ps 1 (PG 23:77a–b).[11] The first fragment follows the source text more closely (with the exception of the omission of τὸν γραπτὸν δηλονότι in the Bible citation ὅτ' ἂν γὰρ ἔθνη τὰ μὴ νόμον ἔχοντα φύσει τὰ τοῦ νόμου ποιεῖ, οὗτοι, νόμον μὴ ἔχοντες, ἑαυτοῖς εἰσι νόμος), while the second fragment omits the first sentence of the commentary. The parallels in both fragments stand out and fragments 13 and 17 treat the same topic of νόμος ... Κυρίου, so it could have been possible for the composer to notice the similarities in content.

Since Theodoret's commentary on Ps 1 is cited almost in full in the course of the catena, it is no surprise that a second doublet based on his text occurs (PG 80:869c–872a). Fragment 22, attributed to Theodoret, and fragment 25, wrongly attributed to Theodore (i.e., of Mopsuestia),[12] comment upon verses 3 and 4 of the first psalm. Fragment 22 is made up almost entirely of biblical citations with an introductory sentence: a paraphrase of the beginning of Theodoret's commentary. Fragment 25 reproduces the entire commentary on both Psalter verses, including the citations already used in fragment 22. Both fragments treat the metaphoric meaning of water mentioned in Ps 1:3, which is not treated in any of the surrounding fragments. Since the only literal parallel between both fragments of the doublet are the Bible citations, the use of the same source text is scarcely noticeable.

From the abovementioned explanation, it is clear that none of the doublets in the commentary on Ps 1 can be explained either by their content or their position in the catena. A mitigating factor is the fact that some of the doublets are not as easily recognisable as others.

---

10. Fragment 16 (f. 8v): ἩΣΥΧΙΟΥ Λοιμοὺς οἶμαι τοὺς ἀμφιβόλους ἀνθρώπους καλεῖ, τοὺς τὴν δικαιοσύνην κατορθοῦντας ἐν σχήματι, τὴν κακίαν δὲ μετιόντας ἐν τοῖς πράγμασιν. Τὸν βίον γὰρ οὗτοι λοιμαίνονται τὸν ἀνθρώπινον. Καθέδρα γὰρ λοιμῶν, ἡ τῶν δικαστῶν τῶν προδιδόντων τὰ δίκαια, καθέδραν λοιμῶν, ὁ τῶν ψευδοδιδασκάλων θρόνος, καθέδρα λοιμῶν, ἡ τῶν ὑποκριτῶν στολή, καθέδρα λοιμῶν, ἡ τῶν ἱερέων ὑπόκρισις, ἐν ταύτῃ κελεύει μὴ καθέζεσθαι. Cf. Hesychius of Jerusalem, *Fragmenta in Psalmos*, ed. Jacques Paul Migne, PG 93 (Turnhout: Brepols, 1978), 1180b.

11. Eusebius of Caesarea, *Commentaria Psalmos*, ed. Jacques Paul Migne, PG 23 (Turnhout: Brepols, 1979).

12. See n. 5.

2. Doublets in the Exegesis of Ps 3

In the commentary on Ps 1, as well as in that on Ps 3, some doublets occur. From the forty-five fragments, eight fragments form four doublets, which can each be traced back to the same source text.

In contrast to the previous doublets, the first doublet of Ps 3 contains two fragments that paraphrase the source text of Didymus the Blind.[13] Fragments 62 and 66 comment upon Ps 3:5 and are correctly attributed to Didymus. They are similar in length and content, but the Bible citation in the heart of the excerpts is the only literal parallel between both fragments. Fragments 61, 62, 64, 65, and 66 all discuss the meaning of ὄρους ἁγίου αὐτοῦ (Ps 3:5), so that this lemma has been treated superfluously and the compiler could have noticed the overlap.

The second doublet fits into the typical pattern of one paraphrased and one literal fragment. The commentary of Theodoret (PG 80:885c) on the fifth verse of Ps 3 is the source text behind fragments 63 and 64, although fragment 64 is wrongly attributed to Theodore instead of Theodoret.[14] Fragment 63 is a paraphrase of the last few lines of Theodoret's commentary on verse 5 with a considerable number of literal parallels. Fragment 64 reproduces the whole commentary, but the part that does not overlap with fragment 63 has nothing in common with any of the preceding or following fragments. Although the fragments of the doublets are placed one after the other, the similarity of source could have been overlooked.

The next doublet is also based on Theodoret's commentary on Ps 3:6 (PG 80:885d–888a). Fragment 67 has an abbreviated attribution that can either be Theodore or Theodoret, while fragment 71 is clearly attributed to Theodoret. Fragment 67, as it can be found in the *Parisinus*, consists of two parts: the first part is a literal reproduction of the commentary that breaks off abruptly with the word διό, while the text φησὶν ἐκοιμήθην τῇ ... τὸν ῥάθυμον cannot be traced back to any known source. In the first part of the fragment, we find two subjects: the first one is repeated in fragment 71, while the second lemma ἐξηγέρθην, ὅτι Κύριος ἀντιλήψεταί μου is new. Compared to the previous doublets, in this case, both the fragments derive their worth from their position in the text. Fragment 67 introduces the subject of sleep, which is continued in fragment 68, a very long fragment attributed to Origen.[15] The topic is taken up again in fragment 70,[16] upon which fragment 71 can be seen as a reaction, introduced by the words Ἄλλος ἔφη.

---

13. Ekkehard Mühlenberg, *Psalmenkommentare aus der Katenenüberlieferung*, vol. 1, PTS 15 (Berlin: de Gruyter, 1975), 126.

14. See n. 5.

15. Origen, *Selecta in Psalmos*, ed. Jacques Paul Migne, PG 12 (Turnhout: Brepols, 1978), 1125a–1129a.

16. Fragment 70 (f. 14r): ΔΙΔ<ΥΜΟΥ> Ἄλλος δὲ τὸ μὲν κοιμηθῇ σημαίνειν φησὶ τὴν ἀνάκλισιν μεθ' ἣν ὁ ὕπνος ἐπιγίνεται, ἐπεὶ οὖν ἑκουσίως τὴν ψυχὴν αὐτοῦ ἔθηκεν, κατὰ τοῦτο

The last doublet in the commentary on Ps 3 is again based on the commentary of Theodoret (PG 80:888a–b). Fragment 81 and 82 comment on Ps 3:8, but only fragment 81 is correctly attributed to Theodoret.[17] The text of the first fragment, which paraphrases a part of Theodoret's commentary, seems to be corrected in the following literal reproduction of his text: the lemma ὀδόντας ἁμαρτωλῶν συνέτριψας is defined by Theodoret through an opposition with the words ἀντὶ τοῦ, which are left out in fragment 81. The topic of ὀδόντας συντρῖψαι was already introduced in fragment 80. Despite their common source, the two short fragments do not have much in common to identify them as a doublet.

Here, in contrast to the previous psalm, we can observe some examples of doublets in which both fragments have their own function in the exegetical text.

3. Doublets in the Exegesis of Ps 5

In the catena on Ps 5, three doublets occur throughout sixty-two fragments—considerably less in comparison with Pss 1 and 3.

The first doublet in the exegesis of Ps 5:4–5 consists of fragments 102 and 104, which are based on the commentary of Theodoret (PG 80:896d–897a). The shortest fragment, fragment 102 (attributed to Theodoret) only paraphrases a few lines of Theodoret's commentary, while fragment 104, wrongly attributed to Theodore,[18] literally reproduces the source text. The second fragment includes an explanation of the word πρωί (Ps 5:4), a topic that recurs in the surrounding fragments.

The next doublet is based on Didymus the Blind's commentary on verses 5–7.[19] Fragments 108 and 113 are both correctly attributed to Didymus and are quite extensive. Each one paraphrases the original commentary and has a similar content: they treat the same subjects of lying, deceiving and killing. The same theme reoccurs in the surrounding fragments. Since the beginning of both fragments is exactly the same, the overlap is easily noticeable.

The last doublet has a special aspect since each of the fragments is attributed to a different author. Fragment 121 is attributed to Didymus; we can indeed find its text in PG 39:1172c–1173a.[20] However, this edition is unreliable and therefore should not be used: the few manuscripts on which it relies are nearly all witnesses

---

κοιμηθεὶς ὕπνωσεν, ἐξεγερθεὶς δὲ ἐκ νεκρῶν, ἀντιλαβομένου Θεοῦ, πρωτότοκος ἐκ νεκρῶν γεγένηται. Cf. Mühlenberg, *Psalmenkommentare*, 1:126.

17. Fragment 82 is attributed to Theodore; see n. 5.
18. See n. 5.
19. Mühlenberg, *Psalmenkommentare*, 1:132.
20. Didymus of Alexandria, *Expositio in Psalmos*, ed. Jacques Paul Migne, PG 39 (Turnhout: Brepols, 1978).

of the catena we are dealing with here.[21] Fragment 124 has an abbreviated attribution that can either be Theodore or Theodoret, but it repeats Theodoret's commentary on verse 9 of Ps 5 (PG 80:897c–900a). According to the similarity in content and in the use of Bible citations, it seems that fragment 121 is a paraphrase of that same passage of Theodoret, and must not be traced back to Didymus. The subject of the κατεύθυνον ἐνώπιόν σου τὴν ὁδόν μου is introduced in fragment 121, taken up again in fragment 124 and continued in fragment 125. Possibly, the difference in attribution could have made the doublet unnoticeable.

4. Composition of the Catena

Since in most cases the content and logical structure of the catena do not offer any reason for the existence of doublets, one might wonder if the catena's composition can help to explain the phenomenon.

The catena in the Paris Psalter is part of a broad and complex tradition of catenae on Psalms.[22] The oldest catena was compiled in the beginning of the sixth century and is named the first Palestinian catena after its geographical origin. This text incorporates patristic authors such as Asterius Sophista, Athanasius of Alexandria, Basil of Caesarea, Cyril of Alexandria, Didymus of Caesarea, Eusebius of Caesarea, Origen, and Theodoret of Cyr. This first catena was completed and enriched a few decennia later in the so-called second Palestinian catena. In this catena, other fragments of already incorporated authors and other authors such as Hesychius of Jerusalem were added to the text of the first Palestinian catena. In order to prove the independence of this second Palestinian catena as separate from the first Palestinian catena, Dorival has already mentioned the existence of doublets in the Paris Psalter.[23] However, for his research, it was not necessary to ask if the composer noticed their presence. In a third stage, some fragments of that second Palestinian catena were combined with a paraphrase of the first Palestinian catena. This phase is called the third Palestinian catena, but its composition cannot be dated precisely.[24]

---

21. PG 39:1155–1156 and Mühlenberg, *Psalmenkommentare*, 1:XVIII–XIX.

22. The catena itself has, apart from the *Parisinus*, twelve other witnesses: *Atheniensis B.N.* 45 (thirteenth century), *Matritenses B.N.* 4702–4704 (sixteenth century), *Mediolanensis Ambrosianus* C264 (sixteenth century), *Monacenses gr.* 12–13 (sixteenth century), *Oxoniensis Nov. Coll.* 31 (sixteenth century), *Oxoniensis Auct. E.* 1.5 (sixteenth century), *Parisinus gr.* 148 (sixteenth century), *Vaticani gr.* 617 (sixteenth century), *Vaticani gr.* 1519 (seventeenth century), *Vaticani gr.* 1677–1678 (sixteenth century), *Vaticani gr.* 1682–1683 (sixteenth century), *Venetus Marcianus gr.* 17 (tenth century).

23. Dorival, *Les chaînes exégétiques*, 1:236–44.

24. More information on the tradition of the Palestinian catenae on the Psalms can be found in Dorival, *Les chaînes exégétiques*, 1:115–324.

In type III of the catenae on Psalms,[25] of which the catena of the *Parisinus* is the most important witness, Athanasius of Alexandria's scholia on the Psalms were added to the third Palestinian catena, only on certain psalms, sometime in the sixth or seventh century.[26] In between the eighth and tenth centuries, a last source has been employed in the compilation of the catena of the *Parisinus*: the commentary on the Psalms by Theodore of Mopsuestia.[27]

The combination of different sources, which treated the patristic commentaries, scholia or homilies in their own way by paraphrasing, shortening or copying, could have led to the presence of doublets. Since the overlap is not always clearly noticeable (see above), the compiler of the catena of the *Parisinus* could have overlooked the doublets, which are based on the same source text, but treated in another way.

5. Concluding Remarks

From the examples cited above it is clear that the existence of doublets, as we observe them now, would not have been so easily recognizable during the composition of the catena. Since the fragments were taken from different sources, which each treated them differently by paraphrasing, shortening or copying, some of those doublets could have been overlooked.

It also seems that the doublets have not been noticed when the *Parisinus* was copied, since I hitherto have not encountered any manuscript[28] where an attempt has been made to remove the doublets by the omission of one of the fragments.

---

25. The catenae on Psalms have been categorized by Karo and Lietzmann into twenty-seven types based on the indices of Pss 22 and 115. The catena of the *Parisinus* is one of type III: see Georgius Karo and Ioannes Lietzmann, *Catenarum Graecorum Catalogus*, Nachrichten von der Königliche Gesellschaft der Wissenschaften zu Göttingen, Philologisch-historische Klasse (Göttingen: Lüder Horstmann, 1902), 25–28.

26. Gilles Dorival, *Les chaînes exégétiques grecques sur les Psaumes: Contribution à l'étude d'une forme littéraire*, vol. 2, Spicilegium Sacrum Lovaniense, Études et documents 44 (Leuven: Peeters, 1989), 350–54.

27. Gilles Dorival, *Les chaînes exégétiques grecques sur les Psaumes: Contribution à l'étude d'une forme littéraire*, vol. 4, Spicilegium Sacrum Lovaniense, Études et documents 46 (Leuven: Peeters, 1995), 174–79.

28. The witnesses of the catena are summed up in n. 21.

APPENDIX[29]

DOUBLET 1: THEODORET ON PS 1:1

1:1 Μακάριος ἀνήρ, ὃς οὐκ ἐπορεύθη ἐν βουλῇ ἀσεβῶν
καὶ ἐν ὁδῷ ἁμαρτωλῶν οὐκ ἔστη
καὶ ἐπὶ καθέδραν λοιμῶν οὐκ ἐκάθισεν[30]

(1) PG 80:866b–869a[31]

Ἐντεῦθεν ῥᾴδιον συνιδεῖν, ὡς πάλαι παρ' Ἑβραίοις τὰς ἐπιγραφὰς εὑρόντες οἱ τὰς θείας ἡρμηνευκότες Γραφάς, ταύτας μετέθεσαν εἰς τὴν Ἑλλάδα φωνήν. Τοῦτον γὰρ καὶ τὸν μετ' αὐτὸν ψαλμὸν ἀνεπιγράφους εὑρόντες ἀνεπιγράφους κατέλιπον· οὐ τολμήσαντές τι προσθεῖναι παρ' ἑαυτῶν τοῖς λογίοις τοῦ Πνεύματος. Τινὲς μέντοι τῶν τὰς ὑποθέσεις τῶν ψαλμῶν συγγεγραφότων ἠθικὴν τοῦτον ἔφασαν τὸν ψαλμὸν περιέχειν διδασκαλίαν· ἐμοὶ δὲ οὐχ ἧττον δογματικὸς ἢ ἠθικὸς ἔδοξεν εἶναι. Περιέχει γὰρ οὐχ ἁμαρτωλῶν μόνον, ἀλλὰ καὶ ἀσεβῶν κατηγορίαν, καὶ παραινεῖ τοῖς θείοις λόγοις προσέχειν διηνεκῶς ἐξ ὧν οὐκ ἠθικὴν μόνον, ἀλλὰ καὶ δογματικὴν ὠφέλειαν καρπούμεθα. Ἁρμοδίως δὲ λίαν ὁ μέγας Δαβὶδ μακαρισμὸν τῆς οἰκείας αὐτοῦ προτέθεικε συγγραφῆς, τὸν ἑαυτοῦ υἱὸν ὁμοῦ καὶ Δεσπότην μιμούμενος, τὸν Σωτῆρα λέγω Χριστόν· ὅστις πρὸς τοὺς ἱεροὺς μαθητὰς διδασκαλίας ἀπὸ μακαρισμῶν ἤρξατο, «Μακάριοι, λέγων, οἱ πτωχοὶ τῷ πνεύματι, ὅτι αὐτῶν ἐστιν ἡ βασιλεία τῶν οὐρανῶν.»[32] Υἱὸς δὲ τοῦ Δαβὶδ ὁ Δεσπότης Χριστὸς ὡς ἄνθρωπος κατὰ τὴν τῶν ἱερῶν Εὐαγγελίων φωνήν·«Βίβλος γὰρ γενέσεως Ἰησοῦ Χριστοῦ υἱοῦ Ἀβραάμ.»[33] Κύριος δὲ αὐτοῦ καὶ ποιητής, ὡς Θεός. Αὐτοῦ γάρ ἐστιν ἡ φωνή· «Εἶπεν ὁ Κύριος τῷ Κυρίῳ μου, κάθου ἐκ δεξιῶν μου.»[34] Μακαρίζει τοίνυν τὸν μήτε τοῖς ἀσεβέσιν ὁδοῦ κοινωνήσαντα, μήτε βεβαίαν τῶν ἁμαρτωλῶν δεξάμενον τὴν βουλήν· τοῦτο γὰρ δὴ στάσιν ἐκάλεσε καὶ τὴν μόνιμον τῶν λοιμῶν φυγόντα διαφθοράν. Τὸ δὲ μακάριος ὄνομα θεία μὲν ὑπάρχει προσηγορία καὶ μάρτυς ὁ θεῖος Ἀπόστολος βοῶν «Ὁ μακάριος καὶ μόνος δυνάστης, ὁ βασιλεὺς τῶν βασιλευόντων, καὶ Κύριος τῶν κυριευόντων.»[35] Μετέδωκε δὲ καὶ ταύτης τοῖς ἀνθρώποις, ὥσπερ καὶ τῶν ἄλλων, ὁ Δεσπότης Θεός· καὶ γὰρ πιστὸς καλούμενος· «Πιστὸς γάρ, φησίν, ὁ Θεός, δι' οὗ

---

29. All the texts in this appendix have been adapted to the standard orthography.

30. The text of the Psalms is a transcription from the *Parisinus* (with standardized orthography).

31. The text of the editions has also been corrected as mentioned in n. 29, but Bible citations that are not cited in the footnotes of the editions, are left out.

32. Matt 5:3.

33. Matt 1:1.

34. Ps 100:1.

35. 1 Tim 6:15.

ἐκλήθητε εἰς κοινωνίαν τοῦ Υἱοῦ αὐτοῦ.»[36] Καὶ ὁ μακάριος Μωσῆς, «Θεός, φησί, πιστός, καὶ οὐκ ἔστιν ἀδικία ἐν αὐτῷ.»[37] Ἐκάλεσε καὶ τῶν ἀνθρώπων πιστοὺς τοὺς ἀναμφιβόλως δεχομένους αὐτοῦ τοὺς λόγους. Οὕτω Θεὸς ὢν καὶ καλούμενος μετέδωκε καὶ ταύτης τῆς κλήσεως τοῖς ἀνθρώποις ὁ μεγαλόδωρος, καὶ βοᾷ·«Ἐγὼ εἶπον, Θεοί ἐστε καὶ υἱοὶ Ὑψίστου πάντες, ὑμεῖς δὲ ὡς ἄνθρωποι ἀποθνῄσκετε.»[38] Τὸ οὖν μακάριος ὄνομα τῆς κατ' ἀρετὴν τελειώσεως ὑπάρχει καρπός. Ὥσπερ γὰρ καὶ ἕκαστον τῶν κατὰ τὸν βίον ἐπιτηδευμάτων εἰς τὸ τέλος ὁρᾷ ἀθλητικὴ μὲν οὖν εἰς τοὺς ἐκ κοτίνου στεφάνους, στρατηγική τε εἰς νίκας καὶ τρόπαια, καὶ μέντοι καὶ ἰατρικὴ εἰς ὑγίειαν καὶ νόσων ἀπαλλαγήν, καὶ ἐμπορικὴ εἰς συλλογὴν χρημάτων καὶ πλούτου περιουσίαν οὕτως καὶ ἡ τῆς ἀρετῆς ἐπιστήμη καρπὸν ἔχει καὶ τέλος τὸν θεῖον μακαρισμόν. Μηδεὶς δὲ ἄνδρα μόνον ὁρῶν ἐνταῦθα μακαριζόμενον, ἐστερῆσθαι νομίσῃ τοῦδε τοῦ μακαρισμοῦ τῶν γυναικῶν τὸ γένος. Οὐδὲ γὰρ ὁ Δεσπότης Χριστὸς ἀρρενικῶς τοὺς μακαρισμοὺς σχηματίσας ἀπηγόρευσε ταῖς γυναιξὶ κτῆσιν τῆς ἀρετῆς. Συμπεριλαμβάνει γὰρ τοῖς ἀνδράσι καὶ τὰς γυναῖκας ὁ λόγος· κεφαλὴ γὰρ γυναικὸς ὁ ἀνήρ,[39] ᾗ φησιν ὁ θεῖος Ἀπόστολος. Συνάπτεται δὲ τῇ κεφαλῇ τὰ μέλη τοῦ σώματος, καὶ κεφαλῆς στεφανουμένης ἀγάλλεται οὕτω καὶ πρός τινα διαλεγόμενοι, καὶ φίλην αὐτὸν κεφαλὴν ὀνομάζοντες, οὐ χωρίζομεν τῶν μορίων τοῦ σώματος, ἀλλ' ἀπὸ μέρους τὸ πᾶν προσφθεγγόμεθα. Οὐχ ἁπλῶς δὲ πρῶτον ὁδοῦ, εἶτα στάσεως, εἶτα καθέδρας ἐμνημόνευσεν· ἀλλ' εἰδὼς ἀκριβῶς, ὡς κίνησιν μὲν πρῶτον ὁ λογισμὸς ὑπομένει, εἴτε φαῦλος, εἴτε σπουδαῖος εἴη· εἶτα στάσιν, εἶτά τινα ἑδραίαν βεβαίωσιν. Παραινεῖ τοίνυν, μήτε τῷ νῷ παραδέξασθαι δυσσεβῆ τινα ἔννοιαν, μήτε ἐπὶ πρᾶξιν ὁδεῦσαι παράνομον. Ἀσεβεῖς δὲ φίλον τῇ θείᾳ Γραφῇ καλεῖν τοὺς ἀθείᾳ, ἢ πολυθείᾳ θρησκεύοντας· ἁμαρτωλοὺς δέ, τοὺς παρανομίᾳ συζῆν προαιρουμένους, καὶ βίον διεφθαρμένον ἀσπαζομένους· λοιμοὺς δέ, τοὺς μὴ μόνον σφᾶς αὐτοὺς λυμαινομένους, ἀλλὰ καὶ ἑτέροις τῆς λύμης μεταδιδόντας, κατὰ τὴν ἐπισκήπτουσαν καὶ ἀνθρώποις καὶ κτήνεσι νόσον, ἧς μεταλαγχάνουσιν οἱ τοῖς νοσοῦσι πελάζοντες. Διὸ φεύγειν ὁ λόγος παρακελεύεται καὶ τὰ τούτων συνέδρια. Ἐπειδὴ δὲ οὐκ ἀπόχρη εἰς ἀρετῆς τελείωσιν τῆς κακίας φυγή·«Ἔκκλινον γάρ, φησίν, ἀπὸ κακοῦ, καὶ ποίησον ἀγαθόν·»[40] καὶ ὁ μακάριος Ἡσαΐας «Παύσασθε, φησίν, ἀπὸ τῶν πονηριῶν ὑμῶν, μάθετε ποιεῖν καλόν·»[41] μάλα εἰκότως ἐπήγαγεν ὁ μακάριος Δαβίδ.

---

36. 1 Cor 1:9.
37. Deut 32:4.
38. Ps 81:6–7.
39. 1 Cor 2:3.
40. Ps 36:27.
41. Isa 1:16–17.

(2) Fragment 5 (f. 8r)[42]

ΘΕΟΔΩΡΗΤ<ΟΥ> Κυρίως δὲ μακάριος ὢν ὁ Θεός, Παῦλος γάρ φησιν, *ὁ μακάριος καὶ μόνος δυνάστης,*[43] μετέδωκε ταύτης τῆς προσηγορίας ἡμῖν, ὡς καὶ πιστὸς καλούμενος. *Πιστὸς γάρ, φησίν, ὁ Θεός, δι'οὗ ἐκλήθητε.*[44] Καί, *Θεὸς πιστός, καὶ οὐκ ἔστιν ἀδικία ἐν αὐτῷ*[45] πειθομένους ἐκάλεσεν. Ὥσπερ οὖν καὶ θεούς, κατὰ τὸ *ἐγὼ εἶπα θεοί ἐστε.*[46] Τὸ οὖν μακάριος ὄνομα τῆς κατ' ἀρετὴν τελειότητος ὑπάρχει καρπός.

(3) Fragment 6 (f. 8r)

ΘΕΟΔΩΡ<ΗΤΟΥ/ΟΥ> Καὶ ἐντεῦθεν ῥᾴδιον συνιδεῖν ὡς πάλαι παρ' Ἑβραίοις τὰς ἐπιγραφὰς εὑρόντες οἱ τὰς θείας ἡρμηνευκότες Γραφάς, μετέθεσαν εἰς τὴν Ἑλλάδα φωνήν. Τοῦτον γὰρ καὶ τὸν μετ' αὐτὸν ψαλμὸν ἀνεπιγράφους εὑρόντες ἀνεπιγράφους κατέλιπον· οὐ τολμήσαντες παρ' ἑαυτῶν τι προσθῆναι τοῖς λογίοις τοῦ Πνεύματος. Τινὲς μέντοι τῶν τὰς ὑποθέσεις τῶν ψαλμῶν συγγεγραφότων ἠθικὴν τοῦτον ἔφασαν τὸν ψαλμὸν περιέχειν διδασκαλίαν, ἐμοὶ δὲ οὐχ ἧττον δογματικὸς ἢ ἠθικὸς ἔδοξεν εἶναι. Περιέχει γὰρ οὐχ ἁμαρτωλῶν μόνον, ἀλλὰ καὶ ἀσεβῶν κατηγορίαν, καὶ παραινεῖ τοῖς θείοις λογίοις προσέχειν διηνεκῶς, ἐξ ὧν οὐκ ἠθικὴν μόνον, ἀλλὰ καὶ δογματικὴν ὠφέλειαν καρπούμεθα. Ἁρμοδίως δὲ λίαν ὁ μέγας Δαυὶδ μακαρισμὸν τῆς οἰκείας προσέθηκε συγγραφῆς, τὸν ἑαυτοῦ υἱὸν ὁμοῦ καὶ Δεσπότην μιμούμενος, τὸν Σωτῆρα λέγω Χριστόν, ὅστις πρὸς τοὺς ἱεροὺς ἀποστόλους διδασκαλίας ἀπὸ μακαρισμῶν ἤρξατο, *μακάριοι, λέγων, οἱ πτωχοὶ τῷ Πνεύματι, ὅτι αὐτῶν ἐστιν ἡ βασιλεία τῶν οὐρανῶν.*[47] Υἱὸς δὲ τοῦ Δαυὶδ ὁ Δεσπότης Χριστὸς ὡς ἄνθρωπος κατὰ τὴν τῶν ἱερῶν Εὐαγγελίων φωνήν, *Βίβλος γὰρ Γενέσεως Ἰησοῦ Χριστοῦ υἱοῦ Δαυὶδ υἱοῦ Ἀβραάμ.*[48] Κύριος δὲ αὐτοῦ καὶ ποιητής, ὡς Θεός. Αὐτοῦ γάρ ἐστιν ἡ φωνή, *εἶπεν ὁ Κύριος τῷ Κυρίῳ μου,*[49] *κάθου ἐκ δεξιῶν μου.*[50] Μακαρίζει τοίνυν τὸν μήτε τοῖς ἀσεβέσιν ὁδοῦ κοινωνήσαντα, μήτε βεβαίαν τῶν ἁμαρτωλῶν δεξάμενον τὴν βουλήν, τοῦτο γὰρ δὴ στάσιν ἐκάλεσεν, καὶ τὴν μόνιμον τῶν λοιμῶν φυγόντα διαφθοράν. Τὸ δὲ *μακάριος* ὄνομα θεία μὲν ὑπάρχει προσηγορία, καὶ μάρτυς ὁ θεῖος Ἀπόστολος βοῶν, *ὁ μακάριος καὶ μόνος δυνάστης, ὁ βασιλεὺς τῶν*

---

42. The text of the fragments of the doublets is a transcription of the catena in the *Parisinus graecus* 139. The other manuscripts of this catena (cf. n. 21), as far as also Mühlenberg (Mühlenberg, *Psalmenkommentare*, 1:XXVI–XXVII) and Dorival (Dorival, *Les chaînes exégétiques*, 1:244–48) stated, depend on the *Parisinus*.
43. 1 Tim 6:15.
44. 1 Cor 1:9.
45. Deut 32:4.
46. John 10:34; Ps 81:6.
47. Matt 5:3.
48. Matt 1:1.
49. Matt 22:44; Mark 12:36; Luke 20:42; Acts 2:34.
50. Heb 1:13.

βασιλευόντων, καὶ Κύριος τῶν κυριευόντων.⁵¹ Μετέδωκε δὲ καὶ ταύτης τοῖς ἀνθρώποις, ὥσπερ καὶ τῶν ἄλλων, ὁ Δεσπότης Θεός, καὶ γὰρ πιστὸς καλούμενος, *πιστὸς γάρ, φησίν, ὁ Θεός, δι' οὗ ἐκλήθη εἰς κοινωνίαν τοῦ Υἱοῦ αὐτοῦ.*⁵² Καὶ ὁ μακάριος Μωυσῆς, *Θεός, φησίν, πιστός, καὶ οὐκ ἔστιν ἀδικία παρ' αὐτῷ.*⁵³ Ἐκάλεσε καὶ τῶν ἀνθρώπων πιστοὺς τοὺς ἀναμφιβόλως αὐτοῦ δεχομένους τοὺς λόγους. Οὕτω Θεὸς καὶ ὢν καὶ καλούμενος μετέδωκε καὶ ταύτης τῆς κλήσεως τοῖς ἀνθρώποις ὁ μεγαλόδωρος, καὶ βοᾷ, *ἐγὼ εἶπα, Θεοί ἐστε καὶ υἱοὶ Ὑψίστου πάντες, ὑμεῖς δὲ ὡς ἄνθρωποι ἀποθνήσκετε.*⁵⁴ Τὸ οὖν μακάριος ὄνομα τῆς κατ' ἀρετὴν τελειώσεως ὑπάρχει καρπός. Ὥσπερ γὰρ ἕκαστον τῶν κατὰ τὸν βίον ἐπιτηδευμάτων εἰς τὸ τέλος ὁρᾷ, ἀθλητικὴ μὲν οὖν εἰς τοὺς ἐν κοτίνῳ στεφάνους, στρατηγική τε εἰς νίκας καὶ τρόπαια, καὶ μέντοι καὶ ἰατρικὴ εἰς ὑγίαν καὶ νόσων ἀπαλλαγήν, καὶ ἐμπορητικὴ εἰς συλλογὴν χρημάτων καὶ πλούτου περιουσίαν, οὕτως καὶ ἡ τῆς ἀρετῆς ἐπιστήμη καρπὸν ἔχει καὶ τέλος τὸν θεῖον μακαρισμόν. Μηδεὶς δὲ ἄνδρα μόνον ὁρῶν μακαριζόμενον ἐνταῦθα ἐστερῆσθαι νομίσῃ τοῦδε τοῦ μακαρισμοῦ τῶν γυναικῶν τὸ γένος. Οὐδὲ γὰρ ὁ Δεσπότης Χριστὸς ἀρρενικοὺς τοὺς μακαρισμοὺς χρηματίσας ἀπηγόρευσε ταῖς γυναιξὶ τὴν κτῆσιν τῆς ἀρετῆς. Συμπεριλαμβάνει γὰρ τοῖς ἀνδράσι καὶ τὰς γυναῖκας ὁ λόγος, *κεφαλὴ γὰρ γυναικὸς ὁ ἀνήρ,*⁵⁵ φησὶν ὁ θεῖος Ἀπόστολος. Συνάπτεται δὲ τῇ κεφαλῇ τὰ μέλη τοῦ σώματος, καὶ κεφαλῆς στεφανουμένης ἀγάλλεται, οὕτω καὶ πρός τινα διαλεγόμενοι, καὶ φίλην αὐτὸν κεφαλὴν ὀνομάζοντες, οὐ χωρίζομεν τῶν μορίων τοῦ σώματος, ἀλλ' ἀπὸ μέρους τὸ πᾶν προσφθεγγόμεθα. Οὐχ ἁπλῶς δὲ πρῶτον ὁδοῦ, εἶτα στάσεως, εἶτα καθέδρας ἐμνημόνευσεν, ἀλλ' εἰδὼς ἀκριβῶς ὡς κίνησιν μὲν πρῶτον ὁ λογισμὸς ὑπομένει, εἴτε φαῦλος, εἴτε σπουδαῖος εἴη, εἶτα στάσιν, εἶτά τινα ἑδραίαν βεβαίωσιν. Παραινεῖ τοίνυν μήτε τῷ νῷ παραδέξασθαι δυσσεβῆ τινα ἔννοιαν, μήτε ἐπὶ πρᾶξιν ὀδεῦσαι παράνομον. Ἀσεβεῖς δὲ φίλον τῇ θείᾳ Γραφῇ καλεῖν τοὺς ἀθείαν, ἢ πολυθείαν θρησκεύοντας, ἁμαρτωλοὺς δέ, τοὺς παρανομίᾳ συζῆν προαιρουμένους, καὶ βίον διεφθαρμένον ἀσπαζομένους, λοιμοὺς δέ, τοὺς μὴ μόνον σφᾶς αὐτοὺς λοιμαινομένους, ἀλλὰ καὶ ἑτέρους τῆς λοίμης μεταδιδόντας, κατὰ τὴν ἐπισκήπτουσαν καὶ ἀνθρώποις καὶ κτήνεσι νόσον, ἧς μεταλαγχάνουσιν οἱ τοῖς νοσοῦσιν πελάζοντες. Διὸ φάσειν† ὁ λόγος παρακελεύεται καὶ τὰ τούτων συνέδρια. Ἐπειδὴ δὲ οὐκ ἀπόχρη εἰς ἀρετῆς τελείωσιν ἡ τῆς κακίας φυγή, *ἔκκλινον γάρ, φησίν, ἀπὸ κακοῦ, καὶ ποίησον ἀγαθόν,*⁵⁶ καὶ ὁ μακάριος Ἡσαίας, *παύσασθαι, φησίν, ἀπὸ τῶν πονηριῶν ἡμῶν [ὑμῶν], μάθετε καλὸν ποιεῖν,*⁵⁷ μάλα εἰκότως ἐπήγαγεν ὁ μακάριος Δαυίδ.

---

51. 1 Tim 6:15.
52. 1 Cor 1:9.
53. Deut 32:4.
54. Ps 81:6–7.
55. 1 Cor 11:3.
56. Ps 33:15; Ps 34:27.
57. Isa 1:16–17.

DOUBLET 2: BASIL ON PS 1:1

1:1 Μακάριος ἀνήρ, ὃς οὐκ ἐπορεύθη ἐν βουλῇ ἀσεβῶν
καὶ ἐν ὁδῷ ἁμαρτωλῶν οὐκ ἔστη
καὶ ἐπὶ καθέδραν λοιμῶν οὐκ ἐκάθισεν,

(1) PG 29:220b–224c

Τῇ φύσει τῶν πραγμάτων ἑπόμενος, τὴν τάξιν ταύτην τοῖς εἰρημένοις ἐπέθηκεν. Βουλευόμεθα γὰρ πρότερον, εἶτα ἱστῶμεν τὸ βούλευμα, εἶτα τοῖς βουλευθεῖσιν ἐναπομένομεν. Πρώτως οὖν μακαριστὸν τὸ ἐν τῇ διανοίᾳ ἡμῶν καθαρόν, ἐπειδὴ ῥίζα τῶν διὰ τοῦ σώματος ἐνεργειῶν τὸ ἐν καρδίᾳ βούλευμα. Ἡ γὰρ μοιχεία, ἐν τῇ ψυχῇ τοῦ φιληδόνου πρῶτον ἀναφλεχθεῖσα, οὕτω τὴν διὰ τοῦ σώματος φθορὰν ἀπεργάζεται. Ὅθεν καὶ ὁ Κύριος φησιν ἔνδοθεν εἶναι τὰ κοινοῦντα τὸν ἄνθρωπον.[58] Ἐπειδὴ δὲ ἀσέβεια κυρίως λέγεται ἡ εἰς Θεὸν ἁμαρτία, μὴ γένοιτο δέξασθαι ἡμᾶς ἐξ ἀπιστίας ποτὲ ἀμφιβολίαν περὶ Θεοῦ! Τοῦτο γάρ ἐστι τὸ πορευθῆναι ἐν βουλῇ ἀσεβῶν, [...] Ἐπανατέλλουσι γὰρ λογισμοὶ πονηροί, ἐκ τῶν παθῶν τῆς σαρκὸς ταῖς ψυχαῖς ἡμῶν ἐντικτόμενοι. Τῷ ὄντι γὰρ ἐλθοῦσα ἡ ἐντολή, τουτέστιν ἡ διάγνωσις τῶν καλῶν, ἐὰν μὴ κατακρατήσῃ τοῦ χείρονος λογισμοῦ, ἀλλὰ συγχωρήσῃ ὑπὸ τῶν παθῶν ἐξανδραποδισθῆναι τὸν λογισμόν· ἀνέζησε μὲν ἡ ἁμαρτία, ἀπέθανε δὲ ὁ νοῦς, νεκρὸς γενόμενος τοῖς παραπτώμασι. Μακάριος οὖν ὁ μὴ ἐγχρονίσας τῇ ὁδῷ τῶν ἁμαρτανόντων, ἀλλὰ λογισμῷ βελτίονι πρὸς τὴν εὐσεβῆ πολιτείαν μεταπηδήσας. [...] ἀλλὰ δι' ὑπομονῆς τὴν ἐλπίδα τῆς σωτηρίας ἀπεκδεχόμενος, καὶ ἐν τῇ ἐκλογῇ τῶν ὁδῶν ἑκατέρων μὴ ἐπιβὰς τῆς ὁδοῦ ἀγούσης ἐπὶ τὰ χείρονα.

(2) Fragment 7 (f. 8r)

ΒΑΣΙΛ<ΙΟΥ> Τῇ φύσει τῶν πραγμάτων ἑπόμενος, τὴν τάξιν ταύτην τοῖς εἰρημένοις ἐπέθηκεν. Βουλευόμεθα γὰρ πρότερον, εἶτα ἱστῶμεν τὸ βούλευμα, εἶτα τοῖς βουλευθεῖσιν ἐναπομένομεν. Πρῶτος οὖν μακαριστὸν τὸ ἐν τῇ διανοίᾳ ἡμῶν καθαρόν, ἐπειδὴ ῥίζα τῶν διὰ τοῦ σώματος ἐνεργειῶν τὸ ἐν τῇ καρδίᾳ βούλευμα. Ὅθεν ὁ Κύριος ἔνδοθεν φησιν *ἐστιν τὰ κοινοῦντα τὸν ἄνθρωπον*.[59] Ἐπειδὴ δὲ ἀσέβεια κυρίως λέγεται ἡ εἰς Θεὸν ἁμαρτία, μὴ γένοιτο δέξασθαι ἡμᾶς ἐξ ἀπιστίας ποτὲ ἀμφιβολίαν περὶ Θεοῦ! Τοῦτο γάρ ἐστι τὸ πορευθῆναι ἐν βουλῇ ἀσεβῶν.

---

58. Matt 15:18.
59. Matt 15:20.

(3) Fragment 9 (f. 8v)

ΒΑΣΙ<ΛΙΟΥ> ΚΑΠ<ΠΑΔΟΚΙΑΣ> Ἀλλὰ καὶ πρῶτον βουλευόμεθα εἶτα ἱστῶμεν τὰς βουλάς, εἶτα ταύταις ἐναπομένομεν, ῥίζα γὰρ τῶν διὰ τοῦ σώματος ἐνεργειῶν τῆς καρδίας τὸ βούλευμα. Ὅθεν ὁ Κύριος φησὶν *ἐξιέναι τὰ κοινοῦντα τὸν ἄνθρωπον*·[60] πρῶτος οὖν ἐν μακαρίοις ὁ μὴ τοῦτο παθών. Ὁδὸς δὲ λέγεται ὁ βίος ἐκ πρώτης γενέσεως πρὸς τελευτὴν ἐπηγόμενος, κἂν μηδεὶς ἐπαισθάνειται καθάπερ οἱ ἐν πλοίῳ καθεύδοντες πρὸς τῶν ἀνέμων ἐπὶ λιμένας ἀγόμενοι, ἀλλὰ καὶ τοῖς ὁδοιπόροις πᾶν ὅπερ ἂν ἴδωσι καθ' ὁδὸν τερπνὸν ἢ δυσχερὲς μετὰ τὴν θέαν παρέρχεται· ὁποῖα τὰ κατὰ τὸν βίον ὡς ἂν ἔχει πέρας λαμβάνοντα. Τὸ δὲ *οὐκ ἔστην* ἐπειδὴ νήπιοι μένοντες ἀδιακρίτως ἔχομεν πρὸς ἀγαθὸν ἢ κακόν. Εἰς ἄνδρα δὲ ἐλθόντες τούτων ἑκάτερα διακρίνομεν, ὥσπερ μέσοι γεγονότες ἀμφοτέρων καὶ δίκην ὑπέχοντες, κατὰ τὸ *ἐλθούσης δὲ τῆς ἐντολῆς ἡ ἁμαρτία ἀνέζησεν, ἐγὼ δὲ ἀπέθανον*,[61] λογισμῷ γὰρ διακρίνας ὁ νοῦς εἰ μὴ φυγὴν ἐνέκρωται ζωὴν ἔχων τὴν ἁμαρτίαν· διττὴ γὰρ ἡ ὁδὸς καὶ δύο τούτων εἰσὶν ὁδηγοί. Τῆς μὲν πλατείας δαιμόνων ἀπατηλὸς διὰ κακίας ἢ δυνούσης ἐπάγων τὸν ὄλεθρον· τῆς δὲ στενῆς ἄγγελος ἀγαθὸς διὰ τῶν τῆς ἀρετῆς ἐπιπόνων πρὸς τέλος ὁδηγῶν τὸ μακάριον. Ἡ δὲ ψυχὴ πρὸς ἑκατέραν τούτων εἰσὶ γῆν ὅταν μὲν ἐνθυμηθῇ τὰ αἰώνια τὴν ἀρετὴν αἱρουμένη· ὅτ' ἂν δὲ πρὸς τὸ παρὸν ἀποβλέψῃ τὴν ἡδονὴν φυλακτέον δὲ μάλιστα τὴν τῶν *λοιμῶν καθέδραν*·[62] ἐξίνουσαν δυσκίνητον. Μακάριον γὰρ τὸ μηδὲ βουλεύσασθαι τὸ κακόν· συναρπαγεὶς δὲ μὴ στῇς ἐπὶ τῆς ἁμαρτίας· καὶ τοῦτο δὲ παθὼν μὴ ἐνιδρυθῇς τῷ κακῷ καθάπερ ἐν λοιμῷ μετάδοσιν ἐξ ἑτέρου λαβών.

DOUBLET 3: ASTERIUS ON PS 1:1

1:1   Μακάριος ἀνήρ, ὃς οὐκ ἐπορεύθη ἐν βουλῇ ἀσεβῶν
      καὶ ἐν ὁδῷ ἁμαρτωλῶν οὐκ ἔστη
      καὶ ἐπὶ καθέδραν λοιμῶν οὐκ ἐκάθισεν,

(1) Richard, *Asterii Sophistae*, 249

Διὰ τῆς καθέδρας τὴν διδασκαλίαν δηλοῖ, ὥς φησιν ἐπὶ τῆς Μωυσέως καθέδρας.[63] Καθέδρα τοίνυν λοιμῶν ἡ διδασκαλία τῶν παρανόμων.

(2) Fragment 10 (f. 8v)

ΑΣΤΕΡΙΟΥ Διδασκαλίας γὰρ ἡ καθέδρα κατὰ τὸ *ἐπὶ τῆς καθέδρας Μωσέως*.[64]

---

60. Matt 15:20.
61. Rom 7:9-10.
62. Ps 1:1.
63. Matt 23:2.
64. Matt 23:2.

(3) Fragment 15 (f. 8v)

ἈΘΑΝΑΣΙΟΥ Διὰ τῆς καθέδρας τὴν διδασκαλίαν δηλοῖ, ὥς φησιν· ἐπὶ τῆς Μωσέως καθέδρας.[65] Καθέδρα τοίνυν λοιμῶν[66] ἡ διδασκαλία τῶν παρανόμων.

DOUBLET 4: EUSEBIUS ON PS 1:2

1:2   ἀλλ' ἢ ἐν τῷ νόμῳ Κυρίου τὸ θέλημα αὐτοῦ,
       καὶ ἐν τῷ νόμῳ αὐτοῦ μελετήσει ἡμέρας καὶ νυκτός.

(1) PG 23:77a–b

Ἐπειδὴ πολλή τίς ἐστι διαφορὰ τῶν φόβῳ τιμωριῶν εὖ πράττειν κατηναγκασμένων καὶ τῶν προαιρέσει αὐτὸ τὸ καλὸν αἱρουμένων, διὰ τοῦτό φησι· Ἐν τῷ νόμῳ Κυρίου θέλημα αὐτοῦ. Νόμον δέ φησιν οὐ πάντως τὸν σκιώδη καὶ τυπικὸν νόμον, πολὺ δὲ πρότερον τὸν ἐν αὐτῷ λεληθότα πνευματικὸν λόγον. Εἴη δ' ἂν νόμος Κυρίου καὶ ὁ κατὰ φύσιν πᾶσιν ἀνθρώποις ἐνεσπαρμένος, δι' οὗ κατορθῶσαι λέγονται οἱ πρὸ τοῦ διὰ Μωυσέως νόμου ἅγιοι· περὶ ὧν φησιν ὁ Ἀπόστολος· Ὅταν γὰρ ἔθνη τὰ μὴ νόμον ἔχοντα, τὸν γραπτὸν δηλονότι, φύσει τὰ τοῦ νόμου ποιῇ, οὗτοι, νόμον μὴ ἔχοντες, ἑαυτοῖς εἰσι νόμος.[67] Ἡ νόμος Κυρίου εἴη ἂν ὁ πρὸς αὐτοῦ τοῦ Κυρίου καὶ Σωτῆρος ἡμῶν πᾶσι τοῖς ἔθνεσι κατηγγελμένος εὐαγγελικὸς λόγος.

(2) Fragment 12 (f. 8v)

ΕΥΣΕΒΙΟΥ ΚΑΙΣΑΡΙΑΣ Καλῶς τὸ θέλημα, διὰ τοὺς εὐπράττοντας ἐξ ἀνάγκης, φόβῳ κολάσεως, μακαριζομένων τῶν προαιρέσει τὸ καλὸν αἱρουμένων, νόμον δέ φησιν οὐ πάντως τὸν σκιώδη καὶ τυπικὸν μᾶλλον δὲ τὸν ἐν αὐτῷ λανθάνοντα λόγον πνευματικόν. Νόμος δὲ Κυρίου[68] καὶ ὁ φυσικὸς καθ' ὃν ἔζησαν οἱ πρὸ Μωσέως εὐαρεστήσαντες, περὶ ὧν μὴ τὸν γραπτὸν νόμον ἐσχηκότων φησιν ὁ Ἀπόστολος ὅτ' ἂν γὰρ ἔθνη τὰ μὴ νόμον ἔχοντα φύσει τὰ τοῦ νόμου ποιῇ, οὗτοι, νόμον μὴ ἔχοντες, ἑαυτοῖς εἰσι νόμος.[69] Λέγοιτο δὲ νόμος καὶ ὁ πᾶσι κατηγγελμένος λόγος τοῦ Χρίστου.

---

65. Matt 23:2.
66. Ps 1:1.
67. Rom 2:14.
68. Ps 1:2.
69. Rom 2:14.

(3) Fragment 18 (f. 8v)

ΕΥΣ<ΕΒΙΟΥ> Νόμον δέ φησιν οὐ πάντως τὸν σκιώδη καὶ τυπικὸν μόνον, πολὺ δὲ πρότερον τὸν ἐν αὐτῷ λεληθότα πραγματικὸν λόγον. Εἴη δ' ἂν *νόμος Κυρίου*[70] καὶ ὁ κατὰ φύσιν πᾶσιν ἀνθρώποις ἐνεσπαρμένος, δι' οὗ κατορθῶσαι λέγονται οἱ πρὸ τοῦ διὰ Μωυσέως νόμου ἅγιοι, περὶ ὧν φησιν ὁ Ἀπόστολος *ὅτ' ἂν γὰρ ἔθνη τὰ μὴ νόμον ἔχοντα, τὸν γραπτὸν δηλονότι, φύσει τὰ τοῦ νόμου ποιεῖ, οὗτοι, νόμον μὴ ἔχοντες, ἑαυτοῖς εἰσι νόμος.*[71] Ἡ νόμος Κυρίου εἴη ἂν ὁ πρὸ αὐτοῦ τοῦ Κυρίου καὶ Σωτῆρος ἡμῶν πᾶσι τοῖς ἔθνεσι κατηγγελμένος εὐαγγελικὸς λόγος.

DOUBLET 5: THEODORET ON Ps 1:3–4

1:3 Καὶ ἔσται ὡς τὸ ξύλον τὸ πεφυτευμένον παρὰ τὰς διεξόδους τῶν ὑδάτων,
ὃ τὸν καρπὸν αὐτοῦ δώσει ἐν καιρῷ αὐτοῦ
καὶ τὸ φύλλον αὐτοῦ οὐκ ἀπορρυήσεται·
καὶ πάντα, ὅσα ἂν ποιῇ, κατευοδωθήσεται.
1:4 Οὐχ οὕτως οἱ ἀσεβεῖς, οὐχ οὕτως,
ἀλλ' ἢ ὡσεὶ χνοῦς, ὃν ἐκριπτεῖ ὁ ἄνεμος ἀπὸ προσώπου τῆς γῆς.

(1) PG 80:869c–872a

Μιμεῖται γὰρ ὑδάτων ἄρδειαν τὰ τοῦ θείου Πνεύματος νάματα· καὶ καθάπερ ἐκεῖνα τὰ παραφυτευόμενα δένδρα τεθηλέναι ποιεῖ, οὕτω ταῦτα παρασκευάζει τοὺς θείους φέρειν καρπούς. Οὗ δὴ χάριν καὶ ὁ Δεσπότης Χριστὸς ὕδωρ τὴν οἰκείαν διδασκαλίαν ὠνόμασεν. «Εἴ τις γάρ, φησί, διψᾷ, ἐρχέσθω πρός με καὶ πινέτω, καὶ ἔσται τὸ ὕδωρ ὃ ἐγὼ δώσω αὐτῷ πηγὴ ὕδατος ζῶντος ἁλλομένου εἰς ζωὴν αἰώνιον.»[72] Καὶ πάλιν· «Ὁ πιστεύων εἰς ἐμέ, καθὼς εἶπεν ἡ Γραφή, ποταμοὶ ἐκ τῆς κοιλίας αὐτοῦ ῥεύσουσιν ὕδατος ζῶντος.»[73] Καὶ μέντοι καὶ πρὸς τὴν Σαμαρῖτιν· «Ὁ πίνων ἐκ τοῦ ὕδατος τούτου διψήσει πάλιν· ὃς δ' ἂν πίῃ ἐκ τοῦ ὕδατος, οὗ ἐγὼ δώσω αὐτῷ, οὐ μὴ διψήσει εἰς τὸν αἰῶνα.»[74] Οὕτω καὶ διὰ Ἡσαΐου τοῦ προφήτου φησίν· «Ὅτι ἐγὼ δώσω ἐν δίψει τοῖς πορευομένοις ἐν ἀνύδρῳ· καὶ ἀνοίξω ἐπὶ τῶν ὀρέων πηγάς, καὶ ἐπὶ τῶν βουνῶν ποταμούς, ποτίσαι τὸ γένος μου τὸ ἐκλεκτόν, τὸν λαόν μου ὃν περιεποιησάμην.»[75] Εἰκότως τοίνυν καὶ ὁ μακάριος Δαβὶδ τὸν τοῖς θείοις λογίοις ἐσχολακότα δένδροις ἀπείκασε παρὰ τὰς τῶν ὑδάτων ὄχθας πεφυτευμένοις, καὶ ἀειθαλῆ μὲν ἔχουσι τὰ φύλλα, τὸν δὲ καρπὸν φέρουσιν εἰς καιρόν. Καὶ γὰρ οἱ τῆς

---

70. Ps 1:2.
71. Rom 2:14.
72. John 7:37; Col 4:14.
73. John 7:38.
74. John 4:13–14.
75. Isa 43:19–20.

ἀρετῆς ἀθληταὶ τῶν μὲν πόνων κατὰ τὸν μέλλοντα βίον κομίσονται τοὺς καρπούς· οἷον δέ τινα φύλλα, τὴν ἀγαθὴν ἐλπίδα διηνεκῶς ἐν ἑαυτοῖς φέροντες τεθήλασι καὶ ἀγάλλονται, καὶ συλῶσι τῇ ψυχαγωγίᾳ τὴν τῶν πόνων βαρύτητα. Ἔχουσι δὲ καὶ τὸν μεγαλόδωρον Δεσπότην τῇ προθυμίᾳ συνεργοῦντα διηνεκῶς· «Τοῖς γὰρ ἀγαπῶσι τὸν Θεόν,» φησὶν ὁ θεῖος Ἀπόστολος, «πάντα συνεργεῖ εἰς τὸ ἀγαθόν.»[76] Διά τοι τοῦτο καὶ ὁ μακάριος ἔφη Δαβίδ·

(2) Fragment 22 (f. 9r)

ΘΕΟΔΩΡΗΤ<ΟΥ> Ἀρδόμενον ἐκ τῆς τοῦ Σωτῆρος διδασκαλίας ἣν ὕδωρ ἐκάλεσε λέγων

εἴ τις διψᾷ ἐρχέσθω πρός με καὶ πινέτω,[77] καὶ ἔσται τὸ ὕδωρ ὃ ἐγὼ δώσω αὐτῷ πηγὴ ὕδατος ζῶντος ἁλλομένου εἰς ζωὴν αἰώνιον.[78] Καὶ πάλιν ὁ πιστεύων εἰς ἐμέ, καθὼς εἶπεν ἡ Γραφή, ποταμοὶ ἐκ τῆς κοιλίας αὐτοῦ ῥεύσουσιν ὕδατος ζῶντος.[79]

(3) Fragment 25 (f. 9r)

ΘΕΟΔΩΡΟΥ Μιμεῖται γὰρ ὑδάτων ἄρδει τὰ τοῦ θείου Πνεύματος νάματα, καὶ καθάπερ ἐκεῖνα τὰ παραφυτευόμενα δένδρα τεθηλέναι ποιεῖ, οὕτως ταῦτα παρασκευάζει τοὺς θείους φέρειν καρπούς. Οὗ δὴ χάριν καὶ ὁ Δεσπότης Χριστὸς ὕδωρ τὴν οἰκείαν διδασκαλίαν ὠνόμασεν. Εἴ τις γάρ, φησίν, διψᾷ, ἐρχέσθω πρός με καὶ πινέτω,[80] καὶ ἔσται τὸ ὕδωρ ὃ ἐγὼ δώσω αὐτῷ πηγὴ ὕδατος ζῶντος ἁλλομένου εἰς ζωὴν αἰώνιον.[81] Καὶ πάλιν ὁ πιστεύων εἰς ἐμέ, καθὼς εἶπεν ἡ Γραφή, ποταμοὶ ἐκ τῆς κοιλίας αὐτοῦ ῥεύσουσιν ὕδατος ζῶντος.[82] Καὶ μέντοι καὶ πρὸς τὴν Σαμαρῖτην ὁ πίνων ἐκ τοῦ ὕδατος τούτου διψήσει πάλιν, ὃς δ᾽ ἂν πίῃ ἐκ τοῦ ὕδατος, οὗ ἐγὼ δώσω αὐτῷ, οὐ μὴ διψήσῃ εἰς τὸν αἰῶνα.[83] Οὕτως καὶ διὰ Ἡσαΐου τοῦ προφήτου φησὶν ὅτι ἐγὼ δώσω ἐν δίψει τοὺς πορευομένους ἐν ἀνύδρῳ, καὶ ἀνοίξω ἐπὶ τῶν ὀρέων πηγάς, καὶ ἐπὶ τῶν βουνῶν ποταμούς, ποτίσαι τὸ γένος μου τὸ ἐκλεκτόν, τὸν λαόν μου ὃν περιεποιησάμην.[84] Εἰκότως τοίνυν καὶ ὁ μακάριος Δαυὶδ τὸν τοῖς θείοις λογίοις ἐσχολακότα δένδρα ἀπείκασε παρὰ τὰς τῶν ὑδάτων ὄχθας πεφυτευμένα, καὶ ἀειθαλῆ μὲν ἔχουσι τὰ φύλλα, τὸν δὲ καρπὸν φέρουσιν εἰς καιρόν. Καὶ γὰρ οἱ τῆς ἀρετῆς

---

76. Rom 8:28.
77. John 7:37.
78. John 4:14.
79. John 7:38.
80. John 7:37.
81. John 4:14.
82. John 7:38.
83. John 4:13–14.
84. Isa 43:20–21.

ἀθληταὶ τὸν μὲν πόνων κατὰ τὸν μέλλοντα βίον κομίσονται τοὺς καρπούς, οἷον δέ τινα φύλλα, τὴν ἀγαθὴν ἐλπίδα διηνεκῶς ἐν αὐτοῖς φέροντες τεθήλασιν καὶ ἀγάλλονται, καὶ συλῶσι τῇ ψυχαγωγίᾳ τῶν πόνων βαρύτητα. Ἔχουσι δὲ καὶ τὸν μεγαλόδωρον Δεσπότην τῇ προθυμίᾳ συνεργοῦντα διηνεκῶς τοῖς γὰρ ἀγαπῶσι τὸν Θεόν, φησὶν ὁ θεῖος Ἀπόστολος, *πάντα συνεργεῖ εἰς ἀγαθόν*.[85] Διά τοι τοῦτο καὶ ὁ μακάριος ἔφη Δαυίδ.

Doublet 6: Didymus on Ps 3:5

3:5   Φωνῇ μου πρὸς Κύριον ἐκέκραξα,
       καὶ ἐπήκουσέ μου ἐξ ὄρους ἁγίου αὐτοῦ.

(1) Mühlenberg, *Psalmenkommentare*, 126

Ἡ ὑπερφυὴς γνῶσις αὐτοῦ δύναται ὄρος ἅγιον εἶναι θεοῦ, ἐξ οὗ εἰσακούει τῶν εὐχομένων θεός, ὁ μονογενὴς υἱὸς αὐτοῦ, περὶ οὗ εἴρηται *Ἔσται ἐμφανὲς τὸ ὄρος κυρίου ἐπ᾽ ἐσχάτου τῶν ἡμερῶν*,[86] δηλούσης τῆς λέξεως ταύτης τὴν γενομένην αὐτοῦ φανέρωσιν κατὰ τὴν ἐπιδημίαν ἐπὶ συντελείᾳ τῶν αἰώνων.

(2) Fragment 62 (f. 14r)

ΔΙΔΥΜΟΥ Λέγοιτο δ᾽ ἂν ὄρος Θεοῦ καὶ ἡ ὑπερφυῆς αὐτοῦ γνῶσις καὶ ὁ μονογενὴς δὲ υἱὸς τοῦ Θεοῦ ἐξ οὗ τῶν εὐχομένων ὁ Πατὴρ ἀκούει περὶ οὗ γέγραπται *ἔσται ἐμφανὲς τὸ ὄρος Κυρίου ἐπ᾽ ἐσχάτου τῶν ἡμερῶν*[87] ἐπὶ συντελείᾳ γὰρ ἡμῖν τῶν αἰώνων ἐφανερώθη.

(3) Fragment 66 (f. 14r)

ΔΙΔ<ΥΜΟΥ> Ὄρος ἅγιον Θεοῦ ἡ ὑπερφυῆς γνῶσις αὐτοῦ δύναται ὄρος ἅγιον τὸ Θεοῦ ἐξ οὗ εἰσακούει τῶν εὐχομένων Θεὸς ὁ μονογενὴς υἱὸς αὐτοῦ περὶ οὗ εἴρηται *ἔσται ἐμφανὲς τὸ ὄρος Κυρίου ἐπ᾽ ἐσχάτων τῶν ἡμερῶν*[88] δηλούσης τῆς λέξεως ταύτης τὴν γενομένην αὐτοῦ φανέρωσι κατὰ τὴν ἐπιδημίαν ἐπὶ συντελείᾳ τῶν αἰώνων.

---

85. Rom 8:28.
86. Mic 4:1; cf. Isa 2:2.
87. Mic 4:1; cf. Isa 2:2.
88. Mic 4:1; cf. Isa 2:2.

DOUBLET 7: THEODORET ON PS 3:5

3:5   Φωνῇ μου πρὸς Κύριον ἐκέκραξα,
       καὶ ἐπήκουσέ μου ἐξ ὄρους ἁγίου αὐτοῦ.

(1) PG 80:885c

Διά τοι τοῦτο μετὰ πάσης προθυμίας προσφέρω σοι τὰς δεήσεις, εἰδὼς ὅτι παραυτίκα τὰς αἰτήσεις παρέξεις. Οὐ φωνὴν δὲ ἐνταῦθα καὶ βοὴν τὴν κραυγὴν νοητέον, ἀλλὰ τὴν τῆς ψυχῆς προθυμίαν. Οὕτω γὰρ καὶ ὁ τῶν ὅλων Θεὸς πρὸς σιγῶντα τὸν μακάριον ἔφη Μωσῆν· «Τί βοᾷς πρός με;»[89] βοὴν τὴν σιγὴν ὀνομάζων διὰ τὴν σπουδαίαν τῆς διανοίας εὐχήν. Τὸ δὲ, «Εἰσήκουσέ μου ἐξ ὄρους ἁγίου αὐτοῦ,» κατὰ τὴν πάλαι κατέχουσαν εἴρηται δόξαν. Ἐνομίζετο γὰρ ἐν τῇ σκηνῇ κατοικεῖν ὁ τῶν ὅλων Θεός, ἐπειδὴ καὶ τοὺς χρησμοὺς ἐκεῖθεν τοῖς ἱερεῦσιν ἐδίδου.

(2) Fragment 63 (f. 14r)

ΘΕΟΔΩΡΗΤΟΥ Ἡ καὶ καθ' ἱστορίαν διὰ τὴν πάλαι κατέχουσαν δόξαν ἐνομίζετο γὰρ ἐν τῇ σκηνῇ τῇ νομικῇ κατοικεῖν ὁ Θεὸς ἐπεὶ καὶ τοὺς χρησμοὺς ἐκεῖθεν τοῖς ἱερεῦσι παρείχετο.

(3) Fragment 64 (f. 14r)

ΘΕΟΔΩΡΟΥ Διά τοι τοῦτο μετὰ πάσης προθυμίας προσφέρω σοι τὰς δεήσεις, εἰδὼς ὅτι παραυτίκα τὰς αἰτήσεις παρέξεις. Οὐ φωνὴν δὲ ἐνταῦθα καὶ βοὴν τὴν κραυγὴν νοητέον, ἀλλὰ τὴν τῆς ψυχῆς προθυμίαν. Οὕτω γὰρ καὶ ὁ τῶν ὅλων Θεὸς προσιόντα τὸν μακάριον ἔφη Μωυσὶν *τί βοᾷς πρός με;*[90] Βοὴν τὴν σιγὴν ὀνομάζων διὰ τὴν σπουδαίαν τῆς διανοίας εὐχήν. Τὸ δὲ *εἰσήκουσέ μου ἐξ ὄρους ἁγίου αὐτοῦ,*[91] κατὰ τὴν πάλαι κατέχουσαν εἴρηται δόξαν. Ἐνομίζετο γὰρ ἐν τῇ σκηνῇ κατοικεῖν ὁ τῶν ὅλων Θεός, ἐπειδὴ καὶ τοὺς χρησμοὺς ἐκεῖθεν τοῖς ἱερεῦσιν ἐδίδου.

DOUBLET 8: THEODORET ON PS 3:6

3:6   Ἐγὼ ἐκοιμήθην καὶ ὕπνωσα·
       ἐξηγέρθην, ὅτι Κύριος ἀντιλήψεταί μου.

---

89. Exod 14:15.
90. Exod 14:15.
91. Cf. Ps 19:7.

(1) PG 80:885d–888a

Νύκτα τὰς συμφορὰς πολλάκις ἡ θεία καλεῖ Γραφή· ἐπειδὴ ὡς ἐν σκότει διάγειν νομίζουσιν οἱ τοῖς ἄγαν ἀνιαροῖς περιπίπτοντες· ταῖς δὲ νυξὶν ὁ ὕπνος συνέζευκται· σημαίνει τοίνυν κατὰ ταυτὸν τὰς θλίψεις, καὶ τὴν τούτων ἀπαλλαγήν. Τὸ γὰρ «Ἐξηγέρθην, ὅτι Κύριος ἀντιλήψεταί μου,» τοῦτο δηλοῖ, ὅτι Τῆς θείας ἀπολαύσας ῥοπῆς κρείττων ἐγενόμην τῶν προσπεσόντων κακῶν. Διό

(2) Fragment 67 (f. 14r)

ΘΕΟΔ<ΩΡΗΤΟΥ/ΩΡΟΥ> Νύκτα τὰς συμφορὰς ἡ θεία πολλάκις καλεῖ Γραφή, ἐπειδὴ ὡς ἐν σκότει διάγειν νομίζουσιν οἱ τῆς ἄγαν ἀρίαρα† περιπίπτοντες, ταῖς δὲ νυξὶν ὁ ὕπνος συνέζευκται, σημαίνει τοίνυν κατὰ ταυτὸν τὰς θλίψεις καὶ τὴν τούτων ἀπαλλαγήν. Τὸ γὰρ ἐξηγέρθην, ὅτι Κύριος ἀντιλήψεταί μου,[92] τοῦτο δηλοῖ, ὅτι τῆς θείας ἀπολαύσας ῥοπῆς κρείττων ἐγενόμην τῶν προσπεσόντων κακῶν. Διὸ φησὶν ἐκοιμήθην[93] τῇ ῥαθυμίᾳ ἐξηγέρθην[94] τῇ μετανοίᾳ ἐκοιμήθην δέ φησι καὶ ὕπνωσα[95] τὴν ἐπὶ πολὺ ῥαθυμίαν αἰνιττόμενος ὅτι Κύριος ἀντιλήψεταί μου ἡ δὲ τοῦ Θεοῦ φιλανθρωπία ἀρκέσει πρὸς ἀρετὴν ἐγεῖραι καὶ τὸν ῥάθυμον.

(3) Fragment 71 (f. 14r)

ΘΕΟΔ<Ω>ΡΗΤ<ΟΥ> Ἄλλος ἔφη νύκτα τὰς συμφορὰς ἡ θεία καλεῖ πολλάκις Γραφή ταῖς δὲ νυξὶν ὁ ὕπνος συνέζευκται δηλοῖ τοίνυν τὰς θλίψεις, καὶ τὴν τούτων ἀπαλλαγήν.

DOUBLET 9: THEODORET ON PS 3:8

3:8   Ἀνάστα, Κύριε, σῶσόν με, ὁ Θεός μου,
       ὅτι σὺ ἐπάταξας πάντας τοὺς ἐχθραίνοντάς μοι ματαίως,
       ὀδόντας ἁμαρτωλῶν συνέτριψας.

(1) PG 80:888a–b

Τελείας μοι τοίνυν μετάδος τῆς σωτηρίας· καὶ καθάπερ πολλάκις ἄδικον κατ' ἐμοῦ δυσμένειαν ἐσχηκότας, καὶ ὁμοφύλους καὶ ἀλλοφύλους, καὶ Ἰσραηλίτας καὶ Ἀμαληκίτας, καὶ μέντοι καὶ αὐτὸν τὸν Σαούλ, ποινὴν εἰσεπράξω τῆς ἀδικίας· οὕτω με καὶ νῦν τῆς σωτηρίας ἀξίωσον. Τὸ δὲ, «Ὀδόντας ἁμαρτωλῶν συνέτριψας,» ἀντὶ

---

92. Ps 3:6.
93. Ps 3:6.
94. Ps 3:6.
95. Ps 3:6.

τοῦ, Πάσης αὐτοὺς ἐγύμνωσας ἰσχύος, ἐκ μεταφορᾶς τῶν θηρίων, ἃ τῶν ὀδόντων στερούμενα, εὐκαταφρόνητα λίαν ἐστὶ καὶ εὐκαταγώνιστα.

(2) Fragment 81 (f. 14v)

ΘΕΟΔΩΡΗΤ<ΟΥ> Ἄλλος τοὺς *ὀδόντας συντρῖψαι*[96] φησὶ τὸ πάσης αὐτοὺς ἰσχύος γυμνῶσαι ἀπὸ μεταφορᾶς τῶν θηρίων ἃ τῶν ὀδόντων στερόμενα, εὐκαταφρόνητα λίαν ἐστιν.

(3) Fragment 82 (f. 14v)

ΘΕΟΔΩΡΟΥ Τελείας μοι τοίνυν μετάδος τῆς σωτηρίας· καὶ καθάπερ πολλάκις ἄδικον κατ' ἐμοῦ δυσμένειαν ἐσχηκότας, καὶ ὁμοφύλους καὶ ἀλλοφύλους, καὶ Ἰσραηλίτας καὶ Ἀμαληκίτας, καὶ μέντοι καὶ αὐτὸν τὸν Σαούλ, ποινὴν εἰσεπράξατο τῆς ἀδικίας· οὕτω με καὶ νῦν τῆς σωτηρίας ἀξίωσον. Τὸ δέ, *ὀδόντας ἁμαρτωλῶν συνέτριψας,*[97] ἀντὶ τοῦ, πάσης αὐτοὺς ἰσχύος ἐγύμνωσας, ἐκ μεταφορᾶς τῶν θηρίων, ἃ τῶν ὀδόντων στερούμενα, εὐκαταφρόνητα λίαν εἰσὶ καὶ εὐκαταγώνιστα.

DOUBLET 10: THEODORET ON PS 5:4–5

5:4 τὸ πρωὶ εἰσακούσῃ τῆς φωνῆς μου,
     τὸ πρωὶ παραστήσομαί σοι καὶ ἐπόψει με.
5:5 Ὅτι οὐχὶ Θεὸς θέλων ἀνομίαν σὺ εἶ,
     οὐ παροικήσει σοι πονηρευόμενος·

(1) PG 80:896d–897a

Θαρροῦσα γὰρ ὡς δέχῃ τὰς ἐμὰς ἱκετείας, εὐθὺς τοῦ φωτὸς ἀνίσχοντος, τῶν βλεφάρων ἀποσεισαμένη τὸν ὕπνον, οἷα δὴ βασιλεῖ καὶ Δεσπότῃ παρίσταμαι, τὴν αἴτησίν σοι προσφέρουσα. Οὐ παντὸς δέ ἐστι λέγειν τῷ τῶν ὅλων Θεῷ, «Παραστήσομαί σοι, καὶ ἐπόψει με·» ἀλλὰ τῶν κατὰ τὸν μέγαν Ἠλίαν διὰ τὴν ἀπὸ τῆς πολιτείας παρρησίαν λέγειν θαρρούντων, «Ζῇ Κύριος, ᾧ παρέστην ἐνώπιον αὐτοῦ σήμερον.»[98]

---

96. Cf. Ps 3:8.
97. Ps 3:8.
98. 3 Kgdms 17:1.

(2) Fragment 102 (f. 18v)

ΘΕΟΔΩΡΗΤ<ΟΥ> Ἐν τισι δὲ γράφεται καὶ ἐπόψει με[99] ὅπερ οὐ παντὸς λέγειν ἀλλὰ τῶν κατὰ τὸν μέγαν Ἠλίαν λέγειν θαρρούντων ἐκ πολιτείας ζῇ Κύριος, ᾧ πάρεστιν ἐνώπιον αὐτοῦ σήμερον.[100]

(3) Fragment 104 (f. 18v)

ΘΕΟΔΩΡΟΥ Θαρροῦσα γὰρ ὡς δέχῃ τὰς ἐμὰς ἱκετείας, εὐθὺς τοῦ φωτὸς ἀνίσχοντος, τῶν βλεφάρων ἀποσεισαμένη τὸν ὕπνον, οἷα δὴ βασιλεῖ καὶ Δεσπότῃ παρισταμένη, τὴν αἴστησίν σοι προσφέρουσα. Οὐ πάντως δὲ ἐστι λέγειν τῷ τῶν ὅλων Θεὸν παραστήσομαί σοι, καὶ ἐπόψει με,[101] ἀλλὰ τῶν κατὰ τὸν μέγαν Ἠλίαν διὰ τὴν ἀπὸ τῆς πολιτείας παρρησίαν λέγειν θαρούντων ζῇ Κύριος, ᾧ πάρεστιν ἐνώπιον αὐτοῦ σήμερον.[102]

DOUBLET 11: DIDYMUS ON PS 5:5–7

5:5   Ὅτι οὐχὶ Θεὸς θέλων ἀνομίαν σὺ εἶ,
      οὐ παροικήσει σοι πονηρευόμενος·
5:6   οὐδὲ διαμενοῦσι παράνομοι κατέναντι τῶν ὀφθαλμῶν σου,
      ἐμίσησας πάντας τοὺς ἐργαζομένους τὴν ἀνομίαν.
5:7   Ἀπολεῖς πάντας τοὺς λαλοῦντας τὸ ψεῦδος·
      ἄνδρα αἱμάτων καὶ δόλιον βδελύσσεται Κύριος.

(1) Mühlenberg, *Psalmenkommentare*, 132

Τούτου ἀληθοῦς ὄντος, οὐκ ἔστιν ἐκ θεοῦ τὸ κακὸν ὡς οἴονται οἱ ἐνυπόστατον τὴν κακίαν τιθέμενοι. Ἐκ στόματος γὰρ Ὑψίστου οὐκ ἐξελεύσεται τὸ κακὸν καὶ τὸ ἀγαθόν.[103] Μόνον γὰρ τὸ ἀγαθὸν εἶναι βούλεται· οὗ ὄντος ἀδύνατον ἔν τινι συστῆναι τὸ κακόν. Ἀπόλλυσιν δὲ Τοὺς λαλοῦντας τὸ ψεῦδος ἢ ψεῦσταί εἰσιν, ἵν' ἐπιγνῶσιν τὴν ἀλήθειαν ἣν καὶ πάλαι ᾔδεισαν. Τὸ γὰρ ἐπιγνῶναι τοῦτο δηλοῖ· οὐδεὶς γὰρ ἀρχὴν ἔχων τοῦ γινώσκειν τι ἐπιγινώσκειν αὐτὸ λέγεται. Πάντων δὲ τῶν λαλούντων τὸ ψεῦδος[104] ὑπὸ θεοῦ ἀπολλυμένων, ἀπολεῖται κἀκεῖνος περὶ οὗ εἴρηται "Ὅτ' ἂν λαλῇ τὸ ψεῦδος, ἐκ τῶν ἰδίων λαλεῖ.[105] Εἰ δὲ τοῦτο, οὐκ ἔστιν κατ' οὐσίαν κακός· οὐ γὰρ

---

99. Ps 5:4.
100. 3 Kgdms 17:1.
101. Ps 5:4.
102. 3 Kgdms 17:1.
103. Lam 3:38.
104. Ps 5:7.
105. John 8:44.

ἅμα τῷ γενέσθαι καὶ εἰς ὑπόστασιν ἐλθεῖν ἀλλὰ μετὰ ταῦτα τραπεὶς ἀρχὴν τοῦ λαλεῖν τὸ ψεῦδος ἔσχεν, ἐσχηκώς ποτε τὸ ἐν ἀληθείᾳ εἶναι. Δηλοῦται δὲ τοῦτο ἐκ τῶν οὕτω περὶ αὐτοῦ γεγραμμένων· Ἐν τῇ ἀληθείᾳ οὐχ ἕστηκεν, ὅτι ἀλήθεια οὐκ ἔστιν ἐν αὐτῷ.[106] ὁ γὰρ ψεκτὸς ὢν διὰ τὸ μὴ ἑστάναι φανερός ἐστιν πειραθεὶς τούτων τῶν διαθέσεων. Κριτέον δὲ ἐκ προθέσεως ἀλλ' οὐκ ἐκ μόνης φωνῆς τὸν ψευδόμενον, ἵνα μὴ ὦσιν ὑπὸ τὴν ἀπειλὴν οἱ οἰκονομικῶς ποτε τοῦτο πεποιηκότες ὡς Ῥαάβ· ἔδοξεν γὰρ ψεύδεσθαι πρὸς τοὺς ἀναζητοῦντας ἐπὶ τῷ ἀποκτεῖναι τοὺς κατασκόπους ἀγαθοὺς ἄνδρας ὄντας· ὑπὸ Ἰησοῦ γὰρ τοῦ Ναβῆ ἀποσταλέντες ἐπαινετοὶ ἦσαν. Τῆς προθέσεως τῆς ἀνθρώπου πολὺ τὸ σπουδαῖον ἐσούσης, οὐκ ἀκόλουθον οὖν ἐστιν τάξαι αὐτὴν ἐν τοῖς ἀπολλυμένοις ἢ ἐν τοῖς τὸ ψεῦδος λαλοῦσιν. Ὥσπερ δὲ οὐχ ὁ ὅπως ποτὲ κτείνων ἄνθρωπον φονεύς ἐστιν, οὕτως οὐ καθάπαξ ὁ ἐκχέων αἵματα αἱμάτων ἀνήρ ἐστιν· οὐ γὰρ λέγομεν φονέας ἢ αἱμάτων ἄνδρας τοὺς κατὰ νόμον θεῖον ἀποκτέννοντας τοὺς ἀξίους τὸ παθεῖν τοῦτο, ἐπεὶ ὥρα λέγειν Σαμουὴλ καὶ Ἠλίαν τοὺς μεγάλους ἄνδρας μαρτυρηθέντας ἐπὶ ἀγαθότητι καὶ προφητείᾳ θείᾳ ὑποκεῖσθαι τοῖς ἐγκλήμασιν τούτοις, ἀλλ' οὐδεὶς τούτων φονεὺς ἢ αἱμάτων ἀνήρ, εἰ καὶ ἔκτειναν τινας ἐπὶ ἀσεβείᾳ καὶ ἐγκλήμασιν μεγίστοις.

(2) Fragment 108 (f. 19r)

ΔΙΔΥΜΟΥ Τούτου ἀληθοῦς ὄντος, οὐκ ἔστιν ἐκ Θεοῦ τὸ κακὸν κατὰ τοὺς λέγοντας ἐνυπόστατον τὴν κακίαν. *Ἐκ στόματος γὰρ Ὑψίστου οὐκ ἐξελεύσεται τὸ κακὸν καὶ τὸ ἀγαθόν,*[107] βουλομένου μόνον εἶναι τὸ ἀγαθόν. Οὗ ὄντος, οὐκ ἂν ἔν τινι συσταίη κακόν. Ἀπόλλυσι δὲ τοὺς ψεύστας καθ' ὃ ψεῦσται πρὸς ἐπίγνωσιν ἀληθείας. *Πάντων δὲ τῶν λαλούντων τὸ ψεῦδος*[108] ὑπὸ Θεοῦ ἀπολλυμένων, ἀπολεῖται καὶ περὶ οὗ φησιν ὁ Σωτὴρ *ὅταν λαλεῖ τὸ ψεῦδος ἐκ τῶν ἰδίων λαλεῖ,*[109] οὐκ οὖν οὐ κατ' οὐσίαν ἐστὶ κακός, τραπεὶς γὰρ ἔσχεν ἀρχὴν τοῦ λαλῆσαι τὸ ψεῦδος. Διὸ φησὶν *ἐν τῇ ἀληθείᾳ οὐχ ἕστηκεν, ὅτι ἀλήθεια οὐκ ἔστιν ἐν αὐτῷ,*[110] ψέγεται γὰρ διὰ τὸ μὴ στῆναι ὡς ἄν ποτε γενόμενος ἐν αὐτῇ, ψεῦδος δὲ λαλοῦντας ἐκ διαθέσεως νοητέον, ἀλλ' οὐ κατὰ ψιλὴν προφοράν, ὅπερ ἄν τις κατ' οἰκονομίαν ποιήσειεν, ὡς ἡ Ῥαὰβ πρὸς τοὺς ἀναζητοῦντας τοὺς κατασκόπους οὐκ ἂν δὲ λέγοις· οὐδὲ φονέας ἢ αἱμάτων ἄνδρας· τοὺς κατανόμον θεῖον ἀποκτείνον τὰς τοὺς ἀξίους· ὡς τὸν Ἠλίαν καὶ Σαμουήλ· ὥστε περὶ τῶν κατανόμου παράβασιν ἀναιρούντων ὁ λόγος· διόπερ αὐτοῖς συνέζευκται καὶ τὸ δόλιος.

---

106. John 8:44.
107. Lam 3:38.
108. Ps 5:7.
109. John 8:44.
110. John 8:44.

(3) Fragment 113 (f. 19r)

ΔΙΔ<ΥΜΟΥ> Τούτου ἀληθοῦς ὄντος, οὐκ ἔστιν ἐκ Θεοῦ τὸ κακὸν κατὰ τοὺς λέγοντας ἐνυπόστατον τὴν κακίαν. *Ἐκ στόματος γὰρ Ὑψίστου οὐκ ἐξελεύσεται τὸ κακὸν καὶ τὸ ἀγαθόν,*[111] βουλομένου μόνον εἶναι τὸ ἀγαθόν. Οὗ ὄντος, οὐκ ἂν ἔν τινι συσταίη κακόν. Ἀπόλλυσι δὲ τοὺς ψεύστας, καθ' ὃ ψεύσται, εἰς ἐπίγνωσιν ἀληθείας. Πάντων δὲ τῶν *λαλούντων τὸ ψεῦδος*[112] ὑπὸ Θεοῦ ἀπολλυμένων, ἀπόλλυται κἀκεῖνος περὶ οὗ εἴρηται *ὅτ ἂν λαλῇ τὸ ψεῦδος, ἐκ τῶν ἰδίων λαλεῖ*[113]· εἰ δὲ τοῦτο, οὐκ ἔστι κατ' οὐσίαν κακός· οὐ γὰρ ἅμα τὸ γενέσθαι καὶ εἰς ὑπόστασιν ἐλθεῖν· ἀλλὰ μετὰ ταῦτα τραπεὶς ἀρχὴν τοῦ λαλεῖν τὸ ψεῦδος ἔσχεν, ἐσχηκὼς ποτὲ ἐν ἀληθείᾳ εἶναι. Δηλοῦται δὲ τοῦτο ἐκ τῶν οὕτω περὶ αὐτοῦ γεγραμμένων *ἐν τῇ ἀληθείᾳ οὐκ ἕστηκεν, ὅτι ἀλήθεια οὐκ ἔστιν ἐν αὐτῷ,*[114] ὁ γὰρ ψεκτὸς ὢν διὰ τὸ μὴ ἑστάναι, φανερῶς ἐστι πειραθῇς τούτων τῶν διαθέσεων. Κριτὲ δὲ ἐκ προθέσεως ἀλλ' οὐκ ἐκ μόνης φωνῆς τὸν ψευδόμενον, ἵνα μὴ ὦσιν ὑπὸ τὴν ἀπειλὴν οἱ οἰκονομικῶς ποτε τοῦτο πεποιηκότες, ὡς Ῥαάβ· ἔδοξε γὰρ ψεύδεσθαι πρὸς τοὺς ἀναζητοῦντας ἐπὶ τῷ ἀποκτεῖναι τοὺς κατασκόπους ἀγαθοὺς ἄνδρας ὄντας· ὑπὸ Ἰησοῦ γὰρ τοῦ Ναυὶ ἀποσταλέντες, ἐπαινετοὶ ἦσαν. Τῆς προθέσεως τῆς ἀνθρώπου πολὺ τὸ σπουδαῖον ἐχούσης, οὐκ ἀκόλουθον ἔσται τάξαι αὐτὴν ἐν τοῖς ἀπολλυμένοις ἢ ἐν τοῖς ψεῦδος λαλοῦσιν. Ὥσπερ δὲ οὐχ ὁπώσποτε κτείνος ἄνθρωπον, φονεύς ἐστιν· οὕτως οὐ καθάπαξ ὁ ἐκχέων αἷμα, ἀνὴρ αἱμάτων ἐστίν· οὐ γὰρ λέγομεν φονέας ἢ αἱμάτων ἄνδρας τοὺς κατὰ νόμον θεῖον ἀποκτένοντας τοὺς ἀξίως παθεῖν τοῦτο· ἐπεὶ ὥρα λέγειν τοῦτο Σαμουὴλ καὶ Ἠλίαν, οἳ ἐπ' ἀσεβείᾳ πολλοὺς ἔκτειναν.

DOUBLET 12: THEODORET ON PS 5:9

5:9   Κύριε, ὁδήγησόν με ἐν τῇ δικαιοσύνῃ σου ἕνεκα τῶν ἐχθρῶν μου, κατεύθυνον ἐνώπιόν σου τὴν ὁδόν μου.

(1) PG 80:897c–900a

Ἔνια τῶν ἀντιγράφων «ἐνώπιόν μου τὴν ὁδόν σου» ἔχει· ἑκάτερα δὲ τῆς εὐσεβοῦς ἔχεται διανοίας. Εἴτε γὰρ ἡ ἡμετέρα ὁδὸς κατευθυνθείη ἐνώπιον τοῦ Θεοῦ, πλάνης οὐ ληψόμεθα πεῖραν εἴτε ἡ τοῦ Θεοῦ ὁδὸς ἐνώπιον ἡμῶν κατευθυνθείη, αὐτὴν ὁδεύσομεν, καὶ πρὸς αὐτὴν προθύμως δραμούμεθα. Αἰτεῖ τοίνυν ἡ κληρονομοῦσα ὁδηγηθῆναι μὲν ὑπὸ τῆς τοῦ Θεοῦ δικαιοσύνης, κατευθυνθῆναι δὲ αὐτῇ τὴν ὁδόν, καὶ ἐξευμαρισθῆναι, ἵνα ῥᾳδίως ὁδεύῃ. Ταύτην ὁ Σύμμαχος τὴν διάνοιαν τέθεικεν· ἀντὶ γὰρ τοῦ, κατεύθυνον, ὁμάλισον εἴρηκεν. Ἀκούομεν δὲ καὶ αὐτοῦ τοῦ Χρίστου διὰ

---

111. Lam 3:38.
112. Ps 5:7.
113. John 8:44.
114. John 8:44.

Ἡσαΐου· «Ἔσται τὰ σκολιὰ εἰς εὐθεῖαν, καὶ ἡ τραχεῖα εἰς ὁδοὺς λείας.»[115] Καὶ ἐν ἑτέρῳ δὲ ψαλμῷ ὁ μακάριος ἔφη Δαβίδ· «Παρὰ Κυρίου τὰ διαβήματα ἀνθρώπου κατευθύνεται, καὶ τὴν ὁδὸν αὐτοῦ θελήσει σφόδρα.»[116] Ταπεινοφροσύνης δὲ μεστὰ τῆς κληρονομούσης τὰ ῥήματα. Οὐ γὰρ αἰτεῖ διὰ τὴν ἑαυτῆς δικαιοσύνην κατευθυνθῆναι αὐτῇ τὴν ὁδόν, ἀλλὰ διὰ τοὺς ἐχθροὺς τοὺς δυσσεβείᾳ συζῶντας, τοὺς ἀδίκως αὐτῇ πολεμοῦντας. Εἶτα αὐτῶν καὶ κατὰ μέρος διδάσκει τὰ τῆς πονηρίας ἐπιτηδεύματα.

(2) Fragment 121 (f. 19v)

ΔΙΔΥΜ<ΟΥ> Ἔν τισι δὲ γράφεται *ἐνώπιόν μου τὴν ὁδόν σου*.[117] Ἐάν τε δὲ ἡμῶν ἡ πλάνης οὐ ληψόμεθα πεῖραν· ἐάν τε τοῦ Θεοῦ ἡ ὁδὸς ἐνώπιον ἡμῶν, αὐτὴν ὁδεύσομεν προθύμως. Ἀντὶ δὲ τοῦ κατεύθυνον, ὁ Σύμμαχος ὁμάλισον εἴρηκεν, κατὰ τὸν Ἡσαΐαν εἰπόντα *ἔσται τὰ σκολία εἰς εὐθείαν, καὶ ἡ τραχεῖα εἰς ὁδοὺς λείας*.[118] Εἴρηται δὲ καὶ ἐν ἑτέρῳ ψαλμῷ *παρὰ Κυρίου τὰ διαβήματα ἀνθρώπου κατευθύνεται*.[119] Οὐκέτι δὲ ταπεινοφρόνως διὰ τὴν ἰδίαν δικαιοσύνην ἡ κληρονομοῦσα κατευθῆναι, διὰ δὲ τοὺς ἀσεβῶς αὐτῇ πολεμοῦντας. Εἶτα κατὰ μέρος ἐπεξέρχεται· τῷ γὰρ ψεύδει συνζῶσιν, καὶ συμφώνους ἔχουσι τῇ γλώττῃ τοὺς λογισμούς, καὶ τὴν δυσωδίαν πρόδηλον ἔχουσιν ἐπὶ λύμῃ τῶν ἄλλων. Λέγει δὲ τὴν κατὰ τοῦ Θεοῦ βλασφημίαν, καὶ τῆς ἀκολασίας τὰ ῥήματα· ἀλλὰ καὶ χαλεπώτερα τῶν προφερομένων ῥημάτων τὰ κεκρυμμένα δόλῳ κατὰ τῶν πέλας τυρεύοντα.

(3) Fragment 124 (f. 19v)

ΘΕΟΔ<ΩΡΗΤΟΥ/ΩΡΟΥ> Ἔνια τῶν ἀντιγράφων *ἐνώπιόν μου τὴν ὁδόν σου*[120] ἔχει· ἑκάτερα δὲ τῆς εὐσεβοῦς ἔχεται διανοίας. Εἶτα γὰρ ἡ ἡμετέρα ὁδὸς *κατευθυνθείη ἐνώπιον τοῦ Θεοῦ*,[121] πλάνης οὐ ληψόμεθα πεῖραν· εἴτε ἡ τοῦ Θεοῦ ὁδὸς ἐνώπιον ἡμῶν κατευθυνθείη, αὐτὴν ὁδεύσωμεν, καὶ πρὸς αὐτὸν προθύμως δραμούμεθα. Αἰτεῖ τοίνυν ἡ κληρονομοῦσα ὁδηγηθῆναι ὑπὸ τῆς τοῦ Θεοῦ δικαιοσύνης, κατευθυνθῆναι δὲ αὐτῆς τὴν ὁδόν, καὶ ἐξευμαρισθῆναι, ἵνα ῥᾳδίως ὁδεύει. Ταύτην ὁ Σύμμαχος τὴν διάνοιαν τέθεικεν ἀντὶ γὰρ τοῦ, κατεύθυνον, ὁμάλισον εἴρηκεν. Ἀκούομεν δὲ καὶ αὐτοῦ τοῦ Χριστοῦ διὰ Ἡσαΐου *ἔσται τὰ σκολία εἰς εὐθείαν, καὶ ἡ τραχεία εἰς ὁδοὺς λείας*.[122] Καὶ ἐν ἑτέρῳ δὲ ψαλμῷ ὁ μακάριος ἔφη Δαυὶδ *παρὰ Κυρίου τὰ διαβήματα ἀνθρώπου κατευθύνεται, καὶ τὴν ὁδὸν αὐτοῦ*

---

115. Isa 40:4.
116. Ps 36:23.
117. Ps 5:9.
118. Isa 40:4.
119. Ps 36:23.
120. Ps 5:9.
121. Cf. Ps 5:9.
122. Isa 40:4.

θελήσει σφόδρα.[123] Ταπεινοφροσύνης δὲ μεστὰ τῆς κληρονομούσης τὰ ῥήματα. Οὐ γὰρ αἰτεῖ διὰ τὴν ἑαυτῆς δικαιοσύνην κατευθυνθῆναι αὐτῆς τὴν ὁδόν, ἀλλὰ διὰ τοὺς ἐχθροὺς τοὺς δυσσεβείᾳ συζῶντας, τοὺς ἀδίκως αὐτῇ πολεμοῦντας. Εἰ τοὺς αὐτῶν καὶ κατὰ μέρος διδάσκει τὰ τῆς πονηρίας ἐπιτηδεύματα.

---

123. Ps 36:23.

The Future Indicative as Imperative in the Septuagint

Anssi Voitila

Abstract: Everyone who has read the text of the Septuagint must have recognized that the future indicative, as an equivalent of the Hebrew *yiqtol*, has an imperative sense in the Septuagint. This use of the future is also attested in Classical and Hellenistic Greek. In fact, we encounter this usage, for instance, in the Greek cultic laws as well. As an imperative the future indicative occurs, obviously, much more frequently in the Septuagint than is customary in the texts directly written in Greek, such as the cultic laws. In this paper, I examine this phenomenon in the Septuagint and in the Greek material. Particular attention is devoted to the contextual and pragmatic factors through which the addressee infers the imperative reading of a future indicative.

Everyone who has read the text of the Septuagint will have recognised that the IND.FUT., as an equivalent of the Hebrew *yiqtol* (and *weqatal*), has an imperative meaning in the Septuagint. This use of the IND.FUT. is also attested in the earliest forms of ancient Greek,[1] even as early as in the Mycenaean tablets,[2] where it is found in one ritual order text. In fact, imperative meanings for future forms are well attested in other languages as well.[3] In this paper, I examine this phenomenon in the Septuagint and compare it with the nontranslated Greek material.

First, we ask what makes a certain IND.FUT. a directive. The future is a morphological marker that, by its very nature, combines temporality and modality. With regard to temporality, it situates the action in the period of time

---

1. See Camille Denizot, *Donner des ordres en grec ancien: Étude linguistique des formes de l'injonction* (Mont-Saint-Aignan: Publications des universités de Rouen et du Havre, 2011), 423–37; Herbert Weir Smyth, *Greek Grammar* (Cambridge: Harvard University Press, 1956), §§1917–18.

2. See Denizot, *Donner des ordres en grec ancien*, 427.

3. See Joan Bybee, Revere Perkins, and William Pagliuca, *The Evolution of Grammar: Tense, Aspect, and Modality in the Languages of the World* (Chicago: University of Chicago Press, 1994), 210–12.

after the moment of speech. In turn, its inherent modality stems from the fact that the future is not as certain to us as are the present and the past. Even though its main use is prediction (as is the case for any true future), the source meaning of the Greek future was to express wish or desire, as noted in Pierre Chantraine's *Grammaire homérique*.[4] The connection between these two uses is clear: If speakers have or think that they have some knowledge of events taking place after the moment of speech, then the future form is interpreted as a prediction. The kind of modality expressed by such prediction, which reflects speakers' attitudes or beliefs regarding the truth of the assertion, is called epistemic modality. This contrasts with deontic modality, which "relates to obligation or permission, emanating" from a source that is external to the relevant individual.[5] Joan Bybee, Revere Perkins, and William Pagliuca include deontic modality in the larger group of Agent-oriented modalities. They define these modalities as follows: "A-o modality reports the existence of internal and external conditions on an agent with respect to the completion of the action expressed in the main predicate"; more specifically, "*obligation* reports the existence of external, social conditions compelling an agent to complete the predicate action."[6] Such directives indicate an existing obligation or permission that is made explicit by, but not imposed by, the speaker. The imperative, however, takes part in speaker-oriented modalities, in which "the speaker grants the addressee permission." "Speaker-oriented modalities do not report the existence of conditions on the agent, but rather allow the speaker to impose such conditions on the addressee."[7] John Lyons defines directives as "utterances which impose, or propose, some course of action or pattern of behaviour and indicate that it should be carried out."[8]

---

4. Pierre Chantraine, *Syntaxe*, vol. 2 of *Grammaire homérique* (Paris: Librairie C. Klinksieck, 1953), §299; against Andreas Willi, *Origins of the Greek Verb* (Cambridge: Cambridge University Press, 2018), §8.13 and p. 441 n. 42 for others. The Greek future is formed by adding a thematic σ-suffix (*-σε/ο- or *-h_iσε/ο-) to the verbal root (CeC-σε/ο-). This means that the future forms are quite often indistinguishable from σ-aorist subjunctives, especially in Homeric Greek, where subjunctive forms with short thematic vowels appear (Willi, *Origins*, §1.13). Therefore, it is also suggested that σ-aorist subjunctive is the starting point of the future forms in *-σε/ο- or *-h_iσε/ο- in classical Greek (see Willi, *Origins*, §8.12 and the literature there). Futures often arise from Subjunctives, at least in Indo-European languages (see Willi, *Origins*, 442 n. 43 for evidence). Nonetheless, this does not change the fact that desiderative (being one of the uses of the subjunctive) would be the source meaning for Future forms in the classical Greek synthetic future.

5. Frank R. Palmer, *Mood and Modality*, 2nd ed. (Cambridge: Cambridge University Press, 2009), 9.

6. Bybee, Perkins, and Pagliuca, *Evolution of Grammar*, 177 (emphasis original).

7. Bybee, Perkins, and Pagliuca, *Evolution of Grammar*, 179.

8. John Lyons, *Semantics* (Cambridge: Cambridge University Press, 1977), 746, cited in Bybee, Perkins, and Pagliuca, *Evolution of Grammar*, 179.

In this study, it will be seen that the IND.FUT. directives, particularly those directed toward a third person, represent mostly agent-oriented modality (the speaker reports an obligation or permission). In other cases, particularly in second-person addressees, speaker-oriented modality (the speaker grants permission, elicits action) is expressed.

What, then, are the criteria for recognising IND.FUT.'s use as a directive? Dominique Maingueneau argues that in the context of a directive, there is a tension between the speaker's actual situation and the realisation of the activity in question.[9] The utterance of the phrase *You will do p* indexes the speaker's power (it is a directive act) or knowledge (it is a prediction). Camille Denizot notes that there are also cases in which these two—power and knowledge—are intertwined.[10] She exemplifies this with Gen 3:16 (in its French form, *Tu enfanteras dans la douleur*, but similar verb forms are employed in Greek and Hebrew), seen in (1).

(1) Gen 3:16
καὶ τῇ γυναικὶ εἶπεν Πληθύνων πληθυνῶ τὰς λύπας σου καὶ τὸν στεναγμόν σου, ἐν λύπαις τέξῃ τέκνα· καὶ πρὸς τὸν ἄνδρα σου ἡ ἀποστροφή σου, καὶ αὐτός σου κυριεύσει
To the woman he said, I will greatly multiply your suffering and your groaning; in suffering you shall bring forth children; and your inclination shall be to your husband, and he shall rule over you.

"In suffering you shall bring forth children" (ἐν λύπαις τέξῃ τέκνα) is a prediction (i.e., the assertion that "the situation in the proposition, which refers to an event taking place after the moment of speech, will hold"[11]), because the addressee does not have control over the action. Moreover, it is also what we call a "commandment," because it is spoken by God. The future, Denizot adds, has performative value here: The divine word is to do things by uttering them.[12] Denizot, following Maingeneau, reasons that the directive value is announcing, without modality ("dépourvue de modalité"), what will be: The speaker places a constraint upon the addressee without necessarily including any indication of will or desire.[13] This seems to indicate deontic meaning for the statement. Maingeneau and Denizot, however, argue that God not only shows a strong commitment to the truth value of this sentence, but its completion in the future is so certain that this is no longer a modal sentence, but rather a statement of fact. This sounds like epistemic modality, which is problematic, because both deontic and epistemic meanings

---

9. Dominique Maingueneau, *Approche de l'énonciation en linguistique française: Embrayeurs, 'temps', discours rapport* (Paris: Hachette, 1981), 76–77; Denizot, *Donner des ordres en grec ancien*, 425.
10. Denizot, *Donner des ordres en grec ancien*, 425.
11. Bybee, Perkins, and Pagliuca, *Evolution of Grammar*, 244.
12. John L. Austin, *How to Do Things with Words* (Oxford: Clarendon, 1962).
13. Denizot, *Donner des ordres en grec ancien*, 425.

would also be a kind of modality. "Without modality" is, therefore, somewhat confusing here.

It is interesting, however, that God's words begin with another IND.FUT. just before, in giving the reason for the affirmations: "I will greatly multiply your suffering and your groaning." God has the greatest authority, and when he predicts something, it will materialise. Thus, his IND.FUT. holds, and this makes it compelling, almost deontic; the obligation is placed upon the agent, and God is the enforcer as the creator of childbirth. This can be read, therefore, as agent-oriented modality. The woman has committed a crime and now she has to pay. God is also bound to the facts of it. This is reminiscent of an interpretation that will be presented shortly concerning Greek legal texts.

Furthermore, Denizot gives the following criteria for recognising the directive use of the future: First, the addressee has some control over the action referred to; and second, the addressee is the (semantic) agent of the action.[14] The latter criterion, Denizot argues, is not always fulfilled, as this depends on the type of text. For example, in administrative or juridical documents (*Les candidats fourniront les pièces suivantes*, "Applicants must submit/provide the following documents"), or in procedural documents (*On prendra pour unité 3 cm.*, "We will take 3 cm. per unit"), the receivers exercise control over the action, but they are not really the addressee(s) ("interlocuteurs") of the intended action. The written document does not specify the proper addressee(s). We often come across this use for the future in inscribed laws and documentary papyri in which the writer orders or instructs the addressee to make sure that a third party completes a certain duty or duties. One example can be seen in (2), which comes from Gortyn in ancient Crete, dated to the middle of the sixth century BCE.

(2) Gortyn Code 3.1–6
... αἰ μὲν κ' ἀμπό]τεροι ἔπον[ται] οἱ ἀλλοῖοι μὴ ἔνδικον ἤμμην, αἰ δέ κα μὴ ἀμπότεροι ὁ [c. 4]ενος τὰν ἀπλόον τι[μα]ν καταστασ[εῖ].
If both the different ones are following, there shall be no legal action; but if both are not, he [the attacking dog's owner?] **shall pay** the simple price.[15]

According to Monique Bile,[16] this form is in variation with the IMP. and the INF. in similar contexts in the Gortyn Code.[17] This occurs only with verbs indicating payment. It expresses obligation, as in *il doit payer*, "he must pay" (in a deontic

---

14. Denizot, *Donner des ordres en grec ancien*, 427.

15. Michael Gagarin, W*riting Greek Law* (Cambridge: Cambridge University Press, 2008), 129.

16. Monique Bile, *Le dialecte crétois ancien: Études de la langue des inscriptions recueil des inscriptions postérieures aux IC* (Paris: Librairie Orientaliste Paul Gauthier, 1988), 254.

17. See also Denizot, *Donner des ordres en grec ancien*, 427–28.

sense), and I am willing to accept the following interpretation: although the law seems to be one of the discourse participants (as the agent giving the order/command/statute), it is only a frame of reference, not a participant, in an actual court situation. The verb appears in the apodosis of a conditional sentence whose protasis explains the reason for the penalty. Bile argues that the IND.FUT. indicates that the action of paying is not considered to involve volition, but rather that it is predictive, in the sense that there is no room for doubt about the realisation of the payment. The text does not even envisage the possibility that an individual could avoid the penalty, if at fault. This sounds to me like yet another instance of the future being used with agent-oriented meaning, that is, the law sets conditions compelling the criminal to complete the predicate action.

The Gortyn Code instances further demonstrate that the law is a characteristic literary context for this usage of the IND.FUT. A law, as a text, has inherent authority. When its "author" uses this authority, this, in turn, prompts a deontic inference for the IND.FUT. Thus, context constitutes the third criterion for interpreting an IND.FUT. as an imperative.

Let us consider yet another instance of directive uses, now in a so-called cultic law, in (3). This text is inscribed into a rock at the entrance to a cave in Thera, dating back to around the beginning of the fourth century BCE.

(3) ΓΕ–ΝΗΤΟΝ Ἀρταμιτίο(υ) τετάρται πεδ' ἰκάδα **θυσέοντι** ἰαρόν, Ἀγορηίοις δὲ [δε]ῖπνο γ [κ]αὶ ἰα[ρ]ὰ πρὸ το(ῦ) σαμηίο(υ).[18]
On the 4th and on the 20th of the month Artemitios, let them offer [lit. they will offer] a sacrifice, on the day of Agoreia, a feast and sacrificial animals before the sign.

The first sentence (ΓΕ–ΝΗΤΟΝ, which is partly damaged) most probably gave the name of the *genos* who gathered there for the sacrificial feast mentioned in the text. In this context, the IND.FUT. refers to a moment beyond the moment of "speech" (a prediction), but because of the cultic context in which it is found, a more compelling reading can be gleaned here: agent-oriented (deontic) modality.

All the Septuagint translators have favoured the IND.FUT. as the most common equivalent of Hebrew *yiqtol*. It seems natural to render *yiqtol* in this way, as it can also have directive value. But what was the translators' interpretation of this form, and how did they intend for readers to understand it? Did they recognise that the IND.FUT. did not have its common predictive meaning in some cases?

In this paper, I will concentrate on instances in Genesis that may be considered anomalies in terms of translators' choices. In these cases, the translators did not use the common equivalent (the one they most frequently used) of the verb form they were translating, but rather chose IND.FUT. Indeed, when the Hebrew verb form alone is not the decisive factor in IND.FUT. usage, other influential factors may come to light. Instances in which Hebrew directives have been

---

18. IG XII, 3 452 (LSCG, 133).

translated with IND.FUT. are particularly useful here. To this end, I will concentrate primarily on the Hebrew IMP. In future studies, however, it would also be interesting to study instances in which the directive *yiqtol* was rendered with the IMP. in Greek, to see which contexts led translators not to use IND.FUT. as an equivalent.

Our first example, in (4), comes from God's instructions concerning the coming flood.

(4) Gen 6:21

וְאַתָּה קַח־לְךָ מִכָּל־מַאֲכָל אֲשֶׁר יֵאָכֵל וְאָסַפְתָּ אֵלֶיךָ וְהָיָה לְךָ וְלָהֶם לְאָכְלָה:

σὺ δὲ **λήμψῃ** σεαυτῷ ἀπὸ πάντων τῶν βρωμάτων, ἃ ἔδεσθε, καὶ συνάξεις πρὸς σεαυτόν, καὶ ἔσται σοὶ καὶ ἐκείνοις φαγεῖν (INF.).

And **take** with you of all food that is eaten, and you shall gather it to you; and it shall be for you, and for them to eat.

Here, the Hebrew IMP. is translated with IND.FUT. In the preceding context, God gives instructions using IND.FUT., and in Hebrew, there are *yiqtols*. In verses 18–19, God tells Noah what he is going to do (1.SG.IND.PRES. + IND.FUT.), and that all living beings are going to die (3.SG.IND.FUT). Next, in the middle of verse 19, God changes the grammatical subject to second-person singular, now saying what Noah is going to do. God has all the power, so this address does not function as mere prediction. It also compels Noah, thereby giving the future a directive meaning (speaker-oriented modality). It is understandable, then, that the translator felt no need to change the mode of the verb in verse 21, although his *Vorlage* would have contained the Hebrew IMP., just as the Masoretic text does. This interpretation is further confirmed in the next verse, in which the narrator says that this was an order (it was what God had ordered: ἐνετείλατο).

In Gen 12:2, God speaks to Abraham. In verse 1, he orders Abraham to leave the land of his father, using IMP. in both languages. In verse 2, he uses three IND.FUT.s (in Hebrew, cohortatives) to tell Abraham how God is going to make a great and successful nation out of him.

(5) Gen 12:2

וְאֶעֶשְׂךָ לְגוֹי גָּדוֹל וַאֲבָרֶכְךָ וַאֲגַדְּלָה שְׁמֶךָ וֶהְיֵה בְּרָכָה:

καὶ ποιήσω σε εἰς ἔθνος μέγα καὶ εὐλογήσω σε καὶ μεγαλυνῶ τὸ ὄνομά σου, καὶ **ἔσῃ** εὐλογητός.

And I will make of you a great nation. And I will bless you and make your name great. And you **will be** blessed.

This is an instance of a shift in grammatical subject. In Hebrew, IMP. is used without, in fact, any directive value. It may be taken as indicating a desired or predicted result. Likewise, in the Greek, the IND.FUT. expresses the same by summarising the preceding blessings. This summarising usage of the IND.FUT. is also not unknown in the Greek texts. After an IMP., an IND.FUT. may have directive value, but it may also indicate that the action(s) that appear as imperative(s) involve(s) some sort of summary,[19] as in (6).

(6) Plato, *Protagoras* 338a
ὡς οὖν **ποιήσετε**, καὶ πείθεσθέ μοι ῥαβδοῦχον καὶ ἐπιστάτην καὶ πρύτανιν ἑλέσθαι ὃς ὑμῖν φυλάξει τὸ μέτριον μῆκος τῶν λόγων ἑκατέρου
So you two **do** as I advised you, and believe me and choose an umpire or supervisor or chairman who will keep watch for you over the due measure of either's speeches. (Advice/counsel > order)[20]

Denizot argues that the IND.FUT. in (6) is not an injunction, because it is not binding; it merely sums up the recommendations Callias has just made, and the IMP. introduces a new aspect in the process.[21]

Spoken by God, the IND.FUT. assures the accomplishment of the prediction. For instance, God gives orders to Abraham concerning circumcision in Gen 17:10, shown in (7).

(7) Gen 17:10
זֹאת בְּרִיתִי אֲשֶׁר תִּשְׁמְרוּ בֵּינִי וּבֵינֵיכֶם וּבֵין זַרְעֲךָ אַחֲרֶיךָ הִמּוֹל לָכֶם כָּל־זָכָר׃
καὶ αὕτη ἡ διαθήκη, ἣν διατηρήσεις, ἀνὰ μέσον ἐμοῦ καὶ ὑμῶν καὶ ἀνὰ μέσον τοῦ σπέρματός σου μετὰ σὲ εἰς τὰς γενεὰς αὐτῶν· **περιτμηθήσεται** ὑμῶν πᾶν ἀρσενικόν.
This is my covenant, which you shall keep, between me and you and your seed after you in their generations. Every male among you **shall be circumcised**.

In Hebrew, an INF.ABS. with directive value is employed. The translator depicts this as IND.FUT. in Greek. The verb, being in passive voice, third-person singular and spoken by God, conveys deontic overtones, as in "every man among you must be circumcised." The obligation is onto Abraham and his family as a covenant (social conditions). God is the other party and the guarantor of the agreement. He seems to impose the directive (hence, this would be speaker-oriented modality), but, in fact, the formulation of the sentence imposes the directive—if they were to disobey the directive, Abraham and his family would violate the covenant. God only reminds the addressee of this, reinforcing it (agent-oriented modality), just as with the IND.FUT. at Gen 3:16 (example [1] above). The IND.FUT. continues to be used throughout the section until Gen 17:14. In Hebrew, both the *weqatal* and *yiqtol* forms are used.

---

19. Similar usage is found at the end of a letter in which the writer asks a banker to make a payment on behalf of his sister and wife, P.Tebt. 3.1.766 (19 Oct. 147 or 16 Oct. 136 BCE): κἀγὼ ἀποστελῶ σοι τῆι λ. τοῦτο δὲ ποιήσας ἔσῃ μοι κεχαρισμένος, "I will send it to you on the 30th. By so doing, you will confer on me a kindness."
20. Denizot, *Donner des ordres en grec ancien*, 431.
21. Denizot, *Donner des ordres en grec ancien*, 431.

This deontic usage of PASS.IND.FUT. has an interesting "parallel" in P.Tebt. I 27:56–59, shown in (8), in which the king's cousin gives instructions to the officials of *toparchias* and their villages.

(8) πλὴν τῶν εἰς [τὰς] τροφὰς τῶν γεωργικῶν κτηνῶν ἃ καὶ με[τὰ] τῶν κωμογραμματέων π[ροσ]χορηγηθήσεται καὶ τῶν ἐγδιοικηθησομ[ένων] ὧν αἱ τειμαὶ καὶ \τούτ/ων αἱ ἀσφάλε[ιαι δο]θεῖσαι κατατεθήσονται ἐπὶ [τ]ῶν τραπεζῶ[ν] πρὸς τὰ καθήκοντα εἰς τὸ βα[σιλικὸν] ἀκολούθως τοῖς προεγδεδομ[έ]νοις χρηματισμοῖ[ς]
except those intended for the fodder of the animals used in agriculture, which **shall be supplied** with the approval of the *komogrammateis*, and except amounts to be collected for which the prices and securities **shall be paid and deposited** at the banks to meet the dues to the treasury in accordance with the regulations previously issued[22]

Next, in (9), Abraham meets the three men under the oak tree of Mamre and addresses them very politely.

(9) Gen 18:5

וְאֶקְחָה פַת־לֶחֶם וְסַעֲדוּ לִבְּכֶם אַחַר תַּעֲבֹרוּ
καὶ λήμψομαι ἄρτον, καὶ **φάγεσθε** (!), καὶ μετὰ τοῦτο παρελεύσεσθε εἰς τὴν ὁδὸν ὑμῶν.
I will get a morsel of bread, so you can refresh your heart (LXX: I will get some bread and **you shall eat**). After that you may go your way.

This case is not directive in the sense that the speaker would have authority over the addressees. Moreover, it is preceded by a predictive IND.FUT. (λήμψομαι), through which the speaker relates what he wants to do next. Rather, the IND.FUT. under discussion can only convey a modal meaning of possibility, indicating a suggestion regarding what the addressees should do, a permission without necessary authoritative social position (speaker-oriented modality).[23] That Abraham's words are only a suggestion is further confirmed when, at the end of verse 5, the three men accept Abraham's suggestion and let him proceed according to his suggestion. Here, in Hebrew, *yiqtol* is used, while in Greek, it appears as IMP.AOR. (כֵּן תַּעֲשֶׂה כַּאֲשֶׁר דִּבַּרְתָּ—οὕτως **ποίησον** καθὼς εἴρηκας— "Very well, **do** as you have said"). The previous Hebrew verse, however, contains two JUSS.s and two IMP.s, which are translated into Greek as IMP. or related forms, including two third-person IMP.s whose proper agents are the servants of Abraham. Abraham expresses his will to serve these holy men.

In this way, the situation in Gen 18:5 resembles the one in Aristophanes, *Lysistrate* 211, seen in (10):

---

22. P.Tebt. 1.27:56–59.

23. Should the speaker have full authority over the addressee, this instance would be interpreted without difficulty as granting permission.

(10) λάζυσθε πᾶσαι τῆς κύλικος ὦ Λαμπιτοῖ· λεγέτω δ᾽ ὑπὲρ ὑμῶν μί᾽ ἅπερ ἂν κἀγὼ λέγω· ὑμεῖς δ᾽ **ἐπομεῖσθε** ταὐτὰ **κἀμπεδώσετε**.
So, grasp the cup, you all, Lampito. One of you, repeat for the rest each word I say. Then **you shall take** oath. And **you shall keep** it securely.[24]

According to Denizot, the context of the scene makes it clear that the speaker is expressing her desire for the others to take an oath.[25] The expression of power over the others is not clear in the text, and it is not necessarily tied to the directive FUT. usage.

The next instance I want to look at, Gen 20:7, is quite different in that the speaker (God, the giver of life) has the authority over the other two agents who are brought into the conversation: the addressee (King Abimelech) and Abraham (the potential prayer). The actions (that Abraham will pray for Abimelech, and Abimelech will stay alive) are presented as possibilities (conditional); they will be realised only if Abimelech makes the right decision. In a way, the sentences with the IND.FUT. serve as motivation for the desired action.

(11) Gen 20:7

וְעַתָּ֞ה הָשֵׁ֤ב אֵֽשֶׁת־הָאִישׁ֙ כִּֽי־נָבִ֣יא ה֔וּא וְיִתְפַּלֵּ֥ל בַּֽעַדְךָ֖ וֶֽחְיֵ֑ה

νῦν δὲ ἀπόδος τὴν γυναῖκα τῷ ἀνθρώπῳ ὅτι προφήτης ἐστὶν καὶ προσεύξεται περὶ σοῦ καὶ **ζήσῃ**.
Now therefore, restore the man's wife. For he is a prophet, and he will pray for you, and **you will live**.

Similarly, in Gen 42:18 (וִֽחְי֑וּ) זֹ֥את עֲשׂ֖וּ—τοῦτο ποιήσατε καὶ **ζήσεσθε**—"Do this and live"), a Hebrew IMP. (now in second-person plural) is rendered with IND.FUT. The speaker (Joseph as the second after Pharaoh in the social hierarchy) has the authority over the addressees. The IND.FUT., which appears after an IMP. in both languages, expresses the result of the realisation of the action indicated by the preceding IMP.: "Do this and you shall live". Like example (11) from Gen 20:7, we may interpret this IND.FUT. not as a directive, but as indicating motivation, future benefit from the actions suggested to the addressee in the narrative sequence that follows. The phrase with the IND.FUT. functions as an apodosis of the previous sentence, which is a sort of protasis that states a condition: "Do this and you shall live" > "If you do this, you will live."

In contrast, in Gen 41:34–35, a sequence of *yiqtol* forms is found rendered with IMP.AOR.3.SG/PLs in a situation where Joseph is making suggestions to Pharaoh concerning the seven coming years of famine. In only the first two is Pharaoh the agent; in the following ones, his servants are to do the actual work: "Let Pharaoh do this, and let him appoint officers over the land, and let them take

---

24. Denizot, *Donner des ordres en grec ancien*, 423.
25. Denizot, *Donner des ordres en grec ancien*, 423.

up the fifth part of the product of the land of Egypt in the seven plenteous years."
This sequence of IMP.s is replaced by the IND.FUT. in verse 36 in Greek, whereas in the Hebrew text, the verse starts with *weqatal* but then continues with *yiqtols*. These IND.FUT.s seem to have a function similar to that of the preceding IMP.s: Namely, they offer instruction or advice (please, give your servants permission to do such and such actions).

Although the situation in the next case, Gen 45:18, shown in (12), resembles that of Gen 18:5, its power structure differs significantly.

(12) Gen 45:18

וּקְחוּ אֶת־אֲבִיכֶם וְאֶת־בָּתֵּיכֶם וּבֹאוּ אֵלָי וְאֶתְּנָה לָכֶם אֶת־טוּב אֶרֶץ מִצְרַיִם וְאִכְלוּ אֶת־חֵלֶב הָאָרֶץ:

καὶ παραλαβόντες τὸν πατέρα ὑμῶν καὶ τὰ ὑπάρχοντα ὑμῶν ἥκετε πρός με, καὶ δώσω ὑμῖν πάντων τῶν ἀγαθῶν Αἰγύπτου, καὶ **φάγεσθε** τὸν μυελὸν τῆς γῆς.

Take your father and your households, and come to me, and I will give you the good of the land of Egypt, and **you will eat** the fat of the land.

In Gen 45:18, the speaker has all the authority, being the Pharaoh himself. However, the Hebrew IMP. and its equivalent, the IND.FUT., are used after a *yiqtol* translated as an IND.FUT. (וְאֶתְּנָה—καὶ δώσω), which has predictive value. Thus, the Hebrew IMP. and its corresponding IND.FUT. in question do not carry obligation inherent to the agent, as in agent-oriented modality, but rather seem to give permission to exploit what has been given as a result of previous actions, thus expressing modality in the speaker-oriented sense. They thus serve as motivation for the earlier actions (go back, take your father, household and belongings, come back to Egypt, and as a reward I give you this land and its riches, so you should eat from it).

In conclusion, the future directive readings in the texts studied in this paper represent, on the one hand, agent-oriented modality (an external agent [e.g., law, social/natural conditions] imposes an obligation on the addressee to perform the predicated action), particularly when the agent is the third person. On the other hand, when the agent is in the second person, they represent speaker-oriented modalities (imperative-like uses: the speaker imposes an obligation on the addressee). Further, it has become evident that the Hebrew directive verb forms have been rendered with IND.FUT. forms that do not seem to convey directive meaning, but rather express results or motivate the addressee, particularly after a period (including its use in the apodosis). The future directive reading emerges when the pure prediction reading is not available. On the other hand, the speaker's position of authority or power over the addressee(s), such that s/he can give orders or instructions to them, does not seem to have had an unequivocal impact on the translation process. IND.FUT. is also used to indicate that permission and suggestions are being given to (an) addressee(s) of a social position that is equal to or higher than that of the speaker. The directive meaning of IND.FUT. is encouraged in legal contexts and in contexts in which other directive verb forms appear. These uses of IND.FUT. also appear in nontranslated Greek texts.

Contributors

Nicholas Peter Legh Allen, North-West University

Elena Belenkaja, Universität des Saarlandes

Eugene Coetzer, University of KwaZulu-Natal

Gunnar M. Eidsvåg, University of Stavanger

Robert J. V. Hiebert, Trinity Western University

Pierre J. Jordaan, North-West University

Gideon R. Kotzé, North-West University

Wolfgang Kraus, Universität des Saarlandes / University of Pretoria

Jonathan M. Robker, University of Münster

Seppo Sipilä, Finnish Bible Society

Satoshi Toda, Hokkaido University, Sapporo

Michaël N. van der Meer, Protestantse Theologische Universiteit, Amsterdam

Leontien Vanderschelden, Katholieke Universiteit Leuven

Anssi Voitila, University of Eastern Finland, Joensuu

Index of Ancient Sources

1. Ancient Near Eastern Texts

Old Babylonian Letters
TCL 17:29   114

Deir Alla Balaam Inscription
Comb. II, 13   111–112, 115

Gilgamesh Epos
Tablet X, lines 301–307   114–115

The Instruction of Ani
17.11–18.4   110–111, 115

KTU/CAT (Cuneiform Alphabetic Texts from Ugarit)
1.23.8–11   113–115

Lamentation over the Destruction of Sumer and Ur
399–401   105

2. Greco-Roman Authors

Aeschylus, *Choephori*
349   59

Aristophanes, *Lysistrata*
211   240–241

Athenaeus, *Deipnosophistae*
5.196a–203b   197

Diodorus Siculus, *Bibiotheca historica*
1.85   195
16.92.5–93.1   197
40.3   203–204

Diogenes Laërtius, *Vitae philosophorum*
1.10   194

Hecataeus, *Aegyptiaca*
264.1   194
264.6   203–204
264 F 25   194

Herodot, *Historiae*
2.58   194
2.63.2   194

Hesiod, *Theogonia*
176–178   90
184–186   90

Homer, *Iliad*
9.410–416   59

Homer, *Odyssey*
7.56–59   89
7.199–200   89
7.204–206   89–90
10.118–120   90

Kallixeinos Rhodius
FGH 627 F 2   197

Manetho, *Aegyptiaka*   185

Pausanias, *Graeciae descriptio*
1.4.4   191
10.23.1–2   191

Plato, *Phaedo*
85e   90

Plato, *Protagoras*
338a   239

Plato, *Sophista*
246a   90

Plato, *Symposium*
211e   184

Plato, *Theaetetus*
155e   90

Plato, *Timaeus*
50c–d   86
51a–b   86–88

Plutarch, *Titus Flaminius*
13.8   61

Plutarch, *Lycurgus*
20.4   61

Sophocles, *Ajax*
465   59

Thucydides, *De bello peloponnesiaco*
6.56–58   196–197

Xenophon, *Hipparchus*
3.2–4   196

3. Inscriptions, Ostraca, and Documentary Papyri

I.Epidaurus A, 33–41   189
IG II/III² 334   196–197
IG XII 3 452   237
I.Gortyn 3.1–6   236–237
I.Lindos D 1–47   191–192
I.Lindos D 94–113   192–193
O.dem.Hor 1   188
OGIS 56 (Canopus)   197–199
P.Brookl. 47.218.3   196
P.Carlsb. 424   187
P.Carlsb. 499   187
P.Carlsb. 559   187

P.Carlsb. 562   187
P.Oxy. 11.1381   189–191, 199
P.Polit.Iud.   67–69
P.Polit.Iud. 4   69
PSI inv. D 60   187
P.Tebt. 1.27.56–59   240
P.Tebt. 3.1.766   239
UPZ I 2–105   186
UPZ I 77–80   187
UPZ I 81   186–187

4. Septuagint (Hebrew Bible)

Genesis
1:2   85–94
3:16   235–236, 239
6:4   89
6:21   238
12:2   238–239
12:7   182
14   127
14:5   89
14:18–20   127
16:2   146, 152
16:3   182
17:1   182
17:10   239
17:14   239
18:1   182
18:5   240
18:24   156
18:28   156
18:29   156
18:30   156
18:31   156
18:32   156
20:7   241
22:14   182
24:5   149
24:39   149
25   77–78
25:6   78
26:2   182
26:24   182
27:12   149
32:20   182–183

32:21	149	33:23	178, 204
32:31	180, 182	34:20	180
35:1	182	34:23	180
35:9	182	34:24	180
36	77–78	34:35	168
41:34–35	241–242	40:35	182
42:18	241		
43:12	154	Leviticus	
45:18	242	9:4	182
46:20	37	16	127
46:27	37	16:2	182, 22
48:3	182		
		Numbers	
Exodus		1:21	57
1:5	37	12	77
2:16	77	12:6–8	178–179
2:22	77	12:7	200
3:6	180	12:8	176, 180, 204
3:16	182	14:14	182
4:1	182	22:6	151–152
4:5	182	22:11	151–152
5:3	76	22:33	159
6:3	182	23:3	150
11:7	169	35:33	38
13:5	49		
13:11	49	Deuteronomy	
14:15	225	4:12	178
16:35	50	4:15	178
17:8–9	76	6:6	123
19:21	180	6:10	49
22:22–24	97	7:1	49
23:15	180	10:18	97
23:17	180	11:29	49
23:30	49	16:16	181
24	127	23:7–8	79
24:9–11	176–177, 201	24:1–4	69
24:10–11	204	30:11	123
24:11	179, 204	31:15	181
24:16	182	32:1	37–38
25:8	182, 201	32:3	36
29:45–46	182, 201	32:4	216–218
32:20	152	32:8	36, 38
33:11–13	176–178	32:9–10	34
33:13	204	32:17	38
33:17–23	176–178	32:16	38
33:20	178	32:25	105

32:37	38	3 Kingdoms / 1 Kings	
32:37–43	34	5:18	138
32:41	35–36, 38	7:15	140
32:43	33–51	8:35	140
33:16	182	8:53	44
34:10	182	11:8	136
		11:14	138
Joshua		11:23	138
9:7	158–159	11:25	138
10:21	169	12:14	168
24:12	156	14:22	136
		15:5	136
Judges		15:9	135
13:22	182–183	15:11	136
		15:25	135
1 Kingdoms / 1 Samuel		15:26	136
1	203	15:27	140
1:7	139	15:33	135, 142
1:22	181	15:34	136
3:21	181	16:6	135
6:5	153	16:7	136
8:8	141	16:15	135
9:6	153	16:16	142
9:7	140	16:17	140
14:6	157	16:19	136
15:22	122–123	16:23	135
21:6	140	16:25	136–137
21:8	140	16:28a(B)	135
23:8	140	16:28b(22:43MT)	136
25:21	147	16:29(Ant)	135
28:13	181	16:30(B=16:39Ant)	136–137
29:4	138	16:38	135
		17:1	227–228
2 Kingdoms / 2 Samuel		18:5	156
7:6	141	18:19	142
11:1	140	18:27	154
13:12	141	18:44	140
14:15	151	20(21):21	140
16:12	157	21(20):1	140
19:4	158	21(20):20	136
19:23	138	21(20):25	136
19:43	141	21(20):31	155
20:15	140	22:17	142
24:21	140	22:18	141
24:25	140	22:19	182
		22:41	135

22:43	136	16:2	136
22:52	135	16:5	140
		16:15	135
4 Kingdoms / 2 Kings		16:16	138
1:13–14	136	16:38	135
1:18b(3:2MT)	136	17	133–144
1:19	135	17:1	135–136
3:2	136	17:2	136–137, 143
3:6	142	17:4	137–140, 144
3:18	136	17:5	140
4:24	140	17:7	140–141
5:23	140	17:14–15	143
6:24–25	140	17:17	136
8:18	136	17:31	139
8:25	135	17:32	143
8:27	136	18:1	135
9:8	140	18:3	136
9:29	135	18:9	140
10:5	136	19:4	155
10:30	136	19:37	139
12:3	136	20:3	136
12:11	140	21:2	136
13:1	135	21:6	136
13:2	136	21:9	136
13:11	135–136	21:15–16	136
14:1	135	22:2	136
14:3	136	23:32	136
14:19	138	23:37	136
14:23	135	24:9	136
14:24	136	24:11	140
14:26	140, 169	24:19	136
15:1	135		
15:3	136	1 Chronicles	
15:8	135	16:28	36
15:9	136	21:5	57
15:13	135	23:34	57
15:15	138		
15:17	135	2 Chronicles	
15:18	136	3:17	167
15:23	135	26:15	181
15:24	136		
15:27	135	1 Esdras	
15:28	136	7:1	166
15:30	138		
15:32	135		
16:1	135		

INDEX OF ANCIENT SOURCES

2 Esdras 1–10 (Ezra)		8:21	167
6:2	125	9:5	90–91
9:2	77	11:36	169
		12:18	168
Judith	161–170	12:25	61
9:6	169	12:38	167
11	165–169	12:42	167
11:6	166–167	12:44	58
11:7	167	13:11	62
11:8	167	13:13	167
11:11	168	14:8	61
11:12	168–169	14:37–46	61–64
11:18	169	14:37	64
11:19	169	14:38	61, 64
11:20–21	166	14:39	62, 64
		14:40	62
Tobit		14:41	62
12:13	169	14:42	62, 64
		14:43	62
1 Maccabees		14:45	62
6:23	166	14:45–46	62
9:34	167	14:46	62
		15:19	57
2 Maccabees	53–65		
1:3–4	99	3 Maccabees	
3	97–98, 203	1	70
3:1–3	55–56	1:9	56
3:2	56	2:22	168
3:6	96	3:26	167
3:10	95–102	7:22	167
3:14–23	56–59		
3:26	96	4 Maccabees	
4:50	61	2:21	168
5:20	60	5:1	167
5:24	167	18:18–19	44
6	59–61		
6:9b–7:42	61	Psalms	
6:18	59–60	1	207–201
6:19	59	1:1	209, 215–221
6:21–22	59	1:2	221–222
6:23	59–60	1:3–4	222–224
6:24–28a	60	3	207, 211–212
6:27	60	3:5	224–225
6:30	60	3:6	225–226
6:31	60	3:8	226–227
7:35–38	60	5	207, 212–213

Index of Ancient Sources

5:4–5	227–228	Job	
5:4	228	1:5	154
5:5–7	228–230	4:12	123
5:7	228–230	14:11	169
5:9	230–232	19:26	181
8:6	44, 46	19:27	181
9:9	50	22:14	181
10(11):7	181	23:9	181
16(17):15	179–180, 184	33:26	181
18:9(19:8)	123	42:1	200
19(20):7	225	42:5	182
26(27):8	182–183		
28(29):1	36	Wisdom of Solomon	
32(33):15	218	18:21–22	58
33(34):6	181		
33(34):27	218	Jesus Sirach	
35(36):27	216	1:6	167
36(37):23	231–232	38–39	200
39(40):7–9	119–131	42:18	167
41(42):3	181		
49(50):7	122	Hosea	
49(50):13	122	8:7	146, 152
50(51):18	122, 129		
62(63):3	181	Amos	
67(68):5	97	5:15	153
67(68):6	97, 101–102	5:22	122
68(69):31	122	9:1	182, 201
81(82):6–7	216, 218		
81(82):6	217	Micah	
83(84):8	181	4:1	224
89–117(90–118)	35		
92(93):1	50	Jonah	
95(96):13	50	1:6	153
96(97):2	167		
96(97):7	33–51	Zephaniah	
99(100):1	215	2:3	153
109(110):1	127		
137(138):1	44, 46	Zechariah	
		5:1–2	121
Odes		9:14	181
2:43	33, 41–51		
		Malachi	
Proverbs		3:1	22
6:22	168	4:5	22
8:22	88		

Isaiah		12:3	153
1:11	122	36:26	131
1:16–17	216, 218		
2:2	224	Daniel	
6:1	182	4:24(Theod)	147
7:6	168	9:10	166
17:7	181, 201	9:13(Theod)	138
31:1	181, 201	9:16(Theod)	138
35:8	22	9:24	169
37:4	158	9:24(Theod)	138
37:38	139		
38	203	5. Second Temple Literature	
38:11	181, 201		
40:3	22	Aristobulus	205
40:4	125, 231		
43:19–20	222–223	Demetrius the Chronographer	67–83

Jeremiah		Ezekiel the Tragedian, *Exagoge*	78
5:4	147		
6:20	122	Josephus, *Contra Apionem*	
9:20	115–116	1.217–218	71, 81–82
14:18	105	1.232–233	185
17:16	166	2.35	67
18:20	168		
20:10	155	Josephus, *De Bello Iudaico*	
21:2	155	2.21.1	18
28(51):8	151	2.487	67
28(51):63	121	7.1	18
33(26):3	149		
43(36):2	121	Josephus, *Antiquitates judaicae*	
43(36):4	121	1.27	91
43(36):32	121	2.224	59
38(31):31–41	123, 131	2.231–232	59
38(31):33	121	4	200
43(36):3	149	12.8	67
43(36):7	149	18.3.3	7
		18.4.1	18
Lamentations		18.5.2	7–27
1:20	103–117	18.7.2	13
3:38	228–230	20.8.10	18
		20.9.1	7, 28
Ezekiel			
2:9	121, 125	Letter of Aristeas	
3:1–3	121, 125	16	172
7:15	105	127	75
		128–170	75

INDEX OF ANCIENT SOURCES 255

Philo of Alexandria, *De opificio mundi*
29   92

Qumran
1QM II, 1–4   200
11QT^a 57   200

6. New Testament

Matthew
1:1   215, 217
3:1–2   22
3:1–12   9
5:3   215, 217
14:1–12   9
15:18   219
15:20   219–220
22:44   217

Mark
1:2–5   22
1:4–9   9
6:14–29   9
12:36   217
23:2   220–221

Luke
3:2–6   22
3:2–20   9
9:7–8   9
20:42   217

John
1:18   203
1:23   22
4:13–14   222–223
4:14   223
7:37   222–223
7:38   222–223
8:44   228–230
10:34   217

Acts
2:34   217
18:14–15   14

Romans
2:14   221–222
7:9–10   220
8:28   223–224
12:1–2   131

1 Corinthians
1:9   216–218
2:3   216
11:3   218

Colossians
4:14   222

1 Timothy
6:15   215, 217–218

Hebrews
1:5   48
1:5–13   42
1:6   33–51
1:13   217
2:5   48–51
2:13   48
3:7–4:13   49
4:1–11   50
4:3   50
4:5   48
4:7   48
5:12   48
6:1   48
6:6   48
6:20   127
7:1–10:18   127
9:6–10   128
9:15   127
9:26   50
9:28   48
10   124, 128
10:5–15   119–131
10:5   48, 50
10:7   124
10:30   48
11:7   50
11:9   49

11:38	50	9.29.16	71, 76
Revelation		*Genzā Rabbā*	12
10:9–10	121		
		Gospel of the Hebrews	12

7. Ancient Christian Texts

Hippolytus, *Fragments*

Asterius sophista, *Commentariorum in Psalmos*

		2.1–8	93
Frg 15 (PG 27:61a)	209–210	Irenaeus, *Adversus haereses*	
Frg on Ps 1:1	220–221	1.11.1.6–12	92

Basil of Caesarea, *Homiliae in psalmos* — Jerome, *Dialogus Contra Pelagianos*

PG 29:220b–224c	209, 219–220	3.2	12

Basil of Caesarea, *Hexaemeron* — Jerome, *De viris illustribus*

2.3.13–14	93	135	163
2.3.20–34	93		

Justin, *Dialogus cum Tryphone*

Clement of Alexandria, *Stromata*

		49	19
1.21.141	71	50	19
5.14.93.5.2–5.14.94.2.1	92–93	84	19

Didymus of Alexandria, *Commentarii in Psalmos* — Origen, *Contra Celsum*

	211		7, 19–31
PG 39:1155–1156	213	1.9	24–26
PG 39:1172c–1173a	212	1.15	22
		1.16	22
		1.22	22
Eusebius of Caesarea, *Commentarii in Psalmos*		1.46	27
		1.47	28–30
PG 23:77a–b	210, 221–222	1.51	23
		1.64	26
Eusebius of Caesarea, *Praeparatio evangelica*		1.71	20
		2.4	22
9.19.4	71, 74	2.7	20
9.21.1	74	2.76	21
9.21.2–3	72	3.22	24
9.21.3	79	3.24	21
9.21.7	75	3.28	24
9.21.9	74	3.34	24
9.21.1–19	71	3.48	26
9.21.11	71	4.11	21
9.21.12	79	4.62	20
9.21.16	73	4.69	21
9.29.1–3	71	5.48	21
9.29.3	78		
9.29.15	71		

Pachomius, *Praecepta*
88	164
92	164

Theodoret of Cyrus, *Commentarii in Psalmos*
PG 80:866b–869a	208–210, 215–218
PG 80:868a–b	208
PG 80:869c–872a	222
PG 80:885c	211
PG 80:885d–888a	211, 226
PG 80:888a–b	212, 226–227
PG 80:896a–897a	212, 227–228
PG 80:897c–900a	213, 230–232

Theophilus, *Ad Autolycum*
2.13.40–45	92

Index of Modern Authors

Abel, F.-M.	61	Blomqvist, J.	148, 158
Abrams, D.	80	Blum, E.	112
Adams, S. L.	101	Bogaert, P.-M.	36, 37, 38, 41, 46, 47, 170
Adler, W.	71		
Aejmelaeus, A.	149, 153, 173	Bons, E.	173
Aḥituv, S.	112	Boon, A.	163, 164
Aitken, J. K.	68, 173	Bornkamm, G.	121, 122
Albrektson, B.	104, 105, 106	Bösenecker, J.	154
Alexander, P. S.	104	Brady, C. M. M.	104
Algra, K.	176	Braun, H.	43, 48
Allen, D. M.	40, 44, 45	Briggs, C. A.	179
Allen, N. P. L.	1, 8, 19, 28	Briggs, E. G.	179
Amphoux, C.-B.	124, 125	Brock, S. P.	199
Anderson, L. B.	146	Brown, W. P.	89
Aneziri, S.	198	Bruce, F. F.	126
Attridge, H. W.	50, 125	Brueggemann, W.	205
Ausloos, H.	173, 174	Buchthal, H.	207
Austin, J. L.	235	Budde, K.	105
Backhaus, K.	50	Budge, E. A. W.	198
Balz, H.	48, 49, 50	Buraselis, K.	198
Barclay, J. M.	68, 69	Burkert, W.	194
Barnes, J.	176	Burkill, A. T.	201
Barthélemy, D.	134, 154, 202	Bury, R. G.	87
Baudissin, W. W. G.	176	Busto Saiz, J. R.	134
Baumgarten, A. I.	202	Bybee, J.	233, 234, 235
Beentjes, P.	167	Callaham, S. N.	109
Berges, U.	106	Chantraine, P.	234
Berlin, A.	106	Charlesworth, J. H.	8
Bertholet, A.	105	Cockerill, G. L.	44, 45, 47, 50
Bertram, G.	172	Cohen, L.	11
Bickerman, E. J.	57, 69, 70, 72, 96, 98	Collins, J. J.	67, 69, 70, 71, 74, 75, 77, 80, 173
Bieler, L.	59		
Bile, M.	236, 237	Colson, F. H.	92
Black, M.	201	Coenen, L.	49, 50
Blau, J.	145	Cook, J.	173, 174, 175, 199
Blinkenberg, C.	191	Corley, J.	162

Cowey, J. M. S.	67, 68, 69	Gagarin, M.	236
Cowley, A. E.	166	García Martínez, F.	200
Craven, T.	162	Gauger, J.-D.	186
Cross, F. M.	105	Geiger, A.	180
Cutler, A.	207	George, A. R.	114
Czerny, J.	195, 196	George, J.	50
Daehner, J.	194	Gibson, J. C. L.	113
Dafni, E. G.	184	Goldstein, J. A.	61
Dahood, M.	106	Gordis, R.	106
Den Hertog, C.	46	Gottlieb, H.	106
Denizot, C.	233, 235, 236, 239, 241	Gräßer, E.	43, 48, 49, 50, 121, 126
Denniston, J. D.	151	Grenfell, B. P.	189
Dijkstra, M.	112	Grimm, L. W.	60, 61
Dillon, J.	176	Grossman, J. B.	194
Dines, J. M.	72	Gruen, E. S.	54, 68, 69, 74, 77, 96, 98
Dodd, C. H.	172	Guignebert, C.	10
Dods, M.	92	Gulde, S. U.	113, 114, 115
Doherty, E.	8, 10	Guthrie, G. H.	43
Dommershausen, W.	96, 97, 98	Gutt, E.-A.	148
Donaldson, J.	92	Gzella, H.	184
Doran, R.	57, 58, 60, 62, 96, 97, 98, 101, 102	Habicht, C.	61
		Hackett, J. A.	112
Dorival, G.	124, 125, 175, 178, 208, 213, 214, 217	Haller, M.	105
		Hanhart, R.	45, 46, 47, 101, 119, 124, 134, 161, 165, 166, 172
Driver, G. R.	109		
Dyserinck, J.	105	Hanson, A. T.	183
Eco, U.	99	Hanson, J.	70
Ehrlich, A. B.	105	Hanson, K. C.	17
Eisele, W.	47, 48, 49	Harl, M.	89, 175
Ellingworth, P.	125	Hatch, E.	147, 166, 167, 168
Engberg-Pedersen, T.	176	Healy, J. F.	113
Engel, H.	162	Hengel, M.	87, 88, 176
Fascher, E.	172	Henrix, H. H.	120
Feldman, L. H.	68	Hermann, M.-L.	45
Fernández Marcos, N.	134	Herter, H.	166
Finkelstein, L.	202	Higbie, C.	191, 192, 193
Flender, O.	49, 50	Hillers, D. R.	105
Foucart, G.	195	Himbaza, I.	183
Frankel, Z.	180	Hoehner, H. W.	17
Fraser, P. M.	67, 70	Hoftijzer, J.	112, 113
Fredriksen, P.	8	Hölbl, G.	188
Frevel, C.	108, 109	Holladay, C. R.	70, 71. 72, 205
Fritsch, C. T.	180, 182, 183	Honigman, S.	68, 69
Fuks, A.	67, 68, 69	Horbury, W.	68
Gäbel, G.	122, 124, 126, 128, 129, 130, 131	Hossfeld, F.-L.	121
		Huehnergard, J.	112

Huß, W.	188	LiDonnici, L. R.	189
Hunt, A. S.	189	Lietzmann, I.	214
Jackson, B.	93	Löhr, H.	126
Jacobsen, H.	78, 79	Lowden, J.	207
Janowski, B.	122	Lundbom, J. R.	35
Jastrow, M.	104	Lyons, J.	234
Jastrup, P. O.	148	Mackenzie, N.	11
Jenni, E.	105, 106	Maingueneau, D.	235
Jenson, P. P.	200	Manion, L.	11
Jipp, J. W.	42	Maresch, K.	67, 68, 69
Jobes, K. H.	72, 124	Mason, S.	9, 10, 18, 202
Joosten, J.	162, 173, 185, 186, 199	Mauersberger, A.	56
Jordaan, P. J.	1, 54, 98, 99	McCarter, P. K.	112
Karo, G.	214	McDaniel, T. F.	106
Karrer, M.	46, 47, 48, 49, 50, 51, 121, 124, 125, 127, 128, 129, 131, 142, 157, 158	McLay, R. T.	43, 44
		Meager, J. C.	15
		Meier, J. P.	8, 10
Kartveit, M.	77	Mertens, D. M.	11
Katz, P.	60	Mettinger, T. N. D.	203
Keel, O.	203	Meyer, R.	37
King, P. D.	108	Michaelis, W.	48
Kipfer, S.	109	Michel, O.	43, 48
Kirby, P.	20	Modrzejewski, J. M.	68, 69, 70, 73
Knipe, S.	11	Moffat, J.	98
Koenen, K.	106, 109	Most, G. W.	90
Koester, C. R.	47, 49, 50	Mühlenberg, E.	208, 211, 212, 213, 217, 224, 228
Kokkinos, N.	7, 16, 17, 18		
Kratz, R. G.	69	Müller, H.-P.	112
Kraus, H.-J.	105, 119, 120, 121, 122, 123, 131, 179	Munnich, O.	175
		Muraoka, T.	56, 85, 109, 145, 147, 149, 150, 151, 154, 156, 157, 158, 159
Kraus, W.	42, 47, 51, 120, 127, 128, 131, 142, 157, 158		
		Murray, A. T.	89, 90
Kreuzer, S.	134, 136, 137, 139, 141, 142	Neusner, J.	202
		Newman, R. C.	17
Kühner, R.	158	Niehoff, M.	69, 70, 71, 72, 75, 76, 77, 83
Labuschagne, C. J.	36, 37, 40		
Lane, W. L.	47, 48, 50, 125	Niehr, H.	113, 203
Lapatin, K. D. S.	194	Nielsen, E.	46
Lauterbach, J. Z.	202, 204	Nigosian, S. A.	36
Le Boulluec, A.	177, 182	Nötscher, F.	176
Lee, J. A.	176	Noy, D.	61, 68
Leidner, H.	8	Nuyts, J.	146, 147, 150
Lemmelijn, B.	173	O'Connor, M.	145
Levy, J.	104, 167	Otto, W.	198
Lewis, N.	186, 189	Otzen, B.	162
Lichtheim, M.	111	Pagliuca, W.	233, 234, 235

Index of Modern Authors

Pakkala, J.   39, 40, 41, 46
Palmer, F. R.   234
Pat-El, N.   111
Pax, E.   193
Perkins, L.   183
Perkins, R.   233, 234, 235
Perles, F.   106
Pietersma, A.   77, 157, 173, 183, 184
Platt, V.   193
Pouliot, V.   11
Price, C. E.   8
Price, R. M.   8, 14, 15
Quack, J. F.   111
Rahlfs, A.   44, 46, 95, 101, 107, 108, 119, 124, 125, 129, 133, 134, 135, 136, 137, 138, 139, 140, 141, 142, 143, 144, 175
Rajak, T.   60, 69
Rakel, C.   162
Rascher, A.   43
Ray, J. D.   188
Redpath, H. A.   147, 166, 167, 168
Reindl, J.   176
Rendsburg, G. A.   111
Renkema, J.   106
Rice, E. E.   197
Richard, M.   209, 220
Ricken, F.   176
Riggenbach, E.   34, 43, 48
Roberts, A.   92
Rofé, A.   40
Rösel, M.   173, 174, 175, 178, 185, 186, 199
Rothschild, C.   14, 15
Rudolph, W.   106
Runia, D. T.   87
Rüsen-Weinhold, U.   129
Ryholt, K.   187
Salmond, S. D. F.   93
Salters, R. B.   110
Sandevoir, P.   177
Schams, C.   54, 59
Schaper, J.   177, 178, 182, 183, 184, 202
Schenker, A.   45
Schlund, C.   178
Schmitz, B.   162
Schneider, H.   44
Schunack, G.   43, 48, 51, 127
Schürer, E.   71, 201
Schwartz, D. R.   55, 58, 82, 96, 97, 98, 101
Seeligmann, I. L.   173, 174, 201
Seow, C.-L.   110
Seybold, K.   35, 119, 120, 121, 122, 123
Siegert, F.   172
Siffer-Wiederholt, N.   125
Sigismund, M.   44
Silva, M.   72
Skehan, P. W.   34, 35, 36, 37, 40, 41, 43, 45
Smith, M. S.   108, 113, 114, 115
Smyth, H. W.   91, 150, 151, 155, 156, 157, 158, 159, 233
Soisalon-Soininen, I.   147
Sollamo, R.   160
Sterling, G.   70, 71, 72, 73, 75, 77, 82
Stern, M.   74
Steyn, G. J.   1, 41, 42, 43, 47, 124, 125, 129, 130
Stolz, L.   48, 49
Swete, H. B.   33
Suys, É.   111
Tajfel, H.   80
Tcherikover, V. A.   67, 68, 69, 96, 100, 101
Thackeray, H. St. J.   81, 91, 134
Thomas, A.   109
Thompson, D.   188
Tigay, J. H.   40
Tigchelaar, E. J. C.   200
Tjen, A.   156, 157
Tov, E.   82
Trebolle Barrera, J.   34
True, M.   194
Tsumura, D. T.   113, 114
Turner, J.   80
Uehlinger, C.   203
Ulrich, E.   34
Van der Heide, A.   104
Vanderhooft, D.   56
Van der Horst, P. W.   85, 86, 87, 88, 90, 91, 92, 93, 94

VanderKam, J. C.   55, 201
Van der Kooij, A.   35, 36, 37, 38, 40,
   45, 173, 175, 186, 199, 201, 202
Van der Kooij, G.   112, 113
Van der Louw, T.   174
Van der Meer, M. N.   174, 175, 186, 201
Van der Merwe, C. H. J.   109
Van Henten, J. W.   54, 61, 98
Van Rooy, R.   146, 151
Venetz, H.-J.   202
Vermes, G.   71, 201
Volten, A.   111
Von Siebenthal, H.   49
Wagner, C.   170
Walter, N.   70, 71
Walters, P.   109
Waltke, B. K.   145
Wander, S. H.   207
Weber, R.   104, 163, 165
Weiß, H.-F.   43, 48, 127
Weitzmann, K.   207
Welles, C. B.   56
Wenham, G. J.   87
Werlitz, J.   136, 137, 141, 142
Wevers, J. W.   78, 86, 177, 178, 182
Whiston, W.   8
Whitaker, G. H.   92
Wilcken, U.   186
Wildeboer, D. G.   105
Willi, A.   234
Williams, R. J.   145
Wilson, W.   93
Wilson-Wright, A.   111
Winter, F.   139
Wolter, M.   50
Wright, B. G.   77, 157
Wright, G. E.   34
Wyatt, N.   113
Yadin, Y.   200
Zenger, E.   121
Ziegler, J.   107, 108
Zindler, F. R.   7, 8, 12, 13, 14, 15

www.ingramcontent.com/pod-product-compliance
Lightning Source LLC
Chambersburg PA
CBHW020113010526
44115CB00008B/814